FLORENCE GREENHOE ʟROBBINS

The Ohio State University

EDUCATIONAL

OCIOLOGY

1 Study in Child, Youth, School,

and Community

GREENWOOD PRESS, PUBLISHERS
NEW YORK

This book is written for four people:

Robbie

"His power comes from some great reservoir of spiritual life else it could not be so Universal and so potent, but the majesty and beauty with which he clothes it are his own."

Nelson and Marguerite

"These are the believers in life and the bounty of life, and their coffer is never empty." [1]

Marguerite Greenhoe Witt

"They also serve who only stand and wait."

[1] Kahlil Gibran, *The Prophet* (New York, Alfred A. Knopf, 1923), p. 24. Used by special permission.

PREFACE

COURSES IN DEMOCRATIC SOCIAL EDUCATION rest
upon three basic assumptions:
1. Respect for the worth and dignity of personality.
2. Faith in the method of intelligence as a way of living and
   working together.
3. Belief in cooperation as a means of implementing decisions
   made in the foregoing atmosphere.

In view of this, it has seemed to educational sociologists at Ohio
State that method or, if you prefer, *course dynamics* was almost if
not quite as important as subject matter. We have, therefore, experimented over the years with various kinds of course procedures.
Sometimes we have leaned toward the more dominative atmospheres, occasionally the laissez-faire atmosphere has been employed
for varying lengths of time. At length the democratic or integrative
course of action has prevailed as our commitment.[1]

Both in classroom groups and in informal groups we have
taken the position that students should, and under guidance are able
and willing to, plan, manipulate, and critically appraise programs
such as the one suggested below.

Having outlined their *aims* and *program,* they may then canvass both the *resources* and the *techniques* available to them. As is
readily seen, these consist of objects and materials as well as persons,
cultural processes, and relationships. Most college communities will
have the following *resources* available:
1. Community centers, relief agencies, correctional institutions,
   research bureaus, psychopathic institutions.
2. Persons within the area available as lecturers or as consult-

---

[1] As will be reported in the body of the book, not a little of this commitment is due to differences in results in learning outcomes, attitude changes,
nd the like, under the different social climate classroom situations.

ants for conferences on current topics and vocational problems.

3. Library reading materials, including newspapers, magazines, books, monographs, government reports—local, county, state, regional, and national—scrapbooks, and photographs.
4. Motion pictures, plays, radio, and television.
5. Maps of all kinds including spot maps, base maps, bar charts, graphs, and other pictorial illustrative material.
6. Class, small group, and individual projects in which data of the above type are collected, portrayed, and interpreted.
7. Student personal experience and observation. In sociology one is faced frequently with the difficulty and the opportunity of giving everyday personal experiences meaning, clarification, and interpretation in a sociological frame of reference.

In the collection, coordination, integration, and preservation of these resources, it is imperative that the work be done by both students and staff members. To present an exhaustive list of the techniques for using these resources is even more difficult than to enumerate the resources themselves. The following techniques are suggestive only and vary from one learning situation to another:

1. Class discussion of the give-and-take variety, small special-interest groups, panels, round tables, etc.
2. Lectures by both instructors and outside persons.
3. Reading of texts, library resources.
4. Agency visits: field trips by the classes, by small groups, and representative committees.
5. Reports, oral and written, presented by the individual or in the more spicy "merry-go-round" fashion.
6. Exhibits of student projects or materials secured from local, state, regional, or other agencies and their studies.
7. Case studies.
8. Uses of radio, television, motion pictures, and dramatizations with proper preparatory and appraisal study.
9. Making of charts, graphs, and maps of the home community of the student.
10. Interviewing of persons who represent various professions for the purpose of student guidance or for securing needed data about social problems.

Experience to date indicates that several values have resulted from these procedures. There is evidence of (*1*) a considerable development of "work skills," such as the ability to organize materials, to generalize, to make application of generalizations, and to interpret social data situations; (*2*) a motivation of civic awareness with consequent improvement of community relationships; (*3*) a vitalization of the subject matter which the usual textbook course can never give; (*4*) a greater amount of purposeful reading; (*5*) exercises in social sensitivity and adjustment due to group projects and committee work as contrasted with work of an entirely individual nature; (*6*) an appreciation of reality on the part of both students and teacher since experiences are derived from student and staff backgrounds; (*7*) considerable increases in factual knowledge.

On the debit side of the ledger we have become impressed with the fact that merely motivating social action is not sufficient. Much time and work are necessary with individuals and small groups if students are to evince any research skill in compiling data or in analyzing and relating the data to other situations. It is necessary to guard continually against jumping too rapidly and deeply into the program because of an enthusiasm that was not supported by readiness to act. If trips and similar activities are not to take on the nature of mere holiday excursions, much planning, study, and direction must be given to preparation for the activity as well as to follow-up programs.

To aid the more eye-minded and/or inexperienced student and teacher in organizing classes along these lines, a student bulletin has evolved and is presented in Appendix A. Suggestions are tentative and incomplete from "malice of foresight" as one instructor once put it.

In other words, the aim is to provide a base from which may spring creativity. A similar viewpoint is taken toward the textbook question. Both students and instructors have agreed that a "source" book is of value for providing orientation and synthesis. It is used also for suggestive purposes. Probably no author would claim that he had dealt with a subject exhaustively. Within the confines of paper and print he has rather tried to open up areas of thought and to motivate further activity and thinking along the lines introduced. Teaching and study aids are offered here to promote extension into areas which could not receive extended attention within the space of this book.

Also no set guide or plan can or should be devised for *all* students everywhere in *any* class. A situational approach demands rather that the observable common repeated elements basic to structure and processes of social groups be utilized for planning, organization, and appraisal in terms of the group structure and processes present. It is for this reason that we urge that the time pressure element be not overlooked in terms of what it will do both to *quantity* and *quality* of the course experience.

We earnestly suggest that two, three, or even more days be allotted for the "getting-acquainted" period, the planning and organization of the class.

This procedure has yielded several benefits: (*1*) There is an opportunity for knowing one another as persons, and for learning one another's backgrounds, and current interests. This contributes markedly both to objectivity, consequent understanding, and respect for students as persons. It allows also for the richer contributions of students as resource persons themselves. (*2*) It allows for what seems to be a necessary "pooling" of ignorance and wisdom of the group. (*3*) The instructor who is interested in counseling has an opportunity to establish a rapport so necessary to successful interpersonal relationships. (*4*) Most important, perhaps, since time has been allotted for this kind of activity, no one feels guilty or that time is just being wasted.

On that basis we present a "tentative" bulletin which has come from the interaction of staff *and* student committees. We invite your questions, comments, and constructive criticisms. Such comments give the "seeing and hearing" instructor an unequaled opportunity to ascertain some of the developmental *levels* and *needs* of students.

This volume on educational sociology is written from the viewpoint presented through courses in educational sociology at The Ohio State University. It is the result of some ten years of teaching and experimentation in teaching.

Thanks to the splendid liberalism of the sociology department chairmen and the equally unusual cooperation, advice, and direction of members in the department of education, the work has been thrilling as well as exacting and satisfying. It may then be worth while to present the viewpoint through a brief résumé of the arisal and development of educational sociology at Ohio State.

As currently defined and implemented at the University, educational sociology is not a "field" as that concept is customarily understood. Rather it is an *area* of interest and study within sociology which has developed here at the suggestion and instigation of people in education.

In the earlier days these people, as has happened in many other institutions, wished their students to experience the so-called social educational outcomes which the application of sociological "principles" to problems of educators might entail.

Accordingly, early emphases were placed upon three main objectives, and courses were set accordingly. The first was to promote interest in and allow for enjoyment of the knowledge gained in a study of personality formation, the working of the social processes, and the like. A second was an endeavor to provide bases for meeting student needs and adjustment problems on an individual and personal level while at college and afterward. A third centered attention on supplying both technical and general understanding of school problems and teacher and community relationships.

For a time the third objective claimed so much attention and effort that we were alluded to as community educational sociologists. From such a beginning, we have widened our areas of interest, study, and investigation to include any educative experience. We make no apology for taking the universe as our laboratory, and we never try to define boundary limits. We try only to maintain some central tendencies which briefly put are these: (1) We are interested and spend much time in general social orientation; (2) we devote considerable attention to social orientation of children; (3) we set aside blocks of time for analysis of the special culture of the school; (4) we still center attention on technical and general understanding of school problems and teacher and community relationships; (5) a current development perhaps a by-product of (4) but coming to stand as a separate entity, is the field of "intergroup education."

As mentioned, all earlier were explored from the standpoint, perhaps bias of theory and practice, of and for educators. More recently the base of operations has been widened to include people outside the College of Education. Hence, while continuing as a service area for a specific group on campus, the approach now aims at three main types of students: prospective teachers, prospective parents of school children, and prospective citizens of the educational community.

It is a major hope that by directing attention along these three viewpoints, by methods to be mentioned later, certain values will obtain:

1. Considerable development of "work skills," such as ability to organize materials, to generalize, to make application of generalizations, and to interpret social data situations.
2. A motivation of civic awareness with consequent improvement of community relationships.
3. A vitalization of the subject matter which the usual textbook course can seldom give.
4. A greater amount of purposeful reading.
5. Exercises in social sensitivity and adjustment through group projects and committee work as contrasted with work of an entirely individual nature.
6. An appreciation of reality on the part of both students and teacher since experiences are derived from student and staff backgrounds.
7. Considerable increases in factual knowledge.

In all this, the role of the instructor is conceived of as that of guide and resource person rather than one of authoritarian role and function.

To obtain these aims has necessitated much experience and experimentation both in subject matter and in classroom methods. Due to the spirit of adventure allowed and encouraged by both departments, many devices have been tried, refined, sometimes abandoned, and occasionally reinstituted in their original form. At present classes proceed, always with deviations in terms of personalities involved, much as described in the student bulletin which is presented in Appendix A. As we shall emphasize again and again, these are tentative arrangements whose chief claim to attention is just this very flexibility and adjustability.

Objective evidence as to their effectiveness has been compiled through several "continuing studies" to be described later. The gains in factual knowledge, social understandings, and skills plus just plain enthusiasm as evidenced through consistently sizable enrollments in what are entirely elective courses have led us to think the effort in social education worth while.

F. G. R.

Columbus, Ohio
November 3, 1952

ACKNOWLEDGMENT

However much one may wish to do so, the acknowledgment of indebtedness to others is seldom complete. As student, teacher, parent, and community member, one draws from all those with whom he comes into contact and interaction. It is possible to mention but a few who have contributed most directly to this undertaking.

The tendency is to think first of great teachers in one's experience who have opened vistas of thought, given guidance and direction, and generally left their influence upon one as a student.

The first of these is David McCamel Trout, now Dean of Students at Mt. Pleasant State Teachers College, Michigan. First as gentleman and scholar and secondly as teacher and counselor par excellence, Dr. Trout remains for all his students a paragon to be admired and remembered.

The second is the late Charles Horton Cooley, Chairman of Sociology, University of Michigan. There was a man of sensitivity, keen insight, and patience as well as scholarly achievement who left his kindly influence on all who knew him.

The third is Lloyd Allen Cook, now Chairman of Educational Sociology at Wayne University, Detroit. Dr. Cook more than any other gave specific purpose and direction as well as competent tutelage when the writer was his student in educational sociology. His interest in and knowledge of the area and his excellent teaching methods provided a long-time challenge and devotion to an area he helped define and develop.

To the following department chairmen with whom I have worked, I am especially grateful for opportunity and freedom to work in the field: Frederick E. Lumley, Perry P. Denune, and Raymond Sletto in sociology and Daniel Eikenberry and Harold Fawcett in education.

Colleagues in sociology who have been of assistance in the teaching and developing of courses include: Melvin Seeman, Christen Jonassen, Robert Bullock, and Charles Westie. I am especially indebted to Brewton Berry who read the manuscript and offered suggestions for its improvement.

Colleagues in education from whom I have derived whatever insight I may have into education include: Laura Zirbes, Ruth Streitz, Harold Alberty, Gordan Hullfish, Earl Anderson, Everett Kircher, Leland Jacobs, Kenneth Arisman, Hugh Laughlin, James Burr, and Lowry Harding.

I am also obligated to Almus Thorp, Rector of St. Stephens Episcopal Church for critical reading of certain portions.

Former graduate students who have been of special help are: Lorraine Lange, New York State Teachers College, Buffalo; Eugenia Hunter, University of North Carolina; Mildred Swearingen, Florida State Teachers College; Janet McCracken, University of Florida; Alberta Lowe, University of Tennessee; Irene Thomas, Coordinator of Elementary Education, Battle Creek, Michigan; Marguerite Frierson, State Teachers College, Fayetteville, South Carolina; Manuel Barkan, Arts-Education, The Ohio State University; Victor Lawhead, Ball State Teachers College, Muncie, Indiana; Mary Jane Loomis and Roberta Utterback, The University School, The Ohio State University; Fern Shipley, Kent State University, Kent, Ohio; Kathyrn Boylan and Mildred McFarland, Shaker Heights schools, Cleveland; Lucetta Gearhart, University of Hawaii; Sara Swickard, Kalamazoo State Teachers College, Michigan; Major Harry Entwhistle, U. S. Army; Ward Cramer, Voice of America, Baghdad; and Hannah Sugantham Charles, St. Christopher's College, Vepery, Madras, India.

Omissions and commissions are peculiarly my own and in no way to be connected with the aforementioned people.

Appreciation is also extended to the numerous authors and publishers who have generously granted permissions to quote from their works. Every effort has been made to give credit meticulously. If omissions have occurred, it is because, as a student committee once wrote, "like Milton we remember too well."

CONTENTS

SCOPE OF EDUCATIONAL SOCIOLOGY

THE HISTORY of childhood has yet to be written. This may be due to two main reasons. First, such a history would be the history of the human race, and, as important, data on childhood are peculiarly in absence.[1]

The Ancients made virtually no records of the life of young children: Classic Rome, for example, furnishes almost no data for child study; legal codes, so fruitful a source of light on many historical topics, have seemed for centuries to recognize children chiefly as channels for the transmission of property. Even medical writings, dealing with problems in which children inevitably occupy a large part, are conspicuous for the relative lack of emphasis they give to children's diseases and the problems of their specific welfare. . . . Despite the gaps, however, there is information on certain specific points such as *status of childhood,* by which is meant the position of children in relation to their parents and the larger social group of which they are a part. . . . (Studies of the literature reveal that). . . . Children constituted a relatively large population element in primitive society; but although they were desired, abortion, infanticide, child spacing, short infancy, and early labor were common in the primitive cultures of the past. . . . Certain changes in the status of children can be noted in the civilizations of classic antiquity. Infanticide often softened into abandonment and exposure, child selling developed as a substitute for both, and emphasis on the duty of children to support their parents became common. However, there remained the sweeping and arbitrary rights of parents to use their child in whatever way was to their advantage.

[1] James H. Bossard, *Sociology of Child Development* (New York, Harper, 1948), p. 598 ff.

The status of the medieval child was the product of a blending of Roman, German, and Christian influences. Childhood was short, rigorous work came early in life, and child rearing was coldly severe and harsh, even at the level of royalty.

Newer attitudes toward children appeared in England during the eighteenth century. Despite the retention of historic practices, parents began to show some conception of their duties to their children. Such changes, however, were limited in scope. . . .

Colonial America reproduced with certain modifications, the European pattern of child status. The colonial family had high status, was patriarchal in form and large in size. Maternal and infant mortality were high. Child labor was common and from an early age. Family discipline was rigid as was that of the school. Colonial law clearly supported both parent and teacher in their disciplinary measures. Manners and courtesy were markedly emphasized. Courtship was controlled closely by parents. Religious experience was emphasized early in the lives of children. Large families seem, however, to have permitted some recreational developments and references to children's games are numerous, even if sometimes in the form of complaints.

Contemporary America is seeing a revolutionary change in the status of children; they are viewed in terms of equality with other members of the family and recognized as coequal personalities in the emerging democracy of the family. Recent years have witnessed notable attempts to revise historic formulations of human rights—to the inclusion of economic and social rights, especially those centering about the development of personality. Emphasis upon the rights of childhood is a phase of this larger program.

The most recent formulation of these rights is that by the Midcentury White House Conference on Children and Youth in December of 1950.

To you, our children, who hold within you our most cherished hopes, we the members of the Midcentury White House Conference on Children and Youth, relying on your full response, make this pledge:

From your earliest infancy we give you our love, so that you may grow with trust in yourself and in others.

We will recognize your worth as a person, and we will help you to strengthen your sense of belonging.

We will respect your right to be yourself and at the same time help you to understand the rights of others, so that you may experience cooperative living.

We will help you to develop initiative and imagination, so that you may have the opportunity freely to create.

We will encourage your curiosity and your pride in workmanship, so that you may have the satisfaction that comes from achievement.

We will provide the conditions for wholesome play that will add to your learning, to your social experience, and to your happiness.

We will illustrate by precept and example the value of integrity and the importance of moral courage.

We will encourage you always to seek the truth.

We will provide you with all opportunities possible to develop your own faith in God.

We will open the way for you to enjoy the arts and to use them for deepening your understanding of life.

We will work to rid ourselves of prejudice and discrimination, so that together we may achieve a truly democratic society.

We will work to lift the standard of living and to improve our economic practices, so that you may have the material basis for a full life.

We will provide you with rewarding educational opportunities, so that you may develop your talents and contribute to a better world.

We will protect you against exploitation and undue hazards and help you grow in health and strength.

We will work to conserve and improve family life and, as needed, to provide foster care according to your inherent rights.

We will intensify our search for new knowledge in order to guide you more effectively as you develop your potentialities.

As you grow from child to youth to adult, establishing a family life of your own and accepting larger social responsibilities, we will work with you to improve conditions for all children and youth.

* * *

Aware that these promises to you cannot be fully met in a world at war, we ask you to join us in a firm dedication to the building of a world society based on freedom, justice, and mutual respect.

So may You grow in joy, in faith in God and in man, and in those qualities of vision and of the spirit that will sustain us all and give us new hope for the future.

Though the above pledge may be accepted by all those who deal with children and youth, there is far from complete acceptance of the "how" to accomplish these promises. The contrasts to be found here are somewhat similar to the cultural lags discussed by students of social change in general.

How much and what shall parents, teachers, and society in general do for children, what status is really "best"for children, are hotly debated questions. What kind of education, meaning largely schools, how concerned, how carried out will best fullfil the pledge?

As is usual in such social dilemma, people in all walks of life elect to "pass opinions" concerning the issue. A few elect to study, compile, and analyze data and attempt interpretations in the light of that data. One such group is known as educational sociologists. As a setting for the study mentioned above, it may be helpful to see how their interest in this area has developed and what their relationships are to the fields from which they extend themselves—education and sociology.

DEVELOPMENTAL PATTERNS OF EDUCATIONAL SOCIOLOGY

RELATION TO SOCIOLOGY

The social-cultural aspects of living are studied and investigated by all the so-called social sciences. Each, however, proceeds in this study from its own particular vantage point. In other words, each has a basic central orientation upon which attention is centered. For example, economics is interested in discovering and postulating the relationships, uniformities, and laws which are repeated in time and space in relation to economic phenomena.

Sociology, on the other hand, may be thought of as a study which attempts to transcend the boundaries of any such compartmentalization as economic phenomena, historical phenomena, or just educational phenomena. It is interested in studying along its specific lines all these compartmentalizations. It attempts to understand not merely the economic specific or the political specific but also the *structures* and *processes* which *act, react,* and *interact* throughout the universe.

This is tantamount to saying that sociology is a generalizing science and in a unique fashion. Economics, geography, and history generalize to the extent that they are interested in finding and presenting uniformities of structure and process which have communality for their particular phenomena. This generalization is different from that mentioned above. Sociology is interested in studying phenomena in a generic sort of way.

It seeks to find not only the nature of society and culture but also the nature of the individual, the *whole individual* in relation to *all* these social-cultural, biophysical backgrounds. Here it should be emphasized that the unique role of sociology is this study of the person and his social-cultural surroundings as wholes in contrast to other views of the individual as a political man or as an economic man.

The person must always be seen *in relation* to all the aspects of his milieu, never isolated from the whole. This suggests that the approach is a situational one, and so it is as opposed to an "atomistic" one, which allows, at the most, understanding of specialized, fragmentized aspects of individual personality, society, and culture.

It should be pointed out, however, that this concept of sociology does not mean that its subject matter is a kaleidoscopic review of all other social sciences and philosophies. Nor does it mean that sociology is not a special science also.

In its generalizing role sociology depends upon the results of experiments, findings, and research of all other sciences, be they physical or social. In turn, sociology fosters their interdependence upon it and its thinking and study outcomes.

Some writers have gone so far as to say that the rise and development of sociology as a systematic science is the story of the "sociologizing" of various other special sciences. This is evidenced not merely by the permeation of social concepts into other areas but also by the rise and flourishing developments of borderline areas, such as social psychology, educational psychology, educational sociology, and others. Even more specific evidences of this assimilation are such movements within areas as that of group dynamics in education colleges.

Unlike some, we do not deplore these trends. If we are really serious about social education, we are more than anxious for the trend toward interdepartmentalism. Who gets the credit is unimportant if the job is well done. It may be, in fact, that the surest sign of successful service of an area is so to "sociologize" the area serviced as to work oneself out of a job.

Sociology is also a special science. It deals with specific kinds of social and cultural phenomena in more intensive fashion. At present these special sociologies include the borderline ones mentioned above plus such as rural sociology, urban sociology, family sociology, sociology of knowledge, criminology, sociology of social disorganization, population study, and the like.

These emphases are well described by Sorokin when he says:

General sociology studies (A) the properties and uniformities common to all sociocultural phenomena in their structural and dynamic aspects as well as the (B) recurring interrelationships between the sociocultural and the cosmic phenomena; the sociocultural and the biological phenomena; the various classes of sociocultural phenomena. *Structural general sociology* studies (A) the structure and composition of the generic sociocultural phenomenon (corresponding to the study of the structure of a cell as a phenomenon of life or that of an atom in physics); (B) the main structural types of the groups of institutions into which human population is differentiated and stratified and their relationships to one another; (C) the main structural types of the cultural systems and their relationships with one another; (D) the structure and types of personality embedded in social groups and cultural systems.

Dynamic general sociology investigates (A) recurring social processes, such as social contact, interaction, socialization, conflict, domination, subordination, adaptation, amalgamation, migration, mobility; how social systems are born, how they acquire and lose members; how they distribute these within the system, how they become organized and disorganized, and how all these processes affect the personality of the individuals involved; (B) recurring cultural processes—invention, diffusion, integration and disintegration, conversion, and the accumulation of cultural traits and systems—and how they affect the personality of the individuals involved; (C) rhythms, tempos, periodicities, trends, and fluctuations in social and cultural processes, together with the general problem of sociocultural change and evolutions; (D) recurring sociocultural processes in persons and how and why persons change.

Special sociologies each do the same in regard to a special class of sociocultural phenomena chosen for intensive study.[2]

By implication educational sociology is then a special sociological area, and by definition, one which deals with the structural and dynamic aspects of the educative process. It is interested in studying this structure to discover the theories and philosophies entailed, its cultural systems, and the structural aspects of personalities and interrelations with the total social scheme. It is likewise concerned with the study of the social and cultural processes and personality processes as they relate to the educative process. And lastly, it is concerned with making application of these findings for the furtherance of democratic values, in short social or democratic education.

[2] Pitirim A. Sorokin, *Society, Culture and Personality* (New York, Harper, 1947), pp. 16–17. Used by permission.

A BRIEF HISTORY OF EDUCATIONAL SOCIOLOGY

EDUCATIONAL SOCIOLOGY like most social inventions appears to have arisen when there was a current need which was not entirely met by existing social institutions. As technological advances and accompanying cultural lags made the process of socialization increasingly "confused and confusing," there was a tendency to dump more responsibility on the existing institution which by name seemed best able to cope with social change. But neither schools nor teachers were by philosophy, training, or practice ready for forthright assumption of such roles in child socialization. Consequently, both by invitation and by attraction, social scientists began paying attention to the problems of schools both within and without from the standpoint of sociological analysis.

If the personalities involved were within education, the educational character rather than the sociological character was stressed by setting the functions of the area to be those of determining educational objectives, shaping of curricula, and what they often call "general sociological orientation" for the school and its program. Writers both past and present who represent this point of view include David Snedden, C. C. Peters, Frederick E. Bolton, and John E. Corbally.

A second trend may be noted toward something like an "applied school" of educational sociology. Sociologists per se make this their center of attention. Here the aim is to supply basic social cultural understandings to school administrators and teachers. This attempt, while still problem-oriented, is interested in adding to the theoretical framework and in using the most scientific study techniques. Some place much, or most, of their emphasis on the school-community orientation, and others pay special attention to extra-school factors, such as movies, comics, and the like. E. George Payne, Harvey Zorbaugh, Lloyd Allen Cook, Joseph S. Roucek, and Leslie D. Zeleny doubtless would not object to being placed in this category.

A third trend, which seems to derive from the foregoing group, tries to present a strictly theoretical point of view. The base of operations here is the development of a sociological theory of educational process. Willard Waller and his interpretation of the school in terms of social roles and statuses was a beginning attempt.

Recent research and practices have seemed to center in the following areas of interest: (1) general social orientation as exemplified by such writers as George Counts and Howard Beale, (2) child socialization as seen in the work of Kingsley Davis, Wm. Foote Whyte, Allison Davis, John Dollard, and James H. Bossard; (3) the culture of the school as portrayed by Willard Waller, Harold C. Hand, Earl C. Kelley, the Warner group, and Hilda Taba and Robert Havighurst; (4) a fourth area entitled interpersonal relations. The work done by Louis Raths under the concept "human relations" and "intergroup education" by L. A. Cook is included here. Others of standing, working in the area, include C. F. Allen, S. R. Slavson, Virginia Axline, Helen Jennings, Newton Kerstetter and Helen Sargent, and Merle Bonney.

The growth of an area may also be viewed from the standpoint of its mention as a needed area by general writers. This phase is usually followed by a "first course," a "first book," a national society, and then by a professional journal or magazine. So it is with educational sociology.

Lester F. Ward is probably the earliest American sociologist to argue the efficacy of social evolution as opposed to those who had posited a relatively uncontrollable biological evolution. Ward anticipated by several generations the current social emphasis in education and urged the use of government planning "guided by realistic *social education.*"

In a more formal sense educational sociology probably had its inception with John Dewey's *School and Society,* which appeared in 1899 and advanced the proposition that the school is a social institution. At about the same time other educators and many sociologists were taking note of the significance of sociology for education. Men such as A. W. Small, E. A. Kirkpatrick, C. A. Ellwood, Alvin Good, and S. T. Dutton were discussing the need of relating education to the experience of the child in the family and community. Again in 1916 Dewey gave new impetus by his *Democracy and Education.* During the 1920's F. R. Clow, David Snedden, Ross Finney, C. C. Peters, C. L. Robbins, Ernest R. Groves, and others continued to write along the lines mentioned above with recognition of the social values of education.

The first course was taught by Henry Suzzalo in 1910 at Teachers College, Columbia University. But it was not until 1917 that

Walter R. Smith published the first text entitled *Introduction to Educational Sociology*. Departments of educational sociology were established at New York University and at Columbia in 1916. A National Society for the Study of Educational Sociology was organized at the annual meeting of the American Sociological Society in 1923. A yearbook was issued from this time annually. *The Journal of Educational Sociology* was undertaken in 1928 under the editorship of E. George Payne. The magazine *Social Education* was begun in 1936. Since 1940 the *Review of Educational Research* has included material related to educational sociology. It can readily be seen that both in point of time and in point of definition of area as well as crystallization of structure and process, educational sociology is a new science.

As someone said a few years back, "It is and has been whatever people say it is." More recently, as Cook has pointed out, there is a movement of educational sociology from the "earlier indefinite status as a rubric under which sociologists offered 'contributions to education'. . ." toward a "special field, the essence of which is the acculturation [3] process as found in schools and schoollike structures." And may we add any other social institutions which assist or impede the socialization process.

The direction which the area has taken at Ohio State has been outlined in the preface. On the basis of that development rests the plan for this book.

Part I, which follows, will deal with the *sociology of the child.* This will be attempted from the situational approach. The method will be the analysis of both structure and process of the various social backgrounds of the child.

Part II will deal with the *sociology of school life.* The point of view will be that of viewing the school as a microcosm. The method will include analysis of "what is" and "what is becoming." That it has both a social structure and well defined processes for implementing is readily apparent to all who teach. Awareness of social outcomes, if not their theoretical aspects, is keen also in children and parents, especially if they are of lower social status. What makes this social world "tick" will be our basic question.

Part III will attempt the integration of the child as we know

[3] The concept "acculturation" as used by Cook is equivalent to our term socialization.

him, the school as a social institution, and the community from which both are derived and into which both return constantly with or without social acceptance and assimilation.

There will be no effort to appear studiously academic or otherwise erudite through the usage of stilted phraseology. Long ago Charles Horton Cooley reminded us as graduate students that the business of language is the communication of ideas not the confusion of them by fancy terms.

PART ONE

‖‖

The Social and Cultural

Orientation of the Child

A THEORY
OF CHILD ORIENTATION

SOCIAL INTERACTIONISM

THE CURRENT INTEREST in this area of educational sociology frequently centers in a problems approach, a "This is what Johnny does, what shall I do about it?" kind of analysis. It is recognized that people must begin "where and when" they are, and this often means the necessary dealing with phenomena as they appear. A more objective and long-range view, however, suggests that it is worthwhile to take a look at a theoretical framework for the study of the child's personality arisal and development. In other words, we need a structure, a plan, or a framework upon which to base a discussion of child orientation.

We do not just solve problems and understand things. We do both in terms of our scheme of social values, our philosophy of living, or if we have not thought that far, in the light of our particular "bag-of-tricks."

The theory and/or bag-of-tricks postulated here is *"social interactionism."* It means that in the light of present knowledge and research, we have abandoned the belief that any one thing is a cause and another an effect. It means further that a one-factor explanation of personal and social outcomes is discarded.

We have learned that everything, every act, be it individual or group, is both cause and effect. This is to say that what appears as one or the other is but a pause in a continuous, on-going *social process* where one thing is the direct result of all that has gone before and in turn gives rise to what follows. To avoid confusion we may say that there are *contributing factors* to personal and social situations. Likewise, there are outcomes which in turn precipitate the next phase or relationship situation.

The view is then that there is a multitude of contributing factors in the arisal and development of child personality and the attending outcomes in his various social relationships. All of these continuously interlace and interact, touching, fusing, differentiating, again contacting in altered ways, and proceeding at varying rates.

A child, a child's personality, is a whole at any given time, for that time and stage of maturity. Some like to think of it as a configuration. Never is it a sum of its parts, or just a part of a larger whole known as society. We must keep in mind that it is not only the sum total of its parts but also, more important, the organizational outcomes, the product of all aspects working together. Sometimes one area assumes ascendancy, again another seems emphasized, but always all *act, react,* and *interact.*

Since most of us are somewhat eye-minded, let us try a diagram as a base for our discussion. It must be remembered that when one diagrams, he always does violence to a whole. In other words, a diagram often makes a thing look as though it is divided into so many parts. This is not what is meant here. The diagram is to be thought of as a "whole" with its divisions to be used as conveniences in understanding the whole.

Students who have worked with the diagram have said that it is easiest understood if one starts at the top, jumps to the bottom of the structure and then considers the in-between.

The *socialized being,* the person, or one's personality is a product. But of what? Current definitions often reply that the personality is the sum total of all the traits which affect relations with others. Such definitions omit the most important concept in the whole process of socialization.

One's personality is not just the color of eyes, plus hair, plus his intelligence, plus various other aspects of his social self. Every day we encounter people who by such criteria should have the same personalities. Instead, though physical and even social characteristics may be so similar as to seem alike, these persons present very different personality composites to the observer. Apparently the integrational processes which have combined these traits, though little understood, are the keys to the product. It is for this reason that we define the socialized being as the *integrated* product, or sum total,

and integration of all those attributes which affect one's relations
with other people.

The product as seen in the diagram has five bases. There may
be more, but at this point we can recognize and deal with these.
Admittedly, they overlap as do most social facts. There is, however,

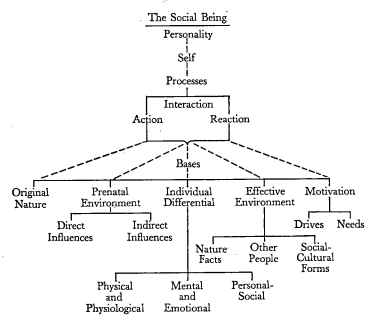

for each a basic central tendency which we may recognize and allow
the boundaries to fall where they may.

ORIGINAL NATURE AS A BASE

The first concept to be considered is *original nature.* What is
this thing? Is it the same as heredity? Is it what we're born with?

The answer is both yes and no. Yes, original nature is com-
prised of the hereditary tendencies and potentialities which have
come down to us through both father and mother lines. No, it is not
that with which one is born.

It can now be shown that original nature exists only for a moment of time, namely, the moment when the sperm and ovum unite to form a new individual. What then, is this original nature, this heredity? What are its structures, its processes? For though it exists for only a moment, its repercussions go down the generations.

Though the answers to these questions form the science of genetics, one of the greatest and most complex of sciences, we can still answer in rather simple and understandable terms.

Human genes, like those in peas, are dominant or recessive. The albinos of circus sideshows are victims of a recessive trait; they have two albino genes. The children of an albino father and a mother with two normal genes have one of each type of gene. Since the normal gene is dominant, they will be normal. But if they marry persons with the same ancestry, their children may have the following types of heredity: (1) two normal genes; (2) a normal gene from father and an albino gene from mother; (3) an albino gene from father and a normal gene from mother; (4) two albino genes. Only the last combination will produce an albino. In other words, the chances are one in four that a grandchild of the original marriage will be an albino— the same three-to-one ratio that Mendel observed in peas.

Not all traits are inherited according to this simple ratio because many of them depend on the interaction of more than one set of genes. But even in the cases where the exact ratios have not yet been discovered, the effects of dominant and recessive genes are evident. For example, curly hair is dominant over straight hair, brown eyes over blue or gray, freckles over unspotted skin, blond or brunette hair over red hair, and some type of baldness over a normal growth of hair.

What Are Genes? Genes are protein molecules five millionths of an inch long. They are difficult to get at not only because of their small size, but also because they lie buried deep in living cells. The heredity-transmitting units do not drift about the cell but come firmly enclosed in "sausage casings." Since these containers absorb different dyes, they are called chromosomes (Greek for "colored bodies").

How You Get Your Genes. The cells of plants and animals have a number of gene-containing chromosomes which are characteristic of the particular species. It ranges from two in a type of roundworm to more than 200 in certain varieties of crayfish. All you inherit is embodied on this quota which you receive from your parents, half from your father and half from your mother.

What Genes Do. Genes are biological architects. Their task is to use material obtained from the environment and build the body according to hereditary blueprints. Every cell in your body contains a full "staff" of 30,000 genes, but which ones work most actively depends on where the cell is located. If your specifications call for brown eyes, a dark complexion, an aquiline nose, and a heavy frame, your genes see to it that the job is done properly. They direct the work of many "craftsmen," including the cells that produce pigments and bone-forming calcium. The parts of the body are so complex, however, that one gene is rarely enough to determine a single trait. At least 150 different genes are required for the construction of the eyes alone, and this total does not include the ones that control eye color.

YOUR GENES AND YOUR CHILDREN

Boy or Girl? The sex of an embryo is determined the instant sperm and egg unite—and the sperm does the determining. All human eggs contain a relatively large body shaped something like an arrowhead and called the X chromosome. But only half the sperm contain this body. If the fertilizing sperm happens to have an X chromosome like that of the egg, the embryo will develop into a girl, because the double-X combination is what produces female characteristics. A Y-containing sperm, on the other hand, results in an XY egg—and a son.

Two of a Kind. One out of every eighty-seven births in the United States results in twins. Usually the reason is that two eggs happen to be released from the ovaries at once, and both are fertilized. Such "fraternal" twins may be of the same or different sexes, depending on the two sperms that penetrate the eggs. The twins may bear no more resemblance to each other than if they had been produced in separate births.

"Identical" twins, however, are always of the same sex and are often mistaken for each other throughout their lives. They come from a single egg. Since this means identical twins have identical sets of genes, they are of special interest in the study of heredity. Detailed life histories of such twins furnish important clues to the interworkings of heredity and environment.

The RH Factor. For many years a mysterious ailment was killing infants in the nation's maternity wards. Most of the victims were born dead; some died a few days after birth. Even in the rare cases where babies survived, the hereditary disease produced permanent after effects, such as deafness and cerebral palsy. There was no effective treatment and no cure.

Then, several years ago, scientists made a discovery that apparently had nothing to do with the disease. They found a new blood group, and called it the RH type (after rhesus monkeys, whose blood was used in the tests). About 85 percent of all Americans have RH blood positive—that is, their red cells contain certain complex substances which had never before been detected. These RH compounds are inherited through dominant genes. But the remaining 15 percent of the population inherit recessive genes. Their red cells lack the RH substances, and they are RH negative.

Doctors meet this situation in two ways. Babies which are born alive but without much chance of surviving may be saved by actually exchanging old blood for new. The infants are given transfusions of fresh blood until all their "bad" blood has been replaced. But, more important, in the long run, parents' blood is typed in advance to find whether or not the danger exists. Then, if there is a risk, doctors can either be prepared for blood transfusion, or else they may advise the couple not to take a chance. RH testing is a standard procedure.[1]

PRENATAL ENVIRONMENT

From the moment of conception the developing, growing fetus and embryo exist in an environment which is most important. "Aha," someone may chortle. "We're back to the old wives' tales of marked babies." But it's not as simple as that. In fact, we are finding that this stage is a frontier in research. What occurs during this period is spoken of as congenital or prenatal inheritance as against germinal inheritance, which refers to potentials in the germ plasms prior to conception. It has been demonstrated that there is no nerve connection between the unborn child and its host. Hence, direct mental influence cannot be applied by the mother, according to present scientific knowledge.

But there are numerous more indirect effects which are generally recognized. These fall into several categories:

1. Certain diseases, such as diabetes, cancer, and syphilitic infections, operate in such a generally deteriorating fashion as to produce many indirect effects. In the main these are much the same as those produced by continued malnutrition. Other diseases such as German measles, we are now told, may affect mentality, sight, and hearing of the unborn child, especially if contracted in the first three months of pregnancy. Reputable physicians are urging that girls be exposed during childhood to the disease to reduce chance contraction during these crucial months.

2. Endocrine imbalances may result in such disorders as cretinism, which is characterized by general retardation, such as emotional and mental subnormalities.

[1] "Genetics—The Science of Heredity," Public Affairs Pamphlet No. 165 (1951), pp. 8–20. Used by permission.

3. The structure of the pelvic region of the mother is also a conditioning factor. Some pediatricians suggest that foot difficulties may be traced to position in the uterine life. Right handedness and left handedness are thought to be more related to congenital position and behavior than to sheer heredity.
4. The shock of being born, birth injuries and the like are suggested as contributing factors to such conditions as those of spastic paralysis, cerebral palsy, and feeblemindedness.

Experiments such as those done by Arnold Gesell and the Fels Institute at Antioch College point up this area of child development as an increasingly important area of research and study with potentials for control.

INDIVIDUAL DIFFERENTIAL

The introduction of the *individual differential* as a base of the socialized individual always brings up a number of questions. Is it the same as the soul? Is it the same as unique experience? Or some more aggressive individual may opine, "I thought this was to be matter-of-fact. Aren't we introducing mystical sociology now?" Perhaps we may clarify better if we say what we find the individual differential is rather than what it is not.

As pointed out earlier, the child lives in groups, and by them he is processed in the light of certain forms of behavior which they have decided are *right, necessary,* and *true.* Some people have gone so far as to say children are shaped by the groups. They believe that the child is a special brand of putty which is molded entirely by the group, its expectations and anticipations. Sometimes such people are called "cultural determinists" and are a good example of one-factor explanations of human behavior, though admittedly their factor is a complex one

Closer examination will reveal, however, that from the moment of birth the child is a growing, developing, dynamic organism. To be sure, he appears powerless against nurses, doctors, and parents who daub his eyes, constrict his movement by clothes, and sometimes allow him to eat only every three or four hours despite the fact that the stomach empties every two. But he is not without resources against these "huge monsters." Valiantly he resists civilization in many ways. He kicks, cries, screams, and on occasion coos, looks angelic, and even smiles to reward the behavior of his caretakers when he approves. But, our critics declare it's a losing battle. Eventually he conforms.

At first he may do just that, conform out of sheer exhaustion, perplexity, and frustration. But as time progresses and his experiences develop, so do his needs, his personal wishes, and his ability at social control not only over his own actions but also over those of others. He does take on gradually the symbols of the group, the words, the gestures, the social tricks of the tribe, but he also becomes a selective agent, often accepting, often rejecting. Most parents know that by the time (varying with maturation rates between sexes as well as just between individuals) he understands language and certainly by the time he uses it, he can and does subtly select, reject, and adapt both persons and forces within his *effective environment*. He learns his objections are not necessarily to be done by crude kicking, yelling, and so forth. Any parent is, or should be, well aware of a child's subterfuges.

The individual differential refers then to the dynamic aspect of personality which is never quite predictable. It is that bit of selfhood which is growing, changing, never completely static (more will be said of this in the discussion on development of the *self*.) Its components are such "traits" as those listed on the chart. Obviously here we do not mean traits as one single discrete item. (If there be social scientists present, let it be said trait is used to include what they would term trait complexes.)

Perhaps the reader wonders why we have included two terms, *physical* and *physiological*. Physical refers to such traits of the individual as his stature, his color of eyes and/or hair. Those who have unusual aspects in any of these areas know how important they can be in the personality adjustment of this individual. A student in one of the classes at Ohio State once illustrated very well what is meant here. He remarked that always he had been too short as measured by the norms for men in our culture. For a long time he had been a "smarty," a bully, and generally, as he put it, an obnoxious little Napoleon. One day, however, an interested and understanding teacher took the time and effort necessary to show him to himself. As a result, he became unusually objective concerning himself. His further remarks might be of interest. Said he, "Even though I am now able to rationalize the matter, I have to admit that I am still irked that I was just too short to play basketball despite my quickness. My legs were too short for track, and I was too slight for football. But the worst of all has always been the fact that all the girls I wanted to date or dance with were just too tall."

Physiological characteristics unlike physical, while not so obvious, are often as, or more, important to the total personality adjustment. The reference here is to the functioning or often malfunctioning of the ductless glands—the endocrine system, which includes the pineal, thyroid, and pituitary glands, the gonads, and the thymus. In certain sections of the country, especially the area of the Great Lakes, thyroid deficiencies and consequent effects are readily noted. These may be mild or extreme. One example will serve to illustrate.

It was summer school time at Columbus with the heat and humidity soaring to their usual heights. Hence one did not wonder too much when a student in the front row seemed on the verge of sleep several days in succession, despite the fact that the discussion was lively and seemingly interesting. On the fourth morning said somnambulant appeared in the instructor's office. She seemed ill at ease and uncertain. After the amenities were over, it became increasingly obvious that she had come with no academic problem. Finally, the reason for her visit came with a rush and bluntly, "I'm so sorry I get so sleepy in your class," she said. "I'm no more bored in it than any other. But I just can't keep awake anywhere if I'm still a minute."

Further discussion developed that she was a school teacher. She taught all the school year, went to school all summer, and then back to teaching in the fall with scarcely a week of vacation. She must go to school to obtain the M.A. so she could secure a larger salary. And going to summer school used up all her money. She felt dull, pushed, tired, beaten, frustrated, caught in a treadmill. She said that while conducting classes, she often gave the children an unplanned recess when she felt she could keep awake no other way.

One might suspect at first glance a disturbed mental condition as primary. Clinic examination, metabolism tests, etc., revealed, however, a glandular disturbance and deficiency. It was indeed amazing to observe what the little white pills did to and for this girl within four weeks. She not only was able to stay awake but also became an active, intelligent participant in discussions.

One word of warning here. It is not suggested, hereupon, that people fly to best sellers on glands as cure-alls. Even in the foregoing case glands were not all in effecting her "cure." Other factors interacted also to aid in the right-about-face. Learning that people were interested in her and her situation, finding that her case was not unusual for the area, plus a realization that even academic and economic factors could be manipulated, gave her a new basis for self-appraisal and realignment of her life pattern.

As the chart suggests and as our example points out, another area for investigation is that of the *mental and emotional.* Here again the principle of interaction is easily illustrated. The physical and physiological often condition, if not determine, reactions in the area. If general physical tone is off center, there are often accompanying repercussions in the areas of irritation, general nervousness, and high emotional response to situations which would ordinarily be taken in stride.

Personal-social traits refer to the child's characteristics which are partly defined by the culture and partly not so defined. For example, the culture mediated through the particular community, family, and other groups prescribes certain attitudes which are to be taken toward not only people but also causes and things.

It also outlines in some detail, depending a great deal upon social class status levels, what one is to consider prime values for living. Some groups value material things, money, increased social prestige. Others play down these values in return for intellectual and or spiritual outcomes. We are all aware of people who remain in an income bracket which fails to provide "things" but allows for richness of thought and interaction with people interested in similar pursuits.

The experience of a six-and-one-half-year-old boy in awakening to these differences between families of playmates will illustrate.

"I do like Tom so well," said he, and then with the seeming irrelevance of childhood, "His father's a minister, isn't he? Why?"

When the slightly nonplussed mother had explained as best she could why people choose various occupations, she was further pushed into a corner by his serious rejoinder.

"Does that make up for never having any money?"

So at an early age without any known direct inculcation, do the money values of the culture impinge upon the growing child. Fortunately for this child, the personal relationships between him and his parents were such that they could discuss this business early and perhaps avoid what the world would term, unhappily, schizoid beliefs concerning such values.

It is such as these very personal-social relationships which are not directly prescribed by the culture. The culture says honor thy father and mother; it does not delineate the ways one will do it. Every counselor who has established a permissive atmosphere has doubtless had the experience of having a counselee say he knows he shouldn't but he hates one or both parents. Usually he is shocked and revolted at what he has said. He has accepted the over-all patterning as to family-parent-child roles, but has worked out the details of the relationship in terms of his own personal-social proclivities.

EFFECTIVE ENVIRONMENT

Let us now center attention upon the *effective environment* which surrounds the individual. First, there are the *nature facts*. The terrain, the geography of the region will condition, though not necessarily determine, many things. We make the qualification between condition and determine for a number of reasons. Many people have thought in the past, and some still do think, that nature facts are all important. These people have said, in effect, "Tell us such things as the topography, the climate, the rainfall, and the earth's resources of the area, and we will tell you what kind of social institutions, customs, and personality types will evolve." In other words, such nature facts are held as determining whether there will be monogamy or polyandrous marriage, whether it will be a capitalistic or some other form of enterprise system, and so on.

At first glance this often seems a good explanation. Closer examination will reveal discrepancies. For example, if nature facts were all, we would expect to find the same or very similar forms in all areas where the same or similar nature facts are found. But this is an invalid assumption.

As even casual visitors to areas can observe, and as social anthropologists have learned, vastly different are the life patterns of the people who inhabit like regions. The differences are found in many areas of living, such as types of clothing, shelter, food, ceremonies, arts and crafts, and child care, to name a few. The Navajo and Hopi Indians of the Southwest provide an excellent illustration of the great cultural divergence of peoples living in similar geographic surroundings within a short distance of each other. The Navajo are a pastoral people doing little or no farming. The Hopi are intensive farmers. The Navajo live in hogans, conical huts made of earth, while the Hopi live in terraced sandstone huts. The Hopi are a completely monogamous people; the Navajo permit polygyny. In Navajo tribes the women do the weaving, but Hopi men perform this function. And finally, the Hopi are traditionally a more peaceful people while the Navajo are traditionally as warlike as any of the Plains Indians.[2]

But as we have indicated above, nature facts do condition behavior. Every teacher or parent knows that nature facts impinge upon "small fry" as well as adults. Humidity and heat set in motion irritability, restlessness, and other socially unacceptable behavior unless there is most careful planning to avoid it. Sports engaged in, manner of dress, types of houses, even menus may be *conditioned* and *delimited* but *not determined* by nature facts.

Another basic conditioning factor is, of course, the culture. Here the viewpoint is that the culture always precedes the individual and is waiting, ready and eager, to process him according to its most cherished patterns.

The term cultural forms refers for sociologists not to refinement and the like but to the way of life of a people. It includes what some students term the *artifacts* and the *immaterial aspects* of a way of life.

Artifacts are simply the material elements of a people. They are the implements one has with which to do his work; the house he lives in; the articles he needs and uses for leisure. But all these "things" are surrounded by idea patterns, by value schemes, and by processes for making them effective. These are the immaterial aspects of cultural forms. Between these two components of the culture there is often much discrepancy both in development and acceptance.

It is a truism that we take on new material objects much more rapidly than we accept new idea patterns. In other words, differential elements of the culture proceed at different rates of speed. The disparities in these rates cause imbalances or cultural lags which may eventuate in tension and conflict action. Thus, we may accept a new artifact, such as a Bendix washer, but still boil clothes all night before using it. When these confusions occur in such areas as standards of child rearing, the focal antagonisms between child and parent may reach considerable sharpness.

[2] For a more complete discussion of geographic factors as limiting rather than determining see Kimball Young, *Sociology, A Study of Society and Culture* (New York, American Book, 1939), Part III "Place and People," pp. 235–399.

The culture then becomes a potent force in orienting the child. As suggested earlier, many people have become so impressed with this fact that they have taken the extreme position that culture *determines* the way the child will live and think. "Give us," they say in effect, "the child as soon as he is born, and what he will become can be determined by the culture which surrounds him." Such cultural determinism is nearly as unreal as geographic or economic determinism.

Closer analysis will reveal that if the bases mentioned are considered, it is evident increasingly that instead of determining, the material as well as the immaterial aspects of the culture *set the stage, limit,* and *influence* but do not determine either personality or cultural developments.

Speaking generally, other *people* are another aspect of the effective environment which surrounds the organism. Some people stimulate a child to better thinking, better acting. "Something" in their make-up gives the child assurance that he is worthwhile, capable, desirable, and accepted. Adults also respond negatively or positively to the total personalities of those who surround them.

Thus, it may be said that *other persons* are of great importance in the stimulation to do or appear at one's best in some instances and in the blocking of activity or in complete negation of it in others.

The social-cultural forms of the diagram include all culturally defined ways of behavior from customs and folkways to mores. One way to view these forms is to say that customs and folkways are to a group what manners are to an individual. In other words, folkways refer to actions which are considered good form but which carry little or no moral sanction.

The mores (singular is *mos,* not *more*) on the other hand are the ways which society has decided *right, necessary,* and *true* for its good and continued existence. Often they have been folkways earlier; by the same token, mores sometimes degenerate into folkways.

In our particular culture the mores have tended to divide themselves into at least three categories. The first includes the *organizational.* Here are included those "musts" of behavior which either through long experience or often as the outcome of crisis have assumed *structure* and *processes* of enforcing the culture. These include monogamy, a modified form of capitalism, etc.

To state it otherwise, the particular ways of doing have been judged of such importance that law has prescribed the structure and the machinery for enforcement with attendant rewards and punishments.

A second category is often spoken of as the *humanitarian* mores. These are those unwritten laws of our society which insist that to some degree we are our brother's keeper; that those of us who are more fortunate have an obligation toward others.

The third category is that of the *scientific* mores. These include the insistence that in a democracy one shall be free to seek the truth through experimentation and research and free to report it without fear of punishment.

Very early we begin to inculcate these values in children, recently, through paper and scrap drives, food and clothing collection and dispersals, and, for slightly more matured youths as well as adults, community chest, Red Cross, charity newsies, and missionary contributions, to mention but a few. The fact that we may sometimes give grudgingly and under pressure only better exemplifies the push and pull of these particular mores.

MOTIVATION

A final area in the consideration of bases of personality is that of the *motivations* which somehow activate this protoplasmic mass known as an infant. Why do we act at all as well as why do we act as we do are worthy questions. Thus far we have talked about the human being as a structural biological organism, to be sure, but one which is always acting in relation to his various environments and necessary adjustment to the same.

It seems imperative *now* to consider this area of action from the standpoint of "What makes it tick?"

It is readily recognizable that "listings" of motives of behavior may, and have, become as numerous as the people interested in listing. To construct new lists seems a waste where acceptable classification exist. Hence, we shall approach this discussion from the combined orientation of two reputable scholars in the field—Kimball Young and Louis Raths.

As suggested in the diagram, there are all kinds of bases and/or motivations to behavior which are both internal and external.

Earlier such motivation was assigned the label of instincts. Why does the infant cry? Why does the growing boy seem obnoxiously aggressive? Why do adults have wars when we know better? Instincts seemed a good answer. It is true that attempts were made to classify them in different ways, but still the word label suggested that all was laid down in the neural patterning of the organism and given a stimulus (some even "forewent" the stimulus) the pattern would unfold like the proverbial rose.

As the inconsistencies of the theory became apparent, the literature dealing with the subject began to acquire such concepts as "instinctive tendencies." By this time the research on animal behavior and infant behavior had indicated that much of what had earlier been considered instinctive was reflex behavior. Likewise, it could be demonstrated that these reflexes could be regulated into habitual behavior. As research accumulated, it was increasingly shown that while the social-cultural conditioning was important and effective, it was not all. The individual differential began to assume its proper place in the analysis of personality arisal and development.

Consequently, authors spoke increasingly of something they labeled wishes and desires, which were culturally and socially defined for the individual by the social group of which he was a member. This type of classification often ignored, or perhaps more accurately assumed, the internal motivations. On the other hand, it did allow for selectivity on the individual's part.

More recently still, the tendency is to avoid the earlier "auras" which clung to such disputed concepts by introducing the terms *drive* and *need.*

Drive is well defined as "a certain state of disequilibrium of the organism setup from within or from without which profoundly influences or directs the course of resopnse, leading usually to a state of equilibrium and adaptation." One great advantage of this approach is that it does not suggest hereditary innateness. Thus, some drives are learned, and some are unlearned.

As these drives become personally, socially, and culturally defined, they take on the character of what we shall here call *needs.* For example, everyone will have physiological drives toward food, rest, and the like. What food will be eaten, how it will be prepared, under what conditions it may be eaten are socially derived and delineated.

This is admittedly a personal bias and an arbitrary classification. Like many another its chief justification is its usability as well as its descriptive ability. If students, after careful thinking, choose to lump the two divisions as *drives* or as just *needs,* or by perchance, a more descriptive set of terms, suggestions are welcome. The important thing is the gaining of insight and understanding concerning all the forces at work.

Kimball Young has provided one of the most challenging arrangements of this kind with relation to *drives*. Paraphrased in terms of the above, it is presented thusly: [3]

A. Physical and Physiological (drives from within)
   1. Respiration and temperature regulation
   2. Hunger and thirst
   3. Eliminative drives
   4. Fatigue and sleep
   5. Sex impulses (which mature after puberty)
B. Physical and Physiological (drives determined by external contacts)
   6. Avoidance of pain, discomfort, or cold—marked by withdrawal reactions
   7. Seeking of comfort, warmth, or pleasant stimulation—marked by approach to the stimulus
   8. Specific pleasures derived from operation of food appetites
   9. Erogenous (sexual) zone pleasure
C. Expressive Reactions
   10. Random vocalization
   11. Random movement of arms and legs, and other associated gross bodily activities, related doubtless to postural tension as well as to interstimulation
   12. Expression of feelings and rudimentary emotions (associated closely with many of those other activities)

In the area of needs as social derivatives Louis Raths and his students have a most provocative listing of needs, as the social and cultural definitions of these physical and physiological disequilibriums.

Children and adults in our culture need: (1) a feeling of belonging, (2) a sense of achievement, (3) a feeling of affection, (4) freedom from fear, (5) freedom from guilt, (6) an opportunity to share in decisions affecting themselves, (7) a feeling of economic security, and (8) integration of attitudes, beliefs, and values.[4]

[3] Kimball Young, *Personality and Problems of Adjustment* (New York, Appleton-Century-Crofts, 1940), p. 62. Used by permission.
[4] Louis Raths and Lawrence Metcalf, "An Instrument for Identifying Some Needs of Children," *Educational Research Bulletin*, Vol. XXIV, No. 7 (Oct. 17, 1945).

But there are other important aspects of motivation to behavior beside those just mentioned. The time element which exists between the drive and its fruition in goal satisfaction is worthy of attention. This is usually referred to as a cycle of activity. Since the discussion of this factor is so well done by Young, we quote him at some length. To avoid confusion it should be noted that Young often uses drive and need interchangeably.

The cycle of activity may be divided, for convenience of description and analysis, into four stages: (*1*) need, want, drive, or physiological tension resulting from disequilibrium set up by internal or external stimuli; (*2*) initial seeking of the stimulus or situation which will satisfy this need—or, per contra, striving to avoid a stimulus if it blocks satisfaction—in short, preparatory effort of some sort; (*3*) final securing of, or avoidance of, the stimulus or situation, often referred to as consummatory activity; and (*4*) the sense of satisfaction, or release of tension or relaxation, associated with the state of equilibrium resulting from the attainment of the goal or end.

The whole cycle may be thought of as a method of releasing tensions, and such release occurs through the consummatory final response—an integrated activity of the highest importance to the balance or the organism. This freedom from strain is a pleasant, serene state, a sort of complacency in the organism which persists until a new cycle ensues. Much of the problem of maladjusted personality rests in the failure of the basic organic tensions to find socially acceptable releases. The partial response is unsatisfactory. Frequently a more or less complete blocking of the releasing responses leads to pathological developments.

There are two other important aspects of the cycle of activity which we must examine. First, no discussion of motivation would be adequate without reference to feelings and emotions. The basic physiological drives connected as they are with the sustaining functions of respiration, circulation, digestion, elimination, sex, and other organic processes—are linked with pleasant or unpleasant feelings and with various emotional states. Moreover, in the striving to attain the goal, or in failure to secure it, the feelings and emotions play important parts. And certainly the sense of release or relaxation which follows the consummatory recourse of events from drive to goal may be greatly influenced by experience or, more technically, by learning. Not only may the drives be modified, elaborated, or acquired by conditioning, but the course of activity from drive to consummation is highly qualified and altered by what we acquire in the way of habits, attitudes, and ideas. Likewise, the goals at which we aim are also profoundly changed and expanded by learning.[5]

THE INTEGRATIVE PROCESSES OF SOCIALI-ZATION

SOCIOLOGY OF LEARNING

The individual is continuously engaged in the process of satisfying these drives and needs. The infant, for example, may become hungry. His stomach empties quickly. The muscles contract when this occurs, and pain results. He needs relief from this unpleasant feeling; he may thrash around in his crib and whimper, and thereby bring someone who will feed him. As his stomach fills, the tension is reduced, and the infant is satisfied and happy. This illustrates the manner in which a "drive" brings about action on the part of the individual. (It should be recognized that *action* does not always indicate physical movement of the body. Similar illustrations could be found where action is not overt in nature.) It demonstrates how a state of disequilibrium, in this case set up from within, influences or directs the response of the individual and leads again to a state of equilibrium.[6]

The newborn infant is very dependent upon society for securing what he needs for a long period of time. It is necessary for him to learn ways by which to satisfy his drives. It is equally important to learn the patterns which are acceptable in his culture. His immediate family group is the agency through which he first begins to learn these methods. If the infant when he awakens squirming and whimpering because he is hungry is presented with food and feels a return to a comfortable state, he begins to learn that squirming and whimpering will bring food. If, however, no food appears when he acts this way and, the tension becoming more acute, his whimpers increase to screams before the food is brought, this infant may learn that screaming is required to bring food.

The family, neighborhood groups, the school, peer groups, and larger community groups all act as agents to teach the child how to behave in ways acceptable in a particular society. The developing self is closely linked with the growing ability of the individual to communicate with others in this constantly broadening environment.

[5] Young, *op. cit.* p. 65 ff.
[6] Janet McCracken, Unpublished paper.

Through the child's identification with, first, his mother and, then, others, he becomes a socialized being.

The child becomes, in rather large measure, his mother, and his mother becomes himself; or to put it more broadly, selfhood is inter-woven with experiencing other individuals. As fast and as deeply as father, brother, sister make their impression on the child, they become parts of him too. This dependence of self upon the percep-tion of others is a primary clue to the social nature of man and to his utter incapacity for any complete autonomy of either perception or action.

Or as G. H. Mead presents it, the socialization of the individual is the "taking over of another person's habits, attitudes, and ideas and the reorganizing of them into one's own system." This results from the playing of many *roles* as he learns to act as others anticipate that he will act. Through the integration of these roles he develops the values and attitudes which form the core of the personality. Jean Piaget's work with Swiss children would indicate that speech of a truly socialized nature develops when he has learned to play the role of another person.

As the socialization of the child proceeds, the child begins to use language as a way to control situations. In the beginning the very young child's adaptations are overt. The two-and-a-half-year old who wants the box another child is sitting in will pull him out by the hair; the five-year old will try to "talk" him out of the box. As three eminent psychologists state it: "Social intercourse as seen in the nursery school shifts from the nonverbal level of smiles, looks, pats, and shoves to 'Can I?' 'What's your name?' 'Don't do that!'"[7] He has begun to learn that words are power devices, that they are definite and efficient in controlling a situation.

During the first weeks of the child's life the vocal chords and the muscles controlling the lungs, tongue, soft palate, and lips are used to make sound of a random nature. Along with these sounds there are many movements of facial muscles, the head, arms, and legs. These random vocalizations and movements of the body are the beginnings of language; they are termed gestures. At first the whole body of the child may be involved in such attempts at com-munication. The stimulus may be the need for food or elimination— internal change—or it may be cold, warmth, or relief from pain—

[7] Gardner Murphy, Lois B. Murphy, Theodore M. Newcomb, *Experimental Social Psychology,* 2d ed. (New York, Harper, 1937), p. 260.

external change. Gestures are related both to internal changes in the organism and external changes in the situation.

Vocalizations are a part of the general activity initiated by such stimuli, and to begin with they have no social significance. However, other people interpret them as having meaning, such as indicating hunger. As a consequence, they react to them and meet a child's smile by an answering smile accompanied by cuddling and the sound of a pleasant voice. When this screwing of his mouth is again and again met by such satisfying experiences, the child begins to screw his mouth, to smile, in order to have the experiences repeated. Blowing out his food, however, may be met by indifference on mother's part; she appears not to notice what is happening. The infant is less apt to repeat this behavior, for neither pleasant nor unpleasant sensations have resulted. Crying, turning aside his head, extending the arms toward a plaything or a person—these are only a few of the gestures a child learns to use in communicating with others.

One little boy, Tommy, who was observed from the time he was nine months of age until he was eighteen months old, used a great variety of gestures. His smile and deep chuckle were signals for a romp. A series of harsh, staccato sounds indicated that he was displeased with something or someone; a toy would be out of reach, the wheel of his kiddie car would be stuck, his own hand might be caught, or he may have wanted someone to play with him. He found that that sound would bring mother to see what had happened and to help where help was necessary. As he learned to walk, he would go find mother and add to his vocalization the grabbing of her skirt to pull her where he wanted her. If it were the opening of a window he desired, he would stand by the window and push up with his hands.

Between the ages of two months and five months, the child begins the babbling or circular-response phase of language development. The gestures do not end at this point as can be seen by the preceding illustration; they become more specific and efficient. In actuality they never completely disappear from the language of an individual. The babbling stage, however, is exceedingly important in the practice gained in the control of the speech mechanisms through the medium of hearing. Susanne Langer pictures this very vividly:

Consider, now, that the vocal play of the infant fills his world with *audible actions;* the nearest and most completely absorbing stimuli, because they are both inner and outer, autonomously produced yet

unexpected, inviting that *repetition* of accidental motions which
Williams James deemed the source of all voluntary acts; intriguing,
endlessly variable noises mysteriously connected with the child himself!
For a while, at least, his idle experiments in vocalization probably fill
his world.[8]

In the same way he will repeat the sounds made by others. This
soon begins to have social implications; when he finds that people
around him will repeat a sound he makes, he will soon produce it
again to gain the approval and the recognition of his mother and
others.

There is a transitional stage between babbling and true speech
which Young calls the imitation phase. Here the child uses the
sounds acquired through the association of hearing and vocalizing
which he has been doing in the babbling stage. This is the time during which the child's random vocalizations begin to become more
specific; from these, "mass activity" responses begin to come differentiated reactions. The child's vocalization may resemble a word
and, therefore, be repeated by another person. The child pronounces
it again and thus begins to isolate the particular vocalization from
the babblings he has been producing so voluminously and so constantly.

The boy mentioned above began to imitate his parents' speech
by repeating the correct number of syllables and with the same inflection but failed to move his lips and tongue in such a way that the
consonant sounds were distinct. Many consonant sounds had been
made during the babbling period; they were not yet attached to the
syllables being pronounced. At the time he was about a year old
he would repeat "Thank you" by almost singing two syllables or
notes, with the first note higher or lower than the second according
to the accent he heard given each word. For several months he continued to do this, gradually increasing the number of syllables he
could repeat and initiating whole sentences of his own. His facial
expression, the tone of voice, and other gestures often indicated the
feelings which accompanied what he was saying. Along with this, a
few words began to be distinguishable; da-da, na-na, Bobby, bye-bye,
ba (for ball), down, and others.

Toward the end of the first year children are found to understand many words even though unable to pronounce them them-

[8] Susanne K. Langer, *Philosophy in a New Key* (New York, Mentor,
1949), p. 101.

selves. At about eleven months Tommy, for instance, gave frequent evidence of understanding a rapidly increasing number of words. At a year of age he crossed a small room to close a door when he was asked, jokingly, to do so. Many words used in his presence brought definite reactions—to say, "Let's go turn on the water for your bath," meant that he left whatever he was doing to go toward the stairs; "ice cream" sent him to the kitchen where he would catch hold of the freezer handle; the names of various toys would be sufficient to send him hunting for them; a particular songbook and a nursery rhyme book were each known to him by particular names.

By means of the circular-response the child moves from the mass activity of random vocalizations to the differentiation of sounds which are favored in his culture. To begin with, children make many sounds which are not used in the language of their own culture. As Young points out, English-speaking children lose the gutterals and many nasal sounds. Or, as Murphy says, each child must make many responses until he hits on one which leads to the reduction of tension. "The process is socially controlled at every stage. It is not enough that the child makes himself understood; he must talk like one of us." [9]

It is interesting to note Susanne Langer's suggestion that there is an optimum period of learning in language development which is closely associated with the lalling or babbling stage. "In a social environment, the vocalizing and articulating instinct of babyhood is fostered by response, and as the sounds become symbols, their use becomes a dominant habit." She continues with the suggestion that in the feral children the babbling stage had been outgrown before it could be exploited for the acquisition of language.

The first words used by a child relate to a general situation; later they assume separate, differentiated meanings. In the child of eighteen months "Car!" is a combination of name and action. It means "Get my hat and coat. There is Daddy's car. Let's go for a ride." Later, it will come to mean a particular object, and other words will be attached to indicate specific feelings and desires related to it. A little girl, sixteen months of age, was already beginning to put words together. Her first combination of words was "Isn't that!" as she pointed to a bright colored picture, to a pretty flower, or any other object which particularly caught her attention. The

[9] Gardner Murphy, *Personality, A Bisocial Approach to Origins and Structure* (New York, Harper, 1947), p. 249. Used by permission.

adjectives were not added to her sentence until several months later.

From this point, the child's vocabulary grows rapidly until by the time he is six or seven years old he is using many thousands of words. A recent study indicates that he can use meaningfully an average of as many as 16,000 words at entrance to school.[10] Furthermore, he uses these words in complete, meaningful sentences.

As the child translates action into gestures and, finally, true language, symbols become increasingly important in managing behavior. In addition, they provide the individual with "the world of meaning, that is, inner anticipatory processes—both conscious and unconscious—which function in the rise of organized inner life and in the prediction of overt adaptation." [11] This second idea has been stated in the following way: "Symbols then, become inner cues to action. The outer symbols used by society have been 'internalized,' 'interiorized' . . . The symbolic organization of the person becomes both a key to, and a factor in the further shaping of, his personality organization." [12] A little later Murphy, describing the way the child learns accepted forms of communication, states:

> But he is highly selective in this process; he learns some words more quickly than others, and develops a rich fund of specialized terms which are his own which portray the deep idiom of his own outlook. He is outwardly and inwardly referring, much of the time, to the goal objects which mean most to him; they are his values and he is defining his values; to do this it is not in the least necessary that the goal objects be physically present. Language then, is one of the richest personality clues that we possess.[13]

Dewey makes the following statement on this point: "Language is similarly not a mere agency for economizing energy in the interaction of human beings. It is a release and amplification of energies that enter into it, conferring upon them the added quality of meaning." [14]

These quotations indicate the importance of the acquisition of language in the developing personality. Words, verbal symbols, provide the most efficient way to manage the environment and, also,

---

[10] Paul Witty, *Reading in Modern Education* (Boston, Heath, 1949), pp. 86–87.

[11] Young, *Personality and Problems of Adjustment,* p. 191.

[12] Murphy, *Personality,* p. 263.

[13] *Ibid.,* p. 266.

[14] Joseph Ratner, *Intelligence in the Modern World: John Dewey's Philosophy* (New York, Modern Library, 1939), p. 808.

are very necessary in enabling the individual to think, to conceive a thing or a situation when it is not actually present. This conception is the basis of the meaning of a symbol. Words become meaningful symbols through relationship with concepts which are related to objects, events, or situations. To conceive a thing is not the same thing as to react to it overtly or be aware of its presence. Talking about things, we use conceptions of them, not the things themselves. The symbols mean the conceptions, not the things.

These concepts are essential in thinking; however, they can easily become divorced from the original concrete experience on which they are based. Where such a thing occurs, they become false and result in vague, unsound thinking. As Murphy states it: "The world of symbols comes from the world of action and returns constantly to the world of action." [15] Without this return, true meaning may become lost or badly distorted.

As the developing human being learns to use language, he increases his ability to reduce the tensions resulting from physiological and social needs. He finds in verbal symbols efficient means of making his needs known, of controlling the behavior of other individuals in the situation, and of understanding the needs of others. He becomes a participant in a cooperative activity in which the behavior of each person in the situation is modified and regulated through social interaction.

Furthermore, through interaction with other human beings, as well as with the material world, he learns the ways of behaving which his society considers suitable and good. As the individual assumes one role and then another, language plays an important part. The words learned are symbols of his identification with the various roles. Through the integration of these roles are developed the attitudes and values which form the heart of the personality.

The particular pattern of symbols or meaning which is internalized is a clue to the values which form the core of the personality. Not only are they clues to the personality, but also they are influential in maintaining and organizing one's values. The following remark is certainly indicative of the personality of a small three-year-old girl as she experienced her first walk in the moonlight. "Look at the moon, Grandmother. See how it makes the whole sky shine." Approximately six months later this same little girl came into her Grandmother's room early one morning, saying, "Words, words,

[15] Murphy, *Personality*, p. 257.

words! My mother and daddy say so many of them. This morning I like my daddy's words more than my mother's." In this statement there is a clear indication of close relationship of words and values and of how a child begins at a very early age to be selective and highly sensitive to the meanings of words, particularly the words of those for whom he has deep affection.

THE SELF

Let us turn to an attempted explanation of the internalization of experience through the action, reaction, and interaction of all the elements thus far discussed.

The dynamics of the social act and, by inference, the creative act proceed first from the general to specialized behavior patterns and from random to planned behavior. This explanation will be based in the main upon the Mead theory of arisal and development of the self.

The self which George Mead posits grows from a social matrix. It develops through action, interaction, and awareness of past action. The self is something which has a development; it is not initially there, at brith, but arises in the process of social experience and activity, that is, develops in the given individual as a result of his relations to that process as a whole and to other individuals within that process.[16] The self has a reflective quality, and in rational conduct the individual takes an objective view of himself. According to Mead, the self develops through social awareness as the individual becomes an object to himself, and he becomes an object to himself only by taking the attitude of other individuals toward himself within a social environment or context of experience and behavior in which both he and they are involved.[17]

Gesture as communication is the basic element in the social act. Communicative gesture, either physical or verbal, makes the action more than an individual act. In the meaning that it conveys it evokes a response, and it is in the response of another organism that the meaning is found. Gesture, then, initiates and elicits response.

The development of the self begins through the assumption of

[16] George H. Mead, *Mind, Self and Society* (Chicago, University of Chicago Press, 1934), p. 135. Used by permission.
    [17] *Ibid.*, p. 138.

roles by the child. The child assumes the roles of several characters. He speaks in one character and responds in another. His response in another character is a stimulus for his action in the first character. His simple role taking develops into play where the attitude of one character calls forth the appropriate attitude of the other. The play develops into a game where the child effects any role at will. He no longer acts as a character but freely assumes the roles of any other involved in the common activity. It is here that he takes on the role of the "generalized other," and in doing so he takes the position of the group and judges his own actions in terms of the social group. The welfare of the others become the object of his own desires. Through his ability to assume the role of the "generalized other" he becomes conscious of his "self."

"What goes to make up the organized self is the organization of attitudes which are common to the group. A person is a personality because he belongs to a community, because he takes over the institutions of that community into his own conduct." [18] Through such a process the individual develops a consciousness of himself. The quality of self-consciousness which develops is the individual's ability to internalize the group of attitudes and responses which belong to the members of the community. The individual is introduced to and comes into a group, and it is through the social process of interaction that his self and his self-consciousness emerges.

Thus, the development of the self occurs in consciousness. Mead differentiates this self into two elements, the "I" and "me." The "I" reacts to the self within, which arises through the taking of the attitude of others. Through taking these attitudes we have introduced the "me," and we react to it as an "I." [19] Both elements are dynamic but each on a different order. The "I" acts for the organism, and in its action it calls forth the attitudes and responses of others. These attitudes and responses are organized into the "me," and the "I" is the answer which the individual makes toward them.

In this process the individual is continuously assimilating the "generalized other" into his "self." "The 'I' both calls out the 'me' and responds to it. Taken together, they constitute a personality as it appears in social experience. The self is essentially a social process going on with these two distinguishable phases. If it did not have

[18] Mead, *op. cit.*, p. 162.
[19] *Ibid.*, p. 174.

these two phases, there would not be conscious responsibility, and there would be nothing novel in experience." [20]

There are several aspects of Mead's concept of the personality which seem important for our purpose. First, the personality develops in a process of social interaction. The individual projects his acts through symbolic communication, and his communications effect responses which are internalized and bear upon his responsive action. Second, the process is an ongoing one, and both the "I" and the "me" are reformed in the ongoing action of the organism. Third, the "I" is the novel in experience. It is the answer which the individual makes toward the attitude of others. The "I" has a sense of freedom and initiative, but its limits are closely circumscribed by the "me." And fourth, the self develops and operates in consciousness with full cognative awareness of the "me" and the "generalized other," for without the other there is no self-consciousness and consequently no self.[21]

Such a theory of the organization of the self is a thrilling one for several other reasons. It's emphasis upon the dynamic, changing aspects and potentials for change are of inestimable importance for social education. The thesis of growth and development through interaction introduces great possibilities for reconstruction.

While we admit the great importance of the formative years, we need no longer despair that the core of personality is so set in early childhood as to be impossible of redirection if not complete re-formation. For social workers, for educators, for parents who feel they got off to a bad start with a child, or any other group which works with children and/or adults, Mead's theory merits extended and intensive study.

The area of language growth and development described above may be taken as an illustration of the processes by which the self organizes.

SUMMARY AND IMPLICATIONS

THE HUMAN INFANT is born human only in form. It takes on personality as it lives and participates in groups.

Hence, the study of personality includes recognition of original

[20] *Ibid.,* p. 178.
[21] Manuel Barkan, Unpublished paper.

nature, prenatal existence, the unique experience or individual differential and its maturation speeds, the pre-existing cultural and social forms as the basic factors from which the specifics are derived through the process of socialization.

The action, reaction, and interaction which go on between and among these aspects to form that organizational outcome known as personality are the basic units of study.

This interaction process may be studied generally in terms of the dynamics of self-development; first, theoretically by the analysis of language and thought growth; and, more specifically and practically, by charting parallelisms in physical and physiological growth rhythms and personal-social outcomes in growth.

These insights need to be further related to the group experiences within which the individual is continually relating himself to others and back to himself, whether consciously or unconsciously, voluntarily or involuntarily.

On the basis now of the theoretical framework presented in this chapter, let us turn to the observation and study of the specific levels of growth and development in the child.

We will need to remember that again we do violence to a whole when we segmentize. Since we can gain insight into the whole, however, only by looking at its components, we will divide the social world in which the individual becomes a person into discussions of family, peer groups, religious groups, and mass media of communication with special emphasis upon the school in Part II.

TEACHING AND STUDY AIDS

1. What is educational sociology? Is it the same as social education? Review briefly its history; present trends in research and classroom procedures and the outlook for the future. The following references will assist you:

    Brookover, W. B., "Sociology of Education: A Definition," *American Sociological Review,* Vol. 14 (June 1949), pp. 407–415.

    Cook, Lloyd A., *A Sociological Approach to Education* (New York, McGraw-Hill, 1950), pp. 484–507.

    Herrington, George S., "Status of Courses in Educational Sociology Today," *Journal of Educational Sociology,* Vol. 21 (November 1947), pp. 129–139.

    ———, "Analysis of Courses in Educational Sociology Changes,"

Journal of Educational Sociology, Vol. 22 (December 1948), pp. 259–275.

2. At this point, examine the plan of the book. Does it seem to you to present a "development flow" of educational sociology? Does it appear to include, or to refer you to, the kinds of "learning outcomes" which you think will be usful to you as a prospective teacher, parent, or community member? If not, where are the lame places? Perhaps you can arrange for special projects which will take account of these areas.

3. What is the difference between an area and a field? Can you make a case for educational sociology as a field?

4. Study, analyze, and compare other theories of personality arisal and development. What are the strengths and weaknesses of the approaches you have contacted? Try outlining your own theory of socialization. Books which will help you include:

Jersild, Arthur T., *Child Psychology,* 3d ed. (New York, Prentice-Hall, 1949).

Linton, Ralph, *The Cultural Background of Personality* (Washington, American Council on Education, 1941).

Murphy, Gardner, Murphy, Lois B., and Newcomb, Theodore M., *Experimental Social Psychology,* 2d ed. (New York, Harper, 1937).

Plant, James, *Personality and the Culture Pattern* (New York, Commonwealth Fund, 1937).

Young, Kimball, *Personality and Problems of Adjustment* (New York, Appleton-Century-Crofts, 1940).

5. Check the literature for studies on prenatal enviromental influences.

6. Knowledge of the motivation of human behavior is of great importance to would-be teachers and parents. Prepare an analysis of motivation, and present it to your class.

7. Respond critically to the viewpoint that the sociology of learning is the study of the development of the self.

8. Check the literature for studies concerning language development. What clues to socialization do you find in such studies?

SELECTED READING REFERENCES

Cooley, C. H., *Human Nature and the Social Order* (New York, Scribners, 1922).

Davis, Kingsley, "Final Note on a Case of Social Isolation." *American Journal of Sociology,* Vol. 52 (1947), pp. 432–437.

Dunn, L. C. *Genetics in the Twentieth Century* (New York, Macmillan, 1951).

Gesell, Arnold, *The First Five Years of Life* (New York, Macmillan, 1930).

Jersild, Arthur T. *Child Psychology,* 3d ed. (New York, Prentice-Hall, 1939).

Langer, Susanne, *Philosophy in a New Key* (New York, Penguin Books, 1948).

Linton, Ralph, *Culture and Personality* (Washington, American Council on Education, 1941).

Mead, George H., *Mind, Self and Society* (Chicago, University of Chicago Press, 1934).

Morgan, J. J. B., *Child Psychology,* 4th ed. (New York, Farrar and Rinehart, 1948).

Murphy, Gardner, Murphy, Lois B. and Newcomb, Theodore M., *Experimental Social Psychology,* 2d ed., (New York, Harper, 1937).

Osborn, Frederick, *Preface to Eugenics* (New York, Harper, 1951).

Piaget, Jean, *The Language and Thought of the Child* (London, Kegan Paul, 1926).

Young, Kimball, *Personality and Problems of Adjustment* (New York, Appleton-Century-Crofts, Inc. 1940).

———, *Sociology* (New York, American Book, 1942).

THE RHYTHMS OF CHILD GROWTH AND DEVELOPMENT

OUTSTANDING men and women who do research concerning child growth and development have always been interested in integrating *what happens* and *when* physically and physiologically with *what happens and when* socially.

Sometimes the research has centered on one phase of these developments and sometimes on another. The job of the educator and the sociologist at this point appears to be that of fitting these studies into a frame of reference which will give direction to teachers and parents who are interested in setting their anticipatory behavior expectations in terms of what research shows is healthful for this dynamic, growing organism.

The material presented below is based upon and adapted from one outstanding attempt at this very aim. The faculty of the Ohio State University School in 1946 on the basis of their own experiments plus a review of the available literature, compiled a monograph entitled "How Children Develop." [1] The timeliness and usefulness of the monograph is attested by it's wide distribution and its translation into other languages.

One of the important contributions of this study is its frame of reference which does not assign the developing child to any watertight compartments. The direction is always in terms of the "developmental flow" of physical growth or maturation and social growth

[1] Material here is adapted and quoted from the bulletin with the permission of the Faculty of the Ohio State University School but should not be considered as a substitute for reading of this excellent bulletin.

and development. This concept allows for variations within and between levels of development and hence is consistent with social education which meets the child where he is and helps him extend himself as he is able toward the goal of optimal development.[2] If it be remembered then that individuals pass through these sequences at faster and slower rates, it will be safe to suggest that there are broad developmental patterns through which each individual passes. One commonly accepted chart for divisions of growth patterns is as follows:

MAJOR DIVISIONS OF PERIODS OF GROWTH

Name of period	*Approximate ages*
Prenatal	0–250 or 300 days
Ovum	0–2 weeks
Embryo	2–10 weeks
Fetus	10 weeks–birth
Birth	Average at 280 days
Neonate	First 2 weeks of postnatal life
Early infancy	First year–3 years
Later infancy	3–6 years
Early childhood	6–9 years
Middle childhood	9–11 years
Later childhood (prepuberal)	11–13 years
Puberty	Average for girls: 12 years
	Average for boys: 14 years
Early adolescence	13–14 years
Middle Adolescence	14–16 years
Later adolescence	16–18 years

The characteristics which may be anticipated for the various periods, as presented below, are adapted from the monograph mentioned previously.

The Prenatal Period—
Neonatal to Early Infancy

AS TOLD in the discussion of original nature, the child is really ages old at the moment of conception. He is not only now biologically older than his parents, but likewise is the carrier of

[2] Optimal is used rather than maximal since it is meant to imply not necessarily "most" but "best for."

SEVEN STAGES IN BOY-GIRL RELATIONSHIP

INFANCY-BABYHOOD
Boy and girl
interested only
in themselves

EARLY CHILDHOOD
Seek companionship
of other children,
regardless of sex

ABOUT AGE EIGHT
Boys prefer to
play with boys,
girls with girls

AGES 10 to 12
Antagonism shown
between sex groups

AGES 13 to 14
Girls become in-
terested in boys,
try to attract
their attention
boys aloof

AGES 14 to 16
Boy group also shows
interest in girls;
some individuals
begin to pair off.

AGES 16 to 17, ON
"Going out in couples"
becomes general

Source: Amram Scheinfeld, *Women and Men* (New York, Harcourt, Brace, 1943), p. 133. Used by permission.

centuries of biological inheritance. Though the combination of two such lines of biological inheritance produces a remarkably unique specimen, there are still great likenesses to parents, siblings, and racial stocks.

Later Infancy   Three to Six Years

I. MAINTAINING PERSONAL HEALTH AND PROMOTING HEALTHFUL LIVING BY:

A. *Meeting needs of rest and diet and freedom from infection. From* dependence on family *through* some independence *toward* eventual complete independence.

Children at this age level are very susceptible to infectious diseases. Respiratory ailments tend to occur in winter and spring, while those of the alimentary tract in summer and fall. Bones are not yet firmly knit, and in line with both this and the fact that more blood is flowing through them to supply materials for growth, there is more predisposition to septic infection. By three years children can feed themselves without spilling, but they still need a selected diet. Often healthy children may eat the same foods as other family members. By three and four children have well-regulated habits of sleeping and toileting. Most three- and four-year olds sleep from eleven to twelve hours at night and from one to two hours during the nap period. Fatigue is usually shown by crossness and restlessness. By the age of six nutritional, toilet, and similar difficulties point "either to deficiencies or—more frequently—to blockings in the total environment."

B. *Achieving optimal physical and organic development. From* rapid growth *through* rapid and uneven growth *toward* relative stabilization.

Heights and weights for children range as follows:

	Height in inches	*Weight in pounds*
3-year-old boys	33–40	26–36
girls	32–40	25–35
4-year-old boys	35–43	29–41
girls	35–43	29–40
5-year-old boys	37–45	43–45
girls	36–46	31–42

By the age of three the full set of temporary teeth is developed. Six-year molars may erupt towards the end of the period. From two

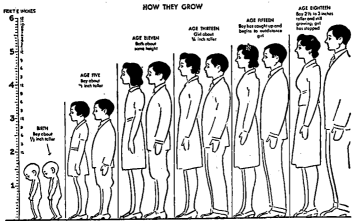

HOW THEY GROW

Source: Amram Scheinfeld, *Women and Men* (New York, Harcourt, Brace, 1943), p. 54. Used by permission.

to five accessory muscles controlling fingers and hands are incomplete in growth and coordination. Right or left handedness occurs by five years. Ninety percent are right handed. Infantile masturbation is practically universal between two and six years. No "rightness" or "wrongness" is attached in his thinking.

C. *Engaging in suitable physical recreational activities.* *From* random manipulation and little social activity *through* hearty physical activity with some controlled manipulation and enjoyment of simple social activity *toward* more controlled manipulation and highly organized activity.

Constant activity such as jumping, climbing, and rhythmic activities are the outstanding characteristics. Three-year olds are interested in imaginative play; four-year olds begin games with others; five-year olds perform the same activities but with a great deal more coordination.

> D. *Developing zeal for promoting healthful living in the immediate and wider community. From an unawareness of health through concern over one's own health toward an awareness of health problems involving the immediate and wider community.*

This age-level child can be taught to use only his own handkerchiefs, towels, etc.

II. ACHIEVING AND MAINTAINING A SENSE OF SECURITY BY:

> A. *Gaining and holding affection, confidence, and esteem. From holding the affection of the family through also gaining and holding the affection, confidence, and esteem of age mates of both sexes toward security in larger social groups.*

These attempts are usually geared toward adult approval rather than peer group sanction. There is no concern for large groups in friendship attempts. But there is a constant hunger in a normally developing social individual for companionship with other children.

> B. *Achieving status. From the egocentric stage through achieving status in the family group and with age mates toward achieving status in the wider community.*

Two- to four-year olds usually are characterized by great resistance to authority. The resistance is usually transitory and needs great understanding. It probably is connected with the difficulties caused because the child does not yet have words to express all his urges and experiences.

The three-year old's life is still centered about his own needs. He is in process of translating "generalized others" into his "me." He wants to participate in all family activities. In fact, status within his family is a major interest with him. He is leaning heavily toward the four-year old's demands that he make decisions for himself. He talks about "how big" he is. Though this may appear to be interest in size only, it has subtler psychological development meanings also. He is ready to begin loosening, if not cutting, the apron strings.

C. *Realizing economic independence. From* dependence upon family *through* some economic independence *toward* complete economic independence.

Most children this age know some coins and what they will do if saved as in a penny bank.

D. *Becoming a social personailty. From* being asocial *through* growing ability to make social responses *toward* adequate and discriminating social response.

Though we maintain that the socialization process begins in rudimentary form at birth, and possibly before, it is true that until about three years the child hits or pushes with little regard for others. He appears selfish because he considers as his whatever he holds or wants; he is resistant and often negative in response to controls exerted upon him. If he is wisely guided, he will gradually work into patterns for getting along comfortably with others. By four years he is eager for other children's company and for their approval. By this age he will engage not only in parallel play but in short-time span games with others. It is perfectly normal for him to have imaginary playmates. His language ability is now such that he can relinquish such attempted controls as crying, hitting, and the like.

The five-year old exhibits a continued development and coordination of all the areas mentioned. He appreciates (if his home and school environments are stable and wisely done) the rights of others. Girls are usually less quarrelsome. Friendships tend to be more stable; imaginary companions should disappear. Organized play in groups of six to eight may be sustained for fifteen minutes or more. The child of this age is embarrassingly blunt, and unless influenced by adults, he has no prejudice concerning race, color, or economic status.

III. DEVELOPING AND MAINTAINING A
SENSE OF ACHIEVEMENT BY:

A. *Gaining a sense of personal adequacy and orientation.
From* a feeling of adequacy through family life *through*
adequate participation in groups beyond the family *toward*
participation in the life of the wider community also.

This goal is advanced in much the same way as mentioned
above with one exception. At this age level he is not likely to have
had community participation unless he has attended nursery school,
kindergarten, or Sunday school.

B. *Understanding and gaining control over the environment.
From* meeting simple wants *through* gaining some control as
a group participant *toward* sufficient understanding of the
environment to solve some of the basic problems of living.

In addition to the accomplishments mentioned above, children
of five can narrate a complete experience, can supply such information as name, address, telephone numbers, and father's name and
business. They are able to manage such home situations as dressing,
setting the table, hanging up clothes, and the like. Opportunities for
these kinds of experiences are of inestimable value in giving the
child a sense of success and achievement so necessary to good mental
health.

C. *Developing sensitivity to the opposite sex. From* social
response without reference to sex *through* social response
excluding the opposite sex *toward* response and adequate
social adjustment to the opposite sex.

IV. DEVELOPING AND MAINTAINING
EVER WIDENING AND DEEPENING
INTERESTS AND APPRECIATIONS BY:

A. *Achieving intellectual and esthetic interests and appreciations. From* satisfactions with immediate sensory experience *through* some attempt to interpret sensory experience

toward sensory experience as contributing to the intellectual and esthetic life.

Children at these ages are highly dramatic and interested in exploring all media of expression. Fortunate, indeed, are youngsters who are provided with opportunities for expression, manipulation, and exploration in music, drawing, painting, and science. At first, interest will be largely centered in activity and materials. Shortly, however, the daubs of paint suggest ideas and gradually increasing, linguistic ability will center on stories of the ideas which their drawings and paintings suggest to them.

B.   *Developing social values and appreciations. From asocial interests through rapidly changing interests and superficial values toward established and more or less permanent interests and social values.*

Increased desire for companionship of other children is usually shown at this time. Though most three-year olds do not share toys readily, they are willing to "help" and participate in familiar family activities. Their interests depend largely upon the quality and diversity of experiences within their family and community. By five most children realize that "things" belong to people and that persons have rights *and* responsibilities if it is constantly called to their attention. They are also ready to respect the wise use of authority.

Early Childhood   Six to Nine Years

I. MAINTAINING PERSONAL HEALTH AND PROMOTING HEALTHFUL LIVING BY:

A.   *Meeting needs of rest and diet and freedom from infection. From dependence on the family through some independence, toward eventual complete independence.*

Children of six to nine years sleep from ten to twelve hours. This is needed to combat the great fatigue they experience in the periods of rapid growth. Generally, they are sturdy and healthy and come through children's diseases well. Accidents are chief death causes at the eight-year-old level because of the adventurous spirit of this age level. If nutritional, toilet, and sleep problems still persist, they may usually be traced to over protectiveness and solicitation on the part of the parents and the resulting tension. These children are capable of considerable independence. They understand about keeping things out of the mouth, wearing of proper clothing, the need to treat cuts for infection, and the like.

B. *Achieving optimal physical and organic development. From* rapid growth *through* rapid and uneven growth *toward* relative stabilization.

Though there are individual differences, an annual growth of two to three inches and an annual weight gain of three to six pounds is to be expected. From five to seven legs lengthen; bodily growth rate slows; the chest becomes larger in circumference than the head or abdomen; the heart is still growing rapidly. Any postural defects show at this period. Six-year-old girls are about as mature as seven-year-old boys. Six-year molars appear between five and six, and the deciduous teeth are lost. While muscular development is incomplete, large muscle control is much more evident than small muscle control. This is a most important fact both for school and home selection of training programs. Eye-hand coordination forges ahead during the latter part of the period. If masturbation has persisted thus far, a sane attitude is necessary to prevent persistence into later developmental periods.

C. *Engaging in suitable physical recreational activities. From* random manipulation and little social activity *through* hearty physical activity with some controlled manipulation and enjoyment of simple social activity *toward* more controlled manipulation and highly organized activity.

Six-year olds have reasonably good basic motor controls and are eager to learn more. They are interested in stunts which involve speed, energy, jumping, and running. They like to be "it" in games and will play team activities such as soccer and football, if rules are "watered" a bit. Girls, especially, enjoy "dressing up" and enacting appropriate parts. Boys identify themselves with cowboys, Indians, cops, and robbers.

> D. *Developing zeal for promoting healthful living in the immediate and wider community. From an awareness of health through concern over one's own health toward an awareness of health problems involved in the immediate and wider community.*

As suggested in another connection, these children will remember to preserve their own health in some ways, and by this age period they will assume responsibility to others to such extents as covering noses and mouths when they sneeze or cough.

II. ACHIEVING AND MAINTAINING A SENSE OF SECURITY BY:

> A. *Gaining and holding affection, confidence, and esteem. From holding the affection of the family through also gaining and holding the affection, confidence, and esteem of age mates of both sexes toward security in larger social groups.*

These are the years when children speed up the establishment of independence from adults. They may do it by refusing to do as asked or told, or by accusing adults of being bossy or not fair. They delight in socially unapproved language, unwashed hands, and remonstrance at "dressing up."

Their contradictoriness is also shown in other ways. They are at loggerheads most with their own siblings yet most sympathetic and kind if siblings are hurt or attacked by others. They are daring, yet have great fears, such as of blood, death, the dark, ghosts, fire, and being alone. Girls are shown to be more fearful than boys. Toward the end of the period the "gang" interest arises and needs to be directed carefully and at once. Jealousy is also characteristic of this period.

Withal there is great need and seeking for adult love and approval. Lucky is the child whose parents and teachers "understand" and really "stand by."

B. *Achieving status. From* the egocentric stage *through* achieving status in the family group and with age mates *toward* achieving status in the wider community.

Boys of six and seven gain prestige by being the largest in the group. Girls are not so concerned over size. By seven and eight all see themselves in relation to the skills of others, and all are sensitive to ridicule, teasing, failure, or loss of prestige. Seven-year olds envy eight-year olds, and they are quite disdainful of what six-year olds can do.

Most children understand competition at this age level, and they engage in it in many ways. The influence of the peer group is in its early stage. By the latter part of the period it is warring for status in decisions of right and wrong conduct, play activities, and types of clothing to be worn.

C. *Realizing economic independence. From* dependence upon the family *through* some economic independence *toward* complete economic independence.

Children of these ages can comprehend "Why we need money?" "Where do we get money?" "How shall we spend it?" They can handle it ably (given some instruction) in shopping situations. They can learn budgeting through a family allowance, and they are now interested in "earning money from small jobs."

D. *Becoming a social personality. From* being asocial *through* growing ability to make social responses *toward* adequate and discriminating social responses.

The child who prefers to be alone at this age is an exception. These children are eager for as many "turns" as possible, and they are able to work out differences more easily. Comradeship still tends to be casual and changing. If the child's behavior is acceptable, children of this age tend not to discriminate on basis of race, creed, or social status unless prejudiced by adults. This fact provides an equaled opportunity for laying foundations of objectivity.

III. DEVELOPING AND MAINTAINING A SENSE OF ACHIEVEMENT BY:

A. *Gaining a sense of personal adequacy and orientation. From a feeling of adequacy through participation in family life through adequate participation in groups beyond the family toward participation in life of the wider community.*

Children of this age are capables of self-criticism and will take that of age mates without too much frustration. They are likewise unblocked in creative and artistic expression. Eight- and nine-year olds tend to have so much self-confidence that they demand to do things beyond their technical ability.

B. *Understanding and gaining control over the environment. From meeting simple wants through gaining some control as a group participant toward sufficient understanding of the environment to solve some of the basic problems of living.*

Six-year olds need the knowledge of handwriting only in relation to such as writing names, dates, and labels. The stage of small muscle coordination is too low to allow for much skill in writing, and if the skill is pushed beyond the readiness level, it may be harmful.

Reading readiness will depend upon the control of the eye muscles and nerves, intellectual abilities and interests, and experiences in relation to cultural background. Some are ready to read by six and one-half years; boys, especially, often are not ready before seven or eight years. Number understanding comes slowly and only with practice and experience in using concrete objects and situations. Six-year olds can work simple problems, such as the absences in the school room or the lunch order problems. Seven-year olds can be expected to count by 1's, 2's, 5's, and 10's; to add and subtract simple combinations; tell time; measure in inches; write numbers and understand meanings of $\frac{1}{2}$, $\frac{1}{3}$, and $\frac{1}{4}$. They are still planning in terms of immediate goals but have a growing realization of time and time sequence.

> C. *Developing sensitivity to the opposite sex. From* social response without reference to sex *through* social response excluding the opposite sex *toward* response and adequate social adjustment to the opposite sex.

At six, boys and girls play with companions of either sex, are not self-conscious about their bodies, nor are they embarrassed by expressed affection. They are now unaffectedly interested in the development of babies, both of the human and animal worlds. By eight and nine they enter a phase of strong attachment for their own sex.

IV. DEVELOPING AND MAINTAINING EVER WIDENING AND DEEPENING INTERESTS AND APPRECIATIONS BY:

> A. *Achieving intellectual and esthetic interests and appreciations. From* satisfactions with immediate sensory experience *through* some attempt to interpret sensory experiences *toward* sensory experiences as contributing to the intellectual and esthetic life.

Children of five, six and seven are interested in nearly everything of the present time and environment. Eight-year olds' interests are extended in both time and space.

Six-year olds strive to reproduce their experiences in drawings and paintings. If the object is recognizable, the proposition is unimportant to them. For example, the man and the house may be the same size and cause no frustration if the child is fortunate enough to be surrounded by people who realize that his expression is more important at this period than how he does it.

Toward the latter part of the period he begins making the transition from this symbolic to the realistic stage. He becomes concerned with relative size, perspective, and correctness of detail. By this time too he can enjoy stories without pictures and "goes in" for jokes, riddles, and humorous stories. His trend toward realism and objectivity is shown by the questions he asks, such as "Where is God?" "What would happen if a flier went on up?" "What is a million?" By now they are gaining respect for skill, and if they live in a democratic atmosphere, ɪ   make their observations with a minimum of envy.

B. *Developing social values and appreciations. From* asocial interests *through* rapidly changing interests and superficial values *toward* established and more or less permanent interests and social values.

The sense of social values in these children includes wanting every one to have both his just rewards and his punishments. They still do not discriminate against children of other races, social positions (unless influenced by adults), but they will discriminate against children who are "outsiders" of their play groups.

C. *Understanding and respect for the cultural heritage. From* lack of concept of culture *through* growing interest in the adventure and drama of building the culture *toward* understanding the contribution of the past to the present, and the desire to contribute to the present culture.

By eight years of age children are able to contrast past, present, and future. They are curious about and interested in comparing the tools, clothing, and household objects of other times and other cultures with their own.

Middle Childhood   Nine to Eleven Years

I. MAINTAINING PERSONAL HEALTH AND PROMOTING HEALTHFUL LIVING BY:

A. *Meeting needs of rest and diet and freedom from infection. From* dependence on the family *through* some independence *toward* eventual complete independence.

Nine-year olds normally sleep about eleven hours, while a ten-year old sleeps about a half hour less. If they are sleeping less, as they often are at this age, the situation needs careful attention. Over stimulation may readily occur at this age since children do not commonly recognize the need for relaxation.

The need for special diets is gone by this age, and normally it is a healthy, sturdy period, freer from diseases than any other. Most children's diseases are over; few "adult" diseases have taken hold. Tuberculosis is still one of the more serious hazards. If the child has lived under the proper atmosphere, his personal hygiene habits are well established.

B. *Achieving optimal physical and organic development. From rapid growth through rapid and uneven growth toward relative stabilization.*

Height and weight growth is now slow and steady. Legs grow faster than trunks; some signs of adolescence often appear. The period of least growth is from nine to ten for girls and from ten to eleven for boys. The sustaining systems—the circulatory, digestive, and respiratory—are mature in function, but growth continues. At ten years eyes have reached adult size and maturity of function. The brain and spinal cord are adult in size, but cellular development is not complete but continuing. Posture is likely poorer than at six or seven. At nine and ten the first and second bicuspids appear; at eleven, the cuspids. Teeth straightening may begin at nine.

C. *Engaging in Suitable Physical Recreational Activities. From random manipulation and little social activity through hearty physical activity with some controlled manipulation, and enjoyment of simple social activity toward more controlled manipulation and highly organized activity.*

The organic need for strenuous physical activity is great and evinces itself in never walking when they can run and never running when they can jump or skip. There is considerable interest in organized games, outdoor activities, and such construction activities as making model airplanes or radio sets. Play they must, and, hence, it is very important that adequate places and opportunities are pro-

vided. Sex differences in interests and behavior are becoming more
noticeable.

> D. *Developing zeal for promoting healthful living in the im-*
> *mediate and wider community. From an awareness of health*
> *through concern over one's own health toward an awareness*
> *of health problems involving the immediate and wider com-*
> *munity.*

These children will take some responsibility for personal hygiene, but they are not much concerned about public health.

> *II*. ACHIEVING   AND   MAINTAINING   A
> SENSE OF SECURITY BY:
>
> A. *Gaining and holding affection, confidence, and esteem.*
> *From holding the affection of the family through also gain-*
> *ing and holding the affection, confidence, and esteem of*
> *age mates of both sexes toward security in larger social*
> *groups.*
> B. *Achieving status. From the egocentric stage through*
> *achieving status in the family group and with age mates*
> *toward achieving status in the wider community.*

Now children demand that they must be in and do "like" the
group. In fact, they are more interested in peer than in other group
approval. Social clubs, secret societies, and scouting organizations
flourish and become more complex in organization. Badges as
symbols of membership are popular. Group size is still small, ranging from four to ten members.

> C. *Realizing economic independence. From dependence*
> *upon the family through some economic independence to-*
> *ward complete economic independence.*

Children of this age have a growing understanding of the
family budget and are anxious to earn money by special jobs, but

they are not too capable of managing their own allowances wisely unless given careful guidance.

> D. *Becoming a social personality. From* being asocial *through* growing ability to make social responses *toward* adequate and discriminating social responses.

Children from nine to eleven are ready for widening contacts, such as visits, camp experiences, and trips. Much of their behavior, especially in club meetings, is characterized by pointless laughter, silly antics, rough-housing, secret codes. The group forces consideration for others in an impersonal and objective fashion. Faults are discussed openly, and discipline is swift and relentless.

> III. DEVELOPING AND MAINTAINING A SENSE OF ACHIEVEMENT BY:
>
> A. *Gaining a sense of personal adequacy and orientation. From* a feeling of adequacy through participation in family life *through* adequate participation in groups beyond the family *toward* participation in the life of the wider community.

Children gain markedly in this respect if they are recognized helpers, planners, and participants in family affairs, actions, and events. Children of this age seem to enjoy an enemy. They are excited by the feeling of solidarity with those on their side.

> B. *Understanding and gaining control over the environment. From* meeting simple wants *through* gaining some control as a group participant *toward* sufficient understandings of the environment to solve some of the basic problems of living.

The vocabulary of an average nine-year old is 10,395 words; that of the ten-year old is 12,460 words, and the average eleven-year old, 13,965 words. Nine-year olds generally read for both information and enjoyment but a four or five year range in reading ability may be expected with some eleven-year olds reading at adult level.

At this time, too, reading disabilities may influence the entire personality adjustment if not carefully handled.

Attention spans increase now, and children are able to fit past events into proper sequences. They are capable of making more longtime plans and can recognize and act upon the principle of division of labor and pooled thinking. Most children of this age level are able and willing under guidance to make decisions affecting their welfare and accept consequences where not too serious.

C. *Developing sensitivity to the opposite sex. From* social response without reference to sex *through* social response excluding the opposite sex *towards* response and adequate social adjustment to the opposite sex.

Sex differences in behavior and interests begin to appear, and boys and girls play less together. Wise schools and homes recognize this trend and gear programs accordingly instead of forcing other kinds of behavior. By eight and one-half boys are strongly attached to boys and girls to girls. This lasts a shorter time for boys than girls. Girls show self-consciousness in playing with boys about (eleven) a year earlier than boys. Girls show their affection by putting arms around one another. Boys do this by punching, wrestling, and tripping. Though they have been interested in an elementary way in reproduction from four years on, they will react now to such explanations with understanding and objectivity.

IV. DEVELOPING AND MAINTAINING EVER WIDENING AND DEEPENING INTERESTS AND APPRECIATIONS BY:

A. *Achieving intellectual and esthetic interests and appreciations. From* satisfaction with immediate sensory experience *through* some attempt to interpret sensory experiences *toward* sensory experiences as contributing to the intellectual and esthetic life.

From nine to eleven imaginative play decreases, and interest in facts and realism increases. A child by the time he is nine seems eager and able to work in more materials. By eleven clay, paint, wood, and musical instruments are used with more discrimination and skill. Help is sought more often, and frequently standards climb so high as to outdistance their skills. The sense of rhythm, sound discrimination, and associative memory have reached adult levels. A good sense of humor is usually developed by nine years of age. As reading ability increases, nine-year olds are eager to learn facts, but they also enjoy the comics, fairy tales, and stories of the "wild" West. By ten they add books of travel, life in other lands, mechanics, and biography to their reading lists. This is the age when lasting interest in science may be developed. By eleven and twelve they show rapid progress in generalizing, making deductions, and solving problems. Abstract principles are still rudimentary.

> B. *Developing social values and appreciations. From* asocial interests *through* rapidly changing interests and superficial values *toward* established and more or less permanent interests and social values.

This is the age of collections. It becomes prevalent about ten years of age for boys and eleven for girls. By ten considerable team-work, loyalty to teams, and better organized games are usual. Though moral codes are obtained largely from home, children of this group are now interested in terms of their own personal experience. They can learn a regard for truth, to be fair and just and not to steal. (Almost every child between six and ten has had one or more experiences in taking things which did not belong to him.) As mentioned, clubs thrive as laboratories for extending the child's independence. A great hazard of the age is that of juvenile delinquency.

> C. *Understanding and respect for the cultural heritage. From* lack of a concept of culture *through* growing interest in the adventure and drama of building the culture *toward* understanding the contribution of the past to the present and the desire to contribute to the culture.

These children are anxious to learn factual information about their culture; they love the adventure which has gone into its construction. They have little interest in its political history as yet.

Later Childhood	Age Eleven to Thirteen Years

I. MAINTAINING PERSONAL HEALTH AND PROMOTING HEALTHFUL LIVING BY:

A. *Meeting needs of rest and diet and freedom from infection.* (To save repetition, remembrance of the "flow" will be assumed henceforth.)

Rest needs now approach those of adults, eight to eight-and-a-half hours of sleep. Boys have much more physical endurance than girls, but both boys and girls are likely to go beyond normal fatigue unless guided carefully. Childhood diseases have about run their course. But resistance to infection is low; hence, there may be many minor illnesses with an attendant need for frequent health examinations. Ravenous but finicky appetites are common. These children are capable of treating minor hurts and realize why it is important to do so.

B. *Achieving optimal physical and organic development.*

This is a rapid growth period with girls usually taller and proportionately heavier than boys. Boys grow broad-shouldered, deep-chested; girls are becoming physically mature—breast and hip development is noticeable. Menstruation may begin and so initiate a most important and hectic adjustment unless there is proper preparation and continued reassurance.

C. *Engaging in suitable physical recreational activities.*

Team games which involve increasing organization are popular now. There is great need for supervision in terms of choice of games which are appropriate to the strength and need for development. Children are now willing to practice and submerge personal ego for the good of the team.

D. *Developing zeal for promoting healthful living in the immediate and wider community.*

At this level the child's concern over his health may manifest in undesirable behavior, such as withdrawal, morbidity, or over-aggression. He understands more about group health problems, such as contagious diseases.

II. ACHIEVING AND MAINTAINING A SENSE OF SECURITY BY:

A. *Gaining and holding affection, confidence, and esteem.*

Status with peers is now more important than adult approval. Desire for group approval increases the amount of club participation. Desire for attention becomes very important with special emphasis on the family's realization of the importance of his affairs and friends. There is a desire for privacy—a room of one's own and private possessions. In the early part of the period there is a tendency to associate with one's own sex. Friendships may be very transitory or remain constant for several months. Socially maladjusted children often gain security by overeating and overactivity.

B. *Achieving status.*

"Dates" are beginning to be a status implement for girls, but boys may lose status if they appear to like girls. Family status should be so clearly defined by now that it will serve as security to back adventures into peer group competition for status.

C. *Realizing economic independence.*

These children can understand the relationship between their wants and the size of the family income. They can distinguish between luxuries and necessities. Some are eager to supplement their allowances by earning money. Some families try to discipline the child of this age by using the allowance as a lever. This possible boomerang should be carefully considered as this age level desires for such things as clothes, movies and "cokes" coincides with an increase in stealing.

D. *Become a social personality.*

By now children will remember to employ the "niceities" in relations with others. They do not criticize each other quite so openly. They are clearly aware of group pressure concerning acceptable behavior and are anxious to stand "right" with their classmates. At this level children of similar interests and problems quite frequently group themselves together. Parties and get-togethers take on added meaning toward the latter part of the period. There is a great attempt to sponser affairs which are more like those of older groups.

III. DEVELOPING AND MAINTAINING A SENSE OF ACHIEVEMENT BY:

A. *Gaining a sense of personal adequacy and orientation.*

Children of this age like to feel their ideas are important in family and group planning. They are eager to do things which yield the satisfaction of achievement and self-improvement. Many get a great feeling of adequacy from living according to the codes of such groups as Boy Scouts, Campfire Girls, and Girl Scouts. Insecurities and feelings of inferiority may develop in both rapidly and slowly maturing individuals.

B. *Understanding and gaining control over the environment.*

Eleven to thirteen year olds evince increasing ability to deal with quantitative aspects of the environment. Words are now their most common medium of expression though they still profit from expressing ideas through tangible materials. Their growing understanding of cause and effect relationships helps them to predict and plan with greater effectiveness. They can and are willing to analyze situations verbally.

C. *Developing sensitivity to the opposite sex.*

In the early part of this age there is a tendency to prefer one's own sex, especially among girls. "Crushes" on both age mates and adults are common. Roughness and rudeness to all females often characterizes a short period for boys. This is followed by a period of overt interest in the other sex. Girls show social awareness earlier than boys. There is a keen interest in their own bodies and in problems related to sex and sex processes of both human beings and all other living organisms.

IV. DEVELOPING AND MAINTAINING EVER WIDENING AND DEEPENING INTEREST AND APPRECIATIONS BY:

A. *Achieving intellectual and esthetic interest and appreciations.*

Imaginative play practically disappears at this age level. Manipulations of things is still enjoyable. There is relatively little interest in art, history, architecture and sculpture, but some interest is manifested in crafts and ornamental art objects. There is an increasing interest in the technical aspects of machinery. Religious interests often become intense during this period.

B. *Developing social values and appreciations.*

After passing through a phase where adult opinions are considered a hindrance, these children may seek adult companionship and guidance. By this period children can learn to do things for others where no immediate and tangible rewards are involved. It is true that this type of behavior is characteristic of children of earlier ages where there is a social education philosophy, but the action is largely initiated, or at least prompted, by others. Cooperative behavior enjoys increasing recognition as a "better" plan of action.

C. *Understanding and respect for the cultural heritage.*

Children of this age are beginning to appreciate the contributions of past achievements to present living. They show continued interest in factual information concerning the building of the culture, in its dramatic, adventureous, and scientific aspects.

Early Adolescence	Thirteen to Fourteen Years
and	
Middle Adolescence	Fourteen to Sixteen Years

I. MAINTAINING PERSONAL HEALTH AND PROMOTING HEALTHFUL LIVING BY:

A. *Meeting Needs of rest and diet and freedom from infection.*

Rest needs are now similar to those of adults. These teen agers feel that they have unlimited resistance and energy and hence are overconfident of their own health care. Growth is rapid, and frequent health examinations are necessary.

B. *Achieving optimal physical and organic development.*

Most girls are taller and proportionately heavier than boys. Differences tend to decrease by fourteen years, and by sixteen a state of relative physical and organic stability has been reached. Growth is rapid through fourteen years. Considerable muscular developments occur, and glandular changes influence the whole tone and effectiveness of the organism. Tiredness and self-consciousness often are accompanied by postural slumps. These may prove unhealthy and must be watched. Skin disorders, especially acne, continue throughout both periods. Girls are approximately a year ahead of boys in both organic and physical maturity as well as mental and emotional stability. Most researchers agree that masturbation is practically universal in boys for varying periods of time and also that more girls masturbate than is commonly supposed. From now on infantile sex expressions tend to become adult. Here, as in earlier levels, other interests can be substituted since sexual tension finds expression in games, dancing, hiking, and the like. As important is a frank, honest, and thoroughgoing sex education program both at home and at school.

C. *Engaging in suitable physical recreational activities.*

In early adolescence the uneven and rapid growth of the individuals causes poor physical coordination. By middle adolescence there is considerable improvement, especially among girls. As co-ordination increases, so does the preference for games requiring higher skill. The differentials in growth and development make difficult a choice of activities to interest all, hence, cliques often develop now.

>   D. *Developing zeal for promoting healthful living in the im-mediate and wider community.*

Children of early adolescence are becoming aware of the theoretical need for proper eating habits and need for rest, but they do not allow this awareness to affect their own behavior. By later adolescence they show concern about such social problems as housing, vaccination, and juvenile delinquency. They will now assume some responsibility for maintaining both their own and group health.

>   *II*. ACHIEVING AND MAINTAINING A SENSE OF SECURITY BY:
>
>   A. *Gaining and holding affection, confidence, and esteem.*

Family security and status are still extremely important. In middle adolescence though he is striving for independence, he still needs understanding adults who know when to hold the line and when to grant freedom, compatible with his maturity level. This is a period of considerable conflict when bad social maladjustments may take firm root unless, as just mentioned, teachers and parents know how to interpret his behavior correctly. Hero worship, so characteristic of the period, may be a godsend if utilized carefully. Parents too often feel affronted when they realize their child will now confide in and take the advice and authority of those not so intimately connected with him. This must be regarded as a normal part of the process of establishing independence.

>   B. *Achieving status.*

The adolescent wants to be considered adult by both his peers and adults. He may try to gain this status by trying to imitate adult vocabulary, dress, and cosmetics. Thirteen- and fourteen-year olds, however, want to retain child status in such areas as home responsibilities. They are continually experimenting with various roles, often changing from a demure to a sophisticated role or from suaveness to "toughness." Children who are slow to grow, especially boys, worry over losing status because of small size. The codes of the peer group seem more important to them than those of parents if conflicts arise and choices must be made.

C. *Realizing economic independence.*

While the major economic security and support continues to come from the family, the youngster often contributes materially by part-time jobs, such as baby sitting, errand boys, and odd jobs. Many are eager for full-time summer employment. Usually they prefer to work for other people. Their growing independence prompts them to want to handle and spend their own money in their own way.

D. *Becoming a social personality.*

Permanent friendships form during this period. There is a tendency for adolescents not accepted by an already established group to drift into groups of their own. The resultant group may go either way, conforming to social codes or becoming antisocial. Children who frequently display regressive forms of behavior tend to become less responsible at this time.

Dating is becoming a common thing now. Girls, especially, cut across grade and age levels as girls tend to date with older boys. Group conformity is so strong that individuals will cheat or lie to protect others in his group.

III. DEVELOPING AND MAINTAINING A SENSE OF ACHIEVEMENT BY:

A. *Gaining a sense of personal adequacy and orientation.*

These children frequently ask for help in learning effective means of group participation, for example, parliamentary procedure, committee, organization, and discussion techniques. Perhaps the greatest seeking is that of finding something at which one can "shine." Concern for the behavior of others is developing at the middle adolescent level, especially.

B. *Understanding and gaining control over the environment.*

Choice of clothing and problems of personal grooming can be handled adequately by this period. As these teen agers approach sixteen, they begin to make more realistic adjustments both to adults and contemporaries. Some are beginning to think about such basic adult problems as marriage, choice of career, vocational plans, and training possibilities.

C. *Developing sensitivity to the opposite sex.*

Puberty is accompanied by increasing sexual impulses. Nearly all normally growing personalities feel a desire to express sincere idealistic affection by some physical means, such as holding hands or kissing. Oversuspicious adults may by the wrong attitude create a sexual consciousness which does not naturally exist. This often leads to experiments with sexual intimacies to allay unconscious self-doubt of sexual adequacy. Similarly, the adolescent may boast of intimacies which he has never experienced.

IV. DEVELOPING AND MAINTAINING EVER WIDENING AND DEEPENING INTEREST AND APPRECIATIONS BY:

A. *Achieving intellectual and esthetic interests and appreciations.*

Sensory impressions and emotions are more complicated as suggested above. By now, intellectual activity is a satisfying end in itself. Boys' reading preferences usually change from adventure stories to stories of real exploits. Girls are usually interested in light fiction. There is considerable interest in all kinds of fads throughout this period.

B. *Developing social values and appreciations.*

The social value of tidiness and grooming is growing apace. Social groups are more stable now. The intellectual interests and abilities are added factors in the establishment of groups. Hobbies are popular. Absorption to the exclusion of all else, however, should be watched as indicative of poor personal adjustment.

C. *Understanding and respect for the cultural heritage.*

These levels are progressing in their understanding that the past is important because of its contribution to the present. Immediate environment is a deep concern. They often investigate such problems as the adequacy with which the school serves the community and pupil-teacher relationships. There is a beginning interest and concern in the social, political, and economic life of the wider community, such as better living and employment conditions for everyone.

Later Adolescence	Age Sixteen to Eighteen Years

I. MAINTAINING PERSONAL HEALTH AND PROMOTING HEALTHFUL LIVING BY:

A. *Meeting needs of diet and rest and freedom from infection.*

Though the rest needs of this age are those of adults, they must be met carefully else there may be serious repercussions. This is especially true since people of this age tend to expend more energy than they possess and are often unwilling to spend time in resting. The growth of the heart often lags behind that of the arteries, so that heart strain is easily possible. It is not uncommon for them to experience faintness, dizziness, and digestive disturbances. Such symptoms are usually indications of immaturity of function.

There is a greater relative freedom from infection at this time. Appetites are now great. Girls are interested in diet and exercise because of weight and figures, boys because of what may be done to condition them for atheletics.

B. *Achieving optimal physical and organic development.*

By eighteen years most young people have achieved mature height and weight; have developed characteristic bodily proportions such as high waistline, high hip line and the like. Boys make considerable gains in muscular strength, and a few will have achieved the physiological maturity of girls. Adult sexual characteristics are pretty well established often with considerable self-consciousness and embarrassment.

C. *Engaging in suitable physical recreational activities.*

Physical coordination and dexterity equals or exceeds that of adults. Some boys still prefer group games but may increase their participation in such individual sports as tennis, swimming, and golf.

Participation in community, school, and church recreational activities reaches its peak. In fact, the problem for normally adjusted children is often one of overstimulation. Dance steps and popular music have their heyday with this age group.

D. *Developing zeal for promoting healthful living in the immediate and wider community.*

These young people are aware of the value of health examinations as a means of protecting both themselves and others. They are interested in and under proper guidance will search out such relationships as those between bad housing and lack of recreation and disease and juvenile delinquency. Smoking and drinking often become symbols of revolt and sophistication.

II. ACHIEVING AND MAINTAINING A SENSE OF SECURITY BY:

A. *Gaining and holding affection, confidence, and esteem.*

These young people are highly sensitive to reactions of all adults toward them though they may not let on. They often seek an outside adult as a confidant. This is especially true if parents refuse to allow them to grow up. If there are younger children in the family, there are often rather severe conflicts at this period. A good bit of security is evident in a highly critical attitude toward themselves, their family, school, and church.

B. *Achieving status.*

These youngsters are anxious to enforce their own privacy and to achieve the status of individuals in their peer groups. They strive to do these things by conforming to the customs of a select group whether they are in juxtaposition to adult customs or not, by paying great attention to personal appearance, by striving to belong to the "right" groups, by boys being afraid to date girls who do not have prestige for fear of losing status. Family success or failure, financial status, and ability in competition influence evaluations of their contemporaries.

C. *Realizing economic independence.*

Many are now investigating college careers with an eye to expense, prestige of institution, and courses of study. All are so interested in achieving financial success and independence that they may take blind-alley jobs.

D. *Becoming a social personality.*

This is a period of ardent love affairs and cliques. Friendships tend to become more lasting. Girls are concerned about the social behavior of boys; they generally admire good looks and careful grooming. Boys are greatly interested in appearing in the approved fashion of the peer group. The group and group status is still their major concern.

III. DEVELOPING AND MAINTAINING A SENSE OF ACHIEVEMENT BY:

A. *Gaining a sense of personal adequacy and orientation.*

Growing adequacy is seen in the desire to give protection instead of receiving it. Some feelings of inadequacy appear in a fear of "graduating." This often initiates conferences to talk about their problems.

B. *Understanding and gaining control over the environment.*

Objectives are now modified by trial-and-error methods. They are slowly building social attitudes which make them more stable in their social relations. These gradually build into personal philosophies of living. There is recognition and willingness to face decisions on education, vocation, sex, marriage, and religion.

C. *Developing sensitivity to the opposite sex.*

These young people begin to think seriously of the qualities desired in prospective mates. Differences in maturity levels of boys and girls are disappearing here as elsewhere. Parties where sexes meet are preferred now by both boys and girls. Girls are very likely at this age to *fall in love* with people older than themselves. Boys generally prefer girls younger than themselves.

IV. DEVELOPING AND MAINTAINING EVER WIDENING AND DEEPENING INTERESTS AND APPRECIATIONS BY:

A. *Achieving intellectual and esthetic interests and appreciations.*

Both sensory impressions and emotions are sharpened and complicated. Greater and deepened interest in both aesthetics and intellectual interests is to be noted. The time is ripe for the development of special talents. Boys tend to avoid writing and substitute talking. Girls like the writing of diaries, letters, and personal experiences. Boys' choice of reading materials often surpasses girls at this period in terms of the intellectual. All are maturing in ability to reason. If properly guided, this growing ability may open a world of intellectual activity and pleasure which will persist whether there is continued formal instruction or not.

B. *Developing social values and appreciations.*

Though many of the values held may still be superficial ones, there is more interest in the intricacies of human behavior. There is improvement in the ability to understand and allow for other peoples' attitudes and beliefs. There is much improvement in the stability of their own social relationships. They begin to realize mutual obligations and responsibilities of persons in these social relationships.

C. *Understanding and respect for the cultural heritage.*

These young people recognize that the data for solving problems of society come from both the past and present and can be used in drawing conclusions concerning the future. Most of them believe that life can be bettered for all and accept the responsibilities and privileges of social progress.

SUMMARY AND IMPLICATIONS

TEACHERS AND PARENTS need to know and understand what the child can and is likely to do at different developmental levels so that they may provide environmental situations which will help the developing child happily to adjust to changing circumstances with a minimum of frustration and difficulty.

This involves the realization that children go from dependence to independence to interdependence. It is necessary for this increasing need to escape from adult domination to be recognized, approved, and provided for without disrupting security and violating attempted self-development and social adjustment.

Physically, intellectually, and emotionally children are able to consider and make decisions on the basis of their experiences. This increasing ability to exercise choice and good judgment in the light of peer group beliefs and judgment is to be considered a sign of progress not one of "sheer cussedness."

Blair and Burton's suggestions to parents and teachers in their reactions to emotional and social difficulties of preadolescents have equal significance for the other developmental levels of children.[2]

1. When children act like children, adults should act like adults.
2. Respect the developing individuality. Do not treat growing boys and girls like adults.

[2] Arthur W. Blair and Wm. H. Burton, *Growth and Development of Preadolescents* (New York, Appleton-Century-Crofts, 1951), pp. 207–216.

3. Use judgment in selecting occasions for discussion, restraint, or punishment.
4. Take the time and trouble to provide opportunity for natural outlets in activity, preferably group activity.
5. Have and express faith in the children, confidence in their growing independence.
6. Act consistently, as fairly as you know how, and without betraying annoyance, or other emotional instability.
7. Do not be fooled into neglecting the child who causes no trouble.
8. Realize that, while possessing certain commonalities, children are different each from the other.
9. Realize that children have feelings, and, in this area, are under a double handicap.
10. Recognize that children are members of a peer society, the aims, values, approvals, disapprovals, of which are far more potent with the child than with the corresponding factors in the adult society surrounding the child.
11. Provide opportunities for boys to have more associations with men.
12. Stop comparing boys with girls during the years when girls' intellectual maturity is on the average about two years ahead of boys.

TEACHING AND STUDY AIDS

1. Consider the growth rhythms presented in this chapter. Locate research which substantiates, extends, or, perhaps, refutes the material presented. The following references will give you a start:
   Gesell, see Selected Reading References.
   How Children Develop (Columbus, Ohio State University School, 1946).
   Jenkins, Gladys, Shacter, H., and W. M. Bauer, *These Are Your Children* (Chicago, Scott, 1949).
   Olson, Willard C., *Child Development* (Boston, Heath, 1949).
2. Arrangements may be made for students to observe children at different levels of development. A log kept of what one would *expect* to find and what one *does find* would provide a means for both teacher and student to check increased insights.
3. Special-interest area committees may be organized along lines of school levels, such as kindergarten, early elementary, later elementary, and junior high and senior high students. For each level records of such maturation and social growth factors as the following might be recorded and analyzed:
   A. Physical size differentials between sexes as well as within the sex grouping.

B. Social maturity differences between boys and girls.
C. Intellectual differences between boys and girls such as reading and writing.
D. Attitudes toward adults (teachers and visitors).
E. Attitudes of boys toward girls and vice versa.
F. Social responsibility of both sexes.
G. Bases for formation of the child groups present.

SELECTED READING REFERENCES

American Council on Education, *Helping Teachers Understand Children* (Washington, 1945).

Barker, Dembo, and Lewin, *Frustration and Regression.* University of Iowa Studies, No. 18, (Ames, Iowa, Child Welfare Station, 1941), p. 314.

Blair, Glenn M., "What Teachers Should Know About the Psychology of Adolescents," *Journal of Educational Psychology* (October 1950), New York, 356–361.

Cole, L. W., *Psychology of Adolescence* (New York, Rinehart, 1942), pp. 133–162.

Davis, Allison, "Grown-Up Children," *Science Digest* (September 1949), p. 38.

Gesell, Arnold, and staff of Child Development Institute:

Published works

1. *The Preschool Child*
2. *The Mental Growth of the Preschool Child*
3. *An Atlas of Infant Behavior*
4. *Feeding Behavior of Infants*
5. *The Psychology of Early Growth*
6. *Biographies of Child Development*
7. *The First Five Years of Life*
8. *Developmental Diagnosis: Normal and Abnormal Child Development*
9. *Infant and Child in the Culture of Today*
10. *The Embryology of Behavior*
11. *The Child from Five to Ten*
12. *Vision: Its Development in Infant and Child* (1949)
13. *Studies in Child Development*

Books in preparation:

1. *The Years from Ten to Sixteen*
2. *The Genesis of Individuality*
3. *Development Trends in Child Rorschach Responses*

Havighurst, Robert J., *Developmental Tasks and Education* (Chicago, University of Chicago Press, 1948), pp. 30–63.

Hurlock, Elizabeth B., *Adolescent Development* (New York, McGraw-Hill, 1949), Chaps. V, VI, VII.

Hymes, James L., Jr., *Enjoy Your Child, Ages 1, 2, and 3,* Public Affairs Pamphlet No. 141 (New York, Public Affairs Committee, 1948).

————, *Three to Six: Your Child Starts to School,* Public Affairs Pamphlet No. 163 (New York, Public Affairs Committee, 1950).

Jenkins, Gladys, Shacter, H., and Bauer, Wm., *These Are Your Children,* (Chicago, Scott, 1949).

Jersild, Arthur T., *Child Development and the Curriculum* (New York, Bureau of Publications, Teachers College, Columbia University, 1946).

Olson, Willard C., *Child Development* (Boston, Heath, 1949).

Child Development Films (16mm)

1. The Growth of Infant Behavior: Early Stages
2. The Growth of Infant Behavior: Later Stages
3. Posture and Locomotion
4. From Creeping to Walking
5. A Baby's Day at Twelve Weeks
6. A Thirty-six Weeks Behavior Day
7. A Baby's Day at Forty-eight Weeks
8. Behavior Patterns at One Year
9. Learning and Growth
10. Early Social Behavior

Life Begins

11. How Behavior Grows
12. The Growth of Motor Behavior
13. The Growth of Adaptive Behavior
14. Infants are Individuals
15. Twins are Individuals
16. The Baby's Bath
17. Bottle and Cup Feeding
18. The Conquest of the Spoon
19. Self-Discovery in a Mirror
20. Early Play
21. Learning to Understand Children (McGraw-Hill Film)

Note: 1–10 are sound films; 11–20 are silent films. You may obtain these movies from: New England Rental Library, 30 Huntington Avenue, Boston 16, Mass.

IV

COMMUNITY BACK-GROUNDS OF CHILDREN IN OUR CULTURE

THE NATURE OF COMMUNITY

"WHAT" AND "WHEN" COMMUNITY

THE CONCEPT COMMUNITY is used and misused by everyone. Its meanings to various users are almost as myriad as the people who employ it. A check of its meaning among students calls forth such replies as "the block I live on," "my end of town," "the town itself," "all who think alike," "people who act together," "those who have something in common."

Curiously enough, each reply has a proverbial grain of truth. For community is associated with place, with the communality of thought and custom, and at length, with action in terms of whatever rules and processes for enforcing them, may exist.

The literature teems with attempts to delimit, and delieneate, the term. If the investigator or discussant is interested, he may follow the lead of Dewey, whose concept suggests no spatial limitations. As he puts it, "There is more than a verbal tie between common, communication, and community." [1]

Other widely used definitions follow a pattern such as that of R. M. MacIver,[2] who wrote that "a community is any circle of people who live together, who belong together, so that they share, not this or that particular interest, but a whole set of interests wide enough and complete enough to include their lives."

Thus, a community might conceivably be two people or 2,000,-

---

[1] John Dewey, *Democracy and Education* (New York, Macmillan, 1924).
[2] Lloyd A. Cook, *A Sociological Approach to Education* (New York, McGraw-Hill, 1950).

000, though the latter part of the definition implies more structuring than the words actually say.

If the writer is interested in a technical study of specific community life patterns, he may outline what seem fundamental characteristics for such endeavor in a highly specific and restricted sense.

A representative of this attempt is Cook, who writes: ". . . This view [reference is to above view of Dewey] like that of place, is extremely important; yet its unbounded sweep limits its usefulness. Any group or institution, any kind of human association, any two friends, is a 'community.'" Unless the concept is more rigorously defined, it can have no precise meaning. From a sociological standpoint a community is a configuration of land, people, and culture, a structural pattern of human relations within a geographic area. In a technical sense the concept has seven fundamental characteristics— (*1*) a population aggregate, (*2*) inhabiting a delimitable contiguous area, (*3*) sharing an historical heritage, (*4*) possessing a set of basic service institutions, (*5*) participating in a common mode of life, (*6*) conscious of its unity, (*7*) and able to act in a corporate way.

Just as the Dewey viewpoint seems impractical so this definition often meets resistance from students. Though it may seem like a fence-straddling procedure, it has seemed best to grant readily that there may well be communality of thought which transcends all boundaries though the chances are that even these may have territoriality, people, and rule aspects in terms of world community.

The suggestion is then that the concept community be defined to mean: (*1*) the people have a certain locus on the land; (*2*) they are subject to rules defined and imposed on the basis of mutual interests, needs, and experience; (*3*) and they are able to act collectively.

Thus, we may speak of and study world community, national community, regional community, and local community. Other subdivisions may occur. At present these are selected because it is possible to glean from the literature studies which have recognized these divisions.

At whatever level community life is to be studied, it then appears that there are the social structures and the social processes which implement it. Though the listing is far from exhaustive it is well to consider each type of community in terms of such basic elements as (*1*) number, composition, and distribution of population and (*2*) the social processes as they relate to such basic areas of living as population, political, economic, religious, educational, and recreational patterns of living.

It must be admitted readily that at the level of world, national, and regional community levels the analyses are fragmentary, evalu-istic, and perhaps even more impressionistic than at the local level, but the need and possibilities for intensive integrative study are none the less important.

Since we must begin where we are, we base the discussion of world community at this point upon Bernard's [3] attempt to analyze in terms of social structure and social process.

World Community

The world has become a community because all of its peoples have acquired common interests. Science has given us many gifts; but it has made the world so small that war is no longer merely the concern of the original combatants; it is the concern of all the citizens of the world community. . . . To live together successfully is a great accomplish-ment. It is true at all levels of association. It does not just happen . . . it has to be learned. We have no choice in the matter. The alternative to living together successfully is not living alone; it is not living at all. . . .

By the end of this century there will be at the very least 500,000,-000 more people on this already crowded globe than there are today. And actually it is probable that unless some world-wide brakes are ap-plied, more than 1,000,000,000 people will be added. . . .

Most of the highly industrialized nations of the world, since they have declining birth rates, look with fear—some even with terror—at a future in which they may be swamped by more fertile people. . . .

The competition among the several nations of the Caucasian races is matched in seriousness by the competition among the major races of the world. During the last three centuries the white race has outbred all other races. This was the natural concomitant of industrialization. . . .

The introduction of power machinery increases wealth; medical science is stimulated as a result; the death rate declines faster than the birth rate; and there is a great spurt in population growth. Warren Thompson has called this time of population growth which follows in-dustrialization the 'swarming period.' It results not from an increased birth rate but from a rapidly declining death rate. The last three cen-turies have been the swarming period for the white races and have be-come the largest single race in the world—1200 million. Industrializa-tion of backward areas may be expected to produce similarly lowered death rates, and lengthened life expectancy.

[3] Jessie Bernard, *American Community Behavior* (New York, Dryden, 1949), p. 634 ff. Used by permission.

The social process of competitiveness in the world community is well illustrated not only in the foregoing description of the racial and ethnic composition of population but also in such areas of international community relations as the economic, political, religious. . . .

The economic competitors in the world community are the several industrialized nations. The objects they compete for are markets, both for acquiring raw materials and for selling their finished products. The usual continuum, ranging from cutthroat competition at one extreme to monopoly at the other, can be found on the international level as well as at home. . . .

There is no formal election in international political competition. The political competition is not for office. It is, however, like all political competition, competition for control of policy. It does not take the shape of an avowed campaign. But it has all the earmarks of a campaign. The two great political competitors today are the United States and Soviet Russia. They are competing for the "votes" of other nations such as Greece, Turkey, Italy, Germany, Japan, Korea, the Latin American Countries—even France and China. Or, as we sometimes say, two ideologies are competing for the allegiance of men everywhere—democracy versus communism, or communism versus non-communism. Specifically, the two nations are trying to "sell" their social and political philosophies. . . .

The techniques used in this great political competitive race are essentially the same as those used in the local community. Propaganda, as in all political competition, is a powerful weapon.

But the most powerful competitive technique in our repertoire, it has been pointed out, is the successful functioning of our own system. The best argument we could use against communism would be prosperity and a successful demonstration of democratic practices.

Nonpolitical relief to disorganized and hungry peoples abroad is advanced as another way in which to demonstrate the superiority of our system. Cold and hungry people, we are told, are susceptible to the lures of communism. If we can rehabilitate them we will have gone a long way, it is argued, toward winning their allegiance. The similarity of this technique to that of the political boss will doubtless strike most readers very forcibly.

The stages in the accommodation continuum for political conflict in the international community range all the way from open warfare to complete union. War, as Clausewitz is quoted as saying, is the continuation of politics with other means. Whatever the causes of war may be, war is itself, like other political conflict, a clash of wills—a political phenomenon. It is an attempt of one nation to impose its will upon another—for whatever reason. We do not drift into wars. We will wars.

Sometimes we may consider war the lesser of two evils. We may hate both. But wars are chosen.

There is, finally, the level of assimilation, where differences disappear and we have actual union. Winston Churchill in June 1940 proposed union between Great Britain and France. There is a movement, headed by Clarence Streit, in behalf of world federation—Federal Union, Inc. Many peace-loving people look forward with a good deal of hope to a union of European nations into a United States of Europe.

Religious competition is related to political competition in its attempt to win followers. As Bernard suggests, although at one time or another Buddhism and Islam were missionary religions, at the present time Christianity is the most aggressive in attempting to win converts. In Asia it competes with Buddhism and Confucianism. In Africa it competes with native religions. In Latin America Protestantism competes with native Catholicism. The techniques include in addition to religious instruction, humanitarian and welfare activities, such as medical care, education, and attacks on social injustice and evil. Famine relief has also been particularly emphasized by the Catholic missionaries.

THE NATIONAL COMMUNITY

THE STUDY of the national community as it relates to child orientation is the attempted study of the ethos of a people. The concept ethos as used by William Graham Sumner means the totality and organizational patterns of all those traits by which one society is recognized as distinct from another. Each nation community has a definite geographical territory, social structures peculiar to its resources and historical development, and social processes which operate in every area of society life.

When national boundaries enclose smaller areas with attendant homogeneity of geographical backgrounds, where invasion and immigration are relatively distant in time and the rate of social change is moderate, it is much easier to delineate the ethos of the nation.

In a country such as the United States with far-flung boundaries, with radically differing terrains, resources, and the like, and with an extreme heterogeneity of population and accompanying cultural patterns, one is better able to define regional ethos than national ethos.

With these limitations in mind we may say that the national communal elements are best expressed in terms of the dominant value patterns within the confines of the nation community. It is readily recognized that these value patterns are often much different in action than in verbalization. Their interpretation and implementation may be conditioned by many social-cultural factors as well as by personal-social ones. Nonetheless, the over-all patterns are fairly discernible. Of the numerous attempts at this type of analysis, the one offered by Cuber and Harper is illustrative. According to them, the seven dominant American value patterns are: [4]

1. Monogamous marriage: that is, one mate at a time, preference for stability and for children to be born within wedlock.
2. Freedom: by which is usually meant holding only minimum arbitrary limitations on the will of people to do as they please.
3. Acquisitiveness: the desirability of securing as great a proportion as possible of income, wealth, and material objects.
4. Democracy: there is a somewhat circumscribed belief that almost everyone should have the right to vote, have access to at least some of the "good things" which the society provides.
5. Education: there is faith that despite its limitations and its needed modifications, the education of as many people as possible, as much as possible, is a worthy objective.
6. Monotheistic religion: adherence to at least some of the traditional tenets of the Christian and Jewish faiths are taken for granted and taught to children.
7. Science: there is great respect for the specific findings of science and the "miracles" which it explained.

When one seeks research findings to supplement authoritative statements such as these, he finds them difficult to locate. One study which deserves mention and offers some fairly objective evidence on the above points is the work of Beery.[5] As the title of the monograph plainly indicates, Berry was interested in finding what this nebulous concept democracy meant to "the people." The items of his questionnaire, however, got at not only value pattern number 4 on the Cuber-Harper list but also 2, 3, and 5, and to a lesser degree, mostly by implication, items 1, 4, and 7.

In other words, in clarifying the concept democracy, people

[4] John F. Cuber and Robert A. Harper, *Problems of American Society* (New York, Holt, 1948), pp. 369–374. Used by permission.
[5] John R. Beery, *Current Conceptions of Democracy,* Teachers College Contributions to Education, No. 888 (New York, Columbia University Press, 1944), pp. 65–69.

also showed agreement and disagreement where the other value areas were concerned. This research, as the author modestly says, has its limitations. The results do not necessarily reflect the views of the whole population of the nation. Not all types of groups are included, and numbers of respondents impose limitations, though statistical procedures took into account the size of the groups. There may well have been more items on which the various groups differed from the average. The results do show a number of interesting things.

There is a large body of democratic theory on which the vast majority of the respondents are agreed. Fifty-two of the items were agreed upon by 95 or more percent of the respondents. The agreement on 157 items was significantly in excess of 75 percent. There were 25 items on which there was sharp disagreement, and a total of 51 items on which the agreement was significantly less than 75 percent.

The groups varied considerably less in the number of items with which they agreed or disagreed to an extent significantly different from the average. The business executives made up the group which was most divergent, and the graduate students were next most divergent. An examination of group alignments revealed that the business executives, the democracy patrons, and the essay contestants tended strongly to agree among themselves and to disagree with the graduate students, the farmers, and the cooperators. These latter groups likewise tended to agree among themselves quite strongly.

The summary of the study points up the ethos or value schemes held in agreement by those tested:

Worth and Dignity of the Individual. The foundation of democracy is faith in the essential worth of each individual human being without regard to occupational, social, economic, or hereditary status.

The maximum development of each individual, when attained without infringing the rights of others, is in the best interests of all.

The state exists for the welfare of the individual, and not the individual for the welfare of the state. Democracy seeks to provide the opportunity for all the people to enjoy the highest values that modern life now affords to the most privileged.

Equality of Individuals. Two kinds of equality are involved in democracy. Strict equality is limited to certain fundamentals, as equality before the law, equality at the ballot box, and equality in basic minimum ways of life. The second kind of equality has to do with aspirations and opportunity. Any individual should be able to aspire to any status or position on the basis of his personal merits.

Liberty. There can be no democracy without the guarantee of civil and religious liberty to every citizen. This includes the right of peaceful assembly and freedom of speech, petition for redress of grievances, safety of life and liberty of person, speedy and fair trials before an impartial jury, freedom to criticize and to propose, freedom of the press, uncensored news, unfettered exchange of ideas and opinions, freedom of choice of mate, of occupation, of movement, of place of residence, of manner of life, and of industrial, political, religious, and cultural affiliations. The right to own private property of the consumers' goods type is included.

Government by the People. A basic premise of democracy is that the great masses of men have an inalienable right to govern themselves. Governments derive their just powers solely from the consent of the governed, and so the people are free to change their government, either in form or in personnel, when such change seems to them to be in their own interests. Governments exist only to serve the people, and the military authority must be subordinate to the civil authority.

Freedom of Experience. Issues which affect human welfare should be decided by reason, not by arbitrary, authoritarian imposition. All controversial matters concerning the general welfare should be fully and publicly discussed before decision is made. The people should discuss important proposed laws being considered by their legislatures.

Democracy implies a faith that social arrangements can always be improved, and that this improvement can be accomplished by peaceful and orderly methods.

Duties and Obligations. Democracy requires that the individual be as conscious of his duties as he is jealous of his rights, for all rights imply obligations. The responsibilities of citizenship are among the highest duties of man, and it is the duty of all to participate in the governing process. The democratic citizen casts his ballot at election time, obeys loyally any law which has reached the statute books, however much he may have been opposed to it beforehand, is ready to accept his full share of the burdens of organized social life, and is willing to give service to the general welfare without personal gain.

And finally, the democratic citizen has faith in the democratic process. He believes it is the best possible form of government and entirely capable of dealing with the most profound and disturbing social and economic issues which may arise.[6]

THE REGIONAL COMMUNITY

IN A COUNTRY as far flung and with as heterogeneous a population as that of the United States, the impingements of the

[6] Beery, *op. cit.,* pp. 65–69. Used by permission.

regional community are often more real and apparent than those of
the national community. Recognition of geographical regions has
been followed more recently by attempts to define and delineate
cultural regions. One of the most extensive of the regional studies
has been done by Odum and Moore and their associates.[7]

The region is considered a unit part of the larger national
community, identifiable first in geographical ways, then on the basis
of economic factors, and finally in terms of cultural likenesses and
dissimilarities.

Rural sociologists have been especially interested in studying
the regional community in terms of major farming areas. These are
not merely academic gymnastics but real attempts to get at areas
which have both physical and cultural components. Such knowledge will be increasingly important in larger scale analyses of needs
and consequent planning for aid and administration at the national
community level.

Here is recognition that very often political boundaries are
merely artificial lines which enclose at best only political units. Cultural areas or regional communities on the other hand cut across
these lines in terms of common customs, racial composition, planes
of living indices, fertility indices, gross incomes, land values per
capita, and physiographic features.

A. R. Mangus, on the basis of these factor analyses, has mapped
both farm and rural cultural areas of the nation. These bear a remarkably close convergence to the seven major types of farming
areas,[8] if one considers that each of the seven types of farming areas
contains one or more cultural regions. Each has distinctive social life
characteristics and a homogeneity in attitudes and social structure reflected by the factor analyses mentioned above. In short, these regional communities represent potential if not always actual, social
systems.

Loomis and Beegle in their study of rural social systems [9] divide
the regions into such categories as the Cotton Belt, the Dairy Belts,
the Wheat Area, the Corn Belt, and the Western Specialty-crop

[7] Howard Odum, *Southern Regions of the United States* (Chapel Hill, University of North Carolina Press, 1936); Howard Odum and H. E. Moore, *American Regionalism* (New York, Holt, 1938).

[8] Carl C. Taylor and others, *Rural Life in the United States* (New York,
Knopf, 1949).

[9] Charles P. Loomis and J. Allen Beegle, *Rural Social Systems* (New York,
Prentice-Hall, 1950), p. 251 ff.

Areas. Within these areas they point to distinctive social life characteristics which accompany ways of making a living.

For example, the Cotton Belt is said to include approximately 33 percent of the farm population of the United States. Population characteristics include high birth rates, mainly native American stock, low planes of living, and large proportions of nonwhites. Social affairs as well as school vacations and church and business activities revolve about the demands of cotton growing and harvesting. Unlike areas where family farming is conducted, only a small minority of the people in the plantation system are active in initiating, promoting or engaging in community action programs.

The Wheat Area has about 4 percent of the farm population of the United States. Its living patterns contrast sharply with those mentioned above. Birth rates are low, planes of living are high, and the rate of ownership both of land and machinery is higher than in the Cotton Belt. Trade centers are important as structuring agencies for social, church, school, and economic life.

In the Corn Belt reside 14 percent of the farmers of the nation. Here the birth rates are low, the planes of living are high and a one-crop economy is not so prevalent. Here too are to be found the one-room neighborhood schools though the trade center rather than the neighborhood is the structuring agency for social and economic affairs. The Farm Bureau, which is the most general farmer's organization, has greatest strength in this region.

The Dairy Belts include about 12 percent of the nation's farmers. As Loomis and Beegle suggest, these areas have several subcultural regions. In the eastern parts, old American and Canadian backgrounds are predominant. These farms are highly mechanized, owned in large part by those who live on them, and social life is much more structured on the old township systems of New England. The Grange is the organization of greatest strength, though many special interest groups are present. Producer's cooperatives are also strong in these parts.

The General and Self-sufficing Areas include about 4 percent of the nation's farm population and cover the greatest land area. Their population has the most diverse cultural backgrounds of any of the areas. These areas are sparsely populated, and neighborhood unity is weak except in the areas with high Indian, Mormon, and Spanish-American blocks of population. With the exception of such areas, birth rates are low, incomes are high, and the "Western pattern" of life prevails.

Western Specialty-crop areas contain approximately 3 percent of the nation's farm population. These areas are relatively small and found within the other farming areas with the exception of California. The family farm is the common unit again with the exception of California, where factory farms occur. Approximately 40 percent of such population aggregates is foreign born, usually with what Loomis and Beegle term strong peasant backgrounds. Again with the exception of the foreign born, there is a high plane of living and low birth rates. Mormon groups combine high planes of living with high birth rates.

With the exception of the Cotton Belt and a few of the Western Specialty-crop Areas, the family farm or ranch is the basic work and economic unit. This kind of rural culture is much different from other rural ways of living. Farmers in such situations are representative of both management and labor and seldom other than conservative in both. In both good times and bad the family unit farm has shown its great superiority over other forms, according to most rural sociologists.

Other kinds of regional community studies include those which are listed as rural trade area studies and metropolitan regional studies. Since these are in the main studies of what we have termed local communities and their service areas, we shall mention them in that connection.

Other studies of a regional character include such as those of Davis and Gardner who were interested in analyzing specialized cultural and social characteristics of a more loosely defined regional community. These also will be discussed later in another connection.

LIVING IN THE LOCAL COMMUNITY

ALL SOCIETIES have social differentiation schemes. In preliterate groupings different functions of individuals were defined largely in terms of age, sex, and strength differentials. Rites of passage from one developmental level to another were clearly defined. Privileges and restrictions could be anticipated and equally looked back upon. One sex would be allowed to do certain things at prescribed times, and there was little chance for maneuvering.

As societies grew in numbers, complexity, and specialization, these differentiations became more fluid, less readily enforceable. Rights and privileges were distributed unevenly with resultant social status systems.

Earlier study and analysis regarded the basis of social distinctions as an economic one expressed in terms of income, wealth, and purchased services. This led to an interpretation of all social structures and processes as one of class struggle. More recent research has centered attention on finding whether we have one or several status systems; what are the identifiable modes of thought and living, and what are their implications for child orientation in our society. This approach suggests the terms caste and class as name tags for a social differentiation which is uneven and unequal in its distribution of privileges.

In the United States caste is equivalent to a color line with castes identifiable as "white" and "other." Within each category are class distinctions. Both caste and class distribute privileges and "things" unequally but with several differences. Caste insists that man is not only born to but must remain within his caste. His attempts at escape are not only disapproved but severely punished. Class mobility, on the other hand, in either direction is possible and attempted. Upward mobility is not only expected but approved and rewarded.

Class is defined in numerous ways. For our purposes it is "the largest group of persons whose members have intimate access to one another." [10] This is tantamount to saying that classes are social-cultural realities; that they are groups of people who experience relatively stable and similar patterns of living, such as occupation, value schemes for their own living and that of their children, who dress, read, talk, and eat with similarity, and who subscribe to similar recreational, religious, and even political behavior. A social scientist can observe, record, and report these likenesses and differences in fairly objective fashion.

CLASS LEVELS

Perhaps the most acceptable study viewpoint at present is that which identifies classes in general as upper, middle, and lower and

[10] Allison Davis, B. B. Gardner, and Mary R. Gardner, *Deep South* (Chicago, University of Chicago Press, 1941), p. 59.

then refines these categories in terms of the particular area studied. Thus, some more complex, long-settled towns might align themselves into as many as six or nine subdivisions, such as upper upper, middle upper, lower upper, upper middle, middle middle, lower middle, upper lower, middle lower, and lower lower. Another might have but an upper and a lower class. It becomes clear then that we have not a class system but class systems within the United States.

As Cooley once phrased it, the factors which affect the variances of the class structure are: (1) great differences in the constituent parts of the population, (2) communication and enlightenment, and (3) the rate of social change.[11]

Warner, Havighurst, and Loeb elaborate the above as follows: [12] "The size of the community, the region in which it is located, the rapidity of growth, the type of growth, and the degree to which its older traditions have held are potent factors in the strength and power of the American Class order."

Since we have emphasized that the possibility of social mobility (both up and down) is characteristic of class as opposed to caste, it is worthwhile to give attention to the "social elevators" [13] which operate in the attempted mobility.

Wealth, income, and occupation are important factors in our class system; yet the possession of great wealth, a large income, and a highly placed occupation do not ensure such a fortunate individual the highest class position. They are important symbols of prestige and arsenals of social power, but by themselves they are not sufficient to give their possessor certain top position. On the other hand, they are sufficient to prevent him from occupying one of the lower rungs of our social ladder.

A man may be the head of an important factory, have a large income and bank account, but he may not necessarily be a member of the upper class of his community. The first generation of a wealthy family is usually not in the highest class. It is necessary for an individual and the members of his family to acquire other symbols of prestige and to participate on the basis of equality, or partial equality, with members of the higher classes. Some of the symbols necessary include the acquisition of outward personal behavior including manners, etiquette, and speech habits which are enforced by inward attitudes and values

[11] Charles Horton Cooley, *Social Organization* (New York, Scribner, 1922), p. 217 ff.
[12] Wm. Lloyd Warner, Robert J. Havighurst, and Martin Loeb, *Who Shall Be Educated?* (New York, Harper, 1944), p. 29 ff. Used by permission.
[13] *Ibid.,* pp. 33–34.

	CLOTHES	FURNITURE	USEFUL OBJECTS	ENTERTAINMENT	SALADS
HIGH-BROW	TOWN — Fuzzy Harris tweed suit, no hat / COUNTRY — Fuzzy Harris tweed suit, no hat	Eames chair, Kurt Versen lamp	Decanter and ash tray from chemical supply company	Ballet	Greens, olive oil, wine vinegar, ground salt, ground pepper, garlic, unwashed salad bowl
UPPER MIDDLE-BROW	TOWN — Brooks suit, regimental tie, felt hat / COUNTRY — Quiet tweed jacket, knitted tie	Empire chair, converted sculpture lamp	Silver cigaret box with wedding ushers signatures	Theater	Same as high-brow but with tomatoes, avocado Roquefort cheese added
LOWER MIDDLE-BROW	TOWN — Splashy necktie, double-breasted suit / COUNTRY — Sport shirt, colored slacks	Grand Rapids Chippendale chair, bridge lamp	His and Hers towels	Musical extravaganza Films	Quartered iceberg lettuce and store dressing
LOW-BROW	TOWN — Leather jacket, woven shoes / COUNTRY — Old Army clothes	Mail order overstuffed chair, fringed lamp	Balsam-stuffed pillow	Western movies	Coleslaw

Though these sketches are not based upon research, they are provocative and illustrative of many of the characteristics discussed under class differences. They were originally suggested by an article of Russell Lynes, "Highbrow, Lowbrow, Middlebrow," which appeared in

DRINKS	READING	SCULPTURE	RECORDS	GAMES	CAUSES
A glass of "adequate little" red wine	"Little magazines," criticism of criticism, avant garde literature	Calder	Bach and before, Ives and after	Go	Art
A very dry Martini with lemon peel	Solid nonfiction, the better novels, quality magazines	Maillol	Symphonies, concertos, operas	The Game	Planned parenthood
Bourbon and ginger ale	Book club selections mass circulation magazines	Front yard sculpture	Light opera, popular favorites	Bridge	P. T. A.
Beer	Pulps, comic books	Parlor sculpture	Jukebox	Craps	The Lodge

Harper's Magazine (February 1949). They appeared in *Life*, Vol. 29 (April 1949), pp. 100–101. (Used by permission of Russell Lynes and *Life* magazine.)

which have become habitual to the individual. Other necessary symbols are a personal and a family environment which symbolize higher position. These include houses, furniture, and similar symbols of status to increase the strength of his claims to higher position.

All this means that a mobile person's money must be translated into a way of life which expresses high status. Such behavior is not sufficient, since, to be rated at the top, it is necessary for him to participate in clique, associational, and often family relations before he is securely placed. These conditions are of greater importance to a woman than to a man. A man is more often forgiven his manners than a woman her etiquette. Wealth is not the only elevator whose power can be used to establish social position. Talents of all kinds which are highly prized raise their possessor's position and make it possible for him to acquire the other necessary symbols and to establish the relations essential to participation in the higher social ranks. A talent for music, singing, painting, acting, writing, or athletics, as well as many other activities, gives the individual prestige in his own profession which may be translated into social position. A rise may or may not be accompanied by the acquisition of wealth.

For a graphic description of one community and how its status systems affect the areas of living, which in turn have an impact upon child life, let us review Yankee City.

Yankee City [14]

The name applied to the upper class of Yankee City is Hill Streeter. An upper-upper man believes himself to be a gentleman, and his wife knows that she is a lady. This aristocratic lineage, which is traced through the father and mother, but preferably through the father, is given the name of the "old family" when the members of a class are identified and separated from the lower-upper and upper-middle classes. The upper-uppers ordinarily live in large and well-conditioned Georgian houses which are along Hill Street or in extensions of Hill Street. The houses of the upper-upper and lower-upper classes, which are the most important symbols of high status, are the most expensive in Yankee City. . . .

The upper-uppers are professional men or proprietors of the larger business and industrial enterprises—the highest brackets in the occupational hierarchy.

The old family group comprises but 1.4 percent of the population, has many more women than men, a smaller proportion of young men and women than any other class, and a higher proportion of old people.

[14] Warner, Havighurst, and Loeb, *op. cit.*, pp. 20–27.

They marry later than any of the other five classes. There are many maiden sisters and unmarried daughters living in the old houses.

The Hill Streeters attend the Episcopal and Unitarian churches and consciously avoid the Catholic churches and such Protestant ones as the Methodist. The minister of one of their churches must be a strong man and of the right class if he is to maintain his own ideas. He continually feels strong social pressure to say "the right things."

It should be remembered that the ranking of churches in the United States varies regionally and locally within the major areas. In the Midwest and the South it is the Holiness and Pentecostal churches which are filled with the lower classes. In southern communities the Methodist churches are often preferred by the local elite, and the Congregational church sometimes is ranked as socially superior.

In Yankee City the upper-upper people participate in associations which are social clubs where topics of interest to the group are discussed. The upper-uppers join with the two classes below them to give charity to the lower groups but refuse to allow these recipients to be members of their charitable organizations. They thereby effectively subordinate the takers of their gifts who cannot return these favors and who feel and are felt to be unworthy of admittance to these organizations of the people who live "in the big houses on Hill Street."

The lower-upper person in Yankee City (his class makes up 1.6 percent of the population) is without a recognized lineage for Yankee City since his family is socially "new" and in the final sense of the word he does not "belong." He feels this and must compensate for it. He tries to give the best parties, to own the finest cars, or become the best in a particular sport, or in some other form of social accomplishment. He continues to try to reach the top, but he can never quite succeed for his judges are his own competitors and those who hold the places above him. Furthermore, the game is stacked against him since he has never had and can never get the one card he must have above all others—gentle birth. Only several generations of living can remedy this matter for him.

The upper-uppers are strong supporters, with a few noteworthy exceptions, of the right wing of the Republican party, but their convictions are tempered with some skepticism about the reasons for their beliefs, and their "liberal education" has made them aware of other points of view which their secure social position allows them to express but not to feel. The lower-uppers are emphatically Republican by vote and by deep conviction; so too are most of the members of the upper-middle class. Those of the lower-upper class who have rebelled from the rule of their elders are anything but Republicans, preferably radical, but these young rebels reverse the position of their elders to demonstrate their freedom from the hateful rule of an inferior upper class which their fellows have accepted in practice.

The lower-uppers share the old Georgian houses with the upper-upper class. Their houses, like those of the old families, have their own lineages which, by the very listing of the names of their occupants, tell a story of superior status and of better living. If one cannot have a family with a lineage, one can buy and maintain with proper respect a house which has a superior one. Furthermore, one can buy a house which is on Hill Street, whose very name symbolizes social superiority and fine living, which places one at least geographically near and, it is to be hoped, socially "near" the old families. Such hopes as these maintain a behavior which, in the generations that follow, ultimately places these new families in the maturity of time among the old families; and in retrospect these present ancestors will rise in the memories of coming generations from new families to old families. Sometimes, to make sure of this, their successors will actually dig up their bones since they are now those of an "old family" and remove them from the more common cemetery and place them in a "better location" in a graveyard where the better people bury their dead. All the old families of today were the new families of yesterday.

The upper-middle class, comprising 10 percent of the people, is a superior group of Side Streeters (they are said to be at the side of and not on Hill Street). The upper-middle class is not fully "socially acceptable" to the two upper classes, but its people are said to be "the good people" and "the respectable people." The manners and tastes of its people are not fully developed in the class sense. In their behavior with those above them, there is a certain giving of precedence by the members of the upper-middle class, there is a masked deference to the words, beliefs, and precepts of the superior classes which helps these middle-class people to gain social acceptance in the larger associations of the upper classes, such as the Women's Club. Not all of this class are mobile; many of them are content, and "these good people" are often the respectable community leaders who are "the salt of the earth" to all classes. This is so because, to their inferiors, "they don't put on airs" and, to their superiors, they are "sound and thoroughly dependable."

The great majority of the homes of this class are medium in size but some are large. The upper-middle people are largely Yankee, with a sizable representation of the Irish and a scattering few of other ethnic groups, such as the Jews and Italians. They marry later than any class below them and at about the same age as the lower-upper class.

They belong to the Protestant churches and not to the Catholic churches. They join such churches as the Congregational, Baptist, and

Christian Science, but not the Episcopal or Methodist. Most of their children go to the local high school, and only a few of the more socially ambitious parents send their children to preparatory schools.

The upper three classes, which compose about 15 percent of the population, look upon the lower-middle members as "respectable" but "belonging to the masses." They are Side Streeters who are in the kinds of organizations where "you never see them."

The lower middles (28.4 percent of the total population) are felt to be the top crust of the lower half of the society by those beneath them, by those above them, and by themselves. The lower-middle-class people live in medium- and small-sized houses which are not in the best condition, and are located nearer "the wrong part of town." Their houses are worth less than those of the three classes above them, but still they are worth considerably more than those of the two classes below them. They are employed in large numbers in the retail stores.

This class has a smaller percentage of Yankees than any of the classes above it. The lower-middle-class marry younger than any of the classes above them and older than either of the two classes beneath them. They belong to the Protestant churches but not to the two Catholic churches.

No class above the lower-middle belongs in significant numbers to fraternal organizations or to auxiliary associations; in fact, these classes avoid such organizations. But the lower-middle-class membership is significantly high for only these two types of associations. There is here a sharp break in the kind of participation the classes below upper-middle enjoy in Yankee City. Furthermore, all the classes above lower-middle are members in significantly high numbers of charitable organizations and social clubs, but the lower-middle class and the other two beneath it are excluded from or avoid such associations.

It is in the lower-middle class that the increase in number of arrests is first noticeable. They account for 8 percent of the arrests of Yankee City. This is four times as much as the upper-middle, but only one third as much as the upper-lower class. The juvenile arrests are far higher than those of the upper classes and much more like those of the two lower classes. It is in the lower-middle class that such organizations as the Society for the Prevention of Cruelty to Children and the truancy officers are able to take effective action in the control of children and to interfere with the role of the parent in the family system.

The members of the upper-lower class are always grouped with the masses by those above them, by those below them, and by themselves, but they are seldom called "Riverbrookers," for they are above them. They are the largest class, having 33 percent of the population.

Half of their houses are small and less than one seventh in good condition. The great majority of the upper-lower class are semiskilled workers, and over 80 percent are above the level of unskilled labor.

The upper-lower class has a greater percentage of ethnic members and a smaller percentage of Yankees than any other class in Yankee City. Only the lower-lower class marries younger than the upper-lower class. It has the smallest percentage of Protestants and is the only class which shows a preference for the two Catholic churches. Only the lowest class has a higher rate of arrest than the upper-lower.

All other classes look down on the lower-lower class. The lower-lower-class people live in the poorest houses in Yankee City and in the "worst areas" in the community. More of their houses are small and in bad condition than any other class. Their houses are located in areas which are considered the worst in the community. They pay their rent by the week and less than all other classes.

Over 60 percent of their people are laborers. More of them are unemployed than all other classes.

The lower-lower class, with 26 percent of the total, is the only one which has more males than females, and it leads all others in number of children. It marries earlier, has a larger percentage of juvenile members, and more married people than other classes. In Yankee City its people prefer the Catholic churches, the Presbyterian, the Methodist, and Baptist churches. They join and avoid associations in about the same way as the upper-lower class.

The lower-lower class is easily the most vulnerable to police interference; 65 percent of all the arrests in Yankee City are from this class and about 11 percent of the members of the lower-lower stratum have been arrested. About one third of the arrested individuals are adolescent. Its family life is more disturbed by the police and its parents are more coerced by the private associations.

It is evident from the foregoing that the several superior and inferior classes of Yankee City, with new and old Hill Streeters at the apex of the hierarchy, with the Homevillers and Side Streeters in the mediate statuses, and the Riverbrookers at the bottom, show a recognition, even if democratically disguised, of a rank order in their lives. Each class in Yankee City is an evaluated way of life in which the several parts tend to conform in value to the general place of a class in the rank order. The class order of Yankee City is a system of interconnected statuses which systematically places the thousands of individuals who live in it and thereby provides these individuals who live in it with a coherent way of life.

CASTE LEVELS

As mentioned previously, the "other" caste also assigns class status. The study of "Old City" will illustrate.[15]

The Negro Class Order

Five social strata may be distinguished in the Negro community of Old City; an upper class, two divisions of the middle class, and two lower classes. In studying the Negro community in Old City it was found that the following traits of individuals of families are the most important bases for clique and social class relationships: the recognized social position of parents; amount of educational achievement; skin color and hair form; church and associational membership; talent; manners and dress; condition and type of house and furnishing.

The members of a social class themselves recognize that the fundamental test of their class status is their ability to participate regularly in the social life of certain other persons. In the colored society, for example, the expression "class with" is used to mean "able to go around with" (socially). One middle-class person will say of another: "Joe can't class with the big folks (upper class), he goes around with the people right here in Turnersville (middle-class neighborhood) just like the rest of us."

In the sense in which a social class is here conceived, therefore, its membership can be identified empirically upon the basis of either of two types of information: (1) records of common participation of individuals in noneconomic groups, such as churches, associations, clubs, large dances, teas, picnics, weddings, and funerals; and (2) the verbal expression by individuals of their willingness to associate with other persons in these social relationships.

The most explicit and detailed expressions concerning class status were made by persons at the top of the colored class structure of Old City. These upper-class persons stated that there were three social classes. They knew and identified the members of the upper class and the highest ranking of the middle class. They also stated their conception of the social traits and techniques by which these individuals had achieved high social status. All the upper-class informants emphasized the weakness, however, of class sanctions.

The colored upper class is divided into two groups: (1) a socially withdrawn group which seems to be essentially fixated upon being white and (2) a socially active group which sometimes attempts to compensate for its not being white by being free in its emotional and sensual expression.

[15] Warner, *et al., op. cit.,* pp. 123–124.

There is no doubt that in the Deep South, as in most colored societies, the chief "weakness" of the class structure lies in the relative lack of economic stratification within the lower caste. As a direct result of caste taboos, for example, colored persons are excluded from all white-collar and professional occupations, except in the few colored businesses or educational institutions. Physicians, dentists, and lawyers, moreover, are relatively few in colored, as compared with white, societies in the South.

The caste system as enforced by the southern state legislatures makes no provision for the education of colored physicians, dentists, or lawyers; and colored people are systematically excluded from white-collar work in business and government. The relative lack of economic or occupational differentiation within colored societies is fundamentally the result of educational deprivation and lack of economic opportunity. Although the operation of the economic system permits a few colored persons to achieve high occupational status, it does not permit a sufficient spread of occupations to allow the development of an occupational hierarchy. In all modern Western class systems, on the other hand, occupational status and economic status are highly correlated with class status. Occupational and economic status may have been acquired from one's ancestors, or be largely honorific, as in the case of the upper-class families who have lost their wealth but have preserved the reputation of wealth and of high occupational status in the past. In any historical view of class, however, there seems no doubt that economic stratification would prove the most nearly constant factor.

Brief and limited in scope though such researches as the above may be, they and others point to a number of impacts upon child life and development.

IMPLICATIONS OF COMMUNITY BACK-GROUNDS FOR CHILD ORIENTATION IN OUR CULTURE

ON THE BASIS of caste and class, the new-born child is endowed with numerous ascribed roles and statuses. Will he be regarded as an asset, a prized objective attained, or as a burden by his family? Will he live in a part of the city, town, or country where he will have light, air, play space, or will he be crowded, breathe impure air, play where every move is a hazard? Will his parents be financially able to buy proper clothing, food, medical attention, both mental and physical, provide wholesome leisure-time pursuits, well-equipped and well-staffed schools, or will the opposite be true? Will he be reared by the small family unit or by a larger kinship grouping? Similar questions and their answers shed light and insight upon one's understanding and appraisal of a child as he operates in a schoolroom, playground situation, or any other social group.

The world community and what goes on in it is now grim reality to the youngest child in our classrooms and homes. Never again will it be sufficient for children to be trained for life in their immediate communities. Never again will they be able to grow, think, and plan in terms of their state, their region, or their nation for long. Not merely the accessibility of nation to nation, but also the highly mobile life they will be living must call for early and consistently developmental growth in perception of wider horizons.

Already there is talk of drafting young women as well as men. Whether we reach that point or not, "the services," diplomatic, medical, recreational, will draw increasingly larger numbers of girls and women. They will be shuttled back and forth across the national community as well as that of the world community. Their sisters who follow soldier husbands will also "see" and bring up their children under highly uncertain, often mobile conditions.

People who must live in such a world must be increasingly able to find a haven from frustration and its satellites within their own center poise of existence, not transitory externals. Important requisites for that type of adjustment are: knowledge of the factors at work; insight into the conflicts in value premises and actional outcomes; appreciation at most, tolerance at the least, of other people, other cultural backgrounds, ways of looking at things, and ways of doing things.

Careful study, as the research accumulates, of the social structures and the processes at work in the various kinds of community backgrounds gives the wherewithal to see the specific social institutions within community relationships, be they immediate and local or farther removed but no less potent in impact. Parents will want to take account of these backgrounds so that in light of them when making decisions and acting upon these decisions they give basic attitudes of curiosity, anxious inquiry, and experience at the child's maturity level. This will require the deliberate planning whereby the parents become aware as early as nursery and kindergarten days of the local social world and how it reaches out into ever-widening social worlds.

Teachers will want to know and understand community backgrounds that they may see the lower-class child who uses" bad words" not as just another bad boy but as one who represents a status level, who is using the only techniques and words he knows, which, incidentally, gain him prestige on his block or in the "street-corner society" which comprises his social-cultural world.

And when they know and understand, perhaps they will find ways and means of helping children and their families to bridge the gaps. Despite the importance of the larger community settings, the particular impingements of immediate community living will rank highest in the thinking of both parents and teachers. We shall close this chapter, therefore, with a summary analysis of some generalizations which seem applicable to the situation. It cannot be overemphasized, however, that these always remain subject to mediation through specific family units.

UPPER-CLASS CHILDREN

Upper-class families regard the child as an immortality agent. He is expected to pass on the family name, its traditions, and be careful to maintain its prestige rating intact. While this attitude toward the child insures him of the best care and opportunities of all sorts, its pressure may rebound in unpleasant ways if the child is not interested or able physically or mentally to function in an approved class manner.

While upper-class children will be taken care of by the immediate family or people in their employ, there is also participation in upbringing by members of the larger kinship group. "What will Grandmother say about it?" "How will other branches of the family regard the action?" are not merely rhetorical questions. One does not act in terms of his immediate family alone but in terms of the norms set by the "clan," the larger kinship grouping whose prestige is also at stake.

Upper-class children usually come to school with a superior linguistic development. They are able not merely to talk but also to express themselves. This ability soon establishes their status. Related to class derivation will be the kinds of words used, the meaning associated with them, the topics discussed, manners, and even curricula will be shaped not merely to promote vocational knowledge but value standards of class. Unless the public school is in effect an area

The home physical plant sets the stage for family life and is an important factor in defining the child's activities, and very often the tone of sibling and parent-child relationships. These children live here, with little or no privacy, with parents lacking time, energy, or interest for supervised leisure activities. There is little medical care and social and cultural advantages. They live in the lower class where there is, in a sense, no "Child's World."

These middle-class children live in the pleasant apartment houses above. Soon they will move to the small but comfortable houses below. In both surroundings each family member will have his own room. The mothers of these children belong to child study groups and child conservation leagues, and they spend untold energy and time in planning for "advantages" for their children. Their children have every medical assistance, and permanency of residence and family relations surrounds them.

These children live here with space inside and outside the home plant. Their family's economic position and relative leisure assure them a full, varied range of activities. They attend private school, travel often and widely, and mingle freely with carefully selected friends. They do not experience the hardships of lower-class children.

school for the upper class, most of these children will not appear in public school. If they go to private school, they will of necessity mingle with children of lower-upper- and aspiring upper-middle-class groups.

As Bossard [16] ably points out,

A problem in parent-child relationships frequently results from the fact that children from the upper-upper and lower-upper classes go to the same private schools and mingle together. Somewhere enroute in their school experience, the lower-upper-class [and we add the upper-middle] children come to sense that the parents are not socially acceptable on the same plane class. This often leads to a situation in which lower-upper-class children develop attitudes of condescension or resentment toward their parents. This is apt to happen wherever children attain a status beyond that of their parents, but it tends to be more conspicuous in the upper class, by way of comparison with the subordination and respect shown by upper-class children toward their parents.

Upper-class children enjoy a large range of activities due not only to their usual economic ability but also to the greater amount of leisure characteristic of the class members. Much of this exclusiveness is doubtless deliberately planned and maintained, but it is due also in large part to [17] "a sorting process carried out by like-minded and like-financed people. Common interests, common traditions, and common capacities, make for a way of socializing which is exclusive. It may be said that the higher ones goes in the social scale, the more social distance is reinforced by geographical separation. Upper-class children tend to live apart both as to section of city, schools attended, amusements. They are largely insulated from contacts outside their class."

MIDDLE-CLASS CHILDREN

Middle-class families truly play an "in the middle" role. Those at middle-middle or above tend to emulate the attitudes of the upper classes toward children. There is general concern for limiting of family size so that resources may be available for activities considered desirable. There is likely to be strong emphasis on enforcing every type of behavior which will hold the line and at the same time increase chances of upward mobility. In fact children are often regarded as a means of fulfilling the hope of class rise.

Especially are the upper-middle brackets anxious to participate in newer ways of child rearing. Here are the child study groups, the

[16] James H. Bossard, *Sociology of Child Development* (New York, Harper, 1948), pp. 306–307. Used by permission.
[17] *Ibid.*, p. 307.

readers of books on child care and development. Here too, unfortunately, are the fadists.

The child in the middle class will be taken care of by the immediate family unless there are extenuating circumstances such as divorce, death, or career mothers. Instead of the wider kinship group influence and determination of goals and the like, the emphasis is on the small, immediate family unit. In fact, there is often keen resentment if in-laws find it necessary to reside with the family. Likewise, no "interference" is brooked or appreciated concerning child care and child rearing. Consequently, children of the middle class are not as apt to feel close ties and obligations to relatives as is the upper-class child. In other words, there may be a feeling of larger kinship solidarity, but it is not the patterned solidarity of the upper class. A relative economic security derived from participation in the professional and salaried occupations may be basic to this more voluntary and casual solidarity.

When the middle-class child enters school, he also carries into the classroom the linguistic equipment characteristic of his status level. In the main, he will speak the language of his teacher since public schools are typically middle-class institutions staffed by middle-class or upper-lower-class teachers. In either case, middle-class values, attitudes, and modes of behavior will be enforced. If at all possible, he will continue his education through high school and college. Post graduate curricula attract many from these class levels. Education is considered the most effective social elevator.

Though middle-class families are seldom able to be "exclusive," as mentioned above, they attempt a rigorous "selective exclusiveness." The activities in which children will engage are carefully chosen in terms of whom they will meet there. Borderline invitational activities, such as dancing schools and riding clubs, are popular.

As several writers point out, the stresses and strains of an activity pattern so directed and so purposive are clearly evident in middle-class children. They might have added that their effects are clearly evident in strain in their parents as well with particular emphasis upon mother's to be discussed later.

LOWER-CLASS CHILDREN

The lower-class child is in a sharply contrasted role to that of the other brackets. His arrival is often regarded as "a sort of inevitable price which fate exacts in payment for sex relations."

Though it is not suggested that lower-class children are all unwanted or rejected, it is true that in the light of economic considerations a new baby presents a crisis in terms of one more mouth to feed, one more person among whom to divide limited resources.

Since in these class groups the rate of divorce and desertion and death is higher, the child's rearing is more likely to be a job of the mother or of mother surrogates, such as older children. Lower-class children must become self-reliant very early, must "help out" either at home or in street trades, and, in a sense, become economic assets to offset their very existence as a burden.

Family loyalty and solidarity of the sort mentioned above are practically impossible to achieve in view of the impermanence of family organization. Where it does exist, it is likely to be based upon common needs for survival rather than upon values, traditions, and rituals from a nostalgic past.

When the lower-class child arrives in the classroom, he, too, brings with him class-oriented language ability. But now it is a penalizing ability. He not only uses the wrong grammatical constructions, but also he uses words which are socially unacceptable to middle-class teachers and/or middle-class children. His topics of discussion are restricted, and his very manner of speaking may invite resistance and resentment.

His chances of health are less, and, hence, his absence record is also greater. He may be forced to stay out of school to work or to care for brothers and sisters. His diet is often insufficient in content or quality to give him the vim needed for average mental work. The "work hard and you'll get somewhere" bromicides are a source of frustration and, later, cynicism. As a consequence, he may snipe at middle-class values which he cannot approach. In more extreme cases delinquent behavior may epitomize his rebellion.

"Now, man-to-man," said the principal to the boy who had appeared numerous times in her office. "Tell me truly, why do you and Miss Smith have trouble living together in the classroom?"

The boy looked up quickly, seemed quietly to decide "Can I trust her" then replied earnestly. "I'll tell you. She keeps telling me, 'You're really bright. If you'd study hard, you'd get somewhere.' And you know as well as I that it's a damn lie for *me*."

For a twelve-year-old child this is indeed a sage verbalization of what many know and feel. And like this child, it need not be so if some one is interested and cares. Suffice it to say, there were those who did. And now what might have been a potential Dillinger is an atomic scientist. But where one is "rescued," all too many become "social waste."

Bossard terms the social activities of lower-class children as residual. By this he means that there is possible or present little selectivity. The child does what is available in terms of settlement house, Big Brother, and similar movements. Parents have neither leisure, money, nor knowledge with which to provide otherwise.

SUMMARY AND IMPLICATIONS

IT SHOULD BE EMPHASIZED strongly that though we may outline class patterns we do not mean to imply that every individual or every family experiences and plays roles in exactly the same way or achieves the same status. Everyone in every status level and in every social group, however small, has many roles and statuses. In one group he may be a follower or member only. In another he may become a dynamic leader and in still others run the gamut in-between. To explain the why of this is difficult. It must obtain from the rearrangements of the aspects of the particular effective environment. Some people stimulate, others block, some physical settings call out activity, others invite lethargy. Familiar customs may stimulate if liked. They may "gag" if engaged in merely because of class pressure.

I don't think I'll ever like to dance after those horrible Saturday afternoons at dancing school. Crawl into dress-up clothes, bow, scrape and mince around, then home and change clothes again. Just because my father and mother went to the same dancing school.

Or witness the opposite effect on the child of a family striving upward and with sacrifice.

I always looked forward to winter and dancing school. When the longed-for invitation came, the whole family celebrated. Father took me out and bought me a whole new outfit. My hair and shoes were always the shiniest there. And you could have cut your hand on the crease in my trousers. I loved every minute of it. Of course, I dreaded intermissions, and I tried to arrive just in time to line up. For the kids gathered in their own little groups then. But I remembered to compliment my girl partners and to be most polite and "not pushing" to the boys. Also, I worked hard at dancing and became very good at it. The teachers would ask me to demonstrate the steps, and gradually first the girls and then the boys began treating me with respect. The girls took me in more than the boys, for they liked my dancing. I never formed any close friends there, but I learned many, many tricks of adjusting there that helped a lot as I grew. And later at college I've met fellows I knew there, and they have been cordial.

Or the third-class adjusted child who wrote:

I'm just amazed at those attitudes. As I look back, I guess my family must have made me a most happy kid. I neither resented nor looked forward especially to such activities. Everybody did them, they were fun; what's next, seems to have been my attitude. It makes my flesh crawl when I hear and read what some of these kids have gone through. I don't like this idea of social distinction at all if it hurts people. But, after all this study I just believe I'll approach marriage rationally. (He means choose a class partner.)

These excerpts point up the remarks that each family tends to have a rank order in its class, and this order determines not only the extent to which it is representative of the class culture, but also its attitude toward other classes and other families in its own class. Lower ranking families in the upper classes are under considerable pressure as a rule; feelings of insecurity manifest themselves in many ways, and the whole atmosphere of the home becomes one of extreme tension. In contrast are the middle-class families who are firmly established in the higher rank orders and who maintain their position with comfort and confidence, secure in the prestige of their relative rank order. The home atmosphere here may be one of ease and contentment. Finally, we may identify the upper-lower class immigrant family, hard-working, living carefully, realizing its class status for the time being, but hopefully anticipating the future. Here is a family obviously on the up.

The child in the American community finds its basic values often at odds with one another. Quietly, subtly, perhaps unconsciously, yet inexorably, or openly and deliberately, he is a social device for congealing and perpetuating class structure on the one hand and on the other for rising in the social structure.

TEACHING AND STUDY AIDS

1. It has been emphasized that the impacts of world community need to be known and understood. How shall we educate at specific developmental levels is a very important question. Too much, too

early will be as bad as too little and too late. A committee organized around this problem could stretch its own mind and that of the class by a round-table or panel discussion presentation of its findings. Starting references for such a project might include:

Association for Supervision and Curriculum Development, Headquarters, 1201 Sixteenth St., N. W. Washington, D. C. *Education for International Understanding*, $1.00.

———, *Living in the Atomic Age*, $.20.

2. All teachers need a more specialized knowledge of various sized communities than this book gives. Organize committees or individually study one or more of the following with an eye to sharing what you have learned with the whole class. Salient points for class discussion may include
   A. How do such variables as size, age, sex, and ethnic composition of population affect patterns of community living?
   B. What evidences do you find of a shift from primary to secondary modes of living in various sized communities? What are the implications of this trend for school people and parents?
   C. Select special areas of living such as family relations, earning a living, etc. and make a cross-analysis in different types of communities.

Open Country and Village Studies

Blumenthal, Albert, *Small Town Stuff* (Chicago, University of Chicago Press, 1932).

Rural Life Studies Series (Washington, Bureau of Agricultural Economics).
   A. *El Cerrito*, New Mexico
   B. *Old Order Amish*, Lancaster, Pennsylvania
   C. Harmony, Georgia

Sherman, Mandel, and Henry, Thomas, *Hollow Folk* (New York, Crowell, 1933).

Smart, Charles, *R. F. D.* (New York, Norton, 1938).

Useem, John, *et al.*, "Stratification in a Prairie Town," *American Sociological Review*, Vol. 7 (June 1942), p. 331 ff.

Warner, Wm. Lloyd, *et al.*, *Democracy in Jonesville* (New York, Harper, 1949.

West, James, *Plainville, U. S. A.* (New York, Columbia University Press, 1945).

Small City

Lynd, Robert and Helen, *Middletown* (New York, Harcourt, Brace, 1929).

———, *Middletown in Transition* (New York, Harcourt, Brace, 1937).

Warner, Wm. Lloyd, *The Social Life of a Modern Community* (New Haven, Yale University Press, 1941).

——, *Social Class in America* (Chicago, Science Research Associates, 1949).

The Larger City

Angell, R. C., "The Social Integration of Cities of More Than 100,-000 Population," *American Sociological Review,* Vol. 12 (June 1947), pp. 335–342.

Drake, St. Claire, and Cayton, H. R., *Black Metropolis* (New York, Harcourt, Brace, 1945).

McKenzie, R. D., *The Metropolitan Community* (New York, McGraw-Hill, 1933).

Mumford, Lewis, *The Culture of Cities* (New York, Harcourt, Brace, 1938).

Zorbaugh, Harvey, *The Gold Coast and the Slums* (Chicago, University of Chicago Press, 1929).

A book which will help tie together what you have learned from these separate studies is:

Bernard, Jessie, *American Community Behavior* (New York, Dryden, 1949).

3. Select several studies of regionalism and make a critical analysis of them. Three references which will give you background are:

Jensen, Merrill, *Regionalism in America* (Madison, University of Wisconsin Press, 1951).

Mangus, A. R., *Rural Regions of the United States* (Washington, Government Printing Office, 1940).

Odum, Howard W., "A Sociological Approach to the Study and Practice of American Regionalism," *Social Forces,* Vol. 20, No. 4 (May 1942).

4. Specific culture areas within cities and within regions are of great interest to the educational sociologist. The children who come from them to the public schools merit great efforts at understanding on the part of their teachers. They are in truth "marginal men," children living often between, but hardly of, two social worlds. Either individually or in groups, study such as the following and analyze the impacts of such community backgrounds upon child socialization:

Stonequist, E. V., *The Marginal Man: A Study in Personality and Culture Conflict* (New York, Scribner, 1937).

Strong, Edward K., *The Second Generation Japanese Problem* (Palo Alto, Stanford University Press, 1934).

Thomas, W. I., and Zaniecki, Florian, *The Polish Peasant in Europe and America,* 5 vols. (Boston, Badger, 1920).

Wernher, Hilda, *My Indian Family* (New York, Day, 1945).

Wirth, Louis, *The Ghetto* (Chicago, University of Chicago Press, 1928).

Young, Pauline V., *The Pilgrims of Russian Town* (Chicago, University of Chicago Press, 1932).

5. Another cultural minority with problems peculiar to it is that of the Negro child. The following books will give you background material for a class report or project:

Brewton Berry, *Race Relations* (Boston, Houghton, 1951).

Davis, Allison, Gardner, B. B., and Gardner, Mary R., *Deep South* (Chicago, University of Chicago Press, 1941).

Dollard, John, *Caste and Class in a Southern Town* (New Haven, Yale University Press, 1937).

Frazier, Franklin E., *The Negro Family in the United States* (Chicago, University of Chicago Press, 1939).

Myrdal, Gunnar, *The American Dilemma* (New York, Harper, 1944).

6. It has been mentioned above that the area of intergroup relations or intercultural relations is of prime importance to all citizens. Organize a committee or individually supplement and extend the above important area by *reading, interviewing,* and visiting those who may shed light on the problems. Executive secretaries of the Urban League, the American Association of Colored People, Young Men's Christian Association, Young Women's Christian Associations, and various other local groups will be glad to perform such a public service.

7. Read Myrdal's *The American Dilemma* and relate its generalizations to child life under such circumstances.

8. Read Geoffrey Gorer's fascinating account *The American People: A Study in National Character,* (New York, Norton, 1948). Make a critical analysis of his findings.

9. Read and evaluate the following approach to the study of status:

Paul K. Hatt, "Stratification in Mass Society," *American Sociological Review, vol* 15 (1950).

Cecil North and Paul K. Hatt, "Jobs and Occupations: A Popular Evaluation," *Opinion News* (Sept. 1, 1947).

10. Read and report on man's adjustment to urban areas as shown in James A. Quinn's *Human Ecology* (New York, Prentice-Hall, 1950), and Lowell Julliard Carr and James Edson Stermer's *Willow Run* (New York, Harper, 1952).

11. Read and report critically on *World Population and Future Resources,* edited by Paul Hatt (New York, American Book, 1951).

V | HOME SOCIAL INTERAC-TION IN RELATION TO CHILD GROWTH AND DEVELOPMENT

FAMILY STRUCTURES AND PROCESSES

THE EARLY FAMILY was a natural biological unit, largely resting in points of origin and development upon the obvious mother-child relationship. Some preliterate peoples are recorded as having little or no notion of the physical connection between the father and the child. Conception was believed to be caused by spirit impregnations of various sorts. One common illustration was the belief that "at high tide the waters were especially charged with impregnating elements and fertilized any female who bathed in them." [1]

This irrevocable mother-child relationship was gradually augmented by a man-woman economic relationship. Women and children needed this economic security, first, because of the inconveniences of pregnancy and second, because of the later helplessness of the human infant. While it is probably true that neither of these factors were as demanding in earlier times as now, the inconveniences and helplessness were present.

From the man's standpoint there must have been complementary satisfactions which entered into decisions to tie himself to other human beings in a permanent relationship. Sex impulses alone would not explain this. Momentary unions even on recurrent bases can and have satisfied this impulse. We may assume that the enlarged family unit occurred also because man needed and derived benefit from

[1] F. E. Lumley, *Principles of Sociology* (New York, McGraw-Hill, 1935), p. 244 ff.

having a woman or women about to cook, to keep the fires, and to assume detail work while he in line with his physical freedom engaged in more exciting activities, such as fishing, hunting, and fighting.

This is tantamount to saying that the extension of the natural family unit to include definite stable relationships between specific individuals made a stronger combination in the struggle for existence. Such observable outcomes of men-women relationships must have gradually reached the level of oral communication.

As was pointed out in Chapter 2, these drives of various sorts cause tension which eventuate in action. Action tends to assume habitual forms and if expedient, may be readily transmitted until group habits grow. When communication is sufficient either at the gestural or verbal level, ways of meeting situations tend to become structural and ways or processes evolve for transmitting these structures which seem right, necessary, and true to the ones involved.

So with the social institution of marriage.[2]

In other words, roles and functions of each family member became defined, sometimes clearly and specifically, in some eras less clearly, with resulting personal and social-cultural implications. Rank or status was also assigned on the basis of attributes considered more or less desirable. Rank in turn allowed for definition of power abilities, privileges, and responsibilities in line with the privileges enjoyed. The goals and/or rewards of the institution were established and a system of rules and punishments for infringements. Loomis adds territoriality or a land locus as a requirement for any social system. When this natural family unit became extended and surrounded by rules, traditions, symbols and ceremonies, it became marriage.

In general usage marriage and family are synonymous terms, but as objects of study, they may be somewhat different. We are interested in family aspects primarily and marriage aspects only as they relate to the developing child. Before discussing the relationship patterns within the modern family, some commonly accepted generalizations about modern kinship systems may be cited.

1. The family is a universal social institution. In no culture do we find complete and unregulated promiscuity.

[2] The records of its growth and development make fascinating reading. See reading list at end of chapter.

2. The structure of the family has varied greatly in various cultures and at various times. Sometimes it has been matriarchal, a form wherein descent is traced in the main through the mother rather than the father. The patriarchal form has often and now most generally predominates. In this form the father name is taken, and descent may be traced only through the father or through mother and father lines.

3. The structure of the marriage relation has also varied greatly from culture to culture. Where more than one wife to a husband has been sanctioned, the form is termed polygyny. Where the reverse is true and more than one husband is sanctioned for one wife, the structure is termed polyandry. Where more than one man marries more than one woman, group marriage is said to have existed. Where one husband and one wife at a time is the custom, the structure is termed monogamy. It is interesting to realize that though the preponderance of married people in the world live monogamously, polygyny is allowed in cultures which contain larger populations than do the cultures which allow only monogamy.

4. Roles and statuses of family members may be very different in different cultures. Functions performed by women in one cultural group may be the functions of men in another. Likewise what is adult role and function in one culture may be the role and function of the child in another.

5. Present trends in a very general sense within our own society and culture include: (A) decline in size and stability of the family, (B) shifts of many earlier roles and functions to other social institutions, (C) a gradual shift away from the father- and/or mother-dominated family toward an equalitarian organization where the needs, hopes, worries and the like of all members of the family are considered of paramount importance, (D) a greater desire for understanding of child development dynamics, and concern for child and adult social adjustment in the light of mental hygiene principles.

These knowledges and trends are causing students increasingly to be interested in examining the kinds of social atmospheres in which children come of age. What are the various kinds of home climates in which children develop? What are their conceptions of child and parent roles and position within the status structure of the home? What are the resulting motivational procedures and finally what are some of the personality outcomes as shown by studies and personal opinion?

HOME SOCIAL CLIMATES

HOME SOCIAL INTERACTION is often said to take place on three levels—sensory, emotional, and intellectual. The sensory level was emphasized in the unfolding of self. The great importance of voice timbre, inflection, and voice attitude, of facial expression with particular emphasis on eye expression, plus an integrated setting with all other gestural communication can hardly be overrated. As one student recalled:

Now that you mention it, I realize that many of the memories I have of my father stem from this level. Even when he was punishing me, his eyes said "This is painful to me, but I love you, so I must do it."

Or listen to another:

I was slow in school and it was a great cross to my mother. I could "feel" the anger and disgust in her as we both struggled "to catch up." I think I've always secretly hated her for it.

It is obvious that these examples are combining at least two, possibly three, levels of interaction. The sense reactions were quickly, perhaps instantly, translated into emotional states which communicated themselves to the children. One suspects that the ideas expressed were also conveyed by chance remarks in general conversation.

These various kinds of actions, reactions, and interactions tend to get themselves structuralized into about three social climates, the authoritarian, the laissez-faire, and the democratic. It is obvious that homes do not always follow one pattern sharply. There will be both deviations and inconsistencies from time to time but there will also be basic tendencies which can be observed, recorded and discussed.[3]

Let us then essay a look at these climates in terms of concepts of the child.

AUTHORITARIAN CLIMATE

In the authoritarian climate the child is considered as a miniature adult. This means that the aims, goals, expectancies, or anticipations set for him will be in terms of adult standards. To a considerable degree he will be expected to react to situations in a so-called

[3] For research findings see R. G. Barker, J. S. Kounin, and H. F. Wright, eds., *Child Behavior and Development* (New York, McGraw-Hill, 1943). Special reference to Lippett and White, Chap. 28.

adult manner, to have interests, even abilities and attention spans, akin to those of adults. A variance of this approach is to consider the child as a vacuum who is to be stuffed with the social heritage as selected and mediated by the family.

If one regards children in this fashion, it is customary to attempt motivation of behavior by a system of rewards and punishments. Depending to some extent upon social-class traditions, these rewards may take such forms as fondling, affection, expressed pride in achievement, privileges or material things ranging from gold star awards through desired toys and clothes to monetary rewards. Punishments, likewise, range from withholding of love, affection, and praise, negative commands, and loss of privileges through to mild or rigorous kinds of corporal punishment.

Observable outcomes of personalities reared in such environments[4] are increased nervous behavior of all sorts, inhibited behavior, and general decreased maturity in behavior. These children are often hesitant, slow to show initiative in situations demanding creative work in the classroom. They are often quarrelsome, annoying, more apt to be disobedient and to resent adult authority.

Other things being equal, these children tend to visit upon people the kinds of attitudes under which they have operated at home. If they are required to be submissive, they may fall into the pattern readily enough in formal situations such as the classroom and "go wild" on the playground.

It should be said in fairness that the interpretation of what is done from the parent standpoint and from that of the child is often quite different. Parents may tell you in all sincerity that they "correct" children in as nice a way as possible whereas children may tell you on a Guess Who test that their parents nag, criticize,[5] and are too strict. This often crystallizes in actual dislike for parents.

Every counselor has doubtless heard this sort of remark from a counselee who in the proper counseling situation feels free from guilt feelings and other social restraints.

I never did like my mother. All she ever did was nag, criticize, and bully me. I always said, never, never will I be like her. But what worries

[4] T. R. Myers, *Intra-Family Relationships and Pupil Adjustment* (New York, Bureau of Publications Teachers College, Columbia University, 1935); M. Y. Radke, *The Relations of Parental Authority to Children's Behavior and Attitudes* (Minneapolis, University of Minnesota Press, 1946).

[5] J. E. Anderson, "Parents' Attitude on Child Behavior: A Report of Three Studies," *Child Development* 17 (1946), pp. 91–97.

me is that I'm afraid I am. I don't seem to know how to do it any other way. Johnny flared up at me just yesterday. "All you do is jaw, 'don't, don't,' I'm sick of you." How can I do it differently?

In terms of growing children, perhaps this effect is as important as any. People tend to establish relationships in line with previous experiences. Another kind of experience or serious thought and study such as the mother in this example was willing to give are the only means of reconstituting the social climate.

On the brighter side it should be pointed out that work by Sewell has suggested that even the authoritarian need not produce all negative effects.

LAISSEZ-FAIRE CLIMATE

As the term has implied historically, the laissez-faire climate is "an every man for himself and the devil take the last one." As Sumner might have put it, its assumption seems to be that that government is best which governs least.

The concept of the child still retains something of the appraisal that he is "like an adult," but unlike the authoritarian climate, goals and aims are not clearly defined for him or strictly enforced. Under a guise of saying that he needs "free expression," he is left to his own devices with but a minimum of, and often inconsistent, guidance. Like the proverbial sponge, the child is supposed to absorb if he is exposed to opportunities. Appraisal and integration are left to chance. One student wrote

I came from such a home. We felt always as though we were at sea without a paddle. If we asked how or what to do, we were told to "figure it out for ourselves," or "do it as we liked." And to make it worse, decisions which were made often were reversed from one day to another. Or if we did figure it out and decide, we were apt to get into hot water. After awhile we took our problems to the minister and the teacher and later the school counselor. Then our parents felt hurt because we never confided in them.

As suggested heretofore, with norms and standards illy defined the motivation is at best a diffused, individualistic, survival one. Trial and error, hard knocks, and frustration gradually mold a "bag-of-tricks" philosophy of living.

These are the children in the classrooms who think teachers too strict if they give direction and positive guidance. "It's a free country; I'll do as I please" attitude is not uncommon. Sometimes, however, the teachers tell us, these adrift children are so glad for the security feeling which the teacher and the classroom living may give that they become so cooperative as to appear almost servile.

In the words of one teacher,

I was glad for the distinctions we made in social climates, especially in dealing with Mark. Only as I realized the difficulty of a child trying to live in two kinds of atmospheres could I understand and help him become more self-reliant as well as group-minded and active.

Or says another,

It took almost the first semester to convince Grace that this was a cooperative-competition in which we engaged. Her unroutinized, free-for-all living, has left deep scars. She is still suspicious of everyone's motives and still fearful of any situation which calls for initiative, planned behavior for the good of all, constructive criticism, and re-planning."

It has seemed to teachers such as these two that far too many so-called democratic homes and schoolrooms are really laissez-faire atmospheres. They are quick to point out that this kind of misconception is not only hard on children but also on schools and teachers who do understand and promote democratic social structures and processes. Teachers often bear the brunt of this wrong definition. Take, for example, one teacher whose schoolroom was really democratic. On the opening day of school she was confronted by a parent with the following:

Oh, yes, you're the teacher from Ohio State who thinks kids should be raised to do as they like. I'm against all of it. My neighbor does that, and her kids are the worst on the block. Why, they even kick their mother on the shins, but she says it's all O.K. because they're supposed to be aggressive at that age. I want none of it. At my house they know who's boss, and they will as long as they put their feet under my table. Where is the principal's office? I hear Miss . . . teaches the same grade, and she's strict.

The results of this atmosphere are readily discernible. Where there is no clear-cut work plan for children, behavior become erratic, frustrated. Frustration leads quickly to aggressive acts of various sorts and back again to frustration until chaos, or at least license, characterizes behavior. An example of how these children react in a classroom will illustrate.

"What happened today at school?" asked the mother.

"Oh, you might know," responded her nine-year-old son, who long accustomed to an orderly democratic existence at home, is thoroughly disgusted and disgruntled at the time and effort wasted in a classroom purporting to be democratic but which in reality is in rank disorder. "Frank talked, interrupted, threw things. Then we spent 15 minutes discussing what to do about Frank. Then he was sent to the first-grade room as punishment. Then we talked and talked again about it, as we've done ever since he came into the room [one year before]. Then Sandy carried on, and it happened all over again. Then the time was gone, so no reading or numbers today. Shop and music and science were O.K., but our room is a mess. All of us but the teacher know all Frank wants is attention and any kind will do. It's so boring. If they'd let us handle him, we'd do better. All he understands is a licking or to be set in a corner and left. When Mrs. L—— substituted, that's what she did and he caught on and behaved. But I do feel sorry for him. What a life he must lead!"

DEMOCRATIC CLIMATE

The thinking exemplified above needs no commentary. The democratic home thinks of the child as a developing, growing, outreaching organism. It recognizes that in no way is he a miniature adult. Study of skeletal structure [6] as well as of growth in rhythm patterns [7] reveals that not even "in looks" is he a small adult.

The democratic home also recognizes that this tiny being as mentioned in Chaper 3 is unsocial, not asocial; is unmoral, not immoral; and therefore, needs guidance and direction as he unfolds and grows. This means that there is room for authority within democracy, and the exercise of authority does not necessarily entail authoritarianism. What authority, by whom, at what time, for what, and how, gradually redefined and redelegated as the maturity level of the child changes, are the important criteria to be considered here.

This conception of the child has paramount influence in the setting of goals, expectancies, and anticipations. It likewise influences the "how" of setting goals.

Anticipatory behavior will be cued by the maturity level of the child. For example, the fact that he may be large for his age will no longer be a signal for ridicule or punishment if he is not ready to act

---

[6] W. C. Olson, *Child Development* (Boston, Heath, 1949), Chaps. 1–5.
[7] See Chapter 3.

mentally, emotionally, and socially as though he were older as well as bigger. A knowledge of muscular coordination rates will preclude setting goals which are too difficult, therefore, frustrating and productive of socially unacceptable behavior.

As emphasized many times before, the development of thought and language, in fact of the whole personality go hand in hand. Therefore, as soon as the child can understand language (and this begins occurring before he can himself manipulate the word symbols), a democratic home begins to include him and his noticed preferences in the setting up of goals.

Several differences distinguish this procedure from that of laissez faire. Though respect for the individual entails recognition of a child's need for self-expression, it also recognizes that this must be channeled. Gone, we hope, is the idea that child-centered means child-monopolized, child-ruled, and child-exploited. In a democratic home the needs of *all* members of the family must be recognized and adjustments made in terms of them.

One of the primary functions of the family unit is to provide a proving ground for adjustments in human relations. A home has surely given a biased viewpoint and experience if the child has operated without reference to the drives, needs, and satisfactions of *all* members of the family, carefully expressed in conferences with children.

It should be hastily reiterated that it is not suggested that small or even older children be expected to make world-shaking decisions. What the democratic home does is to start the education of choice making in areas which are within his experience, interests, and abilities, but are not the crucial areas which would affect his health or safety.

As Dr. Helene Heye of the Ohio State University Nursery School phrases it, "Where health and safety are concerned, our first responsibility is to parents, and children are made to understand that. They can, however, move freely in making play, work, clothing, and even food choices within limitations."

In the home also one needs to learn that "doing as I please" is not democratic but laissez-faire procedure. Freedom is ever freedom within limits—limits set by the group which grants the rights and privileges. Freedom is as a four-year-old kindergartener put it, "doing as we please as long as we don't take other people's pleases."

A frequent question on this point revolves around aren't you really shifting to authoritarianism when "you put your foot down"? The answer is an equally flat No. There is room, even necessity, in democracy for authority. The difference between exercising authority and being authoritarian is largely a matter of attitude, knowledge by the child of the derivation of the authority, and the use to which it is put.

The motivation in the truly democratic atmosphere may have to begin with "things" for the very young child but may and can be moved rapidly toward intrinsic motivation.

"Why are you sweeping the walk?" said one six-year-old child to her neighbor. "My mother promised me a movie. What will you get?"

"Oh," said the second six-year-old girl. "Why should I get something? Everyone at our house does things to help us all. I'm sweeping."

The story might well end there with no comment, but the sequel is worth the recording. At this moment nine-year-old brother of the second child arrived on the scene and said, "Sister, that's hard work for you. Wouldn't you like to rest a minute? I'm through mopping the kitchen floor. I'll sweep for you."

"No, thank you," said his sister. "You did your job, and I like to sweep."

One might conjecture from this isolated incident that these children have had truly pleasant and democratic experiences but that they were overworked. Fuller knowledge reveals that this is carefully guarded against. One has responsibilities in this home but always in terms of strength, ability, and interest. Furthermore, these are not irrevocable tasks. Children need to learn to adjust to change with a minimum of frustration. This can be done in a democratic setting.

"Mowing the lawn is Tom's job, but if he is legitimately busy, his father does it, and Tom does something else," says one mother. "And," she adds smilingly, "if both are busy, I mow it. Washing dishes is my job, but last night I had a meeting so the kids and their father got supper and washed dishes. They report a jolly time."

Children who live and grow in the democratic environment have far better than average chances of a healthy adjustment. Having been respected in their own right, they are willing, even eager to respect the personalities of other people. Having been given a share in decisions concerning themselves, they are able to meet problems with a minimum of frustration. Having learned that the method of intelligence can and will operate, they are not likely to be drawn in first one direction and then another by reliance on mere authority. They are better able to appraise social data critically. "Father, what's your evidence?" may be annoying at times. But as one University School parent says, "It's good insurance for future thinking and action on both our parts."

Theirs is no rote learning but an attitude of mind.

"We won't sing but one of the songs we planned," said the pianist to the cub scout who had carefully planned his announcement in terms of two songs, their histories, etc.

"O.K.," responded the nine-year old as he walked upon the stage. "Ladies and Gentlemen, they've changed the program a bit and there isn't time for our two songs, for which I'm sorry. They're nice songs. We made up the words ourselves." Without embarrassment he told the song his den would sing. Needless to add, the audience saw to it that both songs were sung.

It is true this social assurance was a product of consistent home and school backgrounds, but similar if less pronounced results may be obtained from even one social milieu which operates with understanding and insight.

Perhaps the most frequently asked question in this regard is, "But how will they adjust to real life when they go out from these homes and schools into a highly competitive, even cutthroat world?"

Fortunately we can now answer from the support of both research and common sense appraisals. Several studies point out that when [8] these children go from a democratic school atmosphere to a highly or moderately traditional college they do as well in subject-matter areas as and in most instances better than the control group which has gone from more traditional authoritarian settings. In such areas as initiative, self-reliance, social sensitivity, and responsibility, ability to give and take constructive criticism, ability to express oneself fluently, general poise, and ability not only to plan but carry through, they are rated as superior.

These last ratings are of special importance as relates to the latter part of the question. If the concept of the democratic climate is of any worth at all, its great contribution to personal living should be adjustability. Not in the fluid sense of "Willy-nilly-ness" with a

[8] Class of 1938, University High School, Ohio State University, *Were We Guinea Pigs?* (New York, Holt, 1938). See also studies by Florence Reed, by Wickman, Lewin, *et al.*, as listed for Chapter 8.

"get used to anything attitude" but an intelligent appraisal of situations with consequent wholesome adjustment. Sometimes the wise person may withdraw from a difficult situation, again he may be able to live richly even *within* it without being sufficiently *of* it to be unpleasantly affected by it. This infers an "inner central poise of existence" which relegates annoying details and unpleasantries to their proper sphere—things to be lived with but not "within." This kind of poise is especially necessary in an urbanized environment with its continual overstimulation, its ceaseless barrage from the agencies of mass communication, its confusions and hurry, its emphasis upon "getting somewhere" in a materialistic sense. Ideally "inner poise" is best found in the more pastoral settings of poetic effervescence. Actually, it can be attained in this carefully cultivated attitude of mind and action, conditioned within a truly democratic (not laissez-faire) atmosphere.

And finally the doubters need not worry too much about these children being "cotton wooled." As they grow, in the normal course of events, they spend more and more hours and activities without the home and the school, and their adjustability grows with them. It is not thrust at them "when they get out into the world." This fear seems to arise from a misconception that children are "preparing" for life, that home and school are or can be walled off. In actuality, they are living. They prepare as they live. They meet all the structures and processes of the so-called cutthroat world on their blocks, on their play fields, even within their own schools for far too many children even in modern schools must live in one social world at home and another at school. And thanks to the resiliency of childhood, mental health is no worse than it is!

INTERPERSONAL RELATIONSHIPS WITHIN THE HOME

PARENT-CHILD RELATIONS

In Chapter 2 we emphasized the importance of the drives-needs cycle of activity and inferred that the satisfaction of those needs, such as hunger, is the child's first social act. How these needs will be met we indicated is decided by such contributing factors as the cultural norms, the mores, and the folkways.

But within these larger configurations there are activity cycles which are not culturally delineated, and these we termed personal-

(Reproduced by permission of the artist and *The Saturday Evening Post.* Copyright 1952. The Curtis Publishing Company.)

social. Mother-child, father-child, and sibling relationships are of this nature.

Both popular and scholarly literature of late has devoted much attention to what mothers do or do not do to their children. "Over-protection, rejection, "momism," [9] have become concepts with which to conjure. The result, if parent-teacher study groups and child-conservation league groups are any indication, is often confusion, resentment, and even fear. "They tell us one time to give them love

[9] Edward A. Strecker, *Their Mother's Sons,* 2d ed. (Philadelphia, Lippincott, 1951).

and security; the next time they say we ruin and smother them by lavishing too much affection," as one such club member put it.

Though we nearly all these days sanction the equalitarian home so designed and organized that the needs of all members can be met and though we emphasize that its success is assured only if *every* member acts accordingly, the fact still remains that, in large measure, the mother "keys in" the social climate which will prevail. Though her roles as producer of goods, as teacher, as religious instructor have gradually been taken over in part or *in toto* by other agencies, the affectional role has not been supplanted.

From the child's action, reaction, and interaction with his mother and increasingly, we hope, with his father, the child takes on his attitudes and values. He does this eagerly, for young children are curious, anxious, and unashamed to learn. He likewise does it uncritically, for even the child who is reared in an atmosphere where people are wont to view critically and to weigh evidence before making decisions, starts this procedure in such areas as which toy, which dress—not which religion, which political order, which economic order, or which kind of family climate.

Since this is true, it is easy to see how important are the attitudes laid down at these early ages as to his worth, his importance in the family group, his importance and role in the larger social setting, and as to the ritual of emancipating him from the family.

Many authorities have insisted that the best way to establish from birth on the feeling of emotional, physical, and social security is to breast feed the baby. They cite such facts as those that mother's milk contains elements which will immunize the child in various ways, that it is the most suitable food for the infant. On the social side they assert that being held and fondled in a warm, contact relationship will provide the needed mental, emotional, and social security.

No one will attempt to gainsay such statements. It is worth while pointing out, however, from the personal-social angle that it is not the actual breast feeding but the position in which the child is held, the tonal quality of the voice, the facial expression, and the resulting rapport which are important. Likewise, from the standpoint of father-child relationships, bottle feeding has many worthwhile angles. Some people are coming to think they may outweigh the disadvantages.

"Father" in babyland is often practically an intruder, an outsider, if not "the forgotten man." He is germ-laden and must not come too near baby. He often is around only when baby is eating, or has just eaten, and so baby must not be disturbed. The psychological moments pass, and when children are older, father may wonder wearily why he finds it difficult to meet the child in any way satisfactory to both of them.

If the baby is put on a bottle, the father may participate in baby's living from the moment he arrives from the hospital. He may hold the child in the approved fashion, however awkwardly at first. This kind of activity leads easily and naturally to bathing, changing, playing, and general guidance. The proponents of the Electra and Oedipus complexes to the contrary notwithstanding, children can, under such a scheme, feel equally secure with both parents, unembarrassed, and able to interact freely regardless of sex differentials.

An illustration will point up the desirability of the earliest possible intimate father-child relationships and their contribution to generally excellent general family relationships.

My husband and I both knew that my chances of seeing our children grow up were rather slim. We were very anxious in view of this to create a home situation where either could function in the role of the other. From the time each child was ten days old their father was as active in their care and development as I. He fed them in the morning and at night and oftener over weekends. He changed them, bathed them, and played with them.

One of my greatest satisfactions is the knowledge that if, as, or when I drop out, they can go on adequately. The girl has no hesitancies where her father is concerned nor does she show any unhealthy overattachment tendencies. The same is true of the boy. I am convinced that the best way to make children feel wanted and secure is to proceed in our general fashion.

From time to time inadvertent remarks of theirs have left us with the feeling that we are succeeding. One day a couple came to call. After a bit the boy, then six years, edged up to me and whispered, "Why didn't they bring their kids so we could play?"

"They don't have any," I whispered back and returned to the conversation. Shortly, I felt another nudge, and he said as though he were solving a world problem, "What are they living for then, Mommy?"

One day his sister added to our "treasured sayings" in this wise. "I came over to play because my mother is giving me the dickens. She doesn't like me today," said the little neighbor girl.

"Oh, yes, she does," replied my six-year-old daughter comfortably.

"My mother and daddy give me the dickens too, but I always know they still love me. They just don't like some of the things I do."

It is far too early to predict, of course, but the evidences at present seem to say that they are as secure physically, mentally, emotionally, and socially as is possible in such an age.

On the mental side a problem showed itself early in the boy's development. His parents and most of his aunts and uncles were at the least good students and many were honor students, yet here was a child who had no interest in and showed little readiness or ability in academic subjects. The crowning difficulty came from the cousin whose success was measured by his family in terms of almost entirely academic achievement, which was superior.

"You can't even read; you don't know much," said the cousin one day in some conflict situation where said cousin was not in the lead.

The proverbial straw at that moment broke the patience of our less academic child who squared his shoulders, planted his feet firmly apart, his arms akimbo and replied in obviously rhetorical questions. "Can you make pot holders like the ones my mother uses in the kitchen? Have you ever made ash trays like those? Can you make a lamp that will light like the one I made this year? Can you paint pictures that make you feel good? I'll read when I'm ready, and, what's more, you don't get along with people very well."

The crisis passed and so did the teasing. We, the parents, agreed thereupon that we need not worry about his mental and emotional security. He was learning what we considered important—to accept limitations and live with them, to explore possibilities and how they could widen horizons. We would accept him as he was—and with pride. Social poise and ease seem natural by-products of these other securities.

The little girl may seem to be played down in this narrative, but unintentionally. Since she is a girl, she is better coordinated muscularly. She is also apparently gifted about equally in all areas. At five she announced she wanted to play the piano and added, "Mother, isn't there a picture to show me how?" At six she bounced in one day to say, "I want to read. Come show me how," and forthwith picked up the desired skills not in any genius fashion but with adequacy.

In the area of achieving independence we have tried to follow the same pattern. We assume that one of the most important parent-child relationship functions is an anomalous one. On the one hand we want to give children roots and security and on the other gradually and painlessly free them to outgrow those roots and live their own lives.

In such an age as this we think it almost dangerous for a child to be tied only to the mother and father. Real security demands, we think, that a child be able to feel secure with a wider circle of adults. Then if one of the more loved and depended upon adults (mother or father) is removed, there is not the bottomless void many children experience nor is there so likely to be the overattachment to the one left.

Consequently, we have tried to make it just another natural part of living that one or both of us must be absent from the children, at first for only a short time and then for longer hour spans. Always we have chosen baby sitters with great care for we are convinced that all of the things Bossard emphasizes about servants apply to the occasional baby sitter. We have known of unhealthy superstitions, fears, and worries that were inculcated in our friends' children and have tried to avoid this. This means that baby sitters cost more, but we think it has been worth it.

Also it has seemed a good practice to have the same sitter or sitters most of the time. This gives increased security especially in younger children. Gradually they grow to have a share in choosing which ones will be continued. This also fosters the growing feeling of independence. One day when the little girl had a cold we found it necessary to employ a sitter unknown to us but properly endorsed by a friend. We went early to pick her up and "get acquainted." In the back seat the lady was saying, "I think you and I will get along fine."

"Oh, we'll get along all right," returned Sis, "we always investigate thoroughly anyone who stays with us."

Despite my embarrassment I could not help feeling a glow that she had said not mother or daddy investigate, but the all important "we."

If I were then, by way of analysis, to try to enumerate our "goals" and "methods" as illustrated above, I think they would follow almost exactly those mentioned by Raymond Mangus when he writes:

THE GOALS OF CHILD REARING

For generations most parents have believed that the main goal to be achieved in training children was to make them obedient to parental authority. Beyond the family were the goals of getting ahead in the world in a competitive struggle for wealth, power, and prestige.

These traditional points of view are being replaced by the goal of maturity. What then are some of the marks of a mature person?

1. A person is socially mature when he is able to live easily, comfortably, and harmoniously with other people. Children grow toward social maturity as they learn to play the masculine or feminine role according to their sex; as they gradually emancipate themselves from childish dependence upon their parents; as they learn to love and be loved; and as they learn to be tolerant and at ease with people who differ widely from themselves. The socially mature are free from neurotic necessity to dominate and control others, to be unduly submissive to them, or to withdraw from social contracts.

2. A person is emotionally mature when he is able to control his energies, and manage his fears, hates, resentments, and loves. The child develops in the direction of emotional maturity as he learns to live more in terms of the realities of situations than in terms of his wishes, desires, and prejudices. The emotionally mature person generally feels secure and has a healthy self-respect.

3. A person is intellectually mature when he is able to size up situations and make his own decisions. He makes decisions on the basis of known facts or on the basis of sound principles. He makes decisions with full readiness to assume full responsibility for them.

4. A person is morally mature when he has adopted personally satisfying and socially accepted goals of living, and when he has learned to make wise choices among possible courses of action. He does not make those choices on the basis of whim, fancy, or impulse. Neither does he make them on the basis of rigid rules and taboos handed down through tradition. The morally mature person has a morality based on his own growth needs and on deep concern and consideration for the basic needs of others in any way influenced by his choices.

HUMAN NEEDS

If people are to achieve these goals of maturity they must find fulfillment for their basic needs from early childhood. In addition to the organic needs for food, shelter, rest, and expression, there are certain personal and social needs that must be satisfied if normal development is to be promoted.

Perhaps the most fundamental social needs are two in number. These are:

1. The need for a continuing sense of personal security. This need is one that can never be satisfied by material things alone. It involves a lasting sense of belonging to a warmly acceptant group. Its satisfaction depends upon love and affection and certainty of being wanted by those upon whom one depends.

When the person fails to find satisfaction for his need of security, he is apt to be dominated by fears and anxiety. It is well known that persons dominated by anxiety are vulnerable to ill

There is no more important day in the life of a child or adolescent than its natal day. Its careful observance by peer-group parties and/or family celebrations give an emotional and social security which cannot be overrated. Many child development specialists as well as parents have observed that if circumstances are such that all festive days cannot be observed in like manner, it is desirable, for example, to play down Christmas gifts in favor of birthday gifts and celebration. (Reproduced by special permission of John Falter and *The Saturday Evening Post.* Copyright 1952. The Curtis Publishing Company.)

health, delinquency, intolerance, and a great variety of mental and personality disorders and childish reactions.. Probably the family can give no greater gift to its members than a continuing sense of personal security, and no greater protection than protection from a blighting sense of anxiety.

2. *The second great need of the developing person is the need for a sense of personal worth.* This he gets through recognition and praise for his achievements. To get along in life one must have confidence in oneself and in his fellowmen. He must have a firm belief that he is adequate to stand up to life and meet its problems successfully.

Failure to find fulfillment of this need for adequacy or personal worth is apt to result in a sickening sense of inferiority.

Much of the childish, infantile behavior seen among youths and adults today is in the form of defense against inferiority.

3. There is a third need that all children have today as never before. This is the need for living models of mature, well-adjusted persons after which they can pattern their own lives. Such models they should find in their parents, in their teachers, and in other significant persons with whom they may identify themselves. Children learn better by example than by precept. They unconsciously build themselves in the likeness of those significant adults in their lives. "Do as I say and not as I do," is a difficult lesson for any parent to teach or for any child to learn well.

If children find firm patterns of strength in the characters of their parents, they may adopt those patterns as foundations from which to achieve still higher levels of maturity.

METHODS OF GUIDANCE

With clear understanding of the goals of child rearing and of the needs of children, parents must practice sound methods of child guidance.

Much is written for parents instructing them in methods, procedures, and techniques for bringing up Junior. Much of this is sound advice. For example, the parent is told to be affectionate but not indulgent with the child. To use democratic guidance rather than autocratic commands. To answer the child's questions honestly and frankly. To allow the child to develop at his own speed without forcing him beyond his capacity. To show healthy respect for the child's wishes and desires. To be unshocked by his unacceptable impulses. To give him generous recognition and praise for his real achievements. To give him independence and responsibilities in keeping with his stage of development.

It must be pointed out, however, that there are many instances where parents practice all the "right" methods but have children who turn out badly. Others apparently practice the "wrong" methods but have children who turn out exceedingly well.

This indicates one thing very pointedly. *It is probably even more important that parents be the right persons than that they practice the "right" techniques of child management.* That they have the right attitudes and right feelings toward their children is of basic importance. The child who is fortunate enough to live in a home where it is made to feel wanted, loved, and respected by parents who also love and respect each other is in a happy situation even when wrong external procedures are sometimes fol-

lowed. On the other hand the parents who always follow the recommended external procedures but do so with underlying attitudes
of hostility, resentment, jealousy, and rejection are pretty sure to
cripple the child emotionally. In other words, while adequate
methods of child management are certainly important, the quality
of the parent-child relationship is probably even more important
for normal child development.

A CONCLUSION

For generations American parents have generally hoped for
and expected their children to rise above them on the ladder of
economic success. Now the time has come when parents must
recognize their own personal and social inadequacies and expect
their children to rise above them in achieving more mature ways
of living. This means ways of living that are more perfectly adjusted to the requirements of the modern world. This means ways
of living that avoid the neurotic patterns which so frequently dev-
astate the lives of individuals. It means ways of feeling, thinking,
and doing that will eliminate wars and avoid destructive conflicts
between persons and groups, large and small. It means ways of
living that will make maximum contributions to the all-around
health and happiness of individuals and families everywhere.[10]

THE WORLD OF SIBLING RELATIONSHIPS

THE LITTLE social world of sibling relationships has many
unique and far-reaching influences in the child socialization process.
It is in many instances first in amount of time spent together with
family members.

As children grow, there is a tendency for parents to urge that
"they go play," particularly together. Such close proximity in eating,
sleeping, playing, and perhaps toilet behavior is bound to pose
personality adjustment problems at any age level unless there is
much insight, forbearance, and self-control. All of these qualities are
evidences of maturity—maturity of skeletal coordination, emotional
and social security. Parents who continuously ask the question "Why
do they quarrel?" might better ask "What's wrong if they don't
quarrel?"

[10] A. R. Mangus, *Family Goals for the Rearing of Children* (Columbus,
Ohio, Department of Public Welfare, Division of Mental Hygiene). Used by
permission.

One author suggests wisely that it would be an interesting and illuminating experiment to study and compare the reactions of adults as well as children who were brought together as siblings are through no choice of their own.[11] Within the usual limitations of space, objects, and continuous time the kinds of reactions which would obtain where there are no romantic ties would be interesting to behold.

This inclusiveness and extreme intimacy has many socializing outcomes. Children are frank with one another to the point of cruelty at times; they are realists for where there are siblings, there is little time or chance for much fantasy living. They are adept transmitters of social heritage as they have learned it. They not only may help the younger child to learn academically earlier but also they hand down appraisals of parents and their actions, of the teacher, the minister and even attitudes on social issues are transmitted from child to child.

"See here now, Sister. You sit down and learn this spelling. I know your teacher. She is fine on the arts and social stuff, but she doesn't spend enough time on these things. Look at me," says the 8-year-old brother.

Or

"I'm sick of being just Helen's sister," says another.

Or

"How I loathe my younger brother. Goodie, goodie, studious, and prissy; my family has always held him up to me as an example and never hesitated to rub it in how disgraceful it was to let a younger brother excel me," writes one from the opposite side of the penalization tactic.

Siblings often act as substitute parents. This may be an onerous business entailing the "tagging" along of siblings too much younger for active participation in peer games. Or it may quite baldly present a chance to escape grown-ups. The remark of members of large families to the effect that they always had such wonderful times by themselves may subtly illustrate this. In the process of caring for younger brothers and sisters, children often set up a small social group of their own comparable in many ways to peer groupings.

[11] James H. Bossard, *Sociology of Child Development* (New York, Harper, 1948), p. 97 f.

Brothers and sisters are also sources of security physically, emotionally, and socially. "Here we are, a force united against all comers," they say in effect.

In the sibling world, also, children try out their wings in the striving for status. This may take the form of a healthy rivalry now in one area, now in another, or it may be a bitter struggle to achieve highest status in all respects in the eyes of both parents and siblings. A democratic social climate will encourage rivalry but of the first sort. All members will recognize that every person, child, or adult is important and in terms of what he can be and do, not in terms of what the mother or father or someone else will want him to be and do.

This attitude of "acceptive permissiveness" will allow for a "floating esteem." Johnny can be himself and be unashamed to be so. Susan can proceed at her own faster pace yet feel no superiority in favor with the family. Parents may relax, realizing that both children will be happier, more productive adults. Under this type of emotional climate the ambivalent "trends of opposition and cooperation within" all of us may find healthy outlets and eventual integrated behavior.

If such is not the case, jealousy and envy may arise and become so firmly seated that they are never lost to the detriment of adult sibling relationships. Extremely aggressive children and adults who must be the leaders, who must occupy positions of social ascendency often are acting in compensatory ways to overcome inferior feelings in the sibling world.

SEX DIFFERENTIALS

It is but a commonplace to state that the sex composition of the sibling world is a highly important conditioning factor. Nevertheless, knowledge of some of its specific implications may help parents and teachers to plan in the light of this composition.

If the siblings are all boys, their interests and activities will be much different than when the siblings are all girls or when there are both boys and girls in the same family. These differences will include not only clothing, but also colors, textures, and kinds of clothing and will necessitate careful planning and guidance to supply experiences which a natural setup of boys and girls would supply.

"Would it be all right for me to wear a red hair ribbon in my hair, like sister, if I just do it inside our house?" asked the strongly masculine appearing little boy of four years.

"Why can't I play with dolls too? Why would the boys call me sissy? Fathers play with babies." queried another eight-year-old boy.

"Nanny says she wishes she were a boy. They can do so many things girls can't, but I told her she was crazy. I said, just look, girls can wear boys clothes, but boys can't wear our pretty things. And gee, boys can't have babies," carroled the pretty, well-adjusted little girl of six.

Or consider:

"My best subjects are mathematics and science and how I'd like to be an engineer but do you know what they told me? You might be a dietician, even a chemist or a physicist but change your objectives to fit your opportunities," complained the irate and disgruntled college coed who wished to invade a male professional area.

"She's a fine student and friend, but she's so loud, almost brassy. It's as though she's rebelling against femininity. We just can't pledge her, and she'll be so hurt."

"He's a fine, sensitive young man. Artistic without being sissy, athletic without being obnoxious. He makes me think that a family of two brothers and two sisters is a great combination. They are all such happy people. No jealousy, no fighting, no superior airs. Everyone is thoughtful of everyone else, able to see each other's views."

These brief personal recordings suggest several things concerning the nature and depth of sibling relationships.

Difference in sex of siblings seems to play an important part in determining relationships between them. There is a difference of common interest between the sexes; standards set up for boys are distinctly different from those set up for girls. Boys have privileges which are denied to girls; they are exposed to things from which girls are sheltered. Such distinctions and attitudes influence the relations between the sibs.

Sletto in a study of delinquency came to the following conclusions: [12]

[12] R. F. Sletto "Sibling Position and Juvenile Delinquency, *American Journal of Sociology,* Vol. XXXIX, No. 5 (March 1935), pp. 657–670.

1. Delinquency rates are higher for girls in sib relationships where all sibs are brothers than where sibs are sisters.
2. Delinquency rates are highest for boys where a boy is the middle child and the sibs are brothers.
3. Delinquency rates are high for children who are in sibling positions involving the presence of younger sibs of each sex and low for children in positions involving older sibs of each sex.
4. In general, delinquency ratios are higher for both boys and girls when the elder siblings are of the same sex and younger sibs are of the opposite sex than when the reverse is true.

Studies seem to show also that the sex of the sib nearest the problem child has some relationship. In boys the nearest child above was more often a boy than a girl and nearest below was most often a boy also. With girls there was not too much difference as to the older sib; most often it was a girl. However, in the case of the younger it was most often a boy.[13]

AGE DIFFERENTIALS

Age differentials are of similar importance to sex differences. Much has been said about child spacing as relates to the adjustment of the marriage mates,[14] to the socioeconomic aspects of the marriage, to the health of the mother, and the like. There is very little reference to the effects upon sibling relationships in terms of the amount of time elapsing between births of children.

Family planning might profit greatly if we knew the answers to such questions as: At what age or ages can the first-born adjust most readily to the appearance of another child? Is there a time interval most propitious for the third child in relation to the birth of the second one? Is there a time interval after which children begin to resent quite openly the appearance of another child? If the time interval between children is long, for what dangers ought one to be on the lookout? Where is there danger of the older sibling becoming a parent substitute? At what age can an older child most readily be expected to assume responsibility for a younger brother or sister? Is there any specific age, or is it always a matter of individual variations?[15]

[13] John Levy, "The Impact of Cultural Forms upon Children's Behavior," *Mental Hygiene* (April 1932), pp. 208–211.

[14] Henry A. Bowman, *Marriage for Moderns* (New York, McGraw-Hill, 1948), p. 451 ff.

[15] Bossard, *Sociology of Child Development,* p. 107.

BIRTH POSITION

The impact of ordinal birth position upon the child and sibling relationship has received considerable exploration. Certain generalizations may now be made if we remember that all of them are incident to the social and emotional climate of the home. In other words, in a laissez-faire climate the generalizations are likely to obtain per se. Likewise, the authoritarian setup may drive them deeper unless someone in this structure defines personal-social contacts as mentioned earlier. In a democratic home the minimum of these frustrations may be expected.

The main worth of these "fluid generalizations" is that said knowledge will allow the kind of planning in human relations which will render them invalid!

THE OLDEST CHILD

The first child in homes where he is anticipated with pleasure starts life as the cynosure of attention. His position in family structure is a unique one though various studies and writers ascribe different effects to the position.

He begins life as an only child with all that this may entail in adjustment to adults. For many parents he is "the practice child." They are so anxious to do everything just right to give him a running start. Consequently, he is likely to be trained more rigidly "according to the book," to be treated like choice porcelain.

For a time he is literally enthroned, and then however well he may have been prepared for the new arrival, he is dethroned. He will try to regain his position in any number of ways, depending greatly upon the understanding of parents.

If the insight is not great, he may resort to temper tantrums, bedwetting, actual attacks on the infant, hunger strikes.

If, in addition, the second child arrives just as he is achieving some independence, he may regress acutely. As far as he can see, the baby is the recipient of affection, attention, and care. Playing at being baby is the natural form of behavior to which to revert. He has had to feed himself, to remain dry, to go to bed without fuss, and here is a small being who does none of these things, yet reaps rewards. Unless this experience is carefully handled, the seeds of sibling as well as parent-child bitterness and jealousy will be lushly sown.

As he grows, the oldest child generally accepts family responsibilities first and likewise occupies a leadership role with his brothers and sisters. He is the family pioneer, meeting new situations first. He will have more in common with both parents and siblings than those born years apart. In fact, if there is a difference of as much as ten years, the younger child's relationship with the older sib is comparable to that of an adult. It seems to be most favorable for a child to be born before the first sib is eighteen months old, or after he is three years old.[16] When the child is younger than eighteen months old, he still does not know how it feels to be completely the only child, so he will find it easier to adjust to another sharing his parents attentions. When the child is three, he is ready to make the adjustment of the larger world outside the home, so he doesn't feel so tied to his parents.[17]

In studies made to show how the oldest child compares with the younger in I. Q. tests it is shown that the younger children are higher in I. Q. Since it is improbable that the first child is genetically inferior to later children, it seems that this is due to the younger children gaining from the experiences encountered by the older child.

The oldest child seems more often to be a serious behavior problem. Juvenile delinquency studies have indicated this.

THE MIDDLE CHILD

It has often been said that the second child is truly "in the middle." The older child has at least had the attention, love, and time of his parents centered on him for awhile. The second child is neither first nor is he last, and as a consequence he often feels himself neglected unless parents are sensitive to his position.

He will always be a rival for the parent's love. However, he feels this rivalry less than the oldest because he never had the whole stage. This child fights to be as mature as the oldest child; he tries to compete with him, even outdo him in skills, games, strength, and possessions.[18]

[16] Ernest W. Burgess and E. Locke, *The Family* (New York, American Book, 1950), p. 250.
[17] Manuel C. Elmer, *The Sociology of the Family* (Boston, Ginn, 1945), p. 445.
[18] Allison Davis and Robert J. Havighurst, *Father of the Man* (Boston, Houghton, 1947), p. 125.

From the very first a second or middle child's relationship in the home is different. His parents have already had experience in the rearing of children; therefore, they are more relaxed, confident, and sure about themselves in the rearing of another child. These are not the same parents to whom the first child was born. Not only have they experience in child care, but they have also grown in their own attitudes and beliefs. Frequently the financial situation has changed, especially in middle-class families. This child comes into a home where there is already another child with whom he must compete and share things. In fact, many of the things he gets, may be second-hand. He also has the footsteps of the older child to follow. In some cases this may make it easier for him, for he can learn from the experience of the first; in other cases it may make it more difficult since he may not be able to meet the standards set because of lack of native ability or maturity.

When the problem of the next child comes along, the middle child is dethroned, but there is a difference in the relationship with the dethronement of the first child. Now the middle child has someone above him who is bigger, stronger, more experienced and someone below him who is getting all the attention.

If the second child is a girl and the first a boy with only a year between them, there may be another problem. Because of physiological make-up the girl will exceed the boy until late adolescence. This can increase jealousy, and it may result in the boy's definite resistance to women in general and sister in particular unless wise parents are at hand.

Both parents and teachers often complicate unwittingly the adjustment of the middle children. Student personal experience papers illustrate this.

"Your brother was a straight A student and how we did enjoy working with him. I'm sure you'll do as well," said the teacher on my first day in her room. How I hated her for it. Was I never to be allowed to be myself? Must I always have him held over my head? I studied hard. I would show them I was not only as good but better than he.

Or

What always ruined my day was having both my mother and my teacher call me by my sister's name. I would feel just mean inside and I'd take it out on all of them by faultfinding. They always said, I was so hard to please.

I never minded secondhand toys so much but I never had a really new outfit. Why are parents so stupid? I know it saves money but surely they could plan for now and then something all new.

Or more happily

I was a middle child, but I never minded. My parents made us children realize that their different reactions to us were not due to favoritism but to the fact that we all had different personalities and they were so glad. Each of us was encouraged to go at his own rate and along the lines of his own interest and abilities. Frank was never very good at books, but he was superior with the "things" he could fix and do. Mary was no house helper, but her flower arrangements were lovely. And how she loved to design and make our clothes! Sue was a whiz with the books. As for me, I guess I was never specialized but I always knew how important I was "in general" as mother said, for I could do anything that was needed.

These brief anecdotes suggest the lines of response of the middle child and middle children in general. The first finds himself competing endlessly if unwillingly, the second becomes hypercritical and the third, allows resentment to smoulder and perhaps develop into hatred. The fourth illustrates what an understanding home can do. Parts of the narrative not included here explain how in this home each child was carefully prepared for each new child and inducted into a feeling of acceptance toward him.

THE YOUNGEST CHILD

The last child comes into a complex family situation. There are parents and a child or children above. He is the baby of the family, and as such has certain rights and privileges. He learns from the experiences of his older sibs, and so on tests he seems to have the higher I. Q. The economic condition of the family may be improved even more than in the case of the middle child or children with accompanying cultural advantages for him. Many older children complain that this child is not so strictly disciplined as they were, that he can do more things and at an earlier age, that he is always "the baby" since he is never dethroned.

PARENT-ADOLESCENT RELATIONSHIPS

Though the discussion thus far has aimed at discussing family relationships in general, it applies especially to the younger child.

In our culture the adolescent years are known as the years of special problems, of stress and strain, often of rebellion, of family tension, and especially of parent-adolescent conflict.

Why is this so? In preliterate societies we are told that this is not always the case, that children submit, and apparently with willingness, to any custom, however tiresome or painful.[19]

The viewpoint here in the light of the above discussion is obviously that this conflict need not be so intense, if the factors which condition it are understood. In Chapter 3 we cited the kinds of growth factors from the standpoint of the maturing child which make this a period of potential tension.

Let us now pay special attention to this area. It is well established that preadolescent and adolescent needs and desires are pretty much those of the younger child with the exception that they are intensified by a number of sociological phenomena.[20]

After conning the literature, the analysis of Davis [21] seems still to offer the most briefly thorough sociological analysis of parent-adolescent relations. We quote in detail:

1. *Conflicting Norms.* To begin with, rapid change has given old and young a different social content, so that they possess conflicting norms. There is a loss of mutual identification, and the parent will not "catch up" with the child's point of view because he is supposed to dominate rather than follow. More than this, social complexity has confused the standards within the generations. Faced with conflicting goals, parents become inconsistent and confused in their own minds in rearing their children. The children, for example, acquire an argument against discipline by being able to point to some family wherein discipline is less severe, while the parent can retaliate by pointing to still other families wherein it is firmer. The acceptance of parental attitudes is less complete than formerly.

2. *Competing Authorities.* We took it for granted, when discussing rapid social change, that youth acquires new ideas, but we did not ask how. The truth is that, in a specialized and complex culture, they learn from competing authorities. Today, for example, education is largely in the hands of professional specialists, some of whom, as college professors, resemble the sophists of ancient Athens by virtue of their work of accumulating and purveying knowledge, and who consequently have ideas in advance of the populace at large (i.e.,

[19] Margaret Mead, *Coming of Age in Samoa* (New York, Morrow, 1928).

[20] Ruth Benedict, *Patterns of Culture* (Boston, Houghton, 1934).

[21] Kingsley Davis, "The Sociology of Parent-Youth Conflict," *American Sociological Review* (August, 1940), pp. 523–535. Used by permission.

the parents). By giving the younger generation these advanced ideas, they (and many other extrafamilial agencies, including youth's contemporaries) widen the intellectual gap between parent and child.

3. *Little Explicit Institutionalization of Steps in Parental Authority.* Our society provides little explicit institutionalization of the progressive readjustments of authority as between parent and child. We are intermediate between the extreme of virtually permanent parental authority and the extreme of very early emancipation because we encourage release in late adolescence. Unfortunately, this is a time of enhanced sexual desire, so that the problem of sex and the problem of emancipation occur simultaneously and complicate each other. Yet even this would doubtless be satisfactory if it were not for the fact that among us the exact time when authority is relinquished, the exact amount, and the proper ceremonial behavior are not clearly defined. The adolescent's sociological exit from his family, via education, work, marriage, and change of residence, is fraught with potential conflicts of interest which only a definite system of institutional controls can neutralize. The parents have a vital stake in what the offspring will do. Because his acquisition of independence will free the parents of many obligations, they are willing to relinquish their authority; yet, precisely because their own status is socially identified with that of their offspring, they wish to insure satisfactory conduct on the latter's part and are tempted to prolong their authority by making the decisions themselves. In the absence of institutional prescriptions, the conflict of interest may lead to a struggle for power, the parents fighting to keep control in matters of importance to themselves, the son or daughter clinging to personally indispensable family services while seeking to evade the concomitant control.

4. *Concentration within the Small Family.* Our family system is peculiar in that it manifests a paradoxical combination of concentration and dispersion. On the one hand, the unusual smallness of the family unit makes for a strange intensity of family feeling, while on the other, the fact that most pursuits take place outside the home makes for a dispersion of activities.

5. *Open Competition for Socioeconomic Position.* Our emphasis upon individual initiative and vertical mobility, in contrast to rural-stable regimes, means that one's future occupation and destiny are determined more at adolescence than at birth, the adolescent himself (as well as the parents) having some part in the decision. The necessity of choice at adolescence extends beyond the occupational field to practically every phase of life, the parents having an interest in each decision. A culture in which more of the choices of life were settled beforehand by ascription, where the possibilities were fewer and the

responsibilities of choice less urgent, would have much less parent-youth conflict.

6. *Sex Tension.* If until now we have ignored sex taboos, the omission has represented a deliberate attempt to place them in their proper context with other factors, rather than in the unduly prominent place usually given them. Undoubtedly, because of a constellation of cultural conditions, sex looms as an important bone of parent-youth contention. Our morality, for instance, demands both premarital chastity and postponement of marriage, thus creating a long period of desperate eagerness when young persons practically at the peak of their sexual capacity are forbidden to enjoy it. Naturally, tensions arise—tensions which adolescents try to relieve, and adults hope they will relieve, in some socially acceptable form. Such tensions not only make the adolescent intractable and capricious but create a genuine conflict of interest between the two generations. The parent, with respect to the child's behavior, represents morality, while the offspring reflects morality plus his organic cravings. The stage is thereby set for conflict, evasion, and deceit. For the mass of parents, toleration is never possible. For the mass of adolescents, sublimation is never sufficient. Given our system of morality, conflict seems well nigh inevitable.

Yet it is not sex itself but the way it is handled that causes conflict. If sex patterns were carefully, definitely, and uniformly geared with nonsexual patterns in the social structure, there would be no parent-youth conflict over sex. As it is, rapid change has opposed the sex standards of different groups and generations, leaving impulse only chaotically controlled.

SUMMARY AND IMPLICATIONS

AS HAS BEEN constantly emphasized, the family is first in the life of the child in several ways. As Cooley put it, the family is the cradle of personality. It is primary in point of time in the processing or induction of the child into society and culture. Within its environs all the foundations of personality arisal and development converge. Centuries of biological inheritance and prenatal growth influences produce this new individual which is immediately acted upon by the representatives of society known as parents, siblings, and "other" family members or "fringes." The new individual's basic drives and needs can reach fruition only within the setting provided by these people who surround him. The large cultural roles will be pretty well determined for him. But he is not without resources. His

Camping provides unequaled opportunity for children to plan, execute a program, and evaluate their understandings of themselves, others,
and the outdoors. Many "goings out and comings back" help to reduce
the tension of emancipation from the family.

interpersonal relationships will be enacted not in terms of any cultural determinant alone but in terms of the various individual differentials represented by family members.

Within the family he passes from dependence through varying degrees of independence to interdependence from identification to interidentification with people outside the family group, play groups, gangs, cliques, and formal groupings.

In such an all pervasive setting, he gradually constructs his "own world of habits, attitudes, traits, and values." Thus, we are wont to say that the early childhood years are of extreme importance in laying foundations for one's concept of self, his roles and statuses in numerous groups, and his approach to adjustment problems as they come to him. Though it is not necessarily so in other cultures, the adolescent years in our culture seem often fraught with stress and strain, the "push and pull" of growing up. This period must be regarded and studied as an equally significant period in the laying and reorganizing of foundations of future behavior.

At this time the organic changes furnish new bases for future as well as then present reorganization of behavior. New social contacts and new kinds of social experiences call for reconditioning unless the family setting has been unusually permissive and understanding.

Thus, it appears that as important as the early years are, the years during which physical maturity is being achieved and life decisions concerning work and marriage are being made are among the most important years in the socialization process.

For such reasons the study and further research of the impacts of family backgrounds, the social climates existing therein with all that this means to adjustments, the interpersonal relationships and the patterns by which the child is identified and helped in his assimilation to adult living in his own right are of inestimable value and necessity for the teacher, the parent, and the object of all this concern, the child himself.

VI HOME INTERACTION— SPECIALIZED ASPECTS

"FRINGE" TO CHILD RELATIONSHIPS

CONTRARY to the impression left by some writers, the family impact upon children is not limited to the relationships with just the mother, father, and siblings. There are also "fringes," which exert, if not continual, at least sporadic and significant influences upon children.

There are, at the outer fringe, such contacts as the tradesmen who deliver merchandise, the mailman, storekeeper, the policeman on the beat. These contacts in the rural and small town areas may be undifferentiated since these people may also be neighbors and friends. In urban areas their contacts are of the categoric type. They appear as representatives of ways of living. In their conduct they tend to epitomize places on the social distance scale and attitudes to be taken toward it both by themselves and others.

Other fringe relationships include the music teacher, the dance teachers, the riding or swimming teachers. All of these people are met for short periods but nonetheless communicate not merely the skills for which they are hired but social views as well.

We shall deal here with two of these "fringe" areas. We choose but the two areas of guests and domestic helpers because of space limitations and the fact that the literature has more to offer concerning these areas.

GUESTS

The role of the invited adult guest in the home has been most completely studied by Bossard. He concludes that the guest adds a new factor to the family interactive process, furnishes source material in the learning process for the child, and is manipulated by the parents in the learning process. The role of the guest varies from one family to another, depending upon size of the family, its relative accessibility or isolation, the nature of intrafamily relationships, the number of guests, their relationship with the child and family, the interests of the child, and the child's age and general development.

On the specific side were such findings as the importance of the guest as the personification of some trait, occupation, or personality type; the similar personification of pet aversions and dislikes, the role of the dramatic impression; the guest as a practice person; the emergence of the parent as an adult in the eyes of the child; and the role of the guest in presenting a preview of adult life. The guest is a standard for measuring parents as persons and for seeing the family status in the community. The guest may change the family routine so as to introduce conflicts and increase family tensions, serve as a medium for teaching certain rules of social behavior, or serve as a source for widening the cultural horizon of the family.[1]

Two brief anecdotal reports of students point up a number of the conclusions.

We lived in a section of town where we did not want to live. Father had fallen on hard days and so we moved to the "edge of respectability" as my mother put it. We lived a rather secluded life. My parents must not have been anxious to have our old friends see us thus, and they seldom sought us out. Then one day we received word that an old school chum of my mother was coming to stay over night with us on the way through town. For days we were in a flutter. Every nook and cranny was cleaned and polished. The savings in the teapot were spent for curtains. I knew that money had been put there for mother's needed spring coat, and in a childish way I was worried.

The great day came as did our guest. She was all mother had pictured her, beautifully coiffured and dressed and smelling of such perfume as I had never dreamed of. I listened to her tales of travel and her work as to a fairy princess. It was not until years later that I remembered her impatience with my mother, her condescension with my father. But I did notice how nervous mother was, how apologetic about her poor food, which we had all thought wonderful. I loathed the way my father laughed too loudly and fumbled as he pushed her chair at the table. All in all I felt ashamed of "us." For the first time I became aware that "we" were "poor." For the first time I saw my parents at a disadvantage and was angry as well as humiliated. It must have been

---

[1] James H. Bossard, *Sociology of Child Development* (New York, Harper, 1948), pp. 221–262.

for many weeks that I lived in a "never, never world" worshipping my goddess and thus escaping the half-formed, not to be admitted facts.

If my parents noticed, they gave no sign. As soon as the guest had gone they seemed to return to their usual frugal but contented life. For me it was never the same. I suppose I was bound to awaken sometime, but how I wish she had never visited us.

The second account presents a different picture.

Guests as far as I can remember were as much a part of our family life as school, church, or play. Ours was a jolly, happy family. Mother used to say our house was like Grand Central Station, and she liked it that way. People dropped by to chat on their way "up town." We visited when we were in the yard or in the garden, and at least once a week there were evening guests, sometimes for dinner, for cards, now and then "big" parties, and just to talk.

We children drifted in and out, listened to grown-up conversations or not, so long as we didn't interfere. Father insisted there was "no sense" in company manners. The best at all times is none too good for the family. This did not mean that we couldn't relax but that we always were relaxed.

I realize now that the same kinds of preparations went on whether it was mother's bridge or board tea, the neighbors, the occasional visiting dignitary, or dad's boss.

"People are just people and so are we," was mother and father's viewpoint, and they treated everyone alike. Mother was fully as gracious to the garbage collector as to the supreme court judge. And everyone treated her accordingly. Father made it evident that he was glad you came, and guests seemed to feel likewise.

I realize now that I lived under very fortuitous circumstances. From this situation my sister and I gained an opinion of our parents and of our status as ideal. Since my parents knew many interesting people, I see now that we children sampled many ways of speech, manners, and cultural background. It was all exciting. I could hardly wait to be an adult, and I've never changed my mind.

Unfortunately, research on the importance of the child guest is practically nonexistent. Yet this is an area of extreme importance in child socialization. Fortunate is the child whose parents recognize this and allow, as a natural part of family planning, the planning for child guests. How are guests chosen? For what kinds of activities are they invited? The answering of these questions is a direct channeling of the family and class mores. Below is an account of one student's happy experience with guests of her own age.

One's own special guest, is the biggest event in child life. I can still remember the thrill when my mother said each Sunday at family council, "And now, Sue, who is to be your guest this week?"

Once the choice was done, we would make our own calls. We began this when we were four years old. Then there was the ritual of transportation. Mother would call the guest's mother later and arrange for that. Never, never did she interrupt our conversations. Then we would plan the menu if it were for dinner or the snack if "just for the afternoon." Then came the activities. Sometimes it was a short excursion, but more often we just played. I know now that we were carefully supervised but never openly in such a way as to take away our feeling of "being big."

Finally, we could have overnight guests and then, when we were ready, we could go visiting. Neither was forced. I well remember the day when I was six and a half, and I had been talking to one of my best friends. Our family had best friends, not best friend. I asked Nanny if she would come to play next Tuesday. "Shall I stay all night?" Nanny shocked me by saying.

I was annoyed. I turned at once, wide-eyed and said in awed tones, "She wants to stay all night."

"Would you like that," replied Mother, seemingly unaware of the worldshaking quality of this decision.

"Oh, my yes—only would that mean I would have to go there to stay all night?" I trembled at the thought.

"Not until you are ready to go," said Mother.

Kids liked to come to our house. Mother and father never talked down to them. The atmosphere was relaxed and pleasant. The same cordiality was extended to child guests as adult ones.

I have always traced my social ease and poise to the kinds of experiences listed above. I hope I do as well with my children.

The child's guest plays an important role in his concept of himself, his own worth, and his position in the family and in his peer groupings.

From these interactions he gains a social practice situation of great value. Within it may operate in miniature all the structures and processes of the adult world. It is not only a valuable proving ground but also a means of easy transition from one social stage to another.

One of its most important aspects is derived from the resulting interaction situations in which he is in turn a guest. This business of visiting another child for a short time first and then for longer periods—over night, a week—provides an effective means for helping a child grow out from the family in a painless way. Many experiences in going out from the family while he may still return and repeat the performance, supply a firm base for emancipation from the family nest.

No one is suggesting that children be pushed out or that love and affection be played down. It is necessary to recognize, however, as mentioned in mother-child relationships, that mental health demands that the socialization process be geared in terms of ultimate goals, such as independent, dependable, happy adults. It follows that the job of the home and its interaction is all important in the mental health of children and the adults they will become.

For the beginnings of this process of maturing emancipation lie in the gradually widening and deepening of contacts under pleasant emotional situations such as having guests and being a guest can do. Under such a program carefully planned for, revised on the moment if necessary, the term "homesickness" disappears from the vocabulary.

DOMESTIC HELPERS

The role of the domestic helper in the socialization of the child is so obviously important as to cause wonderment at its apparent lack of interest for researchers.

Again Bossard's [2] study of oral and written autobiographical materials offers the most thought-provoking material in the field to date. He found that all people who lived in homes employing service help felt them definitely a part of their child world. Important factors in the relationship systems include nationality and race. In homes where servants are of another race or of immigrant background, race and minority group status have their impact upon attitudes and values. The nature of the job also affects relationships. Bossard says: [3]

Six definite kinds of family-servant relationships were noted: (*1*) where the servant bears some kinship or social relation to the employer, (*2*) where service has been of long and satisfactory duration so that the servant may be referred to as "a member of the family," (*3*) where the servant is really a fellow employee, (*4*) where the help has a distinct

[2] Bossard, *op. cit.,* p. 200.
[3] *Ibid.* Used by permission.

servant status with the customary symbols of service status, (5) where the servant has a socially distant but personally friendly status, and (6) where the servant bears a marked resentment toward the employer based on relative minority group status.

The roles played in child life by domestic help and their consequent effects are summarized as follows: (1) The servant may be a mother-surrogate; (2) the servant may act as a go-between and mitigator of the harshness of family life; (3) servants provide companionship for the young child; (4) servants may enlarge a child's knowledge of many aspects of life which are alien to him in his own immediate family or from which his parents have carefully protected him; (5) servants may influence sex life and experiences; (6) servants often personify a social type to a child; (7) they may give children an introduction to the meaning of class strife and help to mold their attitudes about these things; (8) the presence of servants can reveal personality traits of family members more clearly to each other; (9) servants of long duration can serve as informal family historians and give the child an "outsider's" view of the family; (10) by adding mere numbers of people to the family circle, servants can increase the complexity of family life; they can also relieve complexity and furnish extra resources for smooth relationships; (11) their presence permits more leisurely parenthood and family life in general; (12) they may make for a certain restraint in family interaction.

Again from our own files of studies made, we present two cases as illustrations of some of the points made above.

Nanny came to live with us before I was born. She was really not related to us, but I never knew this until I grew up. She was the widowed wife of an in-law's brother. She was left suddenly with no money, no training for a job, and no inclination "to battle the world of men." She came to visit and stayed on to help mother when I came. She was so self-effacing, yet so competent and jolly with me, that my parents grew first to depend upon her and then to consider her a necessity. This suited Nanny exactly. When my brother was on the way a final agreement was made, and from that day on life was a bowl of roses for all of us.

She had had no children of her own, and we took their places. Yet she did not spoil us. We must be gentlemen and ladies, and in this she was ruthless. She kept close track of who were our friends and whether they were suitable. She never went against a rule or a demand of our parents, but she could and did soften their application. Our parents might be tired and irritable but never Nanny. I only hope I can keep a similar serene outlook and bearing with my children. How secure and happy she made us, I now realize. I loved my mother, but I think I felt more pride than love. She always looked so beautiful; she sparkled when she "made talks" and everyone said "how dynamic" "how wonderful" until I nearly burst with pride but I took my troubles to Nanny.

Marjorie is an example of the loneliness, frustration, and insecurity caused by rapid servant turnover and family complications.

I shudder as I try to write this. All I remember is how eager I would be when I heard we were to have a new governess. I still don't know if it were I, my parents' selection, or what, but I hated them all, their servility sometimes, their proprietary airs the next. Once I ran away from home to a near-by park where children were playing. I watched two children having a gay time with a pretty young woman. I walked up to them finally and asked, "Where can I get a governess like you?"

The three looked startled; then the little boy hollered, "She's no old governess. She's my mother." The woman looked grave, hushed the boy, took me on her lap, and asked who I was and where I lived. At once she lost her gayness and hurried me home. She explained breathlessly to my father, who happened to be in, how she had found me and brought me at once.

"Why was she in such a hurry to be rid of me," I asked. "Probably afraid someone would think she had kidnapped you," he laughed and went on about his business.

THE ONLY CHILD

CHILD ROLE and status within the interpersonal relationships of the home are often complicated by other specialized factors such as being an "only" or "adopted" child. In the ten years during which we have collected student experience papers, not only their incidence but also the emotional involvement surrounding such children have led us to deem some discussion of them worthy of inclusion. It sometimes happens that such papers prove able summaries of the principal points made by the literature on the subject. Where research is extensive it will be reported, and where less ample, experience papers of the above type will be used.

The first study of only children made in this country was done at Clark University by E. W. Bohannon in 1898. Since it has been so widely quoted, it merits some attention. Bohannon's study was under the direction of G. Stanley Hall, who introduced psychoanlysis into this country when he brought Sigmund Freud from Germany

to give a series of lectures at Clark. Hall is reputed to have said that,
". . . being an only child is a disease in itself." [4]

However one may feel about his method, Bohannon's conclusions merit attention. He found, on the basis of the returns, that:

1. Only children are unmistakably below the average in health and
   vitality.
2. Nervous and physical disorders seem to be unusually common
   in the families.
3. The children appear to enter school later and to be less regular
   in attendance than other children. Success in school is less than
   average.
4. They have less command of themselves socially than other children, and their social relations are therefore more frequently
   characterized by friction.
5. Unusual precocity is common.
6. Many of them indulge in imaginary companionship to compensate for inadequate real companionship.
7. Selfishness is most frequently named among the worst traits and
   affection among the best.
8. As a rule, the home treatment has been that of unthinking in-
   dulgence.[5]

Bohannon's position has found support in the works of Friedjung, Neal, Adler, Fenton the Blantons, Wexberg, and de Saussure,
to name a few. Most of the literature on the only child came out
in the 1920's and 1930's and seems to be due to the concern in testing quantitatively some of the observations of the psychoanalysts
made at an earlier period.

One other consideration which seems to be of importance is
that in 1898 when Bohannon's study was made, this country was
predominantly rural. Accompanying this rurality, it is possible that
there was the attitude which reaches back to Biblical times that large
families are *per se* "good" and small families for the same reason
"bad." In the swing from the "sacred" character of society to the
"secular," the attitude toward small families has changed. Today,
with the higher degree of urbanization, the greater number of city

[4] Ruth B. Guilford, and D. A. Worcester, "A Comparative Study of the
Only and Non-Only Child," *Pedagogical Seminary and Journal of Genetic Psychology,* Vol. 38 (1930), p. 411.
[5] E. W. Bohannon, "The Only Child in a Family," *Pedagogical Seminary
and Journal of Genetic Psychology,* Vol. 5 (1898), p. 477. Used by permission.

dwellers cramped for space, with married women taking part-time positions, a small family is not "looked down upon" and may, on the contrary, be some indication of a family's socio-economic status and a prestige factor in itself. The following are typical reasons for family limitation: "We don't want a large family." "We don't have room here, and besides, we'd rather have one or two children we can bring up well—give advantages to—than many for whom we'd not be able to give these advantages." "Besides, we *both* want to work." [6]

One other point which should be suggested is that there may be, and probably is, a "stereotype" of the "only child" which operates to throw a stigma on all children who are only children regardless of how "well adjusted" they may be. That is, if there is a behavior disturbance on the part of a child and a neighbor or teacher finds out that this child is an only child, this particular factor alone is blamed. One writer says along this line: "The provenance of the belief that only children are maladjusted is apparent enough. Like many other false beliefs it is based largely upon the cumulative effect of observations of single cases of maladjusted only children and upon the common tendency of the scientist as well as the layman to oversimplify a complex phenomenon. Some only children are maladjusted, *ergo* all only children are maladjusted." [7]

Again, it is apparent that what is often taken for self-centeredness, or selfishness, and similar personality attributes may well be just meticulousness. The only child is often an orderly child. When this orderliness is overrun by playmates, the confusion and unrest which it causes may be interpreted wrongly by observers.

When one investigates the researches concerning the only child, he finds them dividing neatly into those who are "fer em" and those who are "agin em." Those who are interested in pursuing specific studies on specific personality traits will find representative references listed at the end of the chapter.

It is difficult to arrive at definite conclusions since there seems to be a division of opinion. Later studies tend to support the idea that the only child has a peculiar problem in that he may be the center of overprotecting parents, particularly if the mother has nothing else to think about but the child, or if either parent, not

[6] From an unpublished paper by Jeannette Searles.
[7] P. A. Witty, "The Only Child of Age 5," *Psychological Clinic,* Vol. 22 (1933–1934), p. 86.

finding satisfaction in the marital relationship, goes to the child for it.

Bohannon's point is well taken when he says, "The constant interference and watchfulness of overanxious parents may deny to the child the range and freedom which his nature calls for at the time and which he must have if he is to develop self-control and self-direction. He must be given some opportunity to choose for himself, to experiment. . . ." [8]

The main dangers to the only child appear to be those quoted by Bohannon—overprotective parents, lack of siblings, etc. Since his study in 1895, however, the urban family today (the family where the only child will be most likely found) has many more contacts; children are sent to nursery school at an early age and are forced, more or less, to play with children their own age. Parents and teachers are probably more aware than ever before of the "dangers" of the only child. None of the recent studies would indicate that the only child is actually in any more "danger" than children in a large family. The dangers are *different,* seems to be the main point. [9]

An article in *Today's Health* summarizes rather well, ". . . it's not the fact that he is the only child in his home that matters. The *quality* of his environment determines the quality of the child—not the quantity of children living at home. Life is full of risks for everybody. Let's give the only child the benefit of the doubt, just as we would other children, and assume that he will come out all right despite the risks and pitfalls that are part of growing up. A normal, healthy child can take them and come out all right in the end. Being an only child is not so very special, so let's not act as if it were." [10]

THE ADOPTED CHILD

ADOPTION is the voluntary acceptance, the transplanting, and the nurturing of a child of other parents into one's family circle and kinship. It is not altruism; it is a permanent and complete filial relationship distinct from guardianship or custody, each being a

[8] Bohannon, *op. cit.,* p. 495.
[9] Searles, *op. cit.*
[10] Elsieliese Thrope, "The Only Child," *Today's Health* (June, 1950), p. 25.

temporary legal arrangement for the protection of a child's person or property.[11]

It is a commonplace to observe that adoption may yield benefits to both the adpotive parents as well as the child. Beyond the usual parents benefits, such as pride and pleasure in the immortality of name and family, the sharing of concerns and interests of child growth and development, possibly sharpened emotional reactions between marriage partners, and ever widening sphere of interests and concerns, there is satisfaction of having a chance to make a unique contribution. For the child, in addition to the many benefits of the natural biological family, there is that of "escaping" institutional life, however good, and of what amounts to "social rebirth."'

If the purposes behind adoption have been sane, appropriate ones, the child may well live and grow in much the same way with essentially the same kinds and degrees of adjustment experiences as any other child.

This suggests, and advisedly, that not all people who wish should adopt a child. As the Brooks suggest,

> Emotional balance and motherliness should outweigh material factors. For sterile couples, if the sterility has a definite psychic basis, its implications and the attitude toward it must be carefully considered. In weighing the matter of age and resources it is to be expected that people in their thirties or possibly early forties—not the impoverished, the very wealthy, the family-tree worshipers, or the superintellectuals—can satisfy the "golden mean" requirements if they have the emotional maturity. The imperatives of a self-inventory for prospective adopters involving motives, attitudes, and habits would be somewhat as follows:
>
> Is the desire but an impulse, or is it rooted in earnest purpose?
>
> Will the result be mere ego satisfaction or continuous socialized investment?
>
> Do we have a genuine interest in children and youth as humanity's richest heritage?
>
> Is our love for each other so sure that a child will bind us even closer without jealousy?
>
> Are we willing to invest twenty years or more of responsibility with many of our former interests displaced by or tributary to the child's welfare?
>
> For better or for worse—since adoptions, like other family rela-

[11] Lee M. Brooks and Evelyn C. Brooks, "Adopting a Child," in Morris Fishbein and Ernest W. Burgess, eds., *Successful Marriage* (New York, Doubleday, 1948); p. 325. Used by permission.

tionships, carry no guarantee of perfection—will we stand by our adopted child in all circumstances as though he had been our physical offspring?

Will we be able to love the child for himself, whatever his background; to guard ourselves resolutely against the projection of our ambitions on to him; and to guide rather than to mold him, thus encouraging his growth power?

Will we aim to grow with him, strive to share our best with him without emphasis on gratitude?

Have we developed tolerance, habitual patience, emotional maturity, and the mental flexibility that ensures against rut-bound middle age?

When our adopted child grows beyond the early need for dependence, will we gradually let him go, confident that into his life has been built the security indispensable to independence? [12]

If the answer "yes" can be given to the ten questions already set forth, the prospective parents will be well prepared for what is ahead in parent-child relationships. However, for the rearing of the adoptive child, there are some aspects that invite special emphasis. In brief they are as follows, again according to Brooks:

Study and Guidance. The waiting period after application has been filed can be likened to pregnancy. This is the preparatory period for study—through books, articles, and possibly child-study groups—on physical care, habit training, the mental growth of children, and mental hygiene itself. Thoughtful, even studious, application is a continuing need for effective parenthood. If they have had no previous experience with children, the prospective parents can make an effort to get acquainted with their friends' children, perhaps borrowing them for short periods. They will want to observe studiously a nursery school or play group, for children cannot be understood or managed solely through books.

The actual techniques of physiological baby care are relatively easy to learn. But psychological adjustment, involving emotions, attitudes, and habits in and between parent and child, comes by no formula. It comes only through patient, intelligent, and continuous effort.

Adaptation and adjustment embrace such questions as these: Should a fragile piece of furniture be replaced with something sturdier? Are the colors too delicate for rough use? Can a meal hour or a social custom be changed happily? The readiness of the new parents may be partially gauged by their attitude toward necessary changes in terms of joyful anticipation or, on the other hand, of sacrifice.

[12] Brooks and Brooks, *op. cit.,* p. 327.

Guidance and advice concerning problems of child nurture are part of the program of authorized child-placing agencies which usually continue supervisory contacts with the adoptive home for six months or a year before the final decree is granted.

The Child's Security. The child has undergone one or more separations and changes. Especially he needs the maximum of that which gives self-security. This comes from well-ordered parental care and affection wherein the main ingredients are a steadiness of head and heart, a gentleness of hand and voice. Thus the child grows happily with a strong sense of belonging: his parents, his home, and his possessions; not "smother-loved" into selfishness but guided into socialized selfhood.

As with the physiological needs of the child, household equipment ordinarily is not a great problem. Adoptive parents can, without much difficulty, learn to accommodate house to child: room and toilet facilities; child-size furniture; toys and play space; and other such matters. But adopters, often a little older than other parents, may have to make effortful changes in habit patterns before they are ready to welcome the child they want. His psychological security is paramount.

From the first day he should be thought of as "one of us." If he is thus closely identified with his adoptive family and is told of his adoption as soon as he understands speech, as matter-of-factly as he learns the color of his eyes, he is no more likely than other children to develop mental or social abberations. The adopted child should not be shielded completely from knowledge of his past but be given strength to face it, to assimilate it through the warmth of constant affection and security. Otherwise there may be unsettling insecurity, even shock and estrangement from his family if unfortunate facts are discovered accidentally.

Growth is the "highest good" for the individual; mutual growth and trust in the parent-child relationship are the "highest good" for any family in the universal quest for security.[13]

The effects of adoption are difficult to appraise since studies in the field are either not available or too fragmentary to be of much more value than autobiographical sketches.

It seems fair to assert, however, that all kinds of results obtain just as they do in the natural biological family and that, as in these families, when attitudes, motives, atmospheres, and the like are of a pattern, similar results may be expected. In short, his position in the family need be no different than that of any other child.

Two sketches presented here may illustrate the points. It so happens that both accounts are those of girls. It is possible that sex

[13] Brooks and Brooks, *op. cit.,* p. 329.

may make some difference but doubtless sex alone is not a determining factor here any more than in the biological family.

I Am Adopted

I was adopted at the age of one year. I can remember very little
of my early years except that I was always given closest care, affection,
and cuddling. I must have been very secure and happy but probably
"overprotected" as we use the term in this course.

Beginning school remains a nightmare to me. I hated it. When my
mother prepared to leave me on the first day, I had hysterics. Apparently
she was equally disturbed at "losing her poor baby." You can well
imagine what followed. I had never played with children (except in
mother's presence) and had never been taken care of by any other adults
than my parents, and I was in a panic of terror.

Somehow I must have lived through those days though I can recall
little specifically.

My first friend was made after Christmas, and I was very happy
when she asked me "home" with her. I was crushed when I was not
allowed to go or to bring her to my house. I see now the pattern, but
then I was only angry and hurt.

My foster mother and father had been pulling apart, and they had
decided to adopt a child to hold their marriage together. I fully agree'
with the authors who insist "having a child" whether naturally or by
adoption to salvage a marriage is a crime against the child in many
ways.

In my home I was a pawn, I feel, between my parents. Each com-
peted for my favor and at the same time made me feel so guilty if I
wanted to be with other children or young people. As a result, I was a
fearfully spoiled brat, and I can see now I must have been a most selfish,
querulous, thoroughly obnoxious child. It is obvious, I guess, that I'm
still "divided," filled with pity for them, much antagonism, and a feeling of great obligation.

I don't know for sure, but I think my antagonism (why not admit
it, my dislike) may go back to that dreadful day in junior high when
a nasty little boy who was angry at me called me a "bastard." I had no
idea what the word meant, but the tone and the expression on the faces
of the group spoke volumes.

In my confusion, I could only say over and over, "I'm not, but you
are."

At that he shook his fist in my face and yelled in triumph, "I'm not
adopted. I got a mother and father."

Mrs. Robbins spoke to us one day about the cruelty of children in
such situations but more especially of the cruelty of parents who had

not prepared children for the meeting of such easily anticipated experiences.

I can now, of course, see why I could never "go with the kids," why we moved from one part of the country to another, and so forth. They didn't want me to know I was adopted. To a teen-ager that meant it was shameful. What I suffered, no one will ever know, but I never mentioned it to my parents. From then on I "acted" the part they wanted me to play, and I must have fooled them well.

On my eighteenth birthday with much trembling, tears, etc. they "told" me and said with pride how they had kept me from knowing to protect me but now I must know. I listened, cold as ice inside, managed to smile, thank them, and escape their sticky, grasping hands. We have never mentioned it since.

When I insisted on going to a college outside the city, they grudgingly agreed. I work every spare moment. I will pay them back. I've gone through school on the accelerated plan in three years. It saved me from summers with them. I think I'll join one of the services and go overseas at that, if I can.

I'll be glad to send them money if they need it. But I spent my youth as a hostage to a miserable marriage, and I have no wish to be the slave of their old age as I know they intended. I've been "used" until I can hardly believe otherwise of anyone.

Adopted and Happily!

I am glad to write this personal experience paper, for it gives me a chance to set down for the benefit of anyone interested what a marvelous thing is adoption. I adopted my parents and they me when I was not quite two. My new parents had decided upon adoption because of a physical sterility which was incurable. It seems to me with what I have read and heard that I was extremely fortunate and still am.

When I reached the age to ask where did I come from, I was told naturally and pleasantly not only where babies come from but where I had come from to this home. I don't remember their words but neither do I remember ever having been shocked or hurt.

From the first it was impressed upon me not only that I had been picked but also that I had picked them. "When we came into the room," said my mother over and over, "you looked at the people with us very solemnly, then laughed, and pointed right at us."

My father says, one of the proudest moments of his life was the time I came home from school and said gleefully, "Francis said to me today, 'You're adopted.'" I can imagine their anxiousness as they asked, "What did you say?" Father says I just grinned and replied, "Oh," I said, "So are my mama and daddy, didn't I pick the best ones?"

There really is little else to say except that I grew, had friends, went places like everyone else.

My mother says she used to be a bit concerned at the "only-child" aspect, but she thought it was taken care of by nursery school, kindergarten, later camps, and a neighborhood where there were lots of children. She says they carefully selected our house with the idea of finding a neighborhood with children of about my age.

Oh, of course there have been "problems" and ups and downs, but everyone has those. It's just a part of living and growing up.

My parents adopted a child because in the natural turn of events they couldn't fit into the larger scheme of things in the usual biological way. I think those two children we heard about earlier illustrate what I mean. The first is the little boy who said to his mother of the couple who had no children, "What are they living for?" In his childish fashion he had stated, I think, a basic truth, and I'm sure my parents felt just that way. As a result, so did I. And like the little girl, I was always sure they loved *me;* they just didn't like occasionally some of the things I did.

Furthermore, I have never felt this overlarge "obligation." Once a visitor said to my mother, "You deserve a special seat in heaven for what you've done for this orphan."

I shall always remember my mother's tinkling laugh as she winked at me and said, "Nonsense. No one owes anyone anything here or hereafter for what anyone of us has done. As I see it, all the younger generation owes the older is to do especially well by the next one."

You can't fail people like that!

THE STEPCHILD

A WIDELY prevalent opinion is that the stepchild is in a uniquely "pestiferous" position. He is stereotyped as a neglected, a misused, unwanted child. He is often considered as a stumbling block to a new marriage, and his own readily recognized unhappiness and general personality difficulties are often stressed as making him a poor marriage risk.

Even the people who hold such views, usually concede, however, that being a stepchild following death of one parent and the remarriage of the bereaved is more propitious than being a stepchild following divorce and consequent remarriage of one or both parents.

As a number of writers have observed the stereotype of the cruel stepmother sets the stage against her. As Smith [14] aptly puts it,

[14] Wm. Carlson Smith, "Remarriage and the Stepchild" in Fishbein and Burgess, *Successful Marriage, op. cit.,* p. 339 ff.

for a long time the older schoolbooks regaled the children with the Cinderella story and its variations in which the stepmother was always a cruel ogress. The child has heard stories about cruel stepmothers from his elders and even his playmates. The imprint of these stereotypes has been deepened by popular usage of the term stepchild. Anything that is considered neglected is called a stepchild. Passenger service has been called the railroad's stepchild because executives give most attention to freight hauling. Reiteration of this idea does much to maintain the stereotype and hang more millstones around the neck of the stepmother and by implication the stepfather.

Factors which complicate the situation are many as recorded by students of the situation. We shall mention a few as indicative of what may occur.

Studies on juvenile delinquency [15] indicate that the step-relationship is a factor in juvenile delinquency and, according to some, more potent for girls than for boys. To conclude, however, that the presence of the stepparent is the causative factor is unwarranted. As suggested many times earlier, the situation surrounding the reasons for the introduction to the idea and the complexity of attitudes surrounding the interpersonal relationships are doubtless the key to the situation.

If the mother parent is absent because of death, there has often been a period when various people have assumed the care of the children. If these are people who understand child development, the transition period may be gotten through with few scars. If they are "hired help," however, they are often likely to assume merely the housekeeper role or perhaps the extreme opposite attitude of "Oh you poor, bereaved dears," and go overboard in pampering.

Relatives, likewise, may be as guilty of extremes in attitudes taken. If the assumption of the duty is undesired, the resulting atmosphere may well be such that a stepmother who is permanent will be welcomed. Again children may resent bitterly any supervision which seems to restrict the freedom of their intermediate period between one home and another.

If divorce has colored the home breakup, the child's adjustment may be complicated. Who was the misused partner, what was the degree of identification with the absent parent, how do relatives view the new alliance, was the new parent introduced gradually as

[15] Smith, *op. cit.,* p. 238.

a friend or abruptly foisted upon the child, what will be the immediacy and character of association with the absent natural parent, will there be two sets of children involved? The answers to all these and many more questions enter into it. A student paper is used here for illustrative purposes.

A Stepchild: That's I

Our home was a happy, happy place. Then one day when I was fifteen years old and my brother was twelve, we were told that mother had been killed in an automobile accident. Father, as well as we children, lived in a daze for weeks. We seemed automatic, numb, lost.

At first a maiden aunt came to stay with us. I guess she meant to be kind. She was always pitying us, but at the same time she nagged us. "Why don't you clean your feet? Have you never been taught to pick up anything? You didn't finish your plate. I suppose I don't cook to suit you . . ." and on and on.

Father seemed less able to adjust than we. For us there were our active friends and activities. In fact, we came gradually to the point where we were home only to eat and sleep. Father tried to take the interest he had always taken, but he went out not at all, withdrew more and more within himself. When he did talk, it was of mother. That would have been O.K., for we liked to talk of her but he always ended such talk by falling into despondency.

At the end of six months, our aunt left. She said we did not appreciate her, we neglected her, and so on. We were secretly glad to see her go. For a while we tried it by ourselves, but it was no good.

Finally, father secured a housekeeper. Within the next two years we had four. Some did their work well; some didn't. Some "liked" us greatly until they saw they couldn't "catch" father.

Then one horrible day father came home all in smiles. Uneasily he reviewed our situation, then blurted, "I'm bringing you a new mother. She has a little girl of six. We'll be one big, happy family."

At first we were too stunned to speak. Then we tried everything. Reproach, tears, bluster, but his mind was made up or perhaps it would be nearer the truth to say made up for him.

I can see now, we never gave her a chance. She was young, pretty, agreeable, but not the caliber of our mother. Her language, even her voice lacked refinement. She was a business associate's filing clerk and our "class consciousness" was outraged.

Furthermore, we had grown accustomed to a rather lax discipline, and she undertook to "discipline" us for our own good. I am ashamed to say we "threw the book at her." What we hoped to gain, I don't know. Perhaps we unconsciously observed and resented the fact that father seemed content with her when one or both of us wasn't around.

Gradually, she began to ignore us. I know now that phase began about the time she became pregnant. How mortified we were by that pregnancy. And to make it even more disgusting, father was delighted and *so* solicitous of her.

Came the birth, and it was twins. Times were tight, and father insisted we take over the house care of our stepsister and those loathsome twins.

Words fail me even now to describe what ensued. Despite the age differences it was really an actual enactment of "your kids and my kids are fighting with our kids." For our stepmother's little girl felt left out and came to ally herself with us.

With five children in the house, and with our approach to maturity, my brother and I did not find it hard to convince father that we should go to live with and take care of our maternal grandfather while my brother finished high school and I transferred to the university.

My brother has now gone into the Navy, my grandfather is dead, and I'm about to finish college. When school is out, I'll be married to an army officer. Often I think of what life would have been like if mother had lived, and when I do, my thoughts turn at once to my possible children. With an army man for a husband, my children could be subjected to much of what I experienced in reverse. I hope I shall be able to remember each mistake.

A second student paper points out not merely a happier side but also offers suggestions concerning the process of inducting both stepparent and stepchild into a new setting.

So I'm a Stepchild

When I was three, my mother told me one day in answer to my question, "Where is daddy?" that daddy was not going to live with us anymore. And when I asked why, she replied that he had found someone he liked better. This I could not comprehend. He had always laughed and played with me a lot. That meant he liked me. Now he no longer came to play so he didn't like me. Just as I was beginning not to care, I was told that daddy would come for me for the day. I was shy at meeting him and sat stiffly erect beside him.

Finally, the zoo and the popcorn made everything seem almost right again. To cut a long story short, my father came to see me every two weeks and feted me for the day. I can see now that it must have been very difficult for my mother after each visit. Daddy came to stand for fun, frolic, excitement, while mother fed, clothed, disciplined, and generally cared for me.

After a few weeks a pleasant and pretty lady would appear at a certain point on our walk in the park. She always had a trinket for me and a smile and was never too busy to spend the rest of the day with us. Then one day we went not to the park or the zoo but to a house. This was where our friend lived, said father, and he now lived there too.

I understand I asked many embarrassing questions at this point. But now I did not look forward so much to "the" day. The "friend" was always pleasant, but the excitement and thrill were gone. When father showed me what he called my new sister, I was very bored. After this the visits got farther and farther apart.

I have always been friendly with my father's family but have never felt any attachment to any of them.

For four years my mother and I held the fort. She worked, of course. (I have since found she worked so that dad might have enough to establish his new family.)

After school I stayed with a neighbor until she could get home from the high school where she taught. I never felt neglected, and if I often felt a "hurt" when I visited other girl's homes where there were nice fathers, I still never grew bitter, thanks to my mother.

When I was nearly ten, we began having a regular guest. This man was a principal at the school where mother taught. His wife was dead, and he had a boy of eight. One day he brought his son to call. We knew each other by sight at school, and soon we were getting along very well.

Now the parties were foursomes. One Sunday afternoon we were all playing flinch. "It's time we left, son, I have some school work to prepare this evening." said our guest.

"I wish you could do it here. I wish we could just stay. It feels like home and our apartment is so lonesome," returned his son.

Mother says the air was electric. Bill turned to her and said, "Tuck spoke my thoughts very well. I wonder how you and Louise feel?"

Before mother could answer, they say I said, "Then it's all settled. Tuck can move into the spare bedroom, and we'll be a family."

Of course, Tuck and I quarreled from time to time but never seriously. Somehow it was an unspoken conspiracy between us to be as helpful as we could so that that Sunday-afternoon atmosphere would last.

Mother and Bill always presented a united front to us and our problems and requests. At the same time they listened to us and consulted with us.

In fact, as I look back over it, I think that was the secret of our successful family life together. Tuck and I had a big stake in it from the first. We were respected as people. We were not thrust into any situation without our consent. It was good to be a family again. Now, according to Bill, he had the daughter he'd always wanted—he never seemed to notice or mind that I never called him father. Now, too, mother agreed it was nice to have a son. One needed men in a house. Unlike me, however, Tuck soon called her "Moppet" which showed his close affection for and with her.

Being a stepchild is no hardship. I can't see what difference any of these "positions" make, if you handle your relations intelligently.

SUMMARY

IT IS BOTH IMPOSSIBLE and undesirable to attempt planning for all areas of child living. One can, however, mitigate, and prepare in advance for such specialized interpersonal relations as those discussed here. If the home atmosphere is permissive and the orientation is in terms of an objective attitude in meeting and working through problems, many adjustment problems may be caught upstream. Sensitivity and awareness of the impacts of these factors may well assure, as the student wrote, "intelligent handling" of human relations with consequent high-level social adjustment.

TEACHING AND STUDY AIDS

1. Singly or as a group make a study of the changing role of the family in different periods of cultural and social change.
2. Make an analysis of the shifts in roles and statuses of family members in the light of the above.
3. Much is said and written these days about the dilemma of the modern woman. Search the literature for studies on this subject and attending implications for child orientation and adjustment. The works by Helene Deutsch and Marynia Farnham are a good beginning place. See also "Adjustment Problems of the Modern Woman," in Kimball Young's *Personality and Problems of Social Adjustment.*
4. Construct an instrument for getting at student home climates and effects upon personality adjustment. Analyze and report your findings to the group.
5. Make a more intensive study than this book has space to give to birth order and position, emphasizing such special positions as the adopted and the foster child's problems, the child of divorce, the institutionalized child, the orphan, the handicapped child, and the child of genius.
6. Suggest some experiences which would bring about the type of adjustment you would want to see in your children.

7. What is your reaction to the suggestions made by the case excerpts presented in the chapters?
8. An area of interest to many people these days is that of finding in an urbanized kind of living ways of integrating not only one's own family living but also that of interfamily integration. An account of one such attempt is contained in "Family Camping—An Experience in Democratic Living," by Florence Greenhoe Robbins, *Elementary School Journal* (January 1950).

SELECTED READING REFERENCES

Anderson, Harold H., "Discipline," Bulletin of the State University of Iowa, based on the Reports of the White House Conference on Child Health and Protection.

Bacal and Sloan, "Ten Ways to Be a Good Parent," *Look* (April and June 1949).

Baruch, Dorothy W., *How to Discipline Your Children*, Public Affairs Pamphlet, No. 154 (New York, Public Affairs Committee, 1949).

Baruch, Dorothy W., *New Ways in Discipline* (New York, McGraw-Hill, 1948).

Benedict, Agnes, and Franklin, Adele, *The Happy Home: A Guide to Family Living* (New York, Appleton-Century-Crofts, 1948).

Bossard, James H., *Sociology of Child Development* (New York, Harper, 1948).

Brown, Morrison, and Couch, "Influence of Affectional Family Relationships on the Character Development," *Journal of Abnormal and Social Psychology*, Vol. 42 (1947), p. 252.

Burgess, Ernest W., and Locke, H. J., *The Family, from Institution to Companionship* (New York, American Book, 1945).

Campbell, A., "Adjustments of Only and Intermediate Children," *Pedagogical Seminary and Journal of Genetic Psychology*, Vol. 43 (1933), pp. 204–205.

Carson, Ruth, *So You Want to Adopt a Baby*, Public Affairs Pamphlet No. 173 (New York, Public Affairs Committee, 1951).

Child Study Association, *When Children Ask About Sex* (New York, 1951).

Davis, Kingsley, "The Sociology of Parent-Youth Conflict," *American Sociological Review* (August 1940), pp. 523–535.

De Saussure, Raymond, "Girlhood Problems of an Only Child," *The Nervous Child*, Vol. 4 (1944), pp. 60–70.

Doyle, Kathleen, *When Mental Illness Strikes Your Family*, Public Affairs Pamphlet No. 172 (New York, Public Affairs Committee, 1951).

Duvall, Evelyn M., *Keeping Up with Teen-agers,* Public Affairs Pamphlet No. 127 (New York, Public Affairs Committee, 1947).

Dyer, Dorothy, "Are Only Children Different?" *Journal of Educational Psychology,* Vol. 36 (1945), pp. 297–302.

Friedjung, J. K., "Die Pathologie des Einzigen Kindes," *Wien. Med. Wodie,* Vol. 41 (1911), pp. 376–381.

Goodenough, F. L., and Leahy, A. M., "The Effects of Certain Family Relationships Upon the Development of Personality," *Pedagogical Seminary and Journal of Genetic Psychology,* Vol. 34 (1927), pp. 45–76.

Goodsell, W., *A History of Marriage and the Family* (New York, Macmillan, 1934).

Groves, Ernest R., and Gladys, *Contemporary American Family* (Philadelphia, Lippincott, 1947).

Guilford, Ruth B., and Worcester, D. A., "A Comparative Study of Only and Non-only Child," *Pedagogical Seminary and Journal of Genetic Psychology,* Vol. 38 (1930).

Lenner, Leo, "Convenience and Convention in Rearing Children," *Scientific Monthly,* Vol. 59 (1944), pp. 301–306.

Kawin, Ethel, *The Wise Choice of Toys,* 2d ed. (Chicago, University of Chicago Press, 1938).

Kemph, V. H., "What About the Oldest?" *American Home,* Vol. 30 (October 1943), pp. 78–80.

Koshuk, Ruth P., *Social Influences Affecting the Behavior of Young Children* (Washington, National Research Council, 1941).

Krout, M. H., "Typical Behavior Patterns in 26 Ordinal Positions," *Journal of Genetic Psychology,* Vol. 55 (1939), pp. 3–30.

Hohman, L. B., "Problems of the Second Child," *Ladies Home Journal,* Vol. 61 (June 1944), pp. 106–107.

Hohman, Leslie, *As the Twig Is Bent* (New York, Macmillan, 1945).

Landis, Paul H., *Adolescence and Youth* (New York, McGraw-Hill, 1947).

Levy, David, *Maternal Over-Protection* (Berkeley, University of California Press, 1943).

Levy, John, "A Comparative Study of Behavior Problems in Relation to Family," *American Journal of Psychiatry,* Vol. 10 (1931), pp. 637–654.

Levy, J. A., "A Quantitative Study of Behavior Problems in Relation to Family Constellation," *American Journal of Psychiatry,* Vol. 10 (1931), pp. 637–654.

Martin, A. R., "Study of Parental Attitudes and Their Influence Upon Personality Development; and Union Settlement," *Education,* Vol. 63 (June 1943), pp. 569–608.

Mead, Margaret, *Male and Female* (New York, Morrow, 1949).

Meyers, C. E., "Emancipation of Adolescents from Home Control," *The Nervous Child,* Vol. 5 (1946), pp. 251–262.

Neisser, Edith G., *Brothers and Sisters* (New York, Harper, 1952).

————, *Mother-in-law and Grandmother,* Public Affairs Pamphlet No. 174 (New York, Public Affairs Committee, 1951).

Neisser, Walter and Edith G., *Making the Grade as Dad,* Public Affairs Pamphlet No. 157 (New York, Public Affairs Committee, 1950).

Nimkoff, Meyer F., *Marriage and the Family* (Boston, Houghton, 1947).

————, "Role of the Family in Personality Development," in Leonard Carmichael, Manual of Child Psychology (New York, Wiley, 1946), pp. 491–497.

Partridge, E. D., *Social Psychology of Adolescence* (New York, Prentice-Hall, 1939).

Reynolds, Martha M., *Children from Seed to Saplings* (New York, McGraw-Hill, 1939).

Ribble, Margaretha A., *The Rights of Infants* (New York, Columbia University Press, 1943).

Riemer, "Loving vs. Spoiling Children," *Mental Hygiene,* 24 (1940), pp. 78–81.

Scott, L. H., "Some Family Life Patterns and Their Relation to Personality Development in Children," *Journal of Experimental Education* (1939), pp. 148–160.

Smart, Charles, "Brother-Sister Act," *Parents* (October 1944), pp. 26–27.

Spock, Benjamin, *Common Sense Book of Baby and Child Care* (New York, Duell, 1946).

Stagner, Ross and Katzoff, E. T., "Personality as Related to Birth Order and Family Size," *Journal of Applied Psychology,* 20 (1936), pp. 340–346.

Stout, Irving W. and Langdon, Grace, "A Study of the Home Life of Well Adjusted Children," *Journal of Educational Psychology* (April 1950), pp. 194–200.

Strain, Frances, *Your Child, His Family, and Friends* (New York, Appleton-Century, 1943).

Symonds, P. M., *The Psychology of Parent-Child Relationships.* (New York, Appleton-Century, 1939), Chap. V, p. 148.

Taylor, Louis, "The Social Adjustment of the Only Child," *American Journal of Sociology,* Vol. 51 (1945), pp. 110–114.

Thorman, George, *Broken Homes,* Public Affairs Pamphlet No. 135 (1947).

Thrope, Elsie, "The Only Child," *Today's Health* (June 1950), p. 25.

Thurstone, L. L., and Thurstone, T. G., "A Neurotic Inventory," *Journal of Social Psychology,* Vol. 1 (1930), pp. 1–30.

Tryon, Caroline E., "How Children Learn Social Adjustment," National Society of Secondary Education Yearbook (1950).

Waller, Willard, *The Family* (New York, Dryden, 1951), Parts I and II.

Ward, Anne, "The Only Child," *Smith College Studies in Social Work,* Vol. 1 (1930–1931), pp. 41–65.

———, "The Only Child of Age Five," *Psychological Clinic,* Vol. 22 (1933), pp. 73–87.

———, "The Personal Adjustments of Only Children," *Psychological Bulletin,* Vol. 31 (1934), pp. 194–200.

Wexberg, John, *Your Nervous Child* (New York, Boni, 1928).

Witty, Paul, "Only and Intermediate Children in the Senior High School," *Journal of Experimental Education,* Vol. 6 (1937), pp. 180–186.

VII CHILD CULTURE AND PEER GROUPINGS

"PUSH AND PULL" OF GROWING UP

BEYOND the parent-child, sibling, other adults' social worlds lie the peer groupings. Toward these groups, their interests, values, and modes of behavior, the child's attention shifts gradually but continuously as the rhythm of growth proceeds. His sibling world took him a step from the adult-dominated world, and peer groups advance his passage toward adulthood many more steps. This passing is not free from strain. Often confusion and resentment result.

Earlier sociological study of peer groups centered largely on the gang, and specifically on the juvenile-delinquent gangs. More recently there has been a growing recognition of a wider range of peer groupings. This range includes the normal and natural social groupings to which children gravitate in the normal process of "growing up and out."

Increasingly the importance of these groups in the socialization process is being recognized. Researchers, discerning teachers, psychiatric social workers, and alert parents are wont to point out that the peer groups are second only to the family, and at certain age levels even have a sharper impact than the family, in their influence upon the developing child.

Understanding of these peer group structures and processes is then a "must" for those who would deal sympathetically, permissively, and intelligently with children.

According to Davis, as pointed out in a preceding chapter, establishment of independence in our culture is a strangely complex, often confusing, and irritating business not only to children but also

Bubble gum may be obnoxious to teachers and parents. It may even be defined as a health hazard. To children, however, it is often one more artifact in their social and cultural world. At certain ages peer group approval of activity looms more important to them than approval of their elders. At preadolescence and adolescence they need adults who understand and guide, not direct.

to adults if they do not know and understand the factors contributing to behavior. When on the other hand, as the better sensitized teachers of today have demonstrated, there is awareness of these sociological factors, the value conflicts of later elementary school, junior high, and senior high children can be eased.

Under guidance these children at their maturity levels have been observed to pose the problems confronting them, analyze them, and if not solve them completely at least learn to live with them in awareness rather than in ignorance, confusion, and resentment.

Writings on peer contacts emphasize that the basis of the formation and unity of these relations is inevitable antagonism and conflict with the adult world—parents, teachers, policemen, group leaders.

The thesis here is obvious. This conflict and antagonism are not inevitable or insoluble when all parties concerned maintain the scientific attitude and method of study concerning them.

TYPES OF PEER GROUPINGS

PEER GROUPS fall into at least two principal categories, the informal and the formal. The informal groups include the play groups, and the gang. They are in the main child-originated, child-constituted, child-directed.

The formal groupings include such as boy and girl scouts, choir groups, clubs, and, at a later age, sororities and fraternities. These are organized for youth, participated in by youth but usually in the shadow of adult advisors, directors, or instructors.

When this guidance is handled skillfully, these groups assume a place in child life equivalent to the informal grouping and offer a superb chance for channeling of thought and behavior along socially acceptable behavior and adjustment. This is not to say that children must be kept surreptitiously from informal groupings. It does imply that natural child groupings can be capitalized upon by wise and cooperative adults and that in such situations children welcome their fruitful participation. Parents should constantly appraise how fast and to what extent child independence is developing and hence how quickly and to what extent adult participation and guidance may progressively withdraw to merely advisor status. This gives both freedom and security to the children.

INFORMAL GROUPS

The Play Group

The play group is a spontaneous grouping which usually forms on the basis of neighborhood proximity. It is outstandingly characteristic of younger children. Its activity pattern may range from the parallel play in which children up to four and five engage through to fairly organized imaginative play. It may be composed of one or both sexes depending upon age and family social status.

As children reach seven to nine years, they make sex distinctions in terms of activities chosen. Some kinds of activities allow for boys, others do not, and vice versa.

Likewise the increase in direction and supervision of children as we go up the social scale is shown in the careful setting of the stage within which children "are free to choose associates at will." Despite the low level of organization in the peer play group, the social attitudes of the larger adult social world begin to be reflected.

There are "rules," often unspoken, such as how one treats children who play "on our lawn," or "things we do and don't do," or "how we use equipment," what kind of language is permissible, what kinds of activities are allowable for boys, for girls, for girls and boys.

It has long seemed to many observers that there exists in the child world an almost separate body of "child culture."

As indicated above much of this is a reflection of the larger social structure and process. There are also customs and social forms which are peculiarly the child's. Examples of these include such as Kings X to hold a favored spot and observance by other children, games such as old cat, tic-tac-toe, take-off's on adults.

The personal-social relations are the transmission agencies and appear to derive from the overlapping of child-sibling generations.

The Gang

The next phase in the natural history of peer groupings is the gang. Early study of this social phenomenon in child life described it as based upon conflict. In view of this belief, gangs were regarded as delinquent groups, and hence "ganging" was defined as "bad." Teachers, parents, and social workers conceived of their roles as "gang breaker-uppers."

In 1936 the extensive work of Thrasher [1] appeared. Though he adhered to the conflict concept as a basis both for formation and integration, his analyses pointed the way to analysis of "ganging" as a natural phenomenon of the maturation process.

His study of the 1,313 gangs in Chicago showed not only the patterns of delinquent behavior but also that children learned in gang living the very values and attitudes that society wished them to learn with one serious exception. They were not oriented in the socially accepted fashion.

To members, the gang participation gave the thrill of new adventure such as "roaming," smoking, petty stealing, and the security of playing pranks and games, of laying siege to other gangs, withstanding adult authority, and other activities.

Its derived values were loyalty to a group, experience in group

[1] Frederic M. Thrasher, *Gang* (Chicago, University of Chicago Press, 1936). Used by permission.

thinking, planning, and concerted action. While elections as such seldom occurred, the rules by which one rose to or fell from leadership
were clearly understood.

This natural need and tendency toward ganging usually takes place
first with the neighborhood play group. If these play groups flourish
in the interstitial areas of a city, in the "cultural no-man's land" around
docks, railroad yards, and the like, the chances of them developing into
juvenile delinquent groups is great.

Usually the juvenile delinquency gang history development is
from play group to truancy then petty stealing to fill the hours of
truancy, alliance with gangs engaged in serious delinquency and finally organized crime.

Of the many studies of gangs and of individuals within gangs,
reported in the literature, that of Rocco is still a classic illustration.

Rocco was born in this country of Italian parentage. His father
came as an adult immigrant 32 years ago and has worked steadily on
railroad section gangs. Five of the seven children in the family had a
grade-school education or better and are now regularly employed and
law-abiding. One brother, Tony, has been "singed with crime," but to
no great extent. The "42" gang had its origins in a typical neighborhood
group of small boys. For ten years it frequented Chicago's West Side.
Though now in virtual eclipse, it has passed on heritage so that "children are growing up into a criminal life." Rocco tells his story in a
matter-of-fact way and with an unusual memory for details.

Beginnings in Truancy. My schooling at Dante was regular, and I
attended to my work while there. I always, from a very small child,
wanted to be an altar boy, and one day when one of the altar boys came
and told me that I was chosen, I was very happy. I went to church every
morning, arose at 6 and served the 7 to 8 o'clock Mass. The altar boys
were my playmates. There was a little clublike room in the basement
where we played games. In the wintertime we went to Hull House and
spent some time in the playroom. Sometimes I went on hikes. I was
never truant from school.

After we moved to Taylor and Sibly, I had to transfer to the Rees
school. I arrived from Dante in the fifth grade and with a good record.
I first met Peter and Louie in this room. At Dante I had never bummed.
At Rees I didn't like the school because I didn't know anybody. Once in
a while we would bum and run back to the old neighborhood. It was
always in the afternoon so I could wait for my friends. We got so we
would go to school only once in a while.

Conflict with the Family. I began to have trouble in school, and it
was reported to my father. He talked to me and punished me. It was

time, too, for my lessons for confirmation, and my father transferred me to Pompeii school. Here I behaved a little better. The principal gave me a talking to right at the beginning. Later I began to find my old friends again. I was kicked out of Pompeii and went back to Rees, where I quit in the seventh grade. By this time we were bumming and stealing.

My parents used to be notified by mail that I bummed yesterday. My mother at first tried talking and pleading with me, sometimes with tears in her eyes. "What's got in your head, Rocky? Why don't you go to school?" "I don't like that school," I said. But she never gave these notices to my father. One day the teacher brought the letter herself. She gave the letter to Albert and asked him to give it to father. He did that night. From then on my father arranged to be notified by the teacher about my absence.

After a few beatings at different times, he got disgusted and let me go. There was nothing said between us; he would just frown at me. At the table I would sit as far away from him as I could. One day he said, "You are not going to school. You are just bumming around. Why don't you go to work?" Then I got my work certificate. From then on I bummed all day every day and at home told them I had a job.

Every morning I was out at 7:30 and returned at 5:30. On Saturday I brought home ten dollars as "pay." When one of them asked me, I told them I was working downtown at the Board of Trade.

How my mother found out that I wasn't working, I don't know. When she did, she began to ask me how I got my money. I tried to lie out of it (stealing). "If your father finds out, he'll kill you. Where did you get your money?" I told her. She cried and said, "Don't do that, Rocky, you'll go to jail and never come out again." It always hurt me to see her cry, but I couldn't change. I met those fellows (the gang) every morning, and when I said I was going to look for a job, they'd laugh at me. Albert's warning has always been "You'll wind up in the gutter." He always had another set of friends.

First Rackets. We first started stealing from clotheslines while bumming from school. The first day we went out west, near Oak Park. We took the street car with a little sack under our arms, filled it, and came home. We "picked" silk shirts and would sell them for only a dollar or two apiece. We would shoot craps on the sidewalk, buy delicatessen, go to shows, and worry the girls.

Our next racket was robbing pennies. One of us would take a sledge hammer and with a partner start down Roosevelt Road looking for penny machines. One smash and the pennies would come rolling out. We would get four or five machines in an evening. If we were chased, we knew the streets like a book and would run through alleys like lightning, or over a fence into an open lot. We used to study get-aways day and night, and we were never caught.

A little later we began to steal bicycles. We would go out to the Oak Park district on the streetcar, take the bikes, and ride them home. We were partners and would use the same basement storeroom. We would sell these bikes, some worth $55 or $65 for $4, $10, or $15. We always had a half dozen bikes in the basement. One day a man came around and said he would give us $9 for a 29 x .4 tire. He told us it was easy. He explained that we could get a bar clip at a hardware store, which we did, and with it take the spare tire off the car. We delivered the tire, and he gave us the $9. Through him another customer heard of us, and these passed us on to still others. We soon got a list of phone numbers of tire customers, leaving orders for sizes in advance. Many of our customers were legitimate working people. We stole tires all over the city. I soon owned a little Ford coupe and we cruised around until we found what we wanted.

In the delicatessen store (gang hangout), we "stoshed" some of our money. I suppose the four of us in good weeks made as high as $200. Our biggest expense then was shooting craps, and we wanted to go with girls like older fellows. We picked up two, one a German and the other Polish. They lived in a hotel. When it got hot for us, we would go over there and stay. We were suckers for those girls, bought them clothes and gave them money.

Trouble with the Police. We got into our first jam when I was about sixteen, and we had been a few months in the tire business. We had our basement fixed up with shelves and marked tire sizes. When a customer wanted a tire, we would take him down, switch on the light, and pull out the right size. Getting into a jam was not new to us, as we had heard a lot from older fellows about fixing the police, springing writs, and getting bail.

We were picked up around the Empire Theater by the old Marmon squad with a gong on each side of the wagon. They took us down to the Desplaines Street station. They thought the Ford I was driving was stolen, and they had us under suspicion for stealing tires. They gave us some beatings, and we didn't know anything. We were booked for disorderly, and the court discharged the case.

After that we began to be watched, and the coppers began to pick us up. I learned that when you are picked up and have money in your pocket, you can fix the cop. Twenty-five dollars will fix it on the spot.

Code of the "42" Gang. When Figlio opened his poolroom, we started hanging out there. The poolroom drew more fellows around the neighborhood who were in little mobs of two and four and eight, and the mobs got close, got acquainted, that way. It was there that the name

"42" sprang up. The bunch were all acquainted; I could approach any fellow and ask him to go on a job. There was an elderly man there we all trusted. We left our guns, left our money to bank, and would drop him a fin or a sawbuck. You could eat there, sleep there; you could get your phone calls and call up the mouthpiece.

If you were "in," the mouthpiece knew that the mob boys were good. He'd spring a writ for you or do anything, and collect afterwards because he knew where to find you and that you'd pay if you belonged to the gang. If you didn't have it (money), the boys would take up a collection.

One time I was pinched seven Sundays in a row. We never talked, no confessions. In some cases, they'd take us down, question us, beat us, and bring us up every two or three hours. One time a young copper came down, first talked rough, then slapped me in the face, but could get nothing on us. He came down later in a kinder mood and told us that he was an ex-hood himself. He did some favors for me, and I met him later when I was out and took him to a good Italian dinner.

Alliance with Politicians. On election day, Vito, Frankie, Bozzi, and Chiochio were busy at the precinct polls. All the others came around. I was an election judge, and Frankie was a worker with a badge. They told me that in the ward it was agreed that votes were to come out 50–50. There would be no trouble that day.

Truck and Auto Rackets. The last six months in the tire business we would go out after 1 P.M. We averaged about $75 a week—all sweet [clear], nobody to pay off. But I thought, "If I went out with the big fellows, I'd be a big shot too." Then we started getting in with the older clique. They hijacked us into their gang, but we wanted to be with them. They were 20 or 21 years of age. They were in the big money, after butter-and-egg trucks, dry goods, and shoes in loads. They were driving Chryslers and having bigger and better times—cabarets, shows, beer joints. We didn't know how to dress, and we felt that they were smarter. They taught me how to match ties and suits, what color shoes and hats to wear.

We were down in the basement at Figlio's. Vito asked me if I wanted to try a pistol, showing me how to aim. Pointing at the target, he showed how a pistol must be aimed lower than the object to always allow for the jump. Later he sold me a .36 Colt's. The older fellows were in the pistol racket (holdups) even then. They went into the pistol racket just as the butter-and-egg business was waning.

I don't remember the first time I went out after a truck, but I can give you an instance. We met one morning at Edgmont and Loomis at the appointed time. We got into Salvi's Ford and cruised around. This cruising around sometimes took an hour before we met up with anything. At Kedzie and Flournoy there stood a truck, butter and eggs. The driver was in the store. I jumped in the truck and drove east, Salvi and the Ford behind me. His work was to cut off anybody following me in a machine by crowding him to the curb.

We had our garage in the neighborhood. Once there, we would unload the stuff and take the truck out of the district. We knew the places where we could dispose of the stuff, and we knew the prices. The two big "fences" would buy anything. You could get money from them any time you brought in the stuff. This racket lasted about a year when I was 19 years old. . . .

We took Gene (a newcomer) for a sucker, but he was a good head for auto work. He took us out to a saloon hangout, and we started taking orders for cars. By this time we knew how to take the ignition switch off, make connections, break the steering lock, and drive away. We would take orders for machines from the saloonkeeper. Bootleggers wanted the numbers changed, and we would have to hold cars until we got numbers from New York. We would write the make, model, and year, and the man would watch for cars of the same description. Then he would send us their license numbers.

Sentences, Paroled, and a Job. In this one (and only) conviction, I got an 18-month sentence to St. Charles (boys' reformatory). First I was downhearted and lonesome. I didn't like the fellows around me. They were punks, wanting to be tough. I attended to work and kept quiet. I was moved to C cottage, where I met some kids from my neighborhood. One day I separated a pair of kids who were fighting, and Colonel Whipp heard about this. He called me to the office and made me a sergeant. I received no punishment in the time I was at St. Charles.

For six months after my release, I reported to a probation officer. That's the guy that got me a job as errand boy. When I went out to an employer, I tried my best not to get the job. Finally, after about four months of stalling, he took me himself. He took me to four places altogether; he pleaded with employers. I never heard anyone lie so much in one day. I worked for two months as errand boy at $15 a week. Of course I did some stealing, just enough to average around $40 a week. I quit the job after my probation period was over.

The Gang in Dissolution. On returning to the mob, I found that it was scattered and broken up. Babe Ruth had been killed by a cop and Jit Pargoni and one of his brothers. The rackets had changed. The trucks had two guys on them. The police had found a way to bring out original numbers on automobiles by using acid. Other numbers hard to find (body numbers) were being put on cars by manufacturers. The police could find them through charts furnished by the company. The chain stores and later the tire war made tires so cheap you could buy legit tires for less than we sold stolen ones. I nosed around among the fellows, but they were all going out with the pistol.

We did our first stick-up in a cigar store. We stayed there a full twenty minutes . . . and we got $700 in money and merchandise. In 1928–1929, I used to go out regularly with the same two fellows. This was on no tips at all, all blind joints. Working on tips is more lousy (dangerous), unless they are the right kind. The tipster may be a stool, leak, or trap. Tipsters and bad luck come together.

We're not gangsters any more. We're just hoodlums. I'm a hoodlum and a small one at that. It would be a good thing if we had a gang and somebody with money to organize us.[2]

FORMAL GROUPS

Clubs

Though the previous discussion of gangs makes it obvious that there is a high degree of organization present in some gangs, they were included among informal groups because of the absence of adult control and/or participation. Let us now consider those equally important peer groupings known as formal clubs, including fraternities and sororities.

It has often been said that boys "gang" and girls "club." In other words, the culture is again reflected especially at middle- and upper-class levels in the difference in freedom allowed boys and girls.

To gang, children need not only the place (usually interstitial areas) but also freedom from adult control. Since girls have this in only relative measure, their tendency at this stage in development is to suit the manner of meeting the need to the surroundings. This means "clubs"—sewing clubs, photography clubs, doll clubs, etc.

With the newer emphasis upon ganging as a natural, wholesome, and desirable means of socialization, a similar outcome is to be noted for boys. Teachers and parents are quick to note the onset of this period and to attempt direction and guidance. A familiar attempt to channel this activity is the cub scout movement.

Boy scouting, as such, missed this highly important, fraught with dynamite, period. Hence, there has developed the cub scout

[2] Quoted by permission from John Landesco, "The Life History of a Member of the '42' Gang," *Journal of Criminal Law and Criminology* (March–April 1943). The arrangement of the material is that of L. A. Cook and Elaine Forsythe Cook in *A Sociological Approach to Education* (New York, McGraw-Hill, 1950), pp 358–363. Used by permission.

movement which aims at this very period, eight to eleven years, when the urge to gang is rampant.

Though those familiar with the program may aver that the organizational pattern has "missed the boat" in many ways, they still agree that, if individual dens are treated in a creative way, they may serve the purpose of the age.

Unfortunately, the cub dens are set up with den mothers, and programs are just replicas of the craft and workshop programs which children in modern schools experience every day. It is to be admitted that they may not be so boring, however, to children whose schools do not provide this kind of educational fare.

A personal experience paper from our files will illustrate the *importance* and the *how* of such formal peer groupings.

Ganging into Clubbing

The parents of the grade in which my eight-year-old son was enrolled were a well-knit, friendly group. Therefore, we knew that our boys were getting "that age."

Nonetheless, we were all somewhat startled to learn from the teacher that several of them were disrupting circle (planning period) and playground and work period situations by their attempts to "start a club."

It was to be secret, they said, to have a treasurer and a name. Not all of the boys in the class would be allowed to join. Such broad outlines spoke their piece. They were ready and willy-nilly; they would "gang." If it were not possible in the open, their natural tendencies would make-shift with an undercover gang.

All parents were busy, or thought they were, and no one wanted to assume the responsibility of being a den mother on the same day each week. Furthermore, this age is noteworthy for its spontaneous expression in terms of noise, tusseling, and the like.

For a few weeks matters drifted; then one night after school, my son said to me, "Mother, we gotta have something 'citing to do and regular. Sam thought it would be fun to go to the 10-cent store and see what we could get. I told him I had no money and he said that didn't matter. He would whoop and holler and run up and down the aisles, and while the clerks watched him, I could pick up things, but it didn't sound right to me."

That did it. One mother agreed to act as titular head, and another agreed to help with the details of phoning, dues responsibilities, and similar activities. A church was found to sponsor the den within its pack structure. As soon as the meetings began several things became apparent. These boys wanted and needed only a minimum of organization procedures. They did not need or want a craft work group. "We do it at school all the time. We want fun."

It was next apparent that these boys needed and wanted male leadership. They were surrounded by women—mothers, women teachers at school, and women teachers at Sunday school.

They did enjoy a bit of ceremony, a short amount of ritual, something "citing" in the way of recreation with their fathers in an ascendent role and food—lots of food.

Gradually we retrenched, rearranged, and reoriented our thinking and our activities with them. Since this is an unusually cooperative parent group, it was done with a minimum of difficulty, but there were grumblings. Some parents thought the boys should be turning out some finished product at each meeting. Some thought they should sit quietly and run a meeting like grown-ups. And one or two objected to the round of "fun," play and entertainment. "My parents never put themselves out like this for me, etc."

Some agreed at once that, if an adult-guided activity were to replace the other kind of ganging, it must be flexible, relaxed, fun, exciting, active, recreational. These people recognized that attention spans at this age would allow for only brief organization work. They saw the need that children in our culture have for "rites of passage" such as the name den, the uniform with its proud array of achievement bars, the brief ceremony of flag saluting, the feeling of "groupness" which holding hands in a circle and repeating a promise, a pledge of allegiance, and a creed together would give. Then, it was time to be about *kid* business and that meant an activity.

So through trial and error, we have evolved a program. It is not foolproof; it has weaknesses, but it gives evidence of meeting these boys' needs. As a parent, I recommend it heartily, the scout organization to the contrary, notwithstanding. And we mothers hope it might prove useful to others who want their boys to be members of gangs under socially acceptable conditions but who are finding, as we did, that the formal programs suggested are not too suitable for boys of this age.

We have two people who assume responsibility for the detail work. Beyond that it is a cooperative venture. The boys and their families take turns at being hosts and providing the recreational project for the day. Fathers take charge of this. In warm weather this ranges from baseball, football, and foot races to swimming and wiener roasts to circus expeditions. In winter there have been home movies, trips to museums, exhibitions, and plays. In other words, the program is entirely up to the father and boy who are hosts, as is the time of meeting.

Dear to the heart of the boy is his uniform, his awards, and his

ceremony, if it is not too long. Each meeting begins with perhaps ten
minutes of formal business meeting, then the boys and fathers take
over. How they whoop, yell, and enjoy themselves!

But this is not "just recreational busywork." They are also learning
—learning skills which will be useful to them recreationally all their
lives and wherever they go. And they are making friends with men—the
fathers of their friends. This promotes their social ease, gives them
added security in adult relationships, provides them, as Mangus suggested, with wholesome adult models of behavior.

There are other by-products. Their sense of loyalty to the larger
whole is great, their pride in their own den in comparison with others
is keen, but not of the cutthroat quality. Their inventiveness and ability
to work cooperatively have been ably shown in the way they "worked"
on skits and pack activities of various sorts.

Furthermore, this approach, we think, has not, as so often happens,
exploited their zest for later real scouting.

CLIQUES

A peer grouping composed of people of similar social class
status with relatively permanent relationships is termed a clique.
Hollingshead's analysis is worthy of repetition.[3]

A clique comes into existence when two or more persons are related one to another in an intimate fellowship that involves "going
places and doing things" together, a mutual exchange of ideas, and the
acceptance of each personality by the others. Perhaps the most characteristic thing about the clique is the way its members *plan* to be together, to do things together, go places together. Within the clique,
personal relations with one another involve the clique mates in emotional and sentimental situations of great moment to the participants.
Confidences are exchanged between some or all members; often those
very personal, wholly private, experiences that occur in the family
which involve only one member may be exchanged with a best friend
in the group. Relations with the opposite sex, with adults, and with
young people outside the clique are discussed and decisions reached
on the action to be taken by the clique, or by a particular member
involved in a situation.

Membership is voluntary and informal; members are admitted
gradually to a pre-existing clique and dropped by the mutual consent
of its participants. Although there are no explicit rules for member-

[3] A. B. Hollingshead, *Elmtown's Youth* (New York, Wiley, 1949), pp.
205–207. Used by permission.

ship, the clique has a more or less common set of values which determines who will be admitted, what it does, how it will censure some member who does not abide by its values.

As the clique comes to be accepted by other cliques as a definite unit in the adolescent society, it develops an awareness of self, a "we feeling," sentiments, and traditions which impel its members to act and think alike. Its members frequently identify their interests with the group in contrast to the interests of the family, other cliques, the school, and society. Generally, clique interests come before those of the individual member or any outside group or interest. This attitude often results in conflicts between the clique and the family, between the clique and the school, or between the clique and the neighborhood. If this conflict element becomes the *raison d'être* of the group, the clique develops into the gang.*

The impact of clique controls on the adolescent produces a sense of his personal importance in his relations with other members, as well as with persons outside the clique, for the clique has a powerful emotional influence on him which he tends to carry over into outside social relations, using it to bolster his own conception of himself. Each member has a group status derived from his ability to achieve some thing or to contribute some thing to the well-being of the clique. This group-derived status is often valued very highly by the boy or girl. Thus, the clique is a powerful influence in the life of the person from its formation in the preadolescent years until it is dissolved by the development of the dating pattern.

Outsiders, especially parents and teachers, often fail to realize the meaning which the clique has for its members; consequently, there is a tendency for them to deprecate it. This may produce more resistance and withdrawal into the sanctuary of the clique on the part of the adolescent, for, in a conflict situation that involves him as a member of the group, the youngster tends to look to the clique for support. The adolescent, bolstered by his sense of belonging to a group that backs him in his efforts to emancipate himself from adult and institutional controls, feels a sense of power, of belonging, of security, and, consequently, makes decisions in collaboration with his clique mates he would never make alone, as long as his decisions meet with clique approval. Each member of the clique, reinforced by the presence of his "pals" and their agreement that some line of action is desirable or un-

* The clique and the gang are closely related social forms, the essential difference between the two being the importance placed upon predacious activity that almost invariably leads to conflict in the gang. The clique is a socially accepted group which normally does not develop conflict relations to the point where an undeclared war exists between itself and society or, for that matter, other cliques.

desirable, that something must be done or undone, produces a cohesive social situation in which the clique acts as a unit. Controls operating in the clique tend to produce uniformity of thought and action on the question at issue. Individuals who do not go along with the decision of the majority are coerced into acquiescence or ostracized since deviation is tolerated only within narrow limits. Adherence to the group code is guarded carefully by the clique's members, for cliques develop reputations and have favorable or unfavorable status attached to them by other cliques, parents, teachers, preachers, and adults on the basis of their membership and activities.

COMMON ELEMENTS IN PEER GROUPINGS AND THEIR IMPACT UPON THE DEVELOPMENT OF CHILDREN

AS THE STUDENT runs through the case studies of individual peer groups, be they the ephemeral play group, the gang, the club, or the clique, and the analysis of their effects on personality, he becomes impressed with the fact that each has its truly unique aspects, its individual differential as it were.

Likewise, he notes that there are common elements, social and cultural, in these cases. He discovers, in other words, that what contributes to delinquency in one child may prove an actual incentive to acceptable behavior for another or just remain in the realm of "uneffective" environment. What makes one child a victim of self-pity, challenges another to do his best. And often the value outcome is the same except in terms of social acceptability.

When taken as sociological phenomena, a number of common outcomes derive. First, peer groupings have a natural history of development. They arise, develop, flourish, and die out or reformulate as adult groups. This is evidently done in relation to the rhythms of growth—physical, mental, and social—as suggested in Chapter 3.

This suggests that their form derives from both personal-social and societal needs. The young child needs activity, release of energy, people his size and shape upon whom to visit what has been visited upon him by huge people. He needs to explore people and relationships as well as things. He needs to experiment, to create, and to synthesize in terms of his own kind. He can do all these things in the ephemeral play group.

As he achieves more specialization in muscular and neural development, as his world of experience widens both physically and

(Reproduced by permission of Norman Rockwell and *The Saturday Evening Post*. Copyright 1952. The Curtis Publishing Company.)

in terms of language and thought development, as he becomes more socially aware, sensitive, and responsible, he needs accompanyingly more complex relationships. At this point just proximity and the like are not sufficient. Similar interests, likes, and dislikes, continued social approval of one's fellows, some escape from adult authority are important in addition to earlier needs. He needs not only more complex and specialized social structures but also permanency and status as evidenced by organizations, with their officers, symbols, and rituals.

This gang (and) or club stage merges sometimes gradually, sometimes abruptly, into a reflection of adult attitudes and beliefs as growth and development point him toward adulthood, its statuses

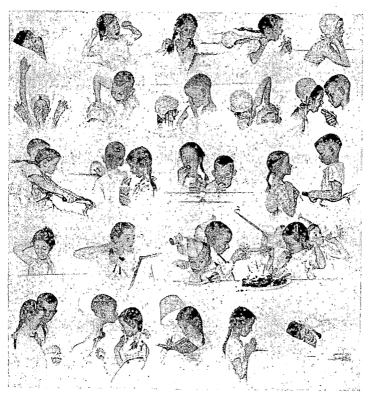

(Reproduced by permission of Norman Rockwell and *The Saturday Evening Post.* Copyright 1952. The Curtis Publishing Company.)

and roles. These relationships are also informal and formal but their character has now changed.

The organization of the play gang is dependent upon the social-cultural milieu in which it arises. It is a social product. If the ganging occurs in socially deprived areas of town, it is always in danger of becoming a delinquent gang. Truancy is one of its first stages. As pointed out in the Rocco case, you have to have something to do, somewhere to go to escape prying eyes. These so-called "risk" areas provide people ready and able to utilize youth's dilemma.

As Bossard says,[4] at least four generalizations may be made

[4] James H. Bossard, *Sociology of Child Development* (New York, Harper, 1948), pp. 501–502.

concerning the role of such factors as race, national origin, and religion in gang development. First, being found most often in first- and second-generation immigrant areas, gangs appear more often among the Polish, Italian, Irish, etc., than among such older groups as the Swedish and the Germans. Second, gang formation and rivalry often result from the carry over of old world antagonisms to the New World. Third, territorial clashes between nationality groups that have become segregated into relatively homogeneous groups often flare forth and at times develop into traditional feuds which are continued on a territorial basis after the originally antagonistic elements have lost their distinctive identity. Fourth, race riots, growing out of the expansion of "Black Belts" in various Northern cities, have gang reverberations.

One of the first values impressed upon the new gang or club member is the realization that he must accept and respect the rights and privileges of others. This means that he must give allegiance to the codes and rules of the group.

Here for perhaps the first time he accepts the control of a group other than the family. He subordinates himself to its rules and codes by giving his loyalty and support and, as he becomes an "old member," his constructive suggestions.

In return the group affords him escape from the adult-dominated world, assigns roles of importance to himself and his group, and assigns a status security such as only peers can bestow.

In our culture these groups with their "secrets," initiation ceremonies and the like are the "only rites of passage our culture affords." They are the proving grounds for idealism. As socializing agencies in the time of preadolescence and adolescence their opinions and ways are often much more important to the child than those of his family members—hence, the so-called age of conflict.

For this reason much stress is laid not upon breaking up these groups but upon attempts to set the stage so they may function wholesomely.

In middle- and upper-status levels this is fairly easy of attainment. In lower-class levels, where as suggested in Chapter 4 parents have neither time, money, knowledge, and often no interest, the job must be performed, if at all, through the school, settlement house, or other community agencies.

In the late adolescent and postadolescent years physical and social development is such that the zenith of gang, or even clique groupings, comes to the end of its natural history. Heterosexual interests intrude; job interest and preparation for careers intervene.

Unless it is a juvenile-delinquent gang which reorganizes now as an adult-criminal gang, the tendency is for the groups to dissolve. Literally, "Wedding bells are breaking up that old gang of mine."

If the group life experience has been directed into organized channels such as scouting, there is a natural flow into adult-oriented forms of the activity. These include such shifts as from scouting to YMCA and YWCA work, from 4-H clubs to Grange and general pushes and pulls toward sorority and fraternity activity, lodges, professional and civic clubs, athletic clubs, or as one youth put it, the "American Legion à la that Great Organizer, Uncle Sam."

How the boy or girl has functioned or not functioned in these groups is of major importance in general social adjustment. Has he or she been excluded from such groups by overprotective parents or by personality aspects which were unattractive? Has he been *in* but not *of* such groups? Has he been so anxious to please that he has been pushed around? Has he always had to be a king pin? Or has he been able to give and take, to respect others, to take a stand without winning and still be happy?

Has the home so set the stage in a democratic framework that his relationships among his peers can be extensions in harmonious fashion or has he lived in such conflicting atmospheres that integration is impossible?

The answers to these and many more questions make of peer group experiences important major life experiences.

TEACHING AND STUDY AIDS

1. Select a natural play group of whatever developmental level you choose. *Be sure* that your observation is unnoticed. Study the social world and special culture as evidenced by the application of the following queries:

   A. On what bases did the group form?
   B. What kinds of activities, ceremonies, and traditions are observable?
   C. What roles and statuses does each member play?
   D. How did he receive his placement?
   E. How do the roles change?
   F. What means of social control were used by group members?

    G. What are the implications of what you have observed for adults who deal with children?

2. A similar project may be planned around observation of a child *club, clique,* or *working committee* within a classroom.
3. Read Wm. Foote Whyte's *Street Corner Society* (Chicago, University of Chicago, Press, 1943). Make a book report on this type of living to the class.
4. Read and critically analyze Thomas Minehan's fascinating book called *Boy and Girl Tramps of America* (New York, Farrar, 1934, and Grosset, 1937).
5. You will sample another world if you read and think upon Paul Cressey's, *The Taxi-Dance Hall* (Chicago, University of Chicago Press 1932).
6. The media of mass communication are currently filled with emphasis upon "dope" and teen-agers. Individually or as a group, study and report the status of the problem for your city or state.
7. Make a study of such national youth organizations as Y-teens, Boy and Girl Scouts, Future Farmers of America, 4-H Clubs, etc. How do they meet the needs of youth? Where do you find gaps or errors in their programs? How could these be remedied?
8. A committee or individual study may be made of the origins of juvenile delinquency, its developmental patterns, and the programs for meeting this social problem. The following references will give you a start: Sheldon Glueck and Eleanor Glurts, *Unraveling Juvenile Delinquency* (New York, The Commonwealth Fund, 1950); Albert Deutsch, *Our Rejected Children* (Boston, Little, Brown, 1950); Wm. C. Kvaiaceus, *Juvenile Delinquency and the Schools* (Yonkers, World Book, 1945).
9. Show the movie *A Criminal Is Born,* shortened version by Metro-Goldwyn Mayer. Lead a discussion concerning it. Re-role the experiences of these boys.

SELECTED READING REFERENCES

Applegate, M. S., *Helping the Boy in Trouble* (New York, Association Press, 1950).

Eckert, Ralph G., *So You Think Its Love,* Public Affairs Pamphlet, No. 161 (New York, Public Affairs Committee, 1950).

Havighurst, Robert J., and Taba, Hilda, *Adolescent Character and Personality* (New York, Wiley, 1949).

Prescott, D. A., *Emotion and the Educative Process* (Washington, American Council on Education, 1938).

Shaw, Clifford, *Brothers in Crime* (Chicago, University of Chicago Press, 1938).

Whyte, Wm. Foote, *Street Corner Society* (Chicago, University of Chicago Press, 1943).

Zirbes, Laura, "Work and Play," *Childhood Education* (December 1948).

VIII RELIGION IN CHILD LIVING

THE CURRENT OUTLOOK

IN EARLIER GENERATIONS when the entire system of
social control was built into and around the religious organization,
it could have been considered only as *the* means of mass communication and influence. Children in that cultural era were faced only
with the need to accept or openly rebel against the prescribed
religious values.

In a secular and sensate culture, such as ours has come to be,
religion in the lives of children, as of adults, has come to occupy an
actually competitive position among the many social agencies of
mass communication and attempted social control, and for those
interested in child development the effects of religion upon parent-
child relations are important.

The traditional approach to religion by many churches, especially
those of an emotional sort, creates a gulf of difference between a youth
and the adults of his family who are established in the faith. This
problem is reflected strikingly in Baldwin's study of youth in Homeland,
a foreign-nationality neighborhood. Research workers reported that
"the self-contained spirituality of the older generation left little opportunity for a sympathetic understanding of the ideals of adolescence."
At the same time adolescents in the community were impatient with
"crystallized dogmas" of their elders. Being confined to the religious
ideologies of the neighborhood, the young people had no chance to
acquire sufficient perspective to analyze and compare their creed with
others. If they rejected the local faith, they had little opportunity to re-
adjust their ideas toward a broader concept of religion. The study also
reports that the adolescents were too emotionally healthy to enter into

the sectarian conflicts which added some vitality to the religious tenets of the elders.

Even where religious ideologies do not produce conflict in the mind of the adolescent and youth, the attempt of parents to project the family religion and its supplementary social taboos onto the child may create strain in adolescent-youth adjustments to out-group patterns.

For the majority of youth, the period of skepticism gradually merges into a period of acceptance, either because they become weary of the struggle with doubt or because they find rational justification for a sufficient number of their beliefs to make the rest acceptable. Others, unable to reconcile religious and scientific views, discard their religion in favor of science. Still others, who have had religion identified with narrow and unreasonable restrictive social taboos, find it necessary to discard the family religion as they leave the family and become participants in more normal social situations. Because their religious training was of negative restrictive taboos rather than of dynamic ideals, their religion ceased to be useful.[1]

The Elmtown study presents timely and enlightening facts about adolescents and religion in one small midwestern town. The researchers point out that practically every student in the school population studied believed in God. Each student thought he was a Christian but only 51 percent participated in any religious activities. The decision to attend or not to attend religious services was left to the parents and in many cases to the children themselves.

The impression gradually grew that religion to these adolescents is comparable in a way to wearing clothes or taking a bath. It is something one has to have or to do to be acceptable in society. The youngsters also assume that Christianity is the one right and true religion. In a vague, almost incomprehensible way, they know of the existence of other religions, but only a few can readily name one of the great historic religions other than Christianity. Moreover, it is rarely that a student understands the difference between a religion and a denomination. This became clear as student after student named a denomination with a local congregation when he was asked what his religion was. Occasionally, a student would volunteer the information, "We are Christians, but there isn't a church here." Here and there is a student who stoutly maintained he did not belong to a church and neither did his family. Such students were asked, "Do you have a religion?" Reactions to this question varied, but, in general, the response was to the

[1] Paul H. Landis, *Adolescence and Youth* (New York, McGraw-Hill, 1945), pp. 187–189. Used by permission. The Homeland study referred to is in *Farm Children* by Bird T. Baldwin, E. A. Fillmore, and Lora Hadley (New York, Appleton-Century, 1930), pp. 30–31.

effect, "I am a Christian, but I don't belong to any church." This way of thinking was impressed upon the child in such an informal way that he assumed he was religious and a church member, when in fact neither he nor his family were affiliated with a church.

Religion to the vast majority is an amorphous body of beliefs symbolized by a number of awesome words, God, Jesus, Christ, Sin, Salvation, Satan, Heaven, Hell. It is given form in a book that embodies all sacred truth, the Bible. . . . But to about 90 percent of the boys and about 80 percent of the girls, religion does not have this compulsive quality. These youngsters believe that a person ought to be religious, but the word does not have any very specific content or meaning except a vague belief in God confirmed by the assertion that they are Christians or belong to a church. . . .

Adolescents who seek an answer to religious questions which trouble them are faced with confusion and contradiction in other areas of the culture. In their formal contacts with the church, they are taught to pray to God for an answer to their prayers when faced by a personal problem. In their high school science courses they are taught cause and effect relationships. The clash of these two thought systems lies at the bottom of most of their religious worries. The Free Methodist minister said to the Sunday school early in February, "Rely upon the infinite wisdom of God; He will show you the way. Follow His path and trouble will never overtake you." The following week a teacher in the science class of the high school stressed cause and effect relationships in nature and used the weather as an example. The weather is of vital importance in this farming community where an early frost may do thousands of dollars' worth of damage to late-maturing crops, or a severe blizzard may kill livestock in unprotected areas. In late January 1942 an unseasonal thaw accompanied by torrential rains produced a sudden flood on a tributary to Indian River. Several hundred livestock on low ground were stranded and many were drowned; one family lost $12,000 worth of cattle in a few hours. This event was fresh in the memory of the children in the science class when the aforementioned discussion of cause and effect took place. At that time a devout Lutheran boy stated that he believed the flood was punishment for our entry into the war. A Free Methodist girl believed the flood could have been averted by prayer. In the course of the discussion, the teacher was alleged to have stated, "There are no miracles," in response to an earnest Lutheran girl's observation that a miracle could have saved the cattle, hay, and grain. This discussion resulted in confusion and some disillusionment for the girl, who later asked the minister, "If there are no miracles, what good are my prayers?" The minister defended his position, and attacked the high school for teaching blasphemous "rot." A

Baptist girl was puzzled by a similar experience. She related, "I was taught when I was a little kid that Christ was conceived by the Virgin Mary. Then in general science (freshman course) I learned there must be fertilization before life begins. A bunch of us kids talked about this the other day. We could not understand it: so I asked Mrs. Block in Sunday School, 'How could Mary have given birth to Christ if she was a virgin?' She was kinda confused for a minute, and she changed the subject. So I still don't know."

It is difficult for the serious student to reconcile the contradictions between what he learns in the religious compartment of his culture with what he is taught in school. His doubts on religious questions are increased particularly when representatives of the church deny facts taught in school without providing any proof beyond assertions that what they believe is "true" and the "facts" of science are "untrue," or when in a shamefaced manner they turn from the question the child asked to some other topic.[2]

Nonparticipation was very strongly associated with lower-class positions and participation with higher-class positions.[3] No significant differences were found for participation or nonparticipation by sex; the girls, however, have a higher participation than the boys in each social class, but the differences were insignificant. Participation was also affected by denominational factors.

From the study it is also apparent that students who participate in religious organizations carry the class system into the church; religious activities and religious clubs are definitely class biased. This undoubtedly explains to some extent the nonparticipation of lower-class groups. Were there both upper- and lower-class churches within denominations, different outcomes might be obtained.

Finally, a barrier exists between these adolescents active in the churches and the ministers. The young people band together and do what their class and age mates do; if they are caught in activities frowned upon by the church, they usually withdraw from the church. More generally, they hide their activities from the minister as they do from their teachers and parents, and happily go with the crowd.

There were differences, however, in attitudes taken by ministers toward youngsters with attendant differences in degrees of intimacy

---

[2] A. B. Hollingshead, *Elmtown's Youth* (New York, Wiley, 1949), pp. 244–245, 247–248. Used by permission.

[3] This is especially interesting in the light of the view of many that religion is an escape mechanism for "have-nots."

between ministers and students. The interested student will find many youth problems in religious areas dealt with at length in *Elmtown's Youth*.

THE ROLE OF RELIGION IN PERSONALITY INTEGRATION

WHAT THEN is or can be the function of religion in establishing standards in the orientation of the child? What is its role as an integrating principle in personality development and adjustment?

One basic assumption still frequently made is that the child must be "sent" to Sunday school with the hope that it will "do him some good." Research might well show that this practice is engaged in increasingly both by "lukewarm" church members and by people who are not on membership roles themselves. What they hope to gain except eventual confusion and bitterness as children grow, it is difficult to see.

As one author suggests, these parents are quietly desperate themselves, helpless against an organizational pattern which refuses to change and yet afraid to withhold religious training entirely. Hence, they send their children alone into what they do not themselves believe or will not participate in and salve their consciences by saying the children can decide for themselves when they are old enough.

Though it is essential to admit that research is not very conclusive on the point, evidence at this time does not indicate an appreciable difference in the real behaviors of church and nonchurch people. For example, marriage prediction studies show that church-connected people have somewhat higher happiness ratings in their marriages, while studies of character traits in Sunday school and non-Sunday school children reveal little difference between the two. Attitude studies have shown that on numerous questions of moral standards and ethical values, no appreciable difference appears between church members and nonmembers so far as their actual conduct is concerned, although differences in verbal response were noted.[4]

This does not say that religion does not affect the actions of children as well as adults. It does suggest that possibly organized

[4] John Cuber, *Sociology* (New York, Appleton-Century-Crofts, 1951).

Even in a secular culture, religion can be "fun" as well as a strong principle of personality integration and adjustment if properly mediated through family tradition and ceremony.

religion and certainly religion influence affect conduct, however indirectly, throughout the community.

Religion and organized religion must not be considered synonomous. If it were possible to conduct valid research in the area, it is not unlikely that large numbers of nonchurch members, especially among more educated levels, would fall well within the religious category. They remain to some extent within so-called Christian beliefs and build their lives around its practices without organized theology. Perhaps they do very well for themselves. Whether they do as well for and with their children remains an unanswerable question except as one receives hints from student papers and general remarks.

In fact, over the years the preoccupation with this area among students is amazing. One suspects that more than a few might echo the account penned by one student.

My parents were in open revolt against all organized religion. What they called the "corruptness of the clergy and the bigotry of the members" had soured them. They called themselves humanists, lived exemplary lives, and surely tried to direct us likewise. But somehow we children always felt something was lacking. I well remember wanting to go to Sunday school so I could sing in the choir and play on the basketball team, as I told my parents. Father was angry and snapped, "You see, just like I told you. No, son, you can go to a singing teacher and play at the school and at camp. Sunday school is just a place where they tell you things that aren't so," he finished. After that I couldn't tell him that I had added the choir and ball part to trick him, that when I had spent the weekend with a friend, I had gone to church with him and had thought the ritual, the pageantry, and the like thrilling. My friend, hesitant at taking me, had warned, "It's beautiful, but symbolic, old man, don't take it all literally." He needn't have worried. In fact, I hardly heard or saw the "words." The building, the atmosphere, the ritual, the symbols, and finally the ideas (with a grain of salt) spelled security roots. Children, I'm sure, need "institutions," family, school, *and church*. To have meaning and persistence ideas must have shape. That guy whose chart we studied was right.[5]

Another student wrote:

I don't know what churches can do to meet this problem of "character building and confidence giving," but I think the suggestions of Landis were very good.

The student was referring to the following analysis by Landis:

In a world of indefinite standards the emphasis upon religious duty and obligation is probably not sufficiently great to help adolescents and youths in maintaining standards. Elasticity in personality is required in a complex society, but few people can maintain integration in their life plan without some core values about which they can build. A religion that fails to provide these core values fails to meet its obligation to youth.

What the church should do to reconstruct its values and clarify its position as a character-building and confidence-giving social institution is a problem beyond the scope of this writing. Some general principles, however, can be enunciated. It is clear that the emphasis by orthodox

[5] Refer to the chart on page 201 by F. Stuart Chapin in *Contemporary American Institutions* (New York, Harper, 1935), p. 16. Used by permission.

TYPE PARTS OF THE STRUCTURE OF THE MAJOR SOCIAL
INSTITUTIONS

Four type parts	Family	Church	Government	Business
I. Attitudes and behavior patterns	Affection Love Loyalty Respect	Reverence Loyalty Fear Devotion	Subordination Cooperatives Fear Obedience	Workmanship Thrift Cooperation Loyalty
II. Symbolic culture traits, "symbols"	Marriage ring Crest Coat of arms Heirloom	Cross Ikon Shrine Altar	Flag Seal Emblem Anthem	Trade-mark Patent sign Emblem
III. Utilitarian culture traits (real property)	Home Dwelling Furniture	Church edifice Cathedral Temple	Public build-ings Public works	Shop Store Factory Office
IV. Code of oral or written specifications	Marriage license Will Genealogy Mores	Creed Doctrine Bible Hymn	Charter Constitution Treaties Laws Ordinances	Contracts Licenses Franchises Articles of incorpo-ration

religion upon certain rigid beliefs, many of them in contradiction to known scientific laws, is productive of mental confusion and unnecessarily puts the young person who accepts them in a position of moral quandary and mental strain. It is questionable that these dogmas have any necessary connection with man's proper relations with his Maker or with improved moral conduct.[6]

If this view is accepted, the next step would seem to be for the church to emphasize the great moral teachings of Christ, their direct application to current social affairs, and to identify religious worship and religious loyalty with the practice of these moral principles. Such a religion has logical validity, is in harmony with the Sermon on the Mount, and embodies the essential spirit of all Christian teaching. Such a religion applied to human relationships could be dynamic in human affairs and give the rising generation a motive for incorporating loyalty to deity in their system of beliefs.

The most reasonable field for the operation of religion in contemporary society seems to lie in providing for the mass organization of the group sentiment of mankind in support of the larger principles

[6] For a brief summary of the evidence indicating that dogmatic religious teaching may actually contribute to criminality, see Harry Elmer Barnes, *Social Institutions* (New York, Prentice-Hall, 1942), pp. 712–714.

of kindliness, sympathy, right, justice, honesty, decency, and beauty.[7]

The difficulty with religion of dogma, even when it succeeds well in indoctrinating children and giving them an effective basis for self-control, is that during adolescence and youth, when scientific understanding develops and the dogma is challenged, the whole foundation of self-control is shattered along with the destruction of faith in the dogmatic principles. The adolescent or youth is then left morally stranded until he re-establishes self-control on a new logical basis.

If the system of religious control could be built on a rational understanding of the laws of man's moral nature and of human obligation from the outset, many could accept the system who do not, and those who do accept would not have to go through the experience of debunking the childhood system of religious beliefs and their sanctions in order to maintain some degree of logical consistency in their views concerning the nature of life, God, and the universe. As it is now, many individuals suffer a great deal in the process of trying to reconstruct the religious foundation. Some are never able to make the reconstruction, and those who are forced to attempt it pass through a period of cynicism and skepticism. For these individuals religion loses in large part its effectiveness as a system of control, its value as a source of inspiration, and its importance as a focal point of character organization.

A second weakness of many denominational religious systems is that their religion is built into a system of narrow and restrictive social taboos that have no moral significance outside the narrow religious sect in which they are practiced. In extreme cases, this even calls for a distinctive dress. As adolescents and youths make the transfer to the out-group, they are forced to discard these restrictive social taboos and, because in their training the taboo was considered an inseparable symbol of piety, their religion goes with the taboo. If religious teaching could be identified with those broader principles of morality by which all civilized men must live—consideration for others, regard for one's own health, kindness, tolerance, etc.—there would never be a reason for discarding it as youth adjusts to the demands of the out-group.[8]

STUDENT CONCERNS IN THE AREA

SOCIOLOGY may be considered by many as merely an analysis of what is, not what to do about it. Students, however, take a more functional viewpoint. In no other area of child orientation do the questions come thicker and faster.

[7] Barnes, *op. cit.*, p. 706.
[8] Landis, *Adolescence and Youth, op. cit.*, pp. 194–196.

Over a three-year period 501 students were allowed to write "personal experiences" papers about any of the areas of child development which had posed greatest worries and problems for them as they grew, for them as parents now, or as parents of the future.

The area of religion and moral training was the sole topic of 121 papers. Only 75 did not mention the area. The remainder discussed it as one of several areas. As might be expected with single students and married students without children, the burthen of the papers dealt with their own doubts, fears, worries, and confusions. Without exception, however, they expressed concern as to how they would meet these problems with their own children. It is perhaps significant that only 16 people felt they had the answer within denominational frameworks from which they came.

Married students with children wrote a slightly different type of paper. They were concerned with their own problems as they related to their specific child or children. Of the married students with children, three retained childhood faith in entirety. They felt it must be passed on to children and felt the problem to be only how to offset hostile influences. The remaining expressed discontent not only with their own backgrounds but also with organized religion's present procedures.

It is interesting to note that students frequently made favorable mention of the trends in church-school nursery and kindergarten departments toward less formalized programs, activity set-ups which utilized craft, recreational, and other "aspects" from modern education. Their greatest concern seemed to center on the adolescent years and their unmet needs within creedal frameworks.

Out of all these papers came only *one* which outlined a deliberate and thoughtful attempt to work through the conflicts. As the writer says in her introduction, the plan undoubtedly has "holes," but, at least, it is a plan.

The curious thing about the paper is the response it has elicited when read to students. They exhibit not only attentiveness and interest in it as a "real life situation," but also often remark that it challenges, whether they agree or disagree with the aims and methods suggested.

We Chose Religion as an Integrating Principle

My husband and I came from what might be termed "indifferent" religious backgrounds. The only time my parents ever darkened church doors was for weddings and funerals and whenever family members were concerned, both kinds of occasions took place within the home.

As a child I was "let go" not "sent" to Sunday school. I liked to go and needed no urging. Until I went away to college I dragged my brother with me. After I left home, he didn't want to go alone, no one urged him, and he is so he now says, "religiously illiterate."

My husband, on the other hand, went to church with his parents if he wished. There was no parental insistence or guidance.

Since our marriage was rather carefully planned, we talked over this area as we did others and decided that we were deeply religious people but we were as yet not ready to select a denomination and assume allegiance to it. We would "check" the situation until children made the issue unavoidable.

It seemed no time at all until the day when the older child, at five a veteran of nursery school and kindergarten, remarked, "Mommy, what's this God business and where's his school? Can I go like Jimmy?" His sister was small; there was a church within a block with a liberal curriculum and so we took the easiest way out by one of us taking him to Sunday school while the other played baby sitter. But our makeshift arrangement backfired. We drew an elderly teacher with equally ancient ideas. Shortly there were for the first time in our experience night dreams, and, of all things, of Hell and fire.

In an attempt to do away with the dreams, we did away with Hell. The dreams stopped, but he no longer wanted to go to Sunday school. Two months later, an elderly neighbor lady died. Through my open window I heard the kids discussing the death. She had gone to heaven, she was happy, and at the thought so were they—all, that is, but one. In amazement I heard my son sobbing hysterically and shrieking, "She's dead and that's it. There's no Hell and so there's no Heaven."

We decided that night we had muddled through long enough. "Who would have thought," we said over and over, "that a just past six-year-old child would reason like that?"

We canvassed the denominations within our community in our thinking, not merely the creeds, but the church plant layouts, the rituals of the services, and, of course, attitudes toward youth groups.

Where creeds seemed liberal enough, we didn't like service rituals, and vice versa. Gradually, we became aware that only one denomination, the one we had visited most when we had attended church, would come near supplying the desired atmosphere by its plant layout, its ritual and pageantry, its symbols and symbolisms.

We would, we decided, face the real issues. We knew some of the dynamics of social change. We were acquainted with the needs of child development as different from those of child care. What we were really concerned about was the finding of a powerful *integrating* force.

We realized that art, social organizations, recreational programs, and the like fill that role for many. They must else why the shift from religion as noted by so many studies. Even textbooks in sociology on child orientation increasingly have no chapter devoted to religion as an important area in child life.

Then we thought over the people we knew who gave this area no place in their lives. Some rode a horse in all directions, "doing good" and then were hurt and angry when efforts were not praised or appreciated or brought no advancement at work or socially. Others were rank materialists. Their good social breeding forbade "bragging," but what brand name did it bear, where was it bought, how expensive was it, who designed it, seemed the value criteria which constantly rose to the surface.

Others were making a veritable religion of Freud, psychoanalysis, et cetera, by whatever name they called it. Others had what they called "philosophies of life" which contained, they told you repeatedly, all the principles of Christianity without the supernaturalism, the medieval trappings, and such infantilisms. They seemed to live pretty well with one another, but, like Shakespeare, we thought they "did protest too much" their adjustment, their happiness, etc.

Why were these various people never satisfied, never content to relax and enjoy, always critical and suspicious of the motives and actions of others? Fighting causes one might understand, but too much seemed to remain on the personality level. Also why were there so many who were willing to talk big in private gatherings, but had not the courage to take a stand publicly and be willing to take the results of the stand? Was expediency the only criterion of their characters? Was there no moral fiber? Were there no strong convictions?

This led easily to a discussion of what personality outcomes did we want. We knew at once that the values of democracy were ours, but we decided democracy was not enough. The people mentioned above believed loudly in democracy. It appeared it might be a cult, but it was still not religion enough to be the sole integrating principle for us. Many were obviously still searching through art, music, and the like. Others had just as obviously given up and had lapsed into cynicism.

Yes, we decided we'd chance religion as a balance wheel for these children and let art, music, and the rest function in complementary and supplementary fashions.

We agreed that Young spoke our viewpoint rather well when he wrote:
"I cannot accept the easy assumption of Freud and his followers that the mysticism and emotional and wishful thought generally found in religious experience constitute an 'escape from reality' or exemplify

but a 'mass neurosis' or a mere 'illusion.' Rather it is my belief that cultural reality, as it may be called, should not be regarded as something material or as made up out of biological reactions to food, drink, and sexual objects. It is at heart mental or psychological. It is a question of beliefs, attitudes, ideas, and meanings. It exists in the minds of men. One cannot, therewith, with Freud blandly dismiss religious experience as an unfortunate illusion without at the same time raising the question whether art, philosophy, and most of the fundamentals of social organization and family life are not likewise 'illusions.' Faithfulness to a mate, loyalty to a country, and belief in a banknote can be shown by this logic to be illusions too. Even material culture disappears without the support of its subjective meaning.

In the light of cultural approval of religious experience—that is, acceptance of this by one's fellow—and in the light of our broader definition of culture as mental or psychological, religious behavior cannot be considered 'an escape' from something superior or better or more real so much as a movement from one aspect of cultural reality to another. To deny the importance of significance of this other phase of reality is tantamount to denying the whole field of subjective thought and action based on personal wishes and fantasy. As Benedict puts it, 'The world man actually lives in—in the sense of his inescapable necessities and the inevitable conditions of life—always bulks very small in relation to the world he makes for himself.' " [9]

We were probably not too academically logical, but this is how we set down our aims, objectives, and procedures.

We felt that these children must be world citizens. This meant, we believed, that an adequate morality and religion could not be conceived of in purely Western terms. Somehow children who will grow to be citizens of a world community must be given insight, and appreciation (not just tolerance) not only of Judo-Christianity and Mohammedanism with their theistic forms, but also of Confucianism, Taoism, Buddhism, and Hinduism with their emphases on esthetic components.

We wanted these children to face life realistically and unafraid, by being able to work out a "unified" ideal, a philosophy of living, on the grounds of which they should be able to perform *constant self-analysis and continual life reconstruction.* We did not want this to remain merely an ethical gymnastic, however. Good works, humanistic enterprise, high moral principles, and the like are laudable enough, we decided, but the primary goal of religion must be growth in the knowledge and experience of the ultimate reality.

If the higher value of life could be established and if they could learn to operate in terms of it, then we felt sure their mental forces

[9] Kimball Young, *Personality and Problems of Adjustment* (New York, Appleton-Century-Crofts, 1940), pp. 788–789. Used by permission.

would be so integrated that conflicts would gradually disappear, and our integrating theory would succeed.

To produce this would mean promoting certain kinds of attitudes and beliefs as well as experiences. For example, intrinsic rewards for the action done rather than external rewards would be one center of attention. We wanted these children to be able to decide upon desirable actions and *perform them without attachment.* To use a commonplace statement, the "getting of the job done well is the important thing, not who gets the credit." Some have told us that such an attitude is impossible for children. We find it is more difficult for adults. Children, we think, are curiously able to take on and live by such concepts—if their total milieu operates that way. And after a time even that consistency isn't too important. For the approach seems to develop a calmness, an internal security, a peculiar, childish maturity, a center poise of existence which is apparent even to the casual onlooker.

So much for the attitude, what would be some fundamental beliefs? Since we are laity, our formulation was simple and went like this.

There is an essential core or unity in all religions. It consists of first, a belief in God as an all pervading force or principle, second, of man as potentially divine or as the children later put it, "a tiny shoot cracks off God and is in us if we can find it."

Therefore, the third important idea would be the establishment of a system of ethical behavior which would "allow" for attunement with the cosmic. The system of ethics could come directly from Christianity, but attunement we felt, must be more specifically trained for than is commonly done in Christian instruction. One does not jump headlong into "meditation" and "effective prayer." These processes must be learned and slowly. Here we would use the methods of the more esthetic religions, for mysticism can be practical and realistic.[10]

Fourth, if these things were so, it would be necessary to study all or many religions, teachers, and/or incarnations with a view to discovering the most effective techniques of attunement for each unique personality.

Fifth, we would be anxious to get across the knowledge that this viewpoint need not stand in the way of participation in organized religion (since alliance with groups seems advisable and desirable for many reasons), if they remembered that there are tenets of action. To most people religious behavior is largely concerned with following specific doctrines, rituals, and so forth. To some it is simply an emotional urge, for others an intellectualization process.

We would start where we were, usually with the use of concrete

---

[10] Edwin J. Dingle, *The Faultless Philosophy of Life* (Los Angeles, Institute of Mental-physics, 1930).

objects as symbols and hope to grow toward the intellectual oneness of life.

In a choice of a church then we would select the one whose ritual, church plant, and the like made the experience most conducive to concentration, meditation, and consequent attunement.

How should we implement the above was the next topic for consideration. Since this family organization was beamed toward democratic ideals and hence equalitarian arrangements, it would have to be a family project. It would have to be approached slowly and given developmental treatment.

Because of the boy's past experiences we expected slow development, possibly resistance. Circumstances decreed otherwise. The minister of the church from whose Sunday school we sought escape came to call. He was most effusive with the children. When he left, I said to the boy, "Son, he seems much interested in children; seems to like you."

He remained sitting with his chin in his hands and replied laconically, "That's 'cause you're here. You ought to see him at church. He bawls us out. I don't care for him."

"What shall we do about Sunday school, son?"

"Why that's easy. Let's go to the one Ace goes to. It's the same kind, and his father likes kids. You can tell, you know. He bawls you out if you need it, but it's different."

It was as easy as that. Ace was his special friend, and Ace's father was a minister. He knew the minister as a father and a person, admired his several talents, and gave evidence that during adolescence when the time came for hero-worship, this man would make an ideal object.

Sundays now had to be replanned, but it seemed worth the effort. Both children liked Sunday school and church when they attended on special days. The Christmas and the Easter seasons brought a multitude of questions. We decided the children's readiness was ripe for putting "meanings" into the scheme. Both Easter and Christmas stories provided a chance to study symbols, first the objects themselves, then their historical meanings and uses. Much of it they would forget until next year, but the "attitude" would remain.

Just as we were thinking that we must provide situations which would foster questions which would take us afield, the boy remarked, "Mike doesn't believe in Christ, but he says he's 'ligious too. Why doesn't he? Is he like those other folks called 'heathen'?"

So we moved into a study of Judo-Christian traditions and then to those "other" people. We could talk of Islam and the Far Eastern religions to adults, but we were stymied on how to introduce these topics to children.

Florence Fitch's books, replete with illustrations, saved the day.

Their historical and elementary theological approaches were just what we needed.

Came the day when the boy remarked, "Lots of things a lot alike in all these 'ligions.'" And not to be outdone his sister remarked, "And I like some of those things real well. Are they just for them? Why can't we do like Mommy when she makes a cake, mix 'em in with ours?"

"And can we leave out some things in ours we don't like? I don't like the cross with Him on it. But just a cross is nice," returned her brother.

A favorite request for the story hour was "tell us about olden times." One night we decided to tell them about really old times and selected the Roman family.

Next day after what was apparently connivance, they wanted to hear more about the household gods, the altar and the customs. Before we finished, one of them observed that a "house God and His altar would be fun."

The development of that altar has been one of the most fascinating family experiences. From what they knew of all the religions they decided to "build" it. What did we have? We had a small table which suited them. We had a raw silk cloth intricately embroidered by a Hindu friend which could serve as an altar cloth. We had a small bell beautifully wrought which had been given us by a Moslem friend. We had a tiny, nicely bound Bible and some candlesticks.

We needed, they thought, a cross and an incense pot. The story of incense and its usages in ritual and ceremony had intrigued them a lot. We undertook a buying excursion. Gravely they inspected the crosses. Which one?

"Not the one with Him on it. He's supposed to take care of you; what can He do up there?" said the sister.

"Yes, let's have it plain," agreed the brother.

The next decision involved what brother termed "background." Should there be a picture, a hanging, or a figure. To cut a long story short, they chose a lovely figurine of the Infant Jesus of Prague, and placed him with a mirror behind him. Why? We had read of an ancient custom which said that when people prayed, they should look searchingly into their own eyes—for obvious reasons.

And, of course, as sister added, "The red and gold on the back show up so pretty in the mirror."

When all was arranged, they decided it should be used, and they slowly evolved how they would do it. Like other "occasions" it must not become commonplace; so Friday night was decided on as a "good time." They never have needed to be reminded that it is Friday.

At first, they took turns lighting candles, everyone sang a song, repeated the Lord's prayer, there was a story, the candles were snuffed, and it was bedtime. Soon innovations began creeping in. They must march in, parts and roles were enacted, and a strange combination of "things" they liked occurred which might look like black magic to the uninitiated. They called this "playing church." Operating on the assumption that there is no irreverence in children, we have gone along with them. . . .

Though we know the difficulty of adult minds when it comes to synthesis, we hope these kinds of experimental backgrounds will provide such a wide area of appreciation and intelligent tolerance as to enable them to sift, sort, and eventually arrive at a working religion which will see them through. In short, we hope that as they grow and develop, they will gradually synthesize the theistic and esthetic components of all the world's great religions. A big order? No doubt, but worth trying for not only on an individual level but also on a world level.

Appraisal as to how we are succeeding has to come from language cues. A couple of recent samples are suggestive.

"Len says he doesn't go to Sunday School. He says it's a place where they tell you things that aren't so," said the sister.

"I asked him what he meant, and he said, 'Like all that about Jesus. My dad says history shows there never even was such a man.' "

"What did you say?" we asked as casually as possible.

"Oh," I just said, "Probably your Dad is nuts, and it doesn't matter whether he lived or not, it's the things he told about living that count." [11]

On the way home from church one morning brother was very quiet. Suddenly he said, "It doesn't make sense to me. It just doesn't make sense."

"What doesn't make sense, Son?"

"They say Nancy is a Catholic, Mike is a Jew, the lady who gave us the cloth is Hindu, and I'm ——————. But what's all the fuss about? There's only one God, and he's the same for all of them, isn't he? Grown-ups can be awfully silly, Mother."

---

[11] This, we gathered, was her response to what they had been told in "preparation" for the one of the circumstances they might expect to meet. Her father had said one night at story time, "Many do not believe that any man of flesh and bones named Jesus ever lived upon this earth plane but rather that some great masters, Avatars, or group of masters evolved the ideal character the ideal personality that became the religious character known as Jesus, and to them this character lives as truly today as the doctrines teach He lived centuries ago. To such people the character, attributes, actions, and doctrines generally attributed to Him are a composite of the ideals, doctrines, and actions of a number of great characters preceding the Christian era. To these people, whether Jesus actually lived as a man is unimportant, the teachings are."

Came the day also when brother remarked in confusion, "I prayed so hard it would happen, and it wasn't answered. I don't understand it."

In as nearly their terms as possible we explained that what many people called no answer was really just not the answer they expected or wanted and that very often that was good.

"Yes," said sister, "Yesterday I wanted that doll in the window and I said, 'Please God,' but I'm glad he said 'No,' 'cause today I saw another I'd rather have."

"Yes," returned her brother, thoughtfully, "But also I guess there are some things you just talk over with him and some you pray for like mother said."

"And don't forget," said small sister, "You have to do it right too; you probably didn't 'release' it right."

Childish wisdom which needs no comment!

Oh, theyll change as they grow. They'll outgrow all the childish customs perhaps, and they'll doubtless plow through agnosticism and even come close to atheism, but we are banking that their present, rather calm, emotional security will hold, that as sister said yesterday when she inspected the first tulip, "Lenny is sure crazy. Nothing as pretty as this 'just happened.'"

In material not recorded here, the student goes on to outline in detail the "method," which the family is using to implement the above premises and equipment. As to this couple's approach, student opinion was well summarized by the husband-wife combination paper stating:

On only one point would we disagree with this account. We feel that all that is necessary is *there* in Christianity, but it is not being dug out. We especially agree that to give it meaning and action the family must become interested in setting up what is in effect a family folk culture system of interpretation and enforcement. It's most attractive elements are that it produces security in the children, makes a working unit of the family group instead of just an aggragation of individuals, and in no way interferes with denominationalism. However modern and effective religious education programs in Sunday schools may be, the time is too short for adequate relation to living unless the family takes over in a very positive way.

SUMMARY AND IMPLICATIONS

IT HAS BEEN EMPHASIZED that in the relating of the individual to his society and culture the family institution is first both in point of time and as a continuing force.

Its role in a stable, sacred society is easily seen and enacted. *The* values, *the* rituals, and *the* rewards and punishments are of external derivation, therefore carefully outlined and, as carefully indoctrinated.

In a sensate, complex society such as ours, however, none of these aspects of living are so stabilized. Instead the growing child and his parents are faced with a wide breadth of choices in all areas, with the task as well as the challenge of achieving a center poise of existence which will provide "home base" from which to operate with a minimum of frustration within the cultural diversity.

It is perhaps worth noting that we do not say "without frustration." As indicated in Chapter 2, such a definition would imply balance and hence no growth. Since we cannot "stand still" by the very nature of the organism and society, retrogression is implied. The well-integrated person is then not the person with no problems but the child or adult who is able to face reality, define the problem, is able to share it with those who by professional training and/or experience are in a position to counsel and guide.

The problems may and will be different, the attitude and approach not so different.

Any churchman will tell you that one of the main functions of organized religion is the development of secure, well-adjusted personalities such as we are describing. Yet large numbers of students at every academic level give evidence of confusion, religious and moral as well as an interest in resolving it. They complain that the churches stress

creedal beliefs and ritualistic nonsense, the sense of sin and the saving of souls as the promise of a future life, that the church has taken a scolding attitude toward human weaknesses, built in complexes of fear and guilt, shame and remorse, with their paralyzing effects on thought and behavior, that it has made supernatural rewards and punishments the great motivations of human conduct, usually ignoring community and local social problems.[12]

Furthermore, studies concerning the impact of religious education on conduct are not impressive since indoctrinating children in religious creeds and ideology made no significant increase in socially approved behavior.[13]

[12] Lloyd A. Cook, *Community Backgrounds of Education* (New York, McGraw-Hill, 1938), p. 288.

[13] Mark, May, and Hartshorne, Hugh, *Studies in Deceit,* Vol. 1 (New York, Macmillan, 1928).

Forward-looking church leaders are well aware of these difficulties with the result that Sunday-school curricula and activities now in use in modern churches, as well as plant layout and methods of teaching, suggest that we are moving, however slowly, toward religious social education programs for children and youth.

On the other side of the ledger it should be noted that the lags and failures in the religious institutions are perhaps no worse, or greater, than in other social institutions. Here as elsewhere much of either success or failure is closely correlated with the clergymen in charge, as described in the Elmtown study. In reference to the local clergyman directly affecting them, one group of students wrote as follows:

Give us a man as priest, rabbi, or minister, who has knowledge of the physical, biological and social sciences; who likes people; who has sympathetic understanding when we go with our difficulties; who is accepting of our frailities; who believes in our sincere if differing viewpoints; who knows better than to use fear and guilt as means of control; who has insight enough to treat us man to man with no "holier than thou" long face. Give us such a human being and we would be willing to meet him more than half way, even to becoming involved in rituals and ceremonies which may have lost their meaning for many of us. In spite of the conflicts, the lags, and other difficulties, more of us would again elect religion as a principle of self-integration and self-adjustment.

TEACHING AND STUDY AIDS

1. What has been the influence of religious education in building character? Search the literature for further studies on this issue.
2. Make a survey of the Sunday school curricula of churches in your area. Do you find a trend away from traditional toward social education programs? Explain.
3. Build a questionnaire and make a survey of college students religious attitudes. Analyze your findings and report them to the class.
4. Make case studies of children, youth, or adults to discover their religious beliefs. Are they consistent with practices?
5. What was your reaction to the woman who wrote that she was trying to reconcile the "esthetic and theistic components of East and West?" Do you think synthesis possible? Why or why not?
6. Read and report on Albert E. Avey's *Re-thinking Religion* (New York, Holt, 1936).

7. Read and report on one of the following:
   F. S. C. Northrup, "Toward A Religion With Worldwide Transforming Power," in Bryson, Finklestein and MacIver, eds. *Conflicts of Power in Modern Culture* (New York, Harper, 1947).
   F. S. C. Northrup—The Meeting of East and West. An Inquiry Concerning World Understanding, 1946. Yale University Press.
8. Individually or as a committee read and critically analyze *Childhood Education Bulletin*, "Religion and the Child," A re-printing of all material published in the magazine relating to this area (Reprint Service Association for Childhood Education, 1946).

SELECTED READING REFERENCES

Akhilananda, Swami, *Hindu Psychology, Its Meaning for the West* (New York, Harper, 1946).

Aurobindo, Sri, *The Divine Life* (New York, Greystone, 1950).

Bernstein, Rabbi Philip S., *What the Jews Believe* (New York, Farrar, Straus & Young, 1951).

Bryson, Lyman, Finkelstein, Louis, and MacIver, Robert M., *Conflicts of Power in Modern Culture* (New York, Harper, 1947), Chaps. XXXV, XXXVI, XXXVII, XXXVIII.

Carlson, A. J., "Science and the Supernatural," *Scientific Monthly*, Vol. LIX (August 1944).

Dawson, Christopher, *Religion and Culture* (New York, Sheen and Ward, 1948).

Dewey, John, *A Common Faith* (New Haven, Yale University Press, 1934). A Report on Conference on Religion and Public Education at Princeton, 1944. American Council on Education.

Everett, J. R., "World Religions in the Building of Peace," in the Eleventh Yearbook of the John Dewey Society (New York, Harper, 1951), pp. 63–73.

Fallow, W., "Gains for Religious Education from Recent Research," *Religious Education*, Vol. 45 (1950), pp. 292–295.

Fitch, Florence, *Allah—The God of Islam* (New York, Lothrop, Lee, Shepard, 1950).

——, *One God—The Ways We Worship Him* (New York, Lothrop, Lee, Shepard, 1945).

——, *Their Search for God—Ways of Worship in the Orient* (New York, Lothrop, Lee, Shepard, 1948).

Folkman, Rabbi and Mrs. Jerome, *Democracy and Religion Begin at Home* (Columbus, Ohio, Committee on Pulpit Publications of Bryden Road Temple, 1948).

Folsom, J. K., "Spiritual Guidance Starts Early," *National Parent Teacher,* Vol. 45 (March 1951), pp. 7–9.

Jensen, J. A., "Interrelations of Religious and Ethnic Attitudes," *Journal of Social Psychology,* Vol. 32 (August 1950), pp. 45–49.

Kubie, L. S., "New Approaches to Old Problems," *Child Study,* Vol. 27, No. 3 (1950), p. 73 ff.

Madden, W., "Education for Religious Quality in Experience," *Harvard Educational Review,* Vol. 21, No. 1 (1951), pp. 14–31.

Magnusson, M. A., "Audio-visual Resource Guide for Use in Religious Education," *International Journal of Religious Education,* Vol. 26 (March 1950), p. 31 ff.

Meyer, H. H., ed., *Education,* Religious education number, Vol. 71 (February 1951), pp. 343–404.

Northrop, F. S. C., *The Meeting of East and West: An Inquiry into World Understanding* (New York, Macmillan, 1947).

"Trends in Religious Education, a Symposium," *Religious Education,* Vol. 46 (January 1951), pp. 7–47.

Tschechielin, M. A., "Educate the Whole Child," *Education,* Vol. 71 (February 1951), pp. 393–396.

Ziegler, J. H., "Is Religious Education Fulfilling Its Function?" *Religious Education,* Vol. 45 (November 1950), pp. 357–362.

IX MASS MEDIA OF COMMU- NICATION AND CHILDREN

BEYOND THE AREAS of person to person interaction, such as family and play groups, lie the vast, often bewildering, increasingly potent purveyors of ideas, the media of mass communication. In the past twenty-five years the literature has been filled with the fears and worries, and later the studies, of the effects of movies, radio, comics, and, more recently, television on childhood. Consequent efforts at control of these impressers of children have taken both censorship and education in the use and evaluation of these various agencies.

Here and there parents and teachers still deplore and look with nostalgia on a day when there were none of these competitors for the time and interest of the child. "Then," say these prophets of doom, "a child could sit down with a good book and think without distraction."

This wish might astonish parents of not so many generations ago who looked upon books themselves as breeders of idleness and daydreaming. When the invention of printing made books available to everyone, pleasure reading was first forbidden, then restricted. Not so many years ago *Gulliver's Travels* and *Huckleberry Finn* were forbidden reading for the young. Today we not only accept books, but also we hope and sometimes insist that our children read them. Indeed, many parents now resist comics, radio, and movies on the ground that they take time which might otherwise be spent with "a good book." Sooner or later, however, we shall probably accept these new developments, too, and learn to use them as we have learned to use books.[1]

[1] Josette Frank, *Comics, Radio, Movies, and Children,* Public Affairs Pamphlets No. 148 (New York, Public Affairs Committee, March 1949). Used by permission.

Educators and parents alike ask in general two questions about mass media. What identifiable effects do they have upon children? What can we do about it?

As we study these problems, students are interested in novel ways of presenting what they find. One such project was the one presented here.

The students who participated investigated children's literature and bibliotherapy, comics, radio, movies, and television, and then decided to present their material in the form of a dramatization. Indicative if not exhaustive in data, it includes the questions we have found often asked in child-study groups. Though this is a departure from traditional textbook form, students have not "winced or cried aloud." We hope its novelty will appeal equally to present readers.

Children's Literature, Comics, Radio, Movies, Television, and Our Children

(All the characters in this play, with the exception of Mr. Baer, are purely the product of the author's imagination; if they resemble any real persons, it is indeed a coincidence. We have tried very hard to give all reference backgrounds for our play. If we have omitted any it is because like Milton, we remember too well. The committee wishes also to make mention of the fact that much of the material on children's reading is based upon class lectures of Dr. Leland Jacobs. Committee members: Sally Casement, Ward Cramer.)

CHARACTERS

MRS. BASEMENT ..... *President of Child-study Group*
DR. BOBBINS .... *Professor of sociology*
DR. JACOBSON .... *Professor of children's literature*
DR. LITTLE .... *Child psychologist*
MR. BAER .... *Comic-strip author*
DR. BALE .... *Social research director*
DR. SOFORTH .... *Dr. Bale's assistant*

SCENE ONE

This scene takes place in the home of Mrs. Basement, where she is entertaining the members of the Child-study Group. It is early in the evening. The parents are seated informally on one side of the room and Mrs. Basement and her guest speakers are seated on the other side of the room, facing the members of the group. As the scene opens, Mrs. Basement is speaking.

MRS. BASEMENT: When I was asked to select the subject matter for this evening's meeting, I was almost at a complete loss. Since this is the last meeting, topics are almost exhausted. I asked not only Mr. Basement for suggestions, but my children as well, and they helped matters very little. Not so long ago, I overheard Billy, a precocious child and playmate of my children, say that I was a dreadful mother because I allowed my children to read comics! I must admit that my children are also ardent radio fans of mystery plays and superman. What worries me is that so many parents, including myself, do not completely understand children's interests. So, tonight, I would like to bring before the group some of these interests, mainly books, radio and comics, and television. It gives me great pleasure to have people of authority on these subject matters, who have kindly accepted the task of giving us information on said subjects. First we have Dr. Bobbins, professor of sociology; next to Dr. Bobbins is Dr. Jacobson, professor of children's literature; on my left is Dr. Little, child psychologist; and next to Dr. Little is Mr. Baer, author of modern comic strips. Dr. Bale, social research director, Dr. Soforth, Dr. Bale's assistant.

(*The group applauds after each introduction, as each guest speaker stands momentarily. Dr. Jacobson remains standing.*)

DR. JACOBSON: It is indeed a pleasure to be here this evening, and I can safely say that we shall all speak as parents, since it is a known fact that Dr. Bobbins, Dr. Little, Mr. Baer, Mrs. Basement and myself are all parents—therefore, we speaketh as parents as well as so-called masters of our professions!

(*Everyone laughs*)

MRS. BASEMENT: Dr. Jacobson, since you have opened the conversation, would you start our discussion tonight? Perhaps books?

DR. JACOBSON: I shall be glad to talk about books, Mrs. Basement. Modern education has made long strides, and children's books have followed its path. Within the past few years there has grown a literature for children which addresses them as intelligent and reasonable people with tastes and interests and pleasures not unlike our own. Educators and psychologists insist upon children's reading not only as an instrument for their education, but also as a necessary part of their emotional experience as well. It is a known fact that we parents try to choose our children's reading material, but it is impossible to restrict their readings to what we choose for them. Therefore, we must both choose books for them and at the same time leave them free to choose their own. If we guide children's interests, we must know their particular tastes and interests, and also what they are likely to want at certain stages of their development. But we must not mold them into preconceived patterns of what the well-read child should read. We should encourage them to find their way to real experiences of their own in this world of books. Their reading guide will guide us.

MRS. BASEMENT: Dr. Jacobson, what shall we expect the children to get from their readings?

DR. JACOBSON: Well, they should get knowledge about the world they live in, and not information only, but interpretation also to satisfy their growing needs to know about people everywhere. Books bring the world to their door. They get a contact with man's treasures of thought, past and present, and reading plays a large part in shaping their thinking, in forming their character, and their standards, ideals and inspirations. And I'm sure that most of you will agree with me that reading itself is a great pleasure for a lifetime; so children read for profit and pleasure as well.

MRS. BASEMENT: Dr. Jacobson, I have been told by many parents that reading makes the child much brighter. Do you agree with that?

DR. JACOBSON: Yes, Mrs. Basement, many parents think that children should read as it is a symbol of intelligence, but whatever they wish, they must not make books the tool of their wishings.

PARENT: Dr. Jacobson, may I ask a question?

DR. JACOBSON: Why yes, please do.

PARENT: Do children read just for information?

DR. JACOBSON: Children read for various reasons. Some read for information, as you mentioned, as they are impelled by desire to know more about the world. Some read for vicarious experiences to push back the boundaries of this circumscribed life. Most children and adults have a yearning and capacity for experience which outruns the limitations imposed upon them by social living. For them books are new worlds to conquer. The ability to imagine oneself the hero or heroine of storied adventure or romance is a priceless gift of childhood. Some children find in reading an escape or a refuge from the humdrum of routine life; they find in reading an outlet for thoughts and emotion of which no overt expression is permissible in civilized living. Such children will seek out stories which mirror their own problems. Identifying themselves with the hero or villain, they may indulge their passions with guilt. Of course, we have children who read chiefly for fun—just to pass the time pleasantly; and then some children read for all these reasons, though not necessarily at the same time.

PARENT: Dr. Jacobson, what kind of books should a child read?

DR. JACOBSON: (laughing) Your question is comparable to one I heard recently from a parent. She asked me what kind of music should her child listen to! There are several types of books. We are all familiar with the classics, such as *Robinson Crusoe, Winnie the Pooh, Hiedi,* and others. Many parents believe that their children should read the classics just because they read them when they were children. Of course, the classics are books which have lived beyond the author's time, and these books have stood the test of time. Also, they are selected by authorities. But we must remember that some of these children's classics were not really written for children but for adults. These books were appropriated by children, such as *Moby Dick.* Most of the classics today are for older children, and few or none were written for the very young child. Our younger readers, ages ranging from two to six years, prefer here and now stories. By that, I mean everyday activities bustling about them. Life is complex and complicated for the youngster who is trying to understand the world about him. They prefer nursery jingle and picture books with or without a brief story that is close to home, such as stories about familiar animals, toys, and children. Children of seven and eight years of age like stories about other children and less familiar animals; also fairy and fanciful tales begin to compete with reality. Stories of the here and now give place to those of long ago. The interest span is lengthening, and stories can carry the attention from one day's reading to the next. The eight or nine year olds demand plenty of action—something has to be happening. Their world widens further, and stories of history and other people's tales are added. The approaching teens, from ten years on, is the age of chivalry, myths, legends, and high adventure on land and sea. This is an age of sampling and discarding, of growing toward tastes and preferences. So you see, age levels certainly must be considered in selecting a book for a child.

PARENT: Dr. Jacobson, I read recently that fairy tales are harmful for children and that they add nothing to their education. Is that true?

DR. JACOBSON: To the child the fairy tale represents art, fantasy, religion—all shock absorbers! So says Fritz Wittels in an article taken from *Child Study.*[2] She also says that the fairy tale in its lonely innocence is in harmony with the mind of the child, compromising the wishes of the child with demands of ethics. The child in his need will create new fairy tales out of his own fantasies, wild products of imagination which would fail to fulfill the aim of the fairy tale with the same utility as do the old motifs, stamped into relatively few forms for countless ages. Fairy tales keep a child from reality, and they cannot be uprooted by our commissaries of progressive education. However, Elsa Naumburg approaches this subject two different ways. The sentimentalist believe fairy tales are a universal literature and language. They help to develop a child's mind, and they embody the concepts of life and characters by which race has explained itself. Also, she says that fairy tales develop ethical standards of right and wrong and they en-

[2] Fritz Wittels, "The Fairytale," *Child Study,* Vol. IX (November 1931), pp. 67–69.

large a child's emotional experiences by introducing him to other homes and customs. The realist looks at fairy tales differently. He believes that fairy tales are a record of a crude past and that they perpetuate the elements of superstition and the animistic attitude toward life. The realist believes that fairy tales depict an unknown environment and confuse a child as to what is real and what is imaginary.

PARENT: Dr. Jacobson, what do *you* mean by fairy tales?

DR. JACOBSON: I think of animal stories, with talking beasts, droll or realistic humorous tales, nursery tales, folk tales, myths, legends, fables, and many others. No doubt, most of you are or have been familiar with *Grimm's Fairy Tales?* Well, if so, think about them as I point out the significant elements of these tales. First, we find a simple plot with few characters. The environment is imaginative and magical, and much exaggeration is used. The whole interest centers around the action of miraculous events and quick transformation; and punishment and reward follow the deed. Children are delighted with animal stories, such as *Three Little Pigs, The Wind in the Willow,* and numerous others. When a young child learns the true characteristics of animals, then he is ready, if he likes, to read stories of talking animals, since he is able to distinguish between the two.

PARENT: Then you believe that fairy tales should be included in a nine-year-old's library?

DR. JACOBSON: Fairy tales affect a child no more than a gangster comic book. This is not true for all children, of course. Parents can usually tell whether the child is sensitive to such reading by reading a few stories to him and watching the results. We should believe in the household tales to the extent that the right child be given them to read. There are some children who might be emotionally unable to read the household tales, and I think that it is the responsibility of the parent who reads such tales to see that the child is not greatly affected by them. These stories have lasted for many years and this is a good argument—because they have been popular for so long. Dr. Little would you make a comment on the subject?

DR. LITTLE: (rising) Within the past few decades the desirability of fairy tales for children has come into serious question from authoritative sources. Psychiatrists and educators have challenged them as offering too easy solutions of life, placing too little premium on effort and endeavor. They say that fanciful literature might tend to confuse the very young listener already struggling to find a footing among the realities of a complex world. This was pointed out also by Mr. Jacobson. These stories help children to experience emotions which otherwise might have been repressed. They are not realistic, but I believe that it is necessary for children to escape reality and daydreams to a certain extent. Of course, this can be carried too far, but most children are adjusted fairly well to the realistic world, and daydreaming is only occasional for children over six or seven.

DR. JACOBSON: Thank you, Dr. Little. (Dr. Little sits down.) I'm afraid that my time is about up, but before I close this talk, I would like to mention briefly something on illustrations in children's literature. Juvenile literature offers simple, imaginative, picturesque, and often aesthetic possibilities in the way of illustrations which few of the best illustrators have been able to resist. You will find the best illustrated books more expensive, but they are good economy in the end since best literature attracts the best artists. Good present-day illustrators for children bear these principles in mind. They think of the interests which children possess and that which will satisfy those interests and at the same time lead toward an appreciation of the highest art. The artist, without being introspective or retrospective, must project his view in such a manner that he contrives to get a child's point of view. If he instructs, he must stock a child's imagination with pictorial facts outside the child's experience. Also, he must train a child's eye to appreciate harmony of color and line, but first of all, he must seek to interest and entertain. The artist does this by producing simple, brightly colored pictures, or suggestive black and white ones in which there is little detail, but much action. In closing I would like to say that one book of pleasing proportions, with good paper, attractive print, wide margins, artistic bindings, and beautifully conceived illustrations which fit a worthwhile book is worth a dozen cheap editions of the same book.

MRS. BASEMENT: Dr. Jacobson, before we leave the topic of children's books, would you give us some guides for selecting them?

DR. JACOBSON: I should be delighted to try that assignment. I think that one might well ask the following questions concerning the book he selects for a child:

1. Is the book suited to the mental age of the child?
2. Is the subject matter interesting to this particular child? Does he really enjoy it?
3. Is the content of the book worthwhile? Will it stand reading and rereading or is it a trivial book that will be looked at once and then put aside?
4. Is the content of the book childlike and desirable *throughout?* Adults sometimes fail to recognize the very important point that books for little children often *go over into action*—the child draws, or dramatizes what is read to him, or incorporates it into his speech.
5. Is the book well bound and durable? Many books come to pieces when children handle them.

6. Is it suitably illustrated? A book should be artistic, but *on the child's level,* not merely pleasing to the adult eye. The pictures must have real meaning for children.
7. Is it well written? If adults would take the time to read through the books which they buy for children, a number of books would be thrown aside on account of careless, slipshod English, lack of anything that lifts the story above the ordinary, or actual "writing down" to the child.[3]

Some other cautions are as follows:

1. Tales of thieves, robbers, dare-devils, brutality, trickery, and immortality should be avoided for they may cause fear or lead older children to perform some of the feats portrayed.
2. Stories of magic may discourage a child to meet difficulties squarely.
3. Books that make real life seem uninteresting should not be given the child.
4. If a child wants to look at books or read all the time, he needs to be encouraged to take part in other activities.

MRS. BASEMENT: Thank you, Dr. Jacobson. Children used to be and still are an added joy to a family. Radio was an added joy to a family, but whether it is still an added joy is an enigma! I would like to read this poem which I once discovered in a magazine.

> Between the dark and the daylight,
> When the night is beginning to lower,
> Comes a pause in the day's occupation,
> That is known as the Children's Hour.
>
> Then endeth the skipping and skating,
> The giggles, the tantrums, and tears,
> When, the innocent voices abating,
> Alert grow the innocent ears.
>
> The little boys leap from the stairways,
> Girls lay down their dolls on the dot,
> For promptly at five o'er the. airways,
> Comes violence geared to the tot.
>
> Comes murder, comes arson, come G-men
> Pursuing unspeakable spies;

[3] Alice Dalgliesh, *First Experiences with Literature* (New York, Scribner, 1932). Used by permission.

Come gangsters and tough-talking he-men
With six-shooters strapped to their thighs;

Comes the corpse in the dust, comes the dictum
"Ya' better start singing, ya' rat!"
While the torturer leers at his victim,
The killer unleashes his gat.

With mayhem the twilight is reeling.
Blood spatters, the tommy guns bark.
Hands reach for the sky or the ceiling
As the dagger strikes home in the dark.

And lo! with what rapturous wonder
The little ones hark to each tale
Of gambler shot down with his plunder
Or outlaw abducting the mail.

Between the news and the tireless
Commercials, while tempers turn sour,
Comes a season of horror by wireless
That is known as the Children's Hour.[4]

DR. BOBBINS: Apparently many of you have experienced this sup-
pertime ritual! The average child of school age spends many hours a
week in listening to radio programs. In some studies the estimate runs
as high as two or more hours per day, but the time varies with different
children and in different localities. In another study it was found that
children of high intelligence in a private school spend only about half
as much time at the radio as did less privileged children in the same
city. In the case of certain types of radio programs, there are definite
age trends in children's interests and differences between the preferences
of boys and girls. However, many programs have a high degree of popularity with children differing in age, sex, socio-economic status, and
intelligence. Popularity depends upon the particular programs that happen to be available in a given locality, the extent to which two or more
popular programs compete with each other at the same period, shifts
in the radio schedule, and other similar factors.

Recent surveys show that a larger proportion of adult programs
are now among children's favorites, partly because there has been some
decline in the number of blood-and-thunder children's programs in re-

[4] Used by special permission of the author and copyright owner, Berton
Braley, 1025 Graybar Bldg. New York City, 17.

cent years. Among programs that decline in popularity as children grow older are dramatizations of fairy tales and other programs of a frankly make-believe sort. Certain adult comedians who supply a relatively broad type of humor, supplemented by slapstick, have a strong appeal at all age levels, while comedians whose humor is of a more subtle variety are likely to rank relatively lower at the early age levels and then gain in popularity with advancing age. Dance music and romantic serials gain an increasing audience in the teens, and there is a rising trend with age in the popularity of sports, quiz programs, general news, and programs dealing with hobbies, historical dramas, and other quality dramas. In general, boys show a higher preference than do girls for crime and violence programs. Girls show a higher preference for domestic drama, crooners, and movie stars. Both boys and girls, however, tend to prefer a cast of characters which includes older children or adults rather than child characters only.

PARENT: Dr. Bobbins, what is the effect of radio programs on a child's fears? Someone told me that children often dream of some of the gruesome stories and characters heard on the radio.

DR. BOBBINS: Many children are frightened while listening to an exciting program, and many of them say that programs, perhaps of a "chiller-killer" nature have influenced their fears and dreams. Sometimes these fears are related specifically to radio programs; but often the radio may have had only an incidental influence on fears and anxieties which spring primarily from other factors in the child's life.

PARENT: Dr. Bobbins, is it up to the parent to help select or encourage certain types of radio programs for their children?

DR. BOBBINS: In many homes there is a discrepancy between the radio tastes of children and their parents, just as there sometimes was a clash between children and parents of an earlier generation on the subject of the dime novel. The programs children like best are the ones some parents dislike most. Johnny may be engrossed over "Superman," but his mother awaits eagerly the end of Johnny's hero. When children in large numbers prefer programs that adults deplore, there may be right and wrong on both sides.

Often times, the adults are prone to judge a program in terms of their own adult point of view. I believe that Dr. Jacobson mentioned this point on book selection. Many parents select a book for a child because they think it is cute or funny or educational; the child's taste and preference were not consulted or respected. A program that seems trashy to an erudite adult may still be suitable for a child, just as a child's dress may fit her well even though it doesn't fit her mother. There is another aspect to this, however. The fact that a child is interested in a program doesn't necessarily mean that the program fills a need. Also, the critical adult has grounds for complaint, not against the child but against the broadcaster, if a children's program simply takes advantage of a child's lack of knowledge and discrimination and plies him with distortions and humbug when a more competent script writer might meet the child on his own ground with a more genuine treatment.

PARENT: Dr. Bobbins, is it true that children listen to radio thrills to escape boredom?

DR. BOBBINS: In seeking vicarious excitement and thrills, children are not showing a novel form of behavior. They seek similar thrills in books, and our mothers and grandmothers similarly found vicarious adventure in their own make-believe. *Treasure Island* and *Tom Sawyer* satisfied the adventurous souls of our parents, and I don't think it ambiguous to say that many youngsters were read *Treasure Island* before they were able to read themselves. If you have an antipathy toward "Superman," you deplore the excitement found in this radio thriller, even though your child can take it in his stride and show no harmful effects.

PARENT: Dr. Bobbins, if we parents aren't more understanding about our children's tastes in radio programs, don't you think that they will have little or no chance of developing fine taste in the arts, music, and dramas when they reach adult maturity?

DR. BOBBINS: (smiling) Since radio is part of our everyday living, so to speak, we must look at it broadly. The child can't be isolated from the bad things of life, but you can expose and interest the child in other interests as well as these radio chillers. In time, the child will have his fill, and he will develop other interests. Of course, if the child has not been taught or encouraged to have other interests, he may be very limited. If the child has nothing better to do, radio programs may become his main interest.

PARENT: Dr. Bobbins, would there be any point in punishing a child if he insists on listening to it for hours?

DR. BOBBINS: Well, that is difficult to say. Many mothers listen to soap operas all day, and when the child is ready to listen to his favorite program at dinner time, it isn't fair to deprive him of the same thing the parent has had all day. Rather than using the term punishment, I like to use guidance, by means of which you can change the child's unfavorable behavior to a better form of behavior. If parents are plagued with the problem of a child over-indulging in radio, they may try to change his interests to other types—such as a workshop, painting or the like—and the best form of interest will win, radio or hobby.

PARENT: Dr. Bobbins, I believe that radio is breaking up home life. (Everyone laughs) I don't mean to be facetious, but I can't help but believe that our children hear nothing but trash day after day.

DR. BOBBINS: In contrast to the many community factors which tend to break up home life, the radio has often been considered a factor for strengthening home life. A study made by Azriel L. Eisenberg in 1936 of more than 3000 children in New York City gives us some information on how the radio influences our home life. The author listed certain favorable influences exerted by the radio. It was pointed out that the radio has tended to provide amusement in the home and has, therefore, influenced people to spend more time at home. Family programs have tended to increase respect for marriage and family life. Certain programs encourage constructive recreational activities and hobbies and thus tend to widen skills and interests of both children and adults.

DR. LITTLE: I would like to add that the widespread use of the radio in school rooms has come so recently that the effect of such teaching instruments has not yet been adequately studied. Dr. Bobbins stated how the radio has influenced family life, but what about television? Of course, it isn't so widespread as the radio but it soon will be. Why, people will even stop going to movies, sports events, and the like. I do believe that more time will be spent at home by all of the members of the family.

DR. BOBBINS: I quite agree with Dr. Little, and I foresee the problem as to what members of the family will be most likely to succeed in selecting programs! (Everyone laughs) I would like to add before concluding my talk that public opinion controls radio programs. Organized resistance by certain groups of parents, of whom the New York Child Study Association is outstanding, has gradually forced commercial advertisers to put fewer vicious programs on the air during the five- to seven-o'clock hours, considered as the children's hour. Comparable to the gradual increase in production of historical or educational commercial movies, the same type of insistence on the part of the radio public has greatly improved the quality of children's radio programs offered by commercial advertisers. It has been seen that children can be helped to like the better programs, and this can be done more effectively if children are stimulated to an interest in the better programs than it can be if adults adopt negative or critical attitudes toward the poorer programs. I have for you some *Teachers' Manuals* of Ohio School of the Air which some of you may be familiar with already. We hope in the future for a more subdued and less nerve-racking children's hour. (Dr. Bobbins sits down.)

MRS. BASEMENT: (rising) Dr. Little, I believe comics are in order.

DR. LITTLE: Thank you, Mrs. Basement. Most children from an early age are interested in comics in the form of comic strips, comic books, and serial comic magazines. And I dare say that just as many adults are interested in the comics. Many people have asked me if comics are harmful. Numerous people flatly blame them as the cause of much juvenile delinquency. Just what do comics have to lure our little readers?

Before we go into more detail, let's go back to the first modern comic book back in 1911 which was a collection of Bud Fisher's "Mutt and Jeff." This comic book was offered to the public for a few cents with six coupons from succeeding issues of the daily paper. These comics sold like "hot cakes," and you know the rapid success of comics since then. It is obvious from the fact that most children, and a large proportion of adults, are drawn to the comics, that there is something in the comic strip format which has a strong appeal. This fact should be taken into account for practical purposes. The comics have been used by some workers in connection with the teaching of reading. A study made by Edward L. Thorndike indicates that the volume of reading material represented by twelve monthly issues of a popular comic serial was equivalent approximately to the contents of two standard-sized fourth-grade readers. In other words, while the pictures no doubt provide the lure, the comic book provides the child with a good deal of opportunity to obtain practice in reading. However, just how much of the printed matter the average child at various age levels actually reads was not ascertained in Thorndike's study.

PARENT: Dr. Little, don't you believe that most of the comic books are harmful for our children and perhaps too excitable?

DR. LITTLE: Sometimes it seems as if comic books are exciting parents more than they are supposed to excite youthful readers. At least there have been quite a number of irate elders and a few psychiatrists breaking into print lately with charges that the comics are totally bad, and that they are corrupting children's taste, degrading their morals, and encouraging crime.

Excitable people frequently accuse certain books, magazines, movies, and plays of doing the same thing to adults. The difference is that parents are inclined to fire a broadside of condemnation at the whole field of comic books rather than concentrate on individual offenders. This approach, we believe, is wrong on three counts.

It implies the need of censorship—a malignancy that can spread rapidly once it gets a start.

It complicates the job of cool-headed civic and parent groups and responsible publishers who are trying to promote the better comic books and discourage the reading of trashy ones. It exaggerates the importance of comics as an evil force in the lives of American children. Any kid needs some vicarious adventure in his life. The comics help fill that need, as the dime novels did before them. A youngster's taste in adventure stories runs to simple problems solved by simple means. Parents often are shocked when these solutions are achieved with the help of fists, knives, and guns. But if a child is healthy and happy, it isn't likely that he is going to absorb enough poison from blood-and-thunder cartoon books to steer him toward a career of crime.

The comics have been held responsible for juvenile murders. Perhaps the children involved thought that they got the inspiration to kill from a comic book. Maybe their parents and the authorities thought so too. We don't. A comic book might provide a suggestion but not a motive. If a youngster shuts himself up in the unreal world of lurid comics to the point where they seem to dictate his actions, there must be something pretty bad in his real world from which he is trying to run away.

Juvenile delinquency is the product of pent-up frustrations, stored-up resentments, and bottled-up fears. It is not the product of cartoons and captions. But the comics are a handy, obvious, uncomplicated scapegoat. If the adults who crusade against them would only get as steamed up over such basic causes of delinquency as parental ignorance, indifference, and cruelty, they might discover that comic books are no more of a menace than *Treasure Island* or *Jack the Giant Killer.*

Many of the questions with respect to standards, good taste, and possible good or harmful effects that arise in connection with the comics are much the same as the questions that arise in connection with radio programs. Through these media of entertainment the child is permitted vicariously to do many things he would not be allowed to do in fact. While parents and teachers are trying to teach the child to be kind, these media sometimes condone cruelty, as when the hero is allowed to knock down his helpless victim or the hapless wolf in the animated cartoon is systematically tortured. While parents and teachers are trying to teach the child not to solve his problems by violence, these media sometimes portray heroes who proceed with brutal force. While the school is seeking to promote good human relationships, these media sometimes have portrayed members of a minority group as being characteristically menial or stupid people. While the home and school have been trying to promote respect for law and order, these media have sometimes glorified crime by portraying criminals in a glamorous light. I have just pointed out that one viewpoint which has been advanced is that crime, physical violence, and various other forms of aggressiveness in children's radio programs, movies, and comics might actually have a good psychological effect.

PARENT: Dr. Little, I don't see any good psychological effect which crime stories in comic books could have on our children.

DR. LITTLE: According to this viewpoint which I have just stated, the child, as he identifies himself with the action, may give play to his aggressive impulses, or wield power which he would like to possess in real life, or satisfy other unfulfilled desires. In a make-believe or vicarious setting, according to this view, he gives vent to feelings which have arisen in response to actual conditions in his everyday life and he thus is relieved from tension and strain. It would be pleasant, indeed, if these media of entertainment thus enabled a child safely and comfortably to "let off steam," to get things off his chest, and so enable him to resume the prosaic business of life in a more serene and relaxed frame of mind. So you see, not all effects of comics are bad.

PARENT: Dr. Little, what are the criticisms of the comics?

DR. LITTLE: Most frequent criticism of the comics is directed at the crudeness of their drawings and drama, at the relatively immature level of their language, humor, and sentiments. There is a tendency to apply to each new form of technique or expression criterions of performances which turn out to be irrelevant. We ignore sometimes what is distinctive and significant in the new medium. The very qualities for which the comics have been condemned by critics give them force and make them socially significant. So, it is these qualities which enabled them to catch and hold interest of children and which today make them more easily apprehended by people of all ages than sermons, political speeches, or the most popular newspapers. In judging the comics and their effect on American youth, I would like to call on Mr. Baer, prominent in this field. Mr. Baer, take over, if you please.

MR. BAER: Thank you, Dr. Little. When we began our comic strip, *The Toodles,* in 1941, husband-and-wife teams in the field were a rarity. Neither of us was able to draw, and we had never written a line for publication, although we had had many years of close contact with cartoonists and syndicate men. We wanted to do a family strip, but crime, blood and thunder, and sex were all the rage. Family life, we were told, was not different enough, not exciting enough to sell to an editor. The American public wanted thrills.

Despite all these warnings and tips from well-meaning, experienced syndicate people we were amateurs enough to venture into this most competitive field of entertainment, in which about a hundred cartoonists attempt to entertain about seventy million people. Even more than that, we insisted on carrying out our idea of doing a continuity strip about modern American family life as we saw it.

Thus, *The Toodles* came into being in the raucous, confused days just before Pearl Harbor. As the war progressed, we were particularly happy that we had stuck to our guns in our choice of subject. Letters from soldiers and sailors all over the world told us that *The Toodles* reminded them of their own families.

Our experienced friends had also warned us to remember to write *down* to the public, which was supposed to have an IQ not above that of the average twelve-year-old child. (Some of our colleagues went so far as to speak of the cartoon audience as morons.) This we refused to believe, or to act upon. There must be, we felt, enough intelligent readers to welcome a sensible, homey, humorous cartoon of everyday life. Producers of plays and movies, we told ourselves, admit that clean, high-grade entertainment has often paid off overwhelmingly.

Yet, in spite of this fact, some movies, radio programs, and comics insist on presenting crime stories exclusively. To get around the censors (or their own consciences), the writers and producers assume that if the guilty man receives his due reward in the end—either being killed by a G-man or going to jail—the story is justified.

To the juvenile or the adolescent mind, however, these endings are inconsequential. All the child understands is that the tough guy is exciting and has exciting experiences. The murderer or thief may even become almost a hero to the child. Do we not all feel sorry for the handsome Jimmy Valentine or the generous, benevolent Robin Hood who steals from the rich to give to the poor?

Undoubtedly World War II had much to do with the avalanche of blood curdling adventure and crime comics which hit our newsstands. During the war so many sensational events were happening in real life that the writers of comic strips found it increasingly difficult to hold the public's interest. The front pages of newspapers blazed away with more gory details than any "crime expert" could dream up, and in order to compete with these actual episodes, the gory comic strips got even bloodier. No crime was too hideous to portray. New methods of killing and also new weapons were introduced to young readers. And the American public finally began to realize that if something were not done quickly, the minds and ideals of youth would soon be corrupted.

No writer of a comic strip today can ignore the recent agitation against these cartooned crimes and criminals. In condemning the bad, however, it is too easy to overlook the good. And there are many good comics today, both in newspapers and in books.

In writing *The Toodles* we have found that there are enough stimulating and exciting experiences in the average family's life to give our strip zest, and it is fairly easy to depict these experiences in an interesting way without having to resort to crime and bloodshed. True, at times one does have to exaggerate and reach out a little for plots which border on the improbable, but it should not be necessary to keep one's characters hanging over a cliff or dangling from a flagpole to sustain interest from Saturday to Monday. An exciting moment in a football game or an unexpected phone call or telegram will do the trick just as well—with much less wear and tear on the juvenile reader.

And it is this juvenile reader of comics whom we writers must particularly consider. He is our adult of tomorrow, our future audience as well as our present one. He will bring home the newspapers his family reads. He will guide his own youngsters' tastes. If he starts out reading good comics, he will pass them on to the next generation.

All recent surveys show that in addition to the millions of boy and girl readers, four out of every five urban adults read comics too. The comics are a part of our American way of living, and we must accept them as such. Moreover, as long as they sell newspapers—and most editors admit they do—they are here to stay!

This is where you parents enter the picture. You alone have it in your power to let these editors know which comics should remain in their papers, for the editors will tell you frankly that they try to print what you, the public, demand. It is up to you to see that the good comics are recognized and the poor ones done away with.

You have it in your power to help the child to discriminate between good comics which will actually enrich his imagination and those that will excite him but lead him nowhere. You can talk over different kinds of comics with your youngsters, perhaps make a game of selecting the best and discarding the worst. Still more important, you can create a home environment in which there is security, self-respect, and challenge so that your children will be emotionally free to make their own choices.

MRS. BASEMENT: Thank you, thank you, Mr. Baer. You have so allayed my fears. It is time now to hear about movies. While we are not so exercised as we were about movies before the Hayes office, we still would like to hear what the studies show. Dr. Bale, will you enlighten us?

DR. BALE: If we are to give a representative, though limited, view of the movies, it will be necessary to determine the numbers of children who are found to attend. Edgar Dale found that in one extensive study involving 20,000 individuals, from 55 to 83 percent of the boys at various ages and from 45 to 70 percent of the girls went to the movies once during the week of investigation. The percentage which never attended ranged from 8 to 2 percent for the boys and from 12 to 2 percent for the girls. At least one percent of all ages attended four or more times during the sample week. From 15 to 25 percent of both sexes attended two to three times per week. The movies have become an important element in the lives of children.

Concerning their likes and dislikes, children were found to prefer love serials, action, and adventure pictures. Girls at or before puberty expressed a preference for love stories, especially if they were laid in the homes of the wealthy. Boys, on the other hand, prefer gangster stories and Westerns. During adolescence the boys too become interested in emotional love stories. Children everywhere, and of all ages, like humor, musical shows, and dancing. Children like newsreels. Dale also found over a period of years that love stories ranked highest in preference, crime, and sex pictures in descending order. This study covered the years 1920–1935.

Herbert Blumer conducted a study to determine what effects, if any, movies had on a group of adolescents, particularly those of positive and negative nature. His conclusions indicate that children receive help in choosing clothes, selecting love techniques, acquiring a philosophy of life, gaining better ideas of modern society, providing for a means of initiative and ambitious effort. They focus attention on family life, its responsibilities and devotions. Loyalty traits are developed, and they help with developing religious and moral attitudes.

High emotional attitudes included daydreaming, terror, sorrow, romantic love, tenseness, and excitement. The movies in these cases provided an escape from the realities of the world. We conclude then that the movies are especially important in stirring the emotions. Sixty-six percent of the children studied gave evidence that they use movie content material in their daydreams. Only 10 percent denied they did any daydreaming. Sixty-one percent of the children's reports indicated reactions of terror and fright. Twenty-two denied this sort of experience.

This evidence again supports the view that mass judgment of the movies is not desirable. Luella Cole proposes that what the child receives from the movies is mainly a crystallization of various points of view and attitudes already existent in the mind of that child. In other words, the pre-delinquent child derives ideas about various techniques used in bank robberies, the child who is sexually aroused finds further excitement from erotic love stories. These same movies, however, furnish other children at the same time not the above mentioned elements but rather ideas for clothing, manners, customs, and styles. Dr. Cole points out that if adolescents are to acquire any knowledge of love making, that they will have to get it from the movies, or from experience, because the home and school give little, if any, assistance in this (at the time) important phase of their life.

Children select from the movies whatever it is they want to learn. In all probability, because of the arousing effect and sometime permanent nature of emotional reactions conveyed by the movies, it would seem desirable to provide better supervision not only of the production itself but also in attendance. Indeed, it is our contention that better films should be presented if for no other reason than to protect those few children who have such emotional defects. Some educators propose that films should be classified into three groups:

1. Those appropriate for children.
2. Those for adolescence.
3. Those for adults.

Cook provides an interesting sidelight concerning the content of movies. He indicates a number of biases which prevail, both national and international. For example, three fourths of the movies studied were held to a locale in the United States. Another bias is that of urbanism. One third of the movies were devoted to life in the city. A third bias concerns economics. Seven out of ten homes in which the plot developed were in the upper class home environment. Coupled with this is the demand for formal and exclusive clothing. A fourth type of bias related to treatment of certain ethnic groups. In forty pictures studied nationalities were depicted. Negroes were usually shown as stupid and sloven. The fifth bias is seen in the way of life pursued by leading characters. Most of the goals of leading men and ladies centered in personal gain, indicated in winning another's love, marriage for love, and professional success. This data would indicate that movies generally are made to pattern, and that there is need for a broadening out. Social behavior of our culture is wider than the movies would have us believe. The implications of this limited scope contributes to the degeneration and misdirection of the wholesome functioning of life.

An interesting study has been conducted by P. W. Holaday and George D. Stoddard, who experimented with 3,000 school children and 200 superior adults. Five important findings were concluded. First, in determining what children learn, and further what they remembered in the movies seen, it was found that children acquire an enormous amount of information from an ordinary movie. W. W. Charters states in this connection that "the eight- or nine-year-old sees half of what is to be seen, the eleven- and twelve-year-old sees two thirds, and the fifteen-and sixteen-year-olds, four-fifths." Second, children tend to accept all information as the truth, whether it is true or false. This comment further supports the view that children's sense of discrimination develops slowly. Third, on the day following the picture's showing, very young children recalled more than one half of what they had seen and recalled it correctly. Six weeks later they recalled nine tenths of what they had seen, supporting the theory that the rate of forgetting is highest immediately after learning. Important implications are found here for the constructive and educative use of motion pictures as a learning instrument, in fact, far superior to that of textbook learning materials. Fourth, it was found that the information best remembered is that which is familiar, emotional in content, and linked with action. Fifth, it was found that when children are properly equated by age, sex, and intelligence, definite differences were discovered. Children from one neighborhood remembered those things which were not remembered with children from different neighborhoods. This would indicate that the child's social surroundings sensitize him to certain stimuli and immunize his reception in others.

Some discussion should be devoted to the effects on children's physical behavior. Investigations have been made in areas of pulse, breathing, and electrical changes of the body while children were viewing certain movies. Young children are affected by the melodramatic movies. Adults are affected to a small degree. Erotic scenes seemed to stir some children as early as nine years, but had their greatest effect on those of fifteen and sixteen years of age. Stimulation was found to be less with adults in this case. Samuel Renshaw, Vernon L. Miller, and Dorothy Marquis found in their studies with children and sleep that the seeing of a motion picture invariably changes the sleep pattern. Further, these effects are found not only that night but also in many succeeding nights as well. Some children showed evidence of this phenomena as long as ten nights later.

In summary then, it may be said, first, that movies are here to stay and that they constitute a potent social force. At their best they carry a high potential value and quality in the entertainment and educative fields. Movies may affect values, attitudes, and ideals as no other medium in our modern culture. We must not discount, however, the other influences upon the life of the child, especially those of the play group, the home, the school, and the community. As yet, we cannot say that any one of these is more powerful than another. I fear I have been too verbose, madam chairman, but there is so much, so very much to say.

MRS. BASEMENT: On the contrary, we have been enlightened a great deal. I think I should change my earlier statement about not worrying so much about movies. And now comes television. Dr. Soforth, what can you say to us about this new invasion of our living rooms?

DR. SOFORTH: The "newness" of television makes my part a very hard one about which to be scientific. Studies are in process but so far results are too fragmentary to be recited authoritatively. Therefore, I should like to read to you from Josette Frank who suggests:

> Television is no longer "just around the corner." It is here— not yet in the homes of tens of millions, as radio is, but available nevertheless in enough homes, shops, and public places to be reaching a very sizable audience, including, of course, children. Whoever installs a television set finds his home immediately inundated by youngsters, especially in the late afternoon hours. Recently, in Hoboken, New Jersey, the police found it necessary to clamp down on some big-hearted saloon keepers who were clearing out their regular patrons

from the bar each afternoon from five to six "to let the kids come in and see the television."

So far, television's "kiddie shows" have shown a marked departure from radio's juvenile programs. Adapting movie and vaudeville techniques, they have offered animated cartoons, puppet shows, children's parties, contests, and amateur hours with audience participation. To date there is a notable absence of box-top appeal, a lack which parents value more than children do. For the most part, these programs have been kept on a childish level, replete with slapstick, nonsense, and hubbub. Even the titles label them as designed for the kindergarten set: "Howdy Doody," "Scrap Book," "Small Fry Club," "Junior Frolics," etc. Irene Wicker's enchanting nursery stories and songs, which have long since disappeared from the air, have been revived for the young television audience. "Howdy Doody," a lively busybody of a puppet, has sprung to instant fame and fortune with a devoted audience of young folks and old.

Like radio, however, television cannot select its audience, and children are not easily pried from their seats after the "kiddie show" is over. Revivals of the old-time western thrillers, intended for adults, are lapped up by the same young audience that has loved the radio adventure serials.

But there is a difference: in television the action is much more graphic. Shooting frays and cafe brawls are vivid, with victims "biting the dust," "dead" riders falling from their horses, guns "pouring lead," murdered corpses being tossed about and frisked—all in the day's work for a ranger. There is nothing new about this type of entertainment, or about the fact that children love it. What is new is that it now becomes available to any three- or four- or five-year-old who happens to be within range.

The problems television raises for parents are, or soon will be, twice as compelling. Young children will have to have their television sessions time scheduled with other activities to take them away from the screen when their show is over. School-age children who have developed a technique for listening to radio along with other activities—homework, for example, or washing dishes—will find that they cannot similarly watch television "out of one eye." Yet, essentially, the parent's job will be the same, calling for sympathy with children's interests, wise management of time, and sane guidance in selection.

For older children and young people, television offers really thrilling fare: *sports,* they can actually watch the World Series, play-by-play, in some distant city; *news,* they can meet face-to-face the personalities who are making world history; *politics,* they can sit in on party conventions and actually watch the wheels go round; *travel,* they can see the native life, as it is lived day by day in India, China,

Mexico, and Palestine; *drama,* they can see the best plays, modern and classical, adapted and beautifully presented with talented acting. What opportunities for expanding young people's experiences and range of vision!

If we are wise, we shall make this fascinating new medium serve our children more fully than radio has. Visual images, it has been said, make deeper and more lasting impressions than auditory ones. Now is the time, while it is still in its early stage, for educators and parents to explore television's possibilities. Instead of blaming bar keepers for letting the children in, we might better see to it that somewhere in the community the children have a chance to see television in suitable places. Instead of berating the showmen of television, as we have in radio and movies, intelligent parents will do better to work with them *now,* developing ways for making the most of this challenging new resource. With intelligence and forethought we can help determine whether television is to be an asset or a nuisance. Skillfully used, at home and at school, television can widen cultural and educational horizons for our children to an extent never before attained by textbooks, movies, or radio.[5]

MRS. BASEMENT: By now, I'm not only exercised but excited about "doing something." What can parents, teachers and community members do about these media? Dr. Bobbins, what *can* parents do?

DR. BOBBINS: What can parents do? They can *listen* and:

1. Try to understand the basic needs of children—and of your own children in particular.

2. Know what your children are reading, seeing, hearing. Listen with them to their preferred programs, or go with them to movies of their own choosing. Introduce them· (not too insistently) to other reading, other programs, other movies which you think they will enjoy. Invite them to listen with you to certain of your favorite programs, or go with you to a movie of your choice.

3. Discuss their favorite programs, comics, movies, with them. Such discussions (if they are without censure or condescension) often help break down barriers and create mutual understanding.

4. Respect their rights and feelings: don't throw away their comics without their consent, don't shut off their radio or interrupt their programs needlessly, don't drag them out of a movie in the middle.

5. Help them develop critical standards by pointing out values, good drawing or good content in a comics magazine, good production or good writing in movies or radio programs. Help them to recognize these differences.

[5] Frank, *op. cit.,* pp. 28–30.

6. Help them budget their time for homework, music practice, outdoor play, necessary chores, allowing for their favorite radio programs, some comics and other reading, and occasional movies.

7. If you find that certain programs or movies upset them, suggest that they skip these for awhile. If they are really disturbed, they will probably be glad to cooperate in this. But if they still seem to want these disturbing programs or movies, you may find that just sitting with them while they are listening or watching will be reassuring. If radio listening or movie going absorbs the children to the exclusion of other interests and activities, talk this over with them too. Together you may arrive at a sensible plan for cutting down or selecting more wisely.

8. See that they have plenty of enjoyable things to do, places to go, wholesome friendships, varied experiences, and real adventures. Encourage their hobbies and help them get the needed "makings." (Puppet making has been greatly stimulated by television.) Include them, too, in your own fun and interests.[6]

MRS. BASEMENT: Now, Dr. Jacobson, what can teachers do?

DR. JACOBSON:

1. Recognize that comics, movies, and radio are prevalent interests and common experiences—don't ignore them.

2. Be familiar with some of the favorite comics and radio programs, at least enough to discuss them with the children and help them grow in their ability to discriminate.

3. Occasionally invite class discussion on these subjects. Encourage the children to expand these interests into more creative activities, using their comics or radio characters as a basis for written stories, dramatizations, puppet shows, drawing, modeling, or painting. They provide a familiar theme on which all the children can contribute.

4. Direct their attention to radio programs or movies they might not know about—not as "required listening," however, but for their fun and interest.

5. Introduce the children to an ever-widening range of interests. As their reading ability grows, help them find books that are inviting, fast moving, easy to read so that reading books too will grow as a pleasurable experience.

6. Suggest that comic magazines be deposited in a safe place, to be reclaimed at the end of the day—if they prove too distracting in class.

7. Make full use of the school radio and movie projector or work toward getting these if there are none in your school. Utilize

[6] Frank, *op. cit.,* pp. 30–31.

whatever school broadcasts are available in your community, tying them in with classroom discussion and study.[7]

MRS. BASEMENT: And now the community, Dr. Bales.

DR. BALES: The community can:

1. Stimulate and promote research by competent specialists to determine more definitely than we know now the effects of various kinds of reading and entertainment on children of various ages. Work out ways for guiding parents and teachers on the basis of these findings.

2. Look over the recreational and cultural activities your neighborhood offers its children. See to it that there is plenty of opportunity for boys and girls of all ages to have fun, creative interests, and satisfying activities.

3. Know what is available to children—on the newsstands, on the air, at the movies—and make your knowledge more than coverdeep.

4. In parent-teacher groups, radio councils, or motion-picture councils, study and discuss the needs of children in these fields and evaluate what is being offered in relation to these needs. (The children might well have a voice in these discussions, since they are the ultimate consumers.)

5. Support with your approval programs, motion pictures, and comic magazines which you believe are maintaining good standards for children's entertainment or education.

6. Express your protest, too, by writing to those responsible for programs, movies, or comics you believe to be harmful or unworthy. Informed, thoughtful criticism is more effective than hysteria.

7. Enlist the cooperation of local radio stations and motion-picture exhibitors in offering programs of special interest and value to children and young people—especially radio programs in which the young people can participate.[8]

MRS. BASEMENT: We thank you more than we can say for your participation here this evening. We feel that by speaking with, as well as listening to, speakers we have a much better understanding of the whys and hows of what you people call mass media of communication. I will not attempt to summarize but only to say from now on we won't just "worry," we'll try to *study, understand,* and *do.*

TEACHING AND STUDY AIDS

1. You will enjoy reading and analyzing the study of Kate Smith's War Bond Drive. It "illuminates the moral dilemma of mass persuasion

[7] Frank, pp. 31–32.
[8] *Ibid.,* p. 32.

by warning how such techniques might be deflected to antisocial ends." See Robert K. Merton, *Mass Persuasion* (New York, Harper, 1946).

2. Another interesting analysis of the effects of radio upon behavior is to be found in the analysis of the Orson Welles show which was a take-off on H. G. Wells, *The War of the Worlds*. See Hadley Cantril, *Invasion from Mars* (Princeton, Princeton University Press, 1940).

3. If there are cooperating schools in your community you may conduct surveys concerning children's likes and dislikes, attitudes and information absorbed from television programs, movies of various types, comic books, and radio programs.

4. Survey periodical literature for studies concerning effects of television on children and adults. What are your conclusions?

5. The people in the case presented in this book suggest that all these media are here to stay. Our job is to learn to live with and control them. Suggest other ways of doing this than those mentioned.

SELECTED READING REFERENCES

Bacmeister, Rhoda W., *Stories to Begin On* (New York, Dutton, 1940).

Bartlett, Kenneth L., *How to Use Radio* (Washington, National Association of Broadcasters, 1938).

Becker, May L., *First Adventures with Reading* (New York, Stokes, 1938).

Blumer, Herbert, *Movies and Conduct* (New York, Macmillan, 1930).

Bryant, Sara Cone, *How to Tell Stories to Children* (Boston, Houghton, 1933).

Cantril, Hadley and Allport, Gordon W., *The Psychology of Radio* (New York, Harper, 1935).

Charters, W. W., *Moving Pictures and Youth* (New York, Macmillan, 1933).

Clark, Weston R., "Radio Listening Habits of Children," *Journal of Social Psychology*, Vol. XII (August 1940), pp. 131–149.

Dale, Edgar, *Children's Attendance at Motion Pictures* (New York, Macmillan, 1933).

Dale, Edgar, *How to Appreciate Motion Pictures* (New York, Macmillan, 1933).

Dalgliesh, Alice, *First Experience with Literature* (New York, McGraw-Hill, 1939).

Eisenberg, Azriel L., *Children and Radio Programs* (New York, Columbia University Press, 1936).

Eisenberg, Philip and Krasno, Becky, *A Guide to Children's Records* (New York, Crown, 1948).

Frank, Josette, *What Books for Children?* (New York, Doubleday, 1937).

Frost, S. E., *Is American Radio Democratic?* (Chicago, University of Chicago Press, 1937).

Gordon, Dorothy, *All Children Listen* (New York, Stewart, 1942).

Harrison, Margaret, *Radio in the Classroom* (New York, Prentice-Hall, 1937).

Hartman, Gertrude, and Schumaker, Ann, *Creative Expression: The Development of Children in Art, Music, Literature and Dramatics* (Milwaukee, Hale, 1939).

Herzog, Herta, *Children and Their Leisure-Time Listening to the Radio* (New York, Radio Council on Children's Programs, 1941).

Hill, Frank, and Williams, W. E., *Radio's Listening Groups* (New York, Columbia University Press, 1941).

Jones, Alma, *Treasures in Books for Boys and Girls* (Ames, Iowa Extension Service Bulletin, 1949).

Koon, Cline M., *The Art of Teaching by Radio* (Washington, United States Government Printing Office, 1933).

Lazarsfeld, Paul F., and Stanton, Frank N., *Radio Research, 1941* (New York, Duell, Sloan and Pearce, 1941).

Lenski, Lois (illustrator), *Read-To-Me Storybook.* Compiled by the Child Study Association of America (New York, Crowell, 1947).

Levenson, William B., *Teaching Through Radio* (New York, Farrar and Rinehart, 1945).

Mahony, Bertha E., and Whitney, Elinor, *Contemporary Illustrators of Children's Books* (Boston, The Bookshop for Boys and Girls, Women's Education and Industrial Union, 1930).

National Broadcasting Company, *How Schools Use Radio* (New York, 1950).

Reid, Seerley, and Woelfel, Norman, *How to Judge a School Broadcast* (Columbus, The Ohio State University, 1941).

Reid, Seerley, *Network School Broadcasts: Some Conclusions and Recommendations,* Bulletin No. 35 (Columbus, The Ohio State University, 1941).

Rowland, Howard, et al., *Criteria for Children's Radio Programs* (Washington, Federal Radio Education Committee, 1943).

Stoddard, G. D., *What Motion Pictures Mean to the Child* (Ames, Bulletin of Iowa State University, 1933).

Weed, F. C., *Choosing Book Friends* (Columbus, Bulletin 180 of the Agricultural Extension Service, The Ohio State University, August 1937).

Woelfel, Norman, and Tyler, I. Keith, *Radio and the School* (Yonkers, World Book, 1945).

X

THE "PRESCHOOL" AS AN AGENCY OF CHILD SOCIALIZATION

DESPITE THE FACT that Part II is devoted to a study of the school per se, we have included consideration of the preschool or kindergarten here on the grounds that it, like the family and the play group, is less formal, less routinized, and more generally connected with initial socialization of the child. Those who would be happier if it appeared under Part II may so use the material without serious violence to either part.

Kindergartens are variously regarded by people and communities. In many areas they have long been a standard part of the educative process. In others there is still strong resistance to the whole idea of the "downward extension of education."

The following case presentation was the outcome of the interest of teachers who found themselves in such an anomalous position. Their community's board of education had voted to reinstitute public kindergartens after their withdrawal some ten years previous. Despite the fact that kindergarten attendance was voluntary, a storm of criticism and debate broke forth in the community. What really was the case, these teachers asked, and they set forth accordingly to visit well-planned and well-conducted preschools as well as to canvass the literature. "Kindergartens on Trial" is their way of presenting what they learned.[1]

The procedure they employed was that of a public hearing before a board of education considering making kindergarten education a part of the community school system. The group in favor of such action was headed by the superintendent of schools and the group opposed, by Mr. Disagree, president of the League Against

[1] Committee Members: Eleanor M. Beyer, Marie L. Ealy, Ruby L. Stimmell.

Tax Levy for the Public Schools. In their panel, as presented below, the president of the board of education is presiding. The other participants in the discussion are as follows:

Name	Address	Occupation
Mr. Lower Middle	Center Boulevard	Clerk, men's clothing store
Mrs. Upper Middle	Successful Circle	Wife of a lawyer
Mr. Middle Middle	Middle Road	Retired farmer
Mr. Disagree	Upper Place	President, League against Tax Levy for Public Schools
Mrs. Upper Upper	Skyline Drive	Wife of president, Capitalistic Bank
Mrs. Lower Lower	Shanty Street	Wife of truck driver
Mrs. Lower Upper	Social Climber Street	Wife of president, Near-the-Top Auto Industry
Miss Teacher	Educational Row	Kindergarten teacher

As the meeting opens, the president of the Board is speaking.

PRESIDENT OF THE BOARD: The gathering this evening is for the purpose of hearing from those who approve of the plan to provide kindergartens in our school system and from those who feel that such action is not only unnecessary but undesirable for children. Each side will state its position and proceed to call upon citizens who support its intent. Mr. Disagree, would you care to begin?

MR. DISAGREE: We wish to prove tonight that kindergartens are unnecessary to the welfare of the child, that money spent on equipment in existing kindergartens is wasted, that the so-called planning of the work period is just a farce, that not enough time is paid to "music work" as an organized art, and that children are institutionalized too early.

PRESIDENT OF THE BOARD: Mr. Superintendent, will you state your position?

SUPERINTENDENT: We on the other hand wish to show that kindergartens provide social security for children, aid in the development and integration of personality, facilitate cooperation between home and school, develop healthful living, instill personal responsibility in the child, encourage creative ability, give the child desirable experiences in music, science, and play with a wealth of well-chosen equipment, and establish democratic ideals in group planning.

PRESIDENT OF THE BOARD: Mr. Disagree, will you proceed?

MR. DISAGREE: I should like to call upon Mr. Lower Middle who lives on Center Boulevard and is a clerk in one of our better clothing stores. Mr. Lower Middle, have you ever sent a child to kindergarten?

MR. LOWER MIDDLE: Yes.

MR. DISAGREE: Do you have a child in kindergarten now?

MR. LOWER MIDDLE: No. All the children do is play, play, play. What good is that to them?

MR. DISAGREE: What do you mean by play, play, play?

MR. LOWER MIDDLE: Well, the one time when I stopped by the kindergarten to pick up my child, all I observed was noise and confusion and play. The whole situation seemed to be noisy and unorganized.

MR. DISAGREE: What were your reactions to this situations?

MR. LOWER MIDDLE: I decided then and there that time spent there was worthless, even bad, so I promptly took my child out of kindergarten.

MR. SUPERINTENDENT: May I ask Mr. Lower Middle a question or two, Mr. President?

PRESIDENT: Please do.

SUPERINTENDENT: Do you enjoy having your little outing with the boys?

ANSWER: Yes.

SUPERINTENDENT: Isn't recreation, after all, an important part of your life?

ANSWER: Well, yes.

SUPERINTENDENT: And, you have heard that all work and no play makes Jack a dull boy, haven't you?

ANSWER: Yes.

SUPERINTENDENT: Well, then, perhaps you can realize that to a child play is the most serious thing in the world. Through it he gains new experiences and thus prepares himself for life. "Through the years, play interest will gradually develop into wholesome pastime which will fill leisure time when the child is grown." [2] Now, Mr. Lower Middle, is your child happy since he is at home alone?

ANSWER: Well, he should be, for I have bought him a swing, a teeter-totter, and a sand box. But he doesn't pay much attention to them.

SUPERINTENDENT: Mr. Lower Middle, "grown-ups" often thoughtlessly underestimate a child's play and think of it merely as a needed device to keep him "amused" or "out-of-mischief" or "out-from-under-foot," forgetting that it is as necessary to his healthy development

[2] Florence C. Weed, *Learning to Live Through Play*, Bulletin 212 (Columbus, Agricultural Extension Service, The Ohio State University, 1945), p. 3. Used by permission.

as food and rest.[3] Now, have you noticed any marked changes in your child since removing him from kindergarten?

ANSWER: Come to think of it, he does cry a good deal, is moody, temperamental, and hard to manage. He gives his mother a bad time most of the day.

SUPERINTENDENT: Did you ever think how unhappy you would be if all your activities were centered around children? By the same token your child can be just as miserable in an adult-centered world. The role that he plays in his home life and that role played when he is with children of his own age is totally different. Other children can help him sense, as no adult can, his place in and his relationship to a group of his contemporaries. We need to take a "child's eye view" to realize the difference in adult and child perspective. To quote from the Association for Childhood Education, Kindergarten Portfolio, Section 6, "Kindergarten is the first big steppingstone away from home and mother. It is a happy situation when social adjustment to a group can be made without the necessity for pressure of learning." [4]

PRESIDENT: Second witness for the opposition, please come forward.

MR. DISAGREE: What is your name?

ANSWER: Mrs. Upper Middle.

MR. DISAGREE: Where do you live?

ANSWER: Successful Circle.

MR. DISAGREE: What is your husband's profession?

ANSWER: He is a lawyer.

MR. DISAGREE: Do you have a child in kindergarten?

ANSWER: Yes.

MR. DISAGREE: Do you visit the kindergarten often?

ANSWER: No.

MR. DISAGREE: Is there a reason for your not visiting your child's kindergarten?

ANSWER: Yes, the work periods seem to lack direction and it seems futile to me to let the child do his own choosing and work in a group. I feel nothing is being accomplished. In my estimation schools are places where children are required to work to their capacity.

MR. DISAGREE: Just what do the children do during a work period?

ANSWER: Some were pounding, others were building with large blocks, while others painted at the easel or colored pictures when I did visit. Some were playing with dolls or putting together puzzles while others were modeling in clay. Why call this a work period? I call it

[3] *Ibid.*, p. 3.

[4] Louise M. Alder and Lorraine Benner, *Portfolio on Kindergarten Extension*, Section 6 (Washington, Association for Childhood Education, 1940). Used by permission.

play. There is too much freedom for the child with the teacher too much in the background. There are no evidences of discipline which I can see.

MR. DISAGREE: In other words, you feel the child is given too much freedom in his own choice and that there is not enough individual direction on the part of the teacher.

ANSWER: Yes.

MR. DISAGREE: That is all. Your witness.

SUPERINTENDENT: Perhaps, Mrs. Upper Middle, you have been expecting too much of your child. No doubt he learned to talk through your efforts at the age of one year.

ANSWER: (*Proudly*) Ten months.

SUPERINTENDENT: No doubt you had him toilet-trained at an early age.

ANSWER: At eighteen months!

SUPERINTENDENT: And even though you may not realize it, you no doubt have an over-anxious child on your hands.

ANSWER: But our status in society compels us to expect and demand certain achievements from our children. We expect them always to do their best with no backsliding.

SUPERINTENDENT: Let me explain to you, Mrs. Upper Middle, and to the assembly, what the purposes of the work and planning period are. From the American Childhood Education Portfolio, Section 12, I quote:

> This is a period in which children are really doing their own thinking and planning as well as their own executing. The children are usually to be found scattered about the room working together on their own or group activities. The teacher is not conspicuously in evidence. She is there helping to keep a workshop spirit in the room and she stands by to suggest, guide, praise, judge, and admire effort and achievement but she does not direct or do work for the children.

According to Mead in *Mind, Self, and Society,* the first stage of the development of self is play where the child assumes the role of other persons. This is brought out in the kindergarten in the housekeeping activities of the doll corner, in the block building, in caring for the animals, etc. These are the ways preschool children re-enact life around them and understand its meaning.

Little children need long periods of time when they can devise their own play, free from too much teacher direction. They also need to make choices whenever possible, for if we expect people to abide by decisions, we should expect to give them a voice in making the decisions.

Bossard says in his *Sociology of Child Development* that the most difficult step in the socialization of the child is the recognition of the rights of others. This process begins, of course, with the child's life with his family, but frequently this group is too small or largely adult; so, it is from experiences in peer groups that the child gains an understanding of the limitations which group life places upon the individual. This is the first lesson learned in living with others, and it can best be learned by experience. At times the activities and interests of the child will be entirely those of his own choosing; at other times he will bend his every effort to cooperate with the group. This is one of the goals of the modern kindergarten.

PRESIDENT: Third witness for the opposition, please come forward.

MR. DISAGREE: What is your name?

ANSWER: Mr. Middle Middle.

MR. DISAGREE: Where do you live?

ANSWER: Middle Road.

MR. DISAGREE: What is your occupation?

ANSWER: I am a retired farmer and president of the League Against the Tax Levy for Public Schools.

MR. DISAGREE: Do you have a child in kindergarten?

ANSWER: No. My children are all grown.

MR. DISAGREE: Do you pay taxes here?

ANSWER: Yes, and they are entirely too high. All of this nonsense and tomfoolery in kindergartens takes too much of my tax money.

MR. DISAGREE: What do you mean by that statement?

ANSWER: Too much fancy equipment for these modern youngsters! All we had when I went to school was a book and a slate, and we got along.

MR. DISAGREE: How do you know what kind of equipment kindergartens have today?

ANSWER: Being an active member of the League against the new tax levy, I made it my business to visit our local kindergarten one day to see just what they do with our tax money. I found that a lot of money is wrapped up in those easels, jungle gyms, paints, clay, toys, musical instruments, gadgets, etc. Why can't the children sit in regular school seats and be satisfied?

MR. DISAGREE: In other words, Mr. Middle Middle, you feel the amount of money spent on equipment is not commensurate with the values gained from the kindergarten activities?

ANSWER: I do.

MR. DISAGREE: That is all. Your witness.

SUPERINTENDENT: Mr. Middle Middle, I understand you have been a very successful farmer.

ANSWER: Yes, I have done well.

SUPERINTENDENT: Did you farm with the same tools and implements which your grandfather used?

ANSWER: No.

SUPERINTENDENT: Why not?

ANSWER: They were not suitable.

SUPERINTENDENT: What kind of equipment did you use to gain the maximum return from your farm?

ANSWER: As modern as I could get, of course.

SUPERINTENDENT: Shouldn't there be advancement in school as well as in farming?

ANSWER: I suppose so, although we got along all right in our school.

SUPERINTENDENT: Just to "get along" isn't good enough any more, Mr. Middle Middle. It paid better dividends in crop harvesting when you had good machinery, didn't it?

ANSWER: Yes.

SUPERINTENDENT: Couldn't the same practice be applied to our local kindergarten?

ANSWER: I suppose so.

SUPERINTENDENT: Let me prove this to you. In the first place small children are very active, and they need plenty of space in which to stretch those large body muscles. They are in the process of perfecting certain body skills and so need space to walk, run, skip, crawl, climb, etc. This rules out the old type of classroom with the screw-down desk where the child had to sit all day, and the teacher was the only one who got any exercise. Now for exhibit "A" (easel paintings and clay models).

Quoting from *Learning to Live Through Play* again, let me say that ". . . just as soon as a little child learns how to manage his body he is ready for excursions into creative expression. Paper and crayons for drawing, pictures to color, paints and paper for painting, clay for modeling—all of these are stepping stones to realistic production." [5] The act of painting improves the muscular coordination of children and is a good means of self-expression. It is important that large pictures be made, for the child of four or five is using his large muscles to a great extent. Clay work is probably the best means towards bringing the young child's muscles under control. Emotional satisfaction is also gained from creating something beautiful to the child, from squeezing and squashing a hunk of clay. Now for exhibit "B" (a wooden table and chair).

Tools are merely a means to an end. They are the means by which children express their ideas in wood. Through using a hammer a child

[5] Weed, *op. cit.*, p. 36.

gains in motor control and coordination of hand and eye. And think of the personal satisfaction to the child of five to be able to create this wooden furniture out of a few pieces of wood and some nails. Look at exhibit "C" (large blocks).

Children need toys for vigorous play, and blocks are perhaps the best materials for young children. The use of blocks provides physical development, stimulates mental processes, and encourages social development. Both large and small blocks have their place in the well-equipped kindergarten. Exhibit "D" (musical instruments).

Children express their feelings in rhythm as in no other way, for they possess a sense of rhythm. Children love various noises and sounds with compelling force. How else provide a child with the necessary implements to serve as an outlet for these hidden urges than to secure the proper media! It is not necessary, however, to obtain the most expensive set of musical instruments. Rather, it is wiser to provide a few with good tone quality. Home-made instruments, some of which the children themselves can make, are more successful. So you see, Mr. Middle Middle, the many gadgets with which you have found fault do have their place and value in a modern kindergarten.

PRESIDENT: First witness for the defense, please.

SUPERINTENDENT: What is your name?

ANSWER: Mrs. Upper Upper.

SUPERINTENDENT: What is your address?

ANSWER: Skyline Drive.

SUPERINTENDENT: What does your husband do?

ANSWER: He is president of the Capitalistic Bank and Trust Company.

SUPERINTENDENT: Do you send your child to kindergarten?

ANSWER: Oh, yes.

SUPERINTENDENT: Why do you send your child there?

ANSWER: Because he is exposed to a well-adjusted social atmosphere where there is a wealth of music situations to which he has learned to respond freely and creatively.

SUPERINTENDENT: In what way do you think music is valuable to your child?

ANSWER: It is important to his physical growth in that it helps large body muscles to develop and helps him to express his imagination creatively.

SUPERINTENDENT: Is the casual observer of a good kindergarten ever apt to be misled by the music program?

ANSWER: Yes, quoting from *Children and Music* of the A. C. E. ". . . a well conceived program of music for children may look like play. It may look inconsequential, unsystematic, and trivial. But it is not trivial for it brings music to children in terms of their own life concerns and interests and doings." [6]

SUPERINTENDENT: That is all. Your witness.

MR. DISAGREE: You haven't mentioned "rhythm bands" in the kindergarten music program. Aren't you interested in rhythm bands?

ANSWER: No, not a band where there are adult-imposed ideas and adult learning, but rather a group where the timing won't dull the creative sensitivity or where children won't become fatigued.

MR. DISAGREE: Wouldn't you be proud to have your child perform in a rhythm band, Mrs. Upper Upper?

ANSWER: No. Children should experiment freely and interchangeably with songs and with bodily movement and with instruments.

MR. DISAGREE: In this way how can you have "music work" in school?

ANSWER: "So-called music work becomes equivalent to singing prescribed songs, to studying an approved instrument, to learning the notations, and very little else. This is the reason why so many children grow to adulthood without the musical heritage which nature has equipped them to possess." [7]

MR. DISAGREE: That is all.

PRESIDENT: Second witness for the defense, please come forward.

SUPERINTENDENT: What is your name?

ANSWER: Mrs. Lower Lower.

SUPERINTENDENT: Where do you live?

ANSWER: We live on Shanty Street.

SUPERINTENDENT: What kind of work does your husband do?

ANSWER: He is a truck driver.

SUPERINTENDENT: Does your child attend kindergarten?

ANSWER: Yes, I have had nine go through kindergarten.

SUPERINTENDENT: What did you like best about the kindergarten program?

ANSWER: Well, with so many children, I found it awfully hard to take care of their teeth and tonsils. Besides, I'm too busy working at my job. I liked the things they told us about health.

SUPERINTENDENT: You feel that your child's health has been improved then?

ANSWER: Yes. Our small income doesn't cover much medical attention; so we were glad to have the school tell us when anything was wrong with our children.

SUPERINTENDENT: In what definite ways have you been helped?

ANSWER: They've all had their teeth and tonsils taken care of, and

[6] Frances Mayfarth, Ellen Olsen, *Children and Music* (Washington, Association for Childhood Education, 1949), p. 10. Used by permission.

[7] *Ibid.*, p. 3.

from the notices sent home my husband and I have found out the importance of vaccination and shots.

SUPERINTENDENT: What do you think of the kindergarten health program regarding food?

ANSWER: I like it fine. It has helped me in planning and cooking our meals. After following these directions, I could see that my family's health was much better.

SUPERINTENDENT: That is all. Your witness.

MR. DISAGREE: Don't you and your husband resent having someone other than your family doctor tell you what to do?

ANSWER: Yes, we did for a while. But after seeing how the other families in our neighborhood were helped, we decided to get help too.

MR. DISAGREE: Aren't you afraid that your child will contract many childhood diseases unnecessarily in kindergarten?

ANSWER: No. They usually get them anyway, and the nurse says that it is better to get these diseases over before they start their reading in regular school.

PRESIDENT: Third witness for the defense. Please come forward.

SUPERINTENDENT: What is your name?

ANSWER: Mrs. Lower Upper.

SUPERINTENDENT: Where do you live?

ANSWER: On Social Climber Street.

SUPERINTENDENT: What is your husband's occupation?

ANSWER: He is president of the Near-the-Top Auto Industry.

SUPERINTENDENT: Do you have any children in kindergarten?

ANSWER: Yes.

SUPERINTENDENT: Do you visit kindergarten often?

ANSWER: Yes.

SUPERINTENDENT: Why?

ANSWER: It has helped me to understand my child. Now that I know John gets along well with other children, I am not worried about his starting in the first grade next fall. I am very interested in school procedures and in what my child is being taught. I have observed how the children make their plans for the work period and how well they share and cooperate. I have found out that kindergarten is not all play, for the children very definitely learn to give attention and consideration to the ideas of others.

SUPERINTENDENT: What do you think of the rest period in kindergarten?

ANSWER: Learning to rest and knowing when to rest are part of the educational values of school for the young child. Sleep cannot be forced, but relaxation can be attained consciously, and relaxing when awake is an important habit for children to acquire.

The rest period is very important, but it is also very difficult to administer it properly. It depends on the kindergarten program and the size of the class and the needs of the children. It can be accomplished either by quiet activity or by a period when the children lie down.

SUPERINTENDENT: Do you know your child's teacher personally?

ANSWER: Yes. She has been a guest in my home, and I consider her a friend and a valuable help in guiding the future of my child. We first became acquainted through the parent-teachers discussion groups and later through home visits.

SUPERINTENDENT: You feel, then, that the kindergarten furnishes the link between the home and later school life?

ANSWER: I do.

SUPERINTENDENT: That is all. Your witness.

MR. DISAGREE: No questions.

PRESIDENT: Fourth witness for the defense, please come forward.

SUPERINTENDENT: What is your name?

ANSWER: Miss Teacher.

SUPERINTENDENT: Where do you live?

ANSWER: Educational Row.

SUPERINTENDENT: Have you found it valuable to learn to know each child's home situation?

ANSWER: Yes, it has helped promote good home-school relationships.

SUPERINTENDENT: Please explain that, Miss Teacher.

ANSWER: The better I know the home situation, the better I can understand and guide the child effectively. This can be done in many ways: through conferences with parents, home visiting and parent observation of kindergarten, parent-teacher study groups, and home interview blanks. We seek advice from the parent and they, in turn, seek advice from the teacher in order to develop a well-integrated personality in the child.

SUPERINTENDENT: Do the methods of controlling the children in your kindergarten vary much or compare favorably with those methods of control in the home?

ANSWER: So many homes have autocratic authority over their children expressed in the father-dominated role. In our public kindergarten our values tend toward democratic ideals which we try to inculcate through planning and sharing, cooperative group work, evaluation techniques, and social understanding.

SUPERINTENDENT: That is all, your witness.

MR. DISAGREE: Don't you think the age of four or five too early an age for a child to start to school?

ANSWER: No, I don't think it is. It tends to make the first grade adjustments more smooth. It helps him to share responsibility, solve problems on his own level, and take care of his own personal needs.

MR. DISAGREE: Don't you think this could be accomplished at home?

ANSWER: Parents often do not realize the social needs of their child, and, consequently, it takes too much of his first year in regular school to make adjustments. A child's personality and conception of himself is well set by the age of four, and too often the only child in a group of adults becomes maladjusted and develops into the well-known "problem child." We feel that kindergarten, where the child can be with his own age level, his peer groups, and can work toward their social approval, starts him on the path of a well-integrated and fruitful life. Quoting from the Association for Childhood Education Kindergarten Portfolio Number 6:

> The kindergarten does what the home rarely can do. It inculcates the first sense of study as well as group discipline, forms proper school habits, correlates mental and physical reactions, and, in uncounted instances gives personal direction to the pupil in his most formative stage. I am convinced that the kindergarten is not an adjunct to education. It is an integral part of it and that very important part, its beginning.[8]

PRESIDENT: We have had the unique opportunity this evening of hearing the carefully thought out and calmly presented view of our citizens on a community issue. We shall now have brief summaries by Mr. Disagree and Mr. Superintendent. You may rest assured that your board in conjunction with its professional and lay advisory committees will give your opinions careful consideration. Mr. Disagree, will you please summarize your viewpoint?

MR. DISAGREE: We have endeavored to prove to you that kindergartens are unnecessary in the life of a small child. The family is the primary social group to which the child belongs first, and it is the most logical group to give him his social training. Whether large or small the family unit knows best the personality of the child and can tell whether any changes need to be effected.

We have also proved that too much money is spent on equipment in existing kindergartens and that such equipment is superfluous for any training that might result.

In the existing kindergartens not enough attention is paid to formalized music, where a child is taught definite instrumental techniques. Too much freedom and choice is allowed.

This excessive freedom is also carried over into all phases of existing kindergarten life, and in our opinion no small child knows well enough what he wants to do to be given a choice.

[8] Alder and Benner, *op. cit.*

No, the opposition feels that kindergartens are unnecessary, expensive, and do not accomplish any given purpose.

SUPERINTENDENT: Kindergartens are a very important step in the education of small children. Where else but in these well-supervised, well-equipped situations could a child better adjust himself socially? Here his peer groups will help him to learn how to become a contributing member in a group and will also stimulate in him a desire to achieve.

Adult guidance is of course essential to the child's development. Quoting from A. C. E. bulletin *Four- and Five-Year Olds:*

> Good guidance demands adults attuned to children, ready at any moment to be observer, parallel worker, auditor, participant, instructor, impartial judge, sympathetic listener, director, appreciative admirer, confessor, dealer in information, advisor, or nurse—whatever the situation may demand for their best development.[9]

And what parent has ever had time to be all of these rolled into one while caring for a house and other members of the family?

As to equipment for kindergartens, a certain amount of well-made equipment is necessary to supply the exploring and questioning phases through which a child begins to learn. As we pointed out in the testimony, expensive equipment is not always advisable, but well-chosen equipment is important.

Because of so many parental conflicts and their negative effect on the child it is necessary to have good rapport between the home and school to better understand personal conflicts which are being created within the child. Many of these conflicts have their start when the child is quite young; therefore, better guidance and understanding fostered by a well-guided home-school program will enable these maladjustments to be corrected before they become too serious.

The programs and standards for kindergartens are based on the developmental needs and individual differences of the children. At this point I should like to submit a well-balanced program taken from a well-conducted Kindergarten:

9:00– 9:45	Work Period
9:45–10:15	Stories
10:15–10:40	Music
10:40–11:00	Lunch
11:00–11:30	Rest
11:30–12:00	Play

Again quoting from A. C. E. bulletin *Four- and Five-Year Olds,* let me say:

[9] Frances Mayfarth, *Four- and Five-Year Olds at School* (Washington, Association for Childhood Education, 1948), p. 8.

Four- and five-year olds, then, need time to grow, adequate space in which to grow, equipment and materials suitable to their age and ability, and perhaps most important of all, other children to play with and the guidance of adults who know what children are like and what they need for growth and development. Public education has assumed responsibility for meeting these needs by establishing kindergartens.[10]

The defense rests.

PRESIDENT: We thank you, one and all. Meeting is adjourned.

TEACHING AND STUDY AIDS

1. If there is a laboratory school on your campus or if there are cooperating public schools, plan a program of visitation for purposes of observation. From your reading, set up criteria for evaluating what you see happening there and share your report with the class. It might be very illuminating to compare the four year old nursery school child and the five year kindergarten child in terms of physical, intellectual, and social characteristics.
2. Make a study of various kindergarten programs for the purpose of being sure you know the philosophy of education behind each pattern.
3. Read and report individually or as a group on one or more of the following selected reading references.
4. Nursery schools are another evidence of the extension downward of education. Make a similar study of the pros and cons of nursery education and present it to the class in whatever form you like.
5. How could the negative side in the case have strengthened its argument?

SELECTED READING REFERENCES

A Good Start for Your Child in School (River Forest, Ill., River Forest Public Schools, 1949.

Alder, Louise M., and Benner, Lorraine, *Portfolio on Kindergarten Extension* (Washington, Association for Childhood Education, 1940).

Baruch, Dorothy, *Understanding Young Children* (New York, Bureau of Publications, Teachers College, Columbia University, 1949).

Berry, Francis and Ewen, Alice, *Portfolio for Kindergarten Teachers.* (Washington, Association for Childhood Education, 1941).

Betzner, Jean (compiler), *School Housing Needs of Young Children* (Washington, Association for Childhood Education, 1939).

[10] *Ibid.*

Dawe, H. C., and Foster, J. C., "The Kindergarten Rest Period," *Child-hood Education* (March 1935).

Equipment and Supplies for Nursery Schools, Kindergartens, and Primary Schools (Washington, Association for Childhood Education, 1948).

Faegre, Marion L., and others, *Your Child From One to Six* (Washington, United States Children's Bureau, Federal Security Agency, 1945), Pub. No. 30.

For Parents Particularly (Washington, Association for Childhood Education, 1949).

Forbes, George, *The Function of the Kindergarten in the Public School* (Washington, National Education Association, 1909).

Foster, Josephine, and Headley, Neith, *Education in the Kindergarten* (New York, American Book, 1948).

Four- and Five-Year-Olds at School, Bulletin (Washington, Association for Childhood Education, 1943).

Frank, Lawrence K., *The Fundamental Needs of the Child* (New York, New York Committee on Mental Hygiene, 1928).

Frank, Mary and Lawrence, *How to Help Your Children in School* (New York, Viking Press, 1950).

Going to Kindergarten in Cincinnati (Cincinnati, Ohio, Cincinnati Public Schools, 1948).

Gregory, Merrill, Payne, and Giddings. *The Coordination of the Kindergarten and the Elementary School* (Washington, National Education Association, 1908).

Hissong, Clyde, *Working with the Child from Two to Six* (Columbus, The Ohio State Department of Education, 1947).

Hymes, James L., Jr., *Being a Good Parent* (New York, Bureau of Publications, Teachers College, Columbia University, 1949).

———, *Discipline* (New York, Bureau of Publications, Teachers College, Columbia University, 1950).

———, "The Forgotten Under-Sixes" *The NEA Journal,* January 1950).

———, *A Pound of Prevention* (New York, New York Committee on Mental Hygiene, 1947).

Kindergarten Hand-book (Madison, Wis., Madison Public Schools, 1950).

Lissim and Silbert, "When Parents Learn with Children" *Childhood Education* (January 1950).

MacLatchy, J. H., *Attendance at Kindergarten and Progress in the Primary Grades* (Columbus, The Ohio State University Press, 1928).

Mayfarth, Frances, ed., *Better School Homes for Children* (Washington, Association for Childhood Education, 1947).

Meeting the Kindergarten (St. Louis County, Mo., Normandy School District, 1949).

Neterer, Elizabeth, and Ewen, Alice, *Portfolios on Materials for Work and Play* (Washington, Association for Childhood Education).

Norton, Edith, "Parent Education in the Nursery School," *Childhood Education International* (1949).

Off to School (Elgin, Ill., Elgin Public Schools, 1948).

Off to School (Richmond, Ind., Richmond Public Schools, 1947).

Pahl, Eleanor, *The Fours and Fives in Action* (Glencoe, Ill., Board of Education, 1947).

Partners in Education (Washington, Association for Childhood Education, 1950).

Primary Manual: A Teacher's Guide: Kindergarten and Grades One, Two and Three. Curriculum Bulletin. (Cincinnati, Ohio, Cincinnati Public Schools, 1947).

Preparing Your Child for School, Pamphlet No. 108 (Washington, Office of Education, Federal Security Agency, 1950).

Recording and Reporting Children's Growth, Leaflet No. 10. Portfolio for Primary Teachers (Washington, Association for Childhood Education, 1945).

Redl, Fritz, *Understanding Children's Behavior* (New York, Bureau of Publications, Teachers College, Columbia University, 1950).

Roy, Katherine, and Associates, *Apply Nursery School Methods of Child Guidance in the Home* (Topeka, Kansas State, 1942).

School Days Ahead (Clayton, Mo., Board of Education, 1949).

Starting to School (Glencoe, Ill., Board of Education, 1948).

Some Special Problems of Children, Aged Two to Five Years (New York, New York Committee on Mental Hygiene, 1947).

The Why and How of Kindergarten Records, Leaflet No. 10, Portfolio for Kindergarten Teachers (Washington, Association for Childhood Education, 1945).

United States Children's Bureau, *Your Child from One to Six* (Washington, Department of Labor, 1945).

Weed, Florence Collins, *Learning to Live Through Play*, Bulletin 212 (Columbus, Agricultural Extension Service, The Ohio State University, 1945).

Working with the Child from Two to Six, Ohio Curriculum Bulletin No. 5 (Columbus, State Department of Education, 1944).

Your Child Goes to Kindergarten: For Parents of Kindergarten Children (Minneapolis, Minneapolis Public Schools, 1947).

Your Child in Kindergarten (Pasadena, Calif., Pasadena Public Schools, 1946).

Your Child Starts to School in Louisville (Louisville, Ky., Board of Education, 1949).

PART II

||||||||||||||||||||||||||||||||||||||||||||||||||||||||||||||||||||||||||||||||||||||||||||||||||||||||||||||||||||||||||||||||||||||||||||||||||||||||||||||||||||||||||||||||||||||||||||

The Social and Cultural

Aspects of the School

XI — THE SCHOOL IN SOCIETY

NATURE OF SOCIAL INSTITUTIONS

SOCIAL INSTITUTIONS, their origins, their development, their variabilities, their possible perfection, have been of interest to people everywhere and in all times.

Some have believed that they were spontaneously created by their gods and then "revealed" to men. Others have given the credit to a master or group of masters who were inspired.

When people subscribe to such beliefs, they are prone to consider institutions inviolate and to retain them as such no matter what social changes may occur and cause lags between the institutions' credo and actual living conditions.

The current sociological agreement today suggests that institutions are the outcomes of man's attempt to meet his needs.[1] This assumes that they change from time to time and take different forms and outlets from one group to another. Since origins are lost in antiquity, attention is settled on what is the nature of social institutions, their variations, their interrelationships, and their tendency to change.

The term social institution is used in many ways by the layman. Whatever has come to be relatively permanent and established with some favor is often called an institution. So-called "characters" of a community are often spoken of in this fashion. The building or buildings which serve as the center of assemblage or the dispensing of functions are often so identified. Churches, synagogues, mosques may be synonymous for many people with religion. The capitol or

[1] See Chapter 3.

the mayor's office may be equivalent to government, and the school house, the college, or the university may connote education.

Again the institutions may be identified with the people, the agents who interpret and enact the institution. In religion this may be thought of as the priest, the minister, the rabbi; in government as the dictator, the president, or chairman; and in education as the teacher, the principal, or the professor.

Sociological definition of social institution is a more specific one. Out of all the definitions proposed by various writers, several characteristics are held in common to distinguish them from other social phenomena. Each has a structure or elements which compose it and are organized and integrated to a degree where certain functions can be performed. These characteristics include:

First, social institutions rest upon and develop from basic human needs, desires, and interests.

Second, each is a configuration of material objects, of their symbolification, attendant beliefs, rituals, and consequent behavior patterns which we term folkways and mores.

Third, there is a degree of permanence and universality in structure which is dependent upon the complexity and specialized nature of the society.

Fourth, these institutions have functions whereby the structure is utilized in performance. In simpler cultures these functions are often sharply differentiated and materially exclusive. Today the opposite is more often the case. It is not too difficult to gain agreement as to central tendencies, but where functions begin and end is often a matter of disagreement. The school ably illustrates this impasse.

All will doubtless agree that one school function is instruction in the basic skills of communication, such as reading, writing, and arithmetic. Shall communication be understood to include the art and science of living successfully and fully in groups through relaxed, socialized classroom activities which vary from art expression through sex education to music instruction, is for many a moot, or more exactly, a highly debatable issue.

All agree that the function of education is the transmission of the social heritage, but whether it is to be done per se or by and with critical analysis with change imminent, will split most drawing room conversation pieces into two politely warring camps.

Not only do social institution structures and functions vary, but they may vary in the same culture at different times in terms of value status.

Religion is accorded an all important role in some societies. In others it occupies a competitive or unpopular role. Within our own society we can readily trace its changed status from the means of personal life and group social control to a purely elective position in a now secular society.

A fifth characteristic of institutional structure and function, as implied above, is change. As one wag has put it, "About the only thing one can be sure of these days is change."

Sociological literature and that of social anthropology is amply supplied with attempts at scientific study and analysis of changes in social institutions. The Middletown studies and community studies in general illustrate this trend.[2]

Somewhat different but equally penetrating analyses of the school as a social institution include Newton Edwards and Herman Richey, *The Role of the School in the American Social Order;* Robert J. Havinghurst, *Who Shall Be Educated?;* Benjamin Fine, *Are Our Children Cheated?*

If there are any general findings which both these general and specific studies of social institutions have in common, it is that in spite of inertia and conservatism changes occur in social structures and their processes of function.

Likewise these changes are not traceable to any one factor or set of factors. Rather it is to be observed that an invention or discovery in one area of life, like the proverbial pebble in the pool, starts reverberations in all other areas, for relationships are reciprocal.

Just as needs, wishes, and interests call forth social structures to satisfy them so will new inventions and discoveries disturb the approached equilibrium and set in motion, if not new needs, newer definitions of them.

If the structure has become so solidified that it will not consider such growth and development, the results may be varied. Stalemate may ensue and/or revolt by smaller or larger segments of those who feel thwarted.

It is important to add that with institutions, as with personality development of the individual, neither the hereditary, the geographical, or the social-cultural factors can be considered as all im-

[2] *See* Chapter 4.

portant. Each influence helps to set the stage as it were, but alone it does not determine.

It is apparent that certain institutions, such as the economic, are more closely related to environmental factors than, say, religion and family are, but these latter are by no means independent of geography. It is also probably true that the simpler societies are closer in their institutional framework to geographical influences than are more complex societies. Man by improvements in his cultural equipment, learns to become less dependent upon his immediate environment, and is even able to alter radically his geographical surroundings by the application of science and technology . . . cultural factors and process play their part too. . . . Every element, material and nonmaterial, that goes into the making of an institution had to be invented somewhere, sometime, and by someone. They have been transmitted from generation to generation for countless centuries, either by imitation or inculcation. They have also been diffused, being carried from their point of origin to the far corners of the earth. . . . To understand any of our institutions, therefore, we need to bear in mind the hereditary, the geographic, and cultural factors that determine its form, that affect its function, and that operate in causing it to change. It is also important that we assess properly the influence of these various factors for they are not all of equal importance, and their significance is not uniform at all times or in all situations.[3]

A BRIEF HISTORY OF THE SCHOOL AS A SOCIAL INSTITUTION

A "RELATIVELY" NEW INSTITUTION

Schools appear to have been one of the later formal social institutions to emerge. In the simpler, smaller, preliterate societies education and socialization were practically synonymous. The family and the intimate and face-to-face, primary group life of the village transmitted the heritage to its children.

Much of this was done by word of mouth where traditions, customs, and the roles and statuses they prescribed for community members were concerned.

As great a portion of the culture was transmitted by the actual performance of duties and activities in company with family or other

[3] Brewton Berry, Part VI, Social Institutions, in Seba Eldridge and Associates, *Fundamentals of Sociology* (New York, Crowell, 1950), p. 492. Used by permission.

community members. Thus a child learned about hunting and fishing by the actual experience of so doing. Here was perhaps the first really progressive schooling where children learned by doing, hearing, and seeing.

In addition, preliterate people recognized the modern fact that changes in physical growth and development entail social growth and development changes.

To emphasize these signs of maturity, to prepare and cause the youth to anticipate these advances, to be certain that cultural facts would be passed on in an approved way and that the new generation would faithfully play the roles assigned, so-called "rites of passage," or initiation ceremonies, were carefully planned and carried out. Tests of physical prowess and endurance as well as of mental attributes were rigorously performed.

In such societies no child could be unsure of his roles and statuses. Nor would he be in conflict over what attitudes to assume, what vocation to choose, what religion to embrace, or what political theory to support. Likewise under this educational system he had no doubts as to when he was adult, when child.

His initiation ceremonies were in effect his graduation exercises and established him securely in his society. This is in sharp contrast to present day ones which often serve, as one student remarked, only to set young people adrift. Mead puts it very well when she says:

So a girl's father may be a Presbyterian, an imperialist, a vegetarian, a tee-totaler, with a strong literary preference for Edmund Burke, a believer in the open shop and a high tariff, who believes that woman's place is in the home, that young girls should wear corsets, not roll their stockings, not smoke, nor go riding with young men in the evening. But her mother's father may be a Low Episcopalian, a believer in high living, a strong advocate of States' Rights and the Monroe Doctrine, who reads Rabelais, likes to go to musical shows and horse races. Her aunt is an agnostic, an ardent advocate of women's rights, an internationalist who rests all her hopes on Esperanto, is devoted to Bernard Shaw, and spends her spare time in campaigns of antivivisection. Her elder brother, whom she admires exceedingly, has spent two years at Oxford. He is an Anglo-Catholic, an enthusiast concerning all things mediaeval, writes mystical poetry, reads Chesterton, and means to devote his life to seeking for the lost secret of mediaeval stained glass. Her mother's younger brother is an engineer, a strict materialist, who never recovered from reading Haeckel in his youth; he scorns art, believes that science will save the world, scoffs at everything that was said and thought before the nineteenth century, and ruins his health by experiments in the scientific elimination of sleep. Her mother is of a quietistic frame of mind, very much interested in Indian philosophy, a pacifist, a strict nonparticipator in life, who in spite of her daughter's devotion to her will not make any move to enlist her enthusiasms. And this may be within the girl's own household. Add to it the groups represented, defended, advocated by her friends, her teachers, and the books which she reads by accident, and the list of possible enthusiasms, of suggested allegiances, incompatible with one another, becomes appalling.[4]

As communities became larger and more closely knit with other communities, as inventions occurred and were diffused, the cultural content gradually became both great enough and specialized enough so that general family and community members could neither know nor be skilled enough in all its aspects to transmit it.

Consequently, as Murdock points out,[5] even advanced primitive peoples began a new and specialized social institution known as the school.

In other words, whenever the existing social institutions can no longer perform all the functions needed, when the culture has become too large, complex, and specialized to be passed on by lay people, a new institution tends to arise. Its structure and its processes reflect those of other institutions within its culture, and its aims are derived likewise from tribal or societal experience. So it was, and is, with the school.

AIMS OF EDUCATION

The aims of preliterate educational practices appear to have been centered upon inducing conformity to group structure and process by securely fitting the individual into the scheme.

Formal agencies of education have also followed this aim in a number of societies. In addition, they have expected the educational system to train for strong physical bodies and alertness in mental ways for the good of the states' military aims. The education system of Sparta is a commonly cited example of this. So important

[4] Margaret Mead, *From the South Seas* (New York, Morrow, 1939), pp. 202–203. Used by permission.

[5] G. P. Murdock, *Our Primitive Contemporaries* (New York, Macmillan, 1934), pp. 384–435.

was the aim that the state took the child from the home at seven years of age for intensive physical culture training as well as that of military science.

Some educational systems have deliberately separated the sheep from the goats in a determined effort to train leaders not only in the military sense but also as leaders in political, economic, and social life.

Salvation has often been the objective of formal education.

Among the early civilization the Jews were somewhat slow in establishing schools, but in the fifth century B.C. the synagogue began to be a center of instruction, and schools were eventually established. The emphasis was upon religion, the Holy Scriptures forming the core of the curriculum. The early history of Christianity offers examples of formal education devoted to religious aims. The rapid spread of Christianity throughout the Roman world following the conversion of the Emperor Constantine in A.D. 312 presented a multitude of problems to the church. The pagan philosophers had to be refuted, converts had to be instructed, Christianity had to be propagated, doctrines had to be expressed in convincing and intelligible language. To these ends the Church developed a variety of schools—catechumenal (for new members), catechetical (for training priests), cathedral (for training bishops) for the purpose of elucidating, propagating, and defending its doctrines.[6]

Throughout history as in more current times, there have been those who sought other utilitarian aims such as most of those mentioned above.

At certain times and in certain places the aim of the school has been to provide a liberal education—that is, to free the individual from the domination of the group; to help him to be informed, articulate, sensitive to life's values, and able to think and act as a responsible being; and to train the mind to be disciplined, curious, sensitive, rational, and skeptical.[7]

Other aims have included such as the belief that all education should be functional in a vocational way. A child should be pointed always toward the niche in society he will fill, should learn to be satisfied with the same and be "A good citizen," whether it is the life of ease and "conspicuous consumption" or that of the vast army which makes the world's goods and performs services.

[6] Berry, *op. cit.,* pp. 538–539.
[7] *Ibid.,* p. 540.

THE SCHOOL IN AMERICAN LIFE: HISTORY OF SCHOOL ROLES AND FUNCTIONS[8]

COLONIAL SCHOOLS

The American colonies must be viewed not as just settlements along the shore edge of a continent but as integral parts of an expanding European civilization.

They were in fact Europe's western frontier, and they were bound in a thousand ways by the traditions and customs of the Old World, by its ideology and by its religious, social, economic, and political institutions. The history of colonial life, therefore, is in no small degree the history of transplanting European culture in American soil. But that is by no means the whole story. The colonists did not hesitate as they struggled to subdue a raw continent to modify inherited ideas, values, and institutions to meet their needs.[9]

One of the inheritances from England was an educational system which reflected the class system. In the early colonies as in the countries from which the settlers were derived, secondary and higher education—Latin grammar schools and colleges—served primarily the needs of a small directive class. Schools concerned with the teaching of reading and writing in English—where they existed at all—were primarily terminal schools for the masses. They were designed to teach the children of the common people to read, to grasp the principles of some religious sect, and to socialize youth in terms of the existing principles of social organization.[10]

When one attempts to trace the development of the early system of education in the New England colonies, he meets with conflicting views. Cubberly regards Massachusett's attempt to establish universal literacy by its Acts of 1642 and 1647 as "not only new educational ideas in the English speaking world, but that they also represent the very foundation stones upon which our American public school systems have been constructed." [11]

The Beards disagree violently.

These laws, which seem to have been honored in the breach as well as in the observance, have been greeted by a modern education as

[8] For a full discussion of the role of the school in developing America, see Newton Edwards and Herman Richey, *The School in the American Social Order* (Boston, Houghton, 1947). Quotations from this book are used by permission.

[9] *Ibid.,* p. 2.

[10] *Ibid.,* p. 14.

[11] E. P. Cubberly, *Public Education in the United States* (Boston, Houghton, 1934), p. 17.

making for the first time in the English language "a legally valid assertion of the right of the state to require of local communities that they establish and maintain schools of general learning." The unwary are liable to be misled by this contention. Unquestionably the first of these acts was conceived partly in the spirit of the English poor law; while the second flowed from a great desire to impose on all children the creed of the Puritan sect. The fact that the education was ordered by "the state" was of no special significance, for the state and church were one in Massachusetts at the time; indeed if the Mathers were to be believed, the church was superior to the state.[12]

Whichever viewpoint may be correct we can be sure that

the men who founded New England, who led Pilgrim and Puritan across the seas to establish Bible commonwealths in the wilderness, had worked out, in their own minds at least, a definite social design. . . . The social order designed by the leaders was a closely knit church-state. As the leaders of New England read their history, sacred and profane, God had never looked with favor on the rule of the many either in church or commonwealth. Consequently, they proposed the establishment and maintenance of a social order in which the popular will have only limited expression.[13]

It is clear that the town schools of colonial New England were designed to meet the needs of a Puritan social order. It is clear, too, that the pattern of these schools was so rigid that it did not yield to the pressures of an emerging capitalistic society.[14]

In the Middle Colonies, no less than in New England and in the South, the transplanted Europeans strove determinedly to maintain the old and familiar culture in new surroundings.

Educational development in each of the colonies established between New England and Maryland was retarded by the disorganizing influences of clashing cultures. In no other section were the people so sharply divided in social origin or in social outlook. In no other section did the Protestant theory of the personal relationship between God and man find such varied expression as in the divided and constantly dividing religious affiliations of the inhabitants. In no other section was the population so heterogeneous with respect to nationality. All mother Europe contributed to the constituency of the population, and the only non-English peoples to found colonies within the limits of the original thirteen established them in this middle region.

[12] As quoted in Edwards and Richey, *op. cit.,* p. 52, from Charles A. and Mary Beard, *The Rise of American Civilization,* Vol. I (New York, Macmillan, 1927), pp. 179–180.

[13] Edwards and Richey, *op. cit.,* pp. 84–85.

[14] *Ibid.,* p. 125.

In the area of private and higher education, considerable progress was made. Over the Middle Colonies, as elsewhere in America, the Renaissance and the Reformation cast long shadows; for many years the classical and religious traditions held education firmly in their grip. As a result, education was, in large measure, divorced from the realities of American life except as it served religious ends or the purposes of a small aristocratic class. Slowly, however, the influence of classicism and ecclesiasticism weakened, and education began to play a more dynamic role in the social and economic life of the people. The private schools and the colleges were the avenues which led away from old inherited European traditions, and nowhere were these institutions more liberal than in the Middle Colonies.[15]

The Southern Colonies presented still another picture.

If any region in the New World was to bear the name "New England," it should have been the area stretching from the Chesapeake Bay southward rather than the northeastern corner of what is now the United States.

Migrants to the South had embraced a much less thoroughgoing Protestantism than those who had taken refuge in New England. By and large, they had no quarrel with the Anglican Church, and few of them were impelled across the sea by the desire for religious freedom. But on the whole, the Anglican clergy in the South were not an impressive lot. Their influence on political development was relatively slight; they tended to follow rather than to shape social policy.

The educational ideals and practices of the Southern colonists were only slightly changed by the transit to America. No phase of Southern life reflected more truly its English origin than did education. A militant middle class was demanding education, but this demand reflected the growing importance of this class rather than the development of any marked democratic or liberal tendencies. Members of this expanding and power-seeking group looked upon education as a means of enhancing prestige and assuring worldly success, but there were as yet few to argue that children generally should be provided with more training than required to fit them to participate, at levels proper to their social stations, in the political, economic, and religious life of the day.[16]

NINETEENTH-CENTURY DEVELOPMENTS

The period from the Revolution to the Civil War was characterized by the formulation and gradual acceptance of the principles of demo-

[15] Edwards and Richey, *op. cit.,* pp. 162–163.
[16] *Ibid.,* pp. 166–168.

cratic liberalism; by the development of a more democratic social structure; by the rise of the common man to a position of importance, politically and otherwise; by a bitter struggle to control the national state on the part of Southern planter interests and the rising capitalistic East; and by the growth of the feeling of national unity. As new forces transformed American life, it became apparent that the educational arrangements designed to meet the needs of colonial society were no longer satisfactory. A few far-sighted leaders saw at an early date that a system of education publicly supported and controlled and free and open to all was required to meet the needs of the emerging democratic state. This point of view, however, found slow acceptance in practice.[17]

Education in the West was slow to develop on a large scale, but from the beginning its purpose and its ideals were more genuinely democratic than was the case in either the South or the East. In the West there was greater emphasis on the preparation of youth to perform their civic duties in a democratic republic, and education was designed more than elsewhere to prevent the rise of social classes, to make social mobility a reality, and to release the moral and intellectual capacities of the individual.[18]

While science and invention, translated into technology, were modifying the foundations of American life, another change, quiet and unheralded but of revolutionary importance, was taking place. As each decade registered a further decline in the birth rate, it became apparent that a demographic revolution was under way. The slowing down of the rate of population growth; the changing age structure of the population; regional, rural-urban, and class differentials in fertility; and internal migration—all these were creating problems of the first magnitude. Scarcely any aspect of public or social policy was left unaffected by population change.

The educational developments that have occurred in the United States during the past three quarters of a century can scarcely be understood unless viewed against this broad background of economic and social change. More important still, educational statesmanship today requires an understanding of the forces that have transformed and are still transforming our traditional pattern of institutional arrangements.[19]

These social changes have had a profound effect upon the development of American educational institutions. They were responsible, in part, for the expansion of the educational enterprise to include within its services most children and youth as well as a large part of the adult population, for the enrichment of the curriculum, for the almost endless attempts to order the instructional program so as to give it system

[17] *Ibid.,* p. 205.
[18] *Ibid.,* p. 319.
[19] *Ibid.,* pp. 439–440.

and co-ordination, for the development of new types of structural organization, for the changing relations of government to education, and for the improvement of the quality of instruction through the scientific study of education and the more effective education of teachers.[20]

The expansion of the educational enterprise was accompanied by ceaseless effort to construct and reconstruct a curriculum to meet the needs of American life as they changed and as they came to be more adequately understood. Fortunately, in the United States no central government has been in a position to control educational policy. Each community has been more or less free to formulate its own educational values and to implement them in such ways as it deemed best. This experimentation, however, has been carried forward within the framework of certain common ideals and has had as its common goal the discovery of a curriculum content—a body of experience—best suited to the changing conditions of American life. Conflict of values and confusion of purpose there have been, but much of this conflict and confusion must be regarded as the product of different ways of arriving experimentally at a common goal.[21]

Structure and function in human institutions are always closely related. Such has been the case with respect to school, college, and university in the United States. As the purpose of education has moved in the direction of a cultural democracy and as attempts have been made to frame programs to meet the changing and varied needs of the people, the structural organization of education has been repeatedly modified in the hope that each unit in the system would perform its own peculiar function more adequately and that a closer articulation and co-ordination of the total program would be achieved.[22]

THE SCHOOL AS A MODERN SOCIAL INSTITUTION

EVEN SO BRIEF an historical examination of the school in relation to American society in different periods points out the action, reaction, and interaction constantly going on between the school and society.

The role and position of the state as a power instrument, the particular stage of development of the economic, religious, and political factors, the concepts of the individual's worth and how he is located in the society's status levels have all been interrelated in

[20] Edwards and Richey, *op. cit.,* p. 667.
[21] *Ibid.,* p. 712.
[22] *Ibid.,* p. 837.

their effects upon the structure and processes of the American school.

The school, in turn, has exerted its influence. Sometimes it has retained structures and processes long after they have outlived their usefulness, thus creating imbalances and lags. Sometimes it has coasted along content with the "present," the status quo, even "intent" upon its sheer perpetuation. Sometimes it has conceived of its role as an active agent in cultural change in one direction or another. Often schools and school people have simply muddled through. Today the issue is no less sharply drawn. Schools make their choices in a changing world along several avenues. Two widely different ones serve a summary purpose.

One purpose of education is to draw out the elements of our common, human nature. These elements are the same in any time or place. The notion of educating a man to live in a particular environment is, therefore, foreign to a true conception of education.

Education implies teaching. Teaching implies knowledge. Knowledge is truth. Truth is everywhere the same. Hence, education should be everywhere the same.[23]

And on the other side:

The school should endeavor to preserve and continually reinterpret and recreate the democratic way of life which has made public education possible. The school has as its basic purpose the creating of a living and learning situation which will provide for the maximum development of the individual and the group in a democratic setting. Recent aims have included the recognition of the human being as a constantly developing organism whose optimal development is desired regardless of his intelligence, social or economic level. Herein the role of the school is thought of as that of the developing and utilizing of the method of intelligence in solving problems of human concern.[24]

Such a school attempts, in the words of Alberty:

1. To provide an educative environment directed toward the optimal development of all American youth regardless of intelligence, level, or social or economic status.

2. To provide for each student the richest possible experience in democratic living within the school and to help the student to intellectualize such experience in terms of democratic values. This calls for

[23] Robert Hutchins, *The Higher Learning in America* (New Haven, Yale University Press, 1936), pp. 66–67.

[24] Harold Alberty, *Reorganizing the High School Curriculum* (New York, Macmillan, 1947), pp. 52–54. Used by permission.

active participation in group living and continuous practice in the re-creation of values.

3. To provide for each student the conditions for optimal physical and mental health defined in terms of adequate functioning in demo-cratic living.

4. To help each student to develop and utilize the method of in-telligence in solving problems of human concern.

5. To help each student to achieve a dynamic understanding of our democratic culture through the intelligent examination of the con-flicting values and practices of the immediate and wider community.[25]

A concrete example of this social educational approach of the present day school is provided in a report to be found in the Ap-pendix which is the result of the cooperative thinking of a school's staff.

THE SCHOOL AS A CURRENT OBJECT OF ATTACK AND CRITICISM

IN AN ERA of rapid and uneven social change cherished in-stitutions of a democratic society are always subject to attack, and the current scene is no exception. In popular magazines, in pam-phlets, in screaming, brightly colored propaganda sheets, in news-papers as well as in some more scholarly publications, one runs head on into attacks on our public schools. In fact, if the reader is at all impressionable, he might readily think that the entire countryside is irate at the schools and clamoring for their complete revision. The thoughtful student, however, is more apt to wish that someone would bring the evidence together, would analyze it in the light of research methods, and in terms of "who," "when," "where," and "by whom sponsored."

The results of such a scholarly attempt may now be read in a monograph entitled "Let's Look at the Attacks on the Schools." [26]

Dr. Alberty and a number of his advanced graduate students undertook this study in order to discover both what the literature would reveal and what a study of their own would contribute. A survey of the literature revealed that there were, in the main, ten basic criticisms levelled at schools as follows:

[25] Alberty, *op. cit.*, p. 54.
[26] Harold Alberty and others, "Let's Look at the Attacks on the Schools," (Columbus, College of Education, The Ohio State University, 1951). Used by permission.

1. Schools are not effectively teaching children the fundamental skills.
2. Schools are not developing obedience, respect for authority, a sense of responsibility, or a sense of the importance of hard work.
3. Schools fail to stimulate competition among students and to reveal to parents the comparative standing of their children.
4. Schools are trying to educate many young people who cannot profit sufficiently from such education.
5. Schools have not been effective in interpreting their programs to the public.
6. Schools fail to develop a wholehearted allegiance to the American way of life.
7. Schools are taking over the functions and responsibilities of the home and other institutions.
8. Schools are not teaching boys and girls to make a living.
9. Schools are not keeping pace with social change.
10. School personnel are not competent to deal with complex problems the modern school faces.

The accompanying data on both sides of these issues points to several conclusions. First, one or another, and in some isolated cases all, of the criticisms may apply to a given school system at one time or another. Also the attacks on the schools as a whole are never substantiated by reputable research findings.

In respect to the first criticism, studies in many communities, both large and small, show that pupils in the newer curricula master reading skills as well or better than comparable pupils in conventional schools.[27]

Since a variety of reading tests were employed in the studies, the consistent trends of evidence seem well established. Also achievement on a variety of arithmetic tests in various communities provides evidence that pupils in the newer curricula are attaining standards equal or superior to comparable pupils in conventional schools at both the elementary and secondary levels. In general, the newer curricula produce pupils who surpass pupils of the conventional curriculum in language skills and usage. In spelling achievements there is no difference. In secondary schools studies of English are also favorable to the newer curricula.

One very important further point made by the authors in their survey of the basic skills should be given much consideration. They

[27] See Lowry W. Harding, "How Well Are Schools Now Teaching the Basic Skills?" *Progressive Education,* Vol. 29, No. 1 (October 1951), pp. 7–15.

find that not only are the so-called basic skills not neglected but the newer curricula are emphasizing the broadening of the number of basic skills to include, such as initiative, social responsibility, ability to work cooperatively with others, and a concept that leadership resides in all and therefore the person must assume responsibility for his actions, to mention but a few.

Incidentally, the discovery of these curricular aims and outcomes is in itself able answer to criticisms two and three. When you know what grades on a grade card, with attendant cut-throat competition, can do to a child's honesty, his happiness, and his general outlook on life, the reader is apt to conclude that evidence has to be interpreted in the light of education aims. If one assumes the values assigned to traditional schools of "hard work at an assigned task" whether it has meaning or not to the student, then it is probable that students are not so engaged in modern schools. But if one takes the viewpoint that "learning is most effective when the task is accepted by the learner as being worthwhile and when its accomplishment is accompanied by a feeling of genuine achievement," then modern schools are doing an excellent job.

The criticism that schools are trying to educate many who cannot profit therefrom seems aimed mainly at secondary education for even these critics agree on the need for a literate population. The criticism appears to say "that the schools should be geared to the needs of the few, the intellectual elite" rather than to the needs of *all* American youth as democratic ideals would hold.

It is undoubtedly true that so long as curricula remain pointed toward college entrance requirements while the larger percentage of graduates finish their formal schooling at this level, schools are not giving the kind of secondary education which provide for needs and hence optimal development, nor are they preparing youth to make a living by such tactics. But the answer is not less education but "redirected education toward meeting the needs of all youth."

On the issue of the failure of schools adequately to interpret the American way of life, the workshop group points out that merely saluting the flag and reciting the Preamble to the Constitution does not insure appreciation unless effort is made to interpret and relate the principles learned to daily living.

The modern high school student knows the dangers of totalitarian government and has had practice in recognizing and evaluating propaganda for what it is. He is not likely to become a victim of this and other vicious schemes that are utilized by totalitarian governments. Loyalty to the American way of life goes deeper than a pledge of allegiance, beautiful words, and flag waving. One must experience democratic practices and living (in schools) if these values are to be protected, retained, and extended.[28]

Analysis of the literature on this criticism suggests that much of it is springing from "front" organizations and/or from such individuals as Allen A. Zoll.

The studies suggest that many schools have been remiss in the interpretation of their aims, programs, and the like to their constituents. There is evidence also to show, however, that school people are increasingly aware of and interested in this area. In fact, some have gone so far as to say that an enlightened citizenry is one of the best means both of avoiding and of fighting these attacks on the schools. However people may feel, if they do not have the facts they cannot adequately support their schools and school people. And in the lapse of time often necessary to become armed with these facts, the attacking forces enlist many well-meaning but naive citizens.

The criticisms concerning the taking over of home functions and the failure to keep pace with social change are closely interrelated. The increasing urbanization, development of technology, speed up of communication and transportation, and general increase in complexity and specialization of the culture tend to lead us from primary to secondary ways of living. It is a commonly accepted sociological datum that when this occurs, institutional structures as well as processes of functioning will be affected. Some functions will no longer be feasible for one institution but will be so for another. Very often what seems a lost function is but a difference of performance in the function. For example,

"Doesn't it make you mad to have a teacher send home word that your boy should have glasses or that he doesn't get along well with the kids and the school suggests he be allowed to be seen by their social worker?", raved the discontented parent.

"It would not bother me in that way at all," responded the second parent at the meeting. "In this complicated business of living these days I should be eternally grateful that people who could look at him objectively and with superior training, took such an interest and had such concern for my child. I should know that they want for him what

[28] Alberty, "Let's Look at the Attack on the Schools," *op. cit.,* p. 86.

I want for him, adjustment and happiness. No, they aren't taking away our functions, they are re-enforcing them and evidently better than we if our children have reached them in the state you describe."

On the issue of the quality of teacher personnel, the study indicates that although the teaching profession is not up to the standards that many think desirable, there is evidence of improvement as higher salary scales are achieved, as better facilities and equipment become available, as requirements in training advance, and as staff relations improve. It is worth noting that in a nation-wide survey of student reaction to teachers the students, representing all types of schools, liked three out of four of their teachers and considered them helpful, interesting, stimulating, democratic, and intelligent. Their dislike for the fourth teacher was related mostly to temperament and personality. Only one tenth of the reasons for dislike included "too old fashioned, too old to be teaching, or doesn't know the subject."

And finally, what do laymen say when surveyed by such as the Elmo Roper study for *Life* magazine? Roper's data showed that a majority (67 percent) believes that children today are being taught more worth while things than children were twenty years ago. Almost all parents think the school should play as important a role in the socialization of children as the home. A rather large number (67 percent) feel that teachers are more competent than they were in 1930. This is not to say that the respondents did not find weaknesses in the schools. They did and do. This is healthy and necessary if criticisms are made in relation to specific as well as general situations and are of a constructive nature. For the very nature of social living demands constant examination, re-examination, sometimes deletion, often extension as communities perform what well-adjusted, growing personalities must also continually perform—life reconstruction.

TEACHING AND STUDY AIDS

1. What have been the various aims of education in different cultures and ages? How have these aims influenced concepts of teacher- and school roles, status, and classroom methods?
2. What would you say are some of the conflicting views at present as to roles and functions of schools in the social order?
3. What is your personal concept of what schools should be and do?

SELECTED READING REFERENCES

A Laboratory School Evaluates Its Contributions to Teacher Education. (Columbus University School, College of Education, The Ohio State University, 1943).

Alberty, Harold, *Reorganizing the High School Curriculum* (New York, Macmillan, 1948).

Bode, Boyd H., *How We Learn* (Boston, Heath, 1940).

Brubacher, John S., *A History of the Problems of Education* (New York, McGraw-Hill, 1947).

Burr, James B., Harding, Lowry W., and Jacobs, Leland B., *Student Teaching in the Elementary School* (New York, Appleton-Century-Crofts, 1950).

Butts, R. Freeman. *A Cultural History of Education: Reassessing Our Educational Traditions* (New York, McGraw-Hill, 1947).

Collaborators in Child Growth and Development, *Child Growth and Development Emphases in Teacher Education* (Oneonta, N. Y., American Association of Teachers Colleges, 1944).

Cubberly, E. P., *Public Education in the United States* (Boston, Houghton, 1934).

Edwards, Newton and Richey, Herman. *The School in the American Social Order* (Boston, Houghton, 1947).

General Education in a Free Society, Report of the Harvard Committee (Cambridge, Harvard University Press, 1945).

Good, Harry G., *The Development of Education in the Twentieth Century* (New York, Prentice-Hall, 1950).

Hambly, W. D., *Origins of Education Among Primitive Peoples* (New York, Macmillan, 1926).

Hulburd, D., *This Happened in Pasadena* (New York, Macmillan, 1951).

Hullfish, G. H., *Education in Philosophy and Interaction* (Columbus, Ohio, Educational Collections, 1944).

———, "What Kind of Education?" *Educational Research Bulletin,* Vol. 26 (May 1947), p. 118.

Kilpatrick, W. H., *Source Book in the Philosophy of Education* (New York, Macmillan, 1948).

Melby, E. O., *American Education Under Fire* (New York, Anti-Defamation League, 1951).

Presey, Sidney and Robinson, F. P., *Psychology and the New Education* (New York, Harper, 1944).

Roper Study. "What the U. S. Thinks about Its Schools." *Life,* Vol. XXIX, No. 16 (Oct. 16, 1950), pp. 11–18.

Smith, Preserved, *A History of Modern Culture* (New York, Holt, 1930).

Strang, Ruth, "What Did You Get on Your Report Card?" *National Parent Teacher,* Vol. XLIV (March 1950), p. 26.

Thayer, V. T., *The Attack upon the American Secular School* (Boston, Beacon, 1951).

Todd, W. H., *What the Citizens Know about Their Schools* (New York, Columbia University Contributions to Education, No. 279. Bureau of Publications).

XII

THE SCHOOL AS A SOCIAL WORLD

NATURE AND CHARACTERISTICS[1]

LIKE OTHER social worlds, the school social world is a unity of interacting personalities. It is, in effect, a "closed system of social interaction."

Though it centers attention upon the giving and receiving of instruction, it carries with it also a whole system of activities which are clustered about it but may have little relation to mere classroom instruction.

As a social institution, the school has several characteristics which set it apart as a social unity. It has (1) a definite population, (2) which is oriented into a clearly defined political structure, arising from the mode of social interaction characteristic of the school and influenced by numerous minor processes of interaction; (3) there is a nexus of a compact network of social relationships, (4) a pervasive "we" feeling, and (5) a culture that is definitely a separate one from that of nonschool social unities.

Different types of schools include these characteristics in greater or lesser degrees and within settings which are related to the social differentiation scheme which supports them. Private schools, especially boarding schools, include all of them. In the boarding school the population is relatively stable and homogeneous because of the social status and economic factors which have operated to select and elect those who will be allowed to attend. These factors operate in

[1] This section is based upon and occasionally adapted from Waller's widely quoted analysis. W. W. Waller, *Sociology of Teaching* (New York, Wiley, 1932). Materials from Waller used by permission.

a two-way fashion. Not only does the family social and economic status operate, but also the school itself may so set its criteria as to exclude the new rich or those whose intellectual possibilities are not such as to uphold creditably the reputation of the school. Their political structure is clearly defined by "a book of rules and a long line of precedents." The feeling of "we-ness" is promoted by uniforms or distinctive dress, by extremely close and intimate association, by relative isolation from other social worlds and the community in general, and by an unconscious or often deliberately fostered feeling of being "different," sometimes translated "better." The culture content, thus, easily comes to be unique and distinctive, to say the least.

In the private day school a somewhat different situation is likely to obtain. It may become almost as closed a corporation as the boarding school. When people do not live together, that is, eat, sleep and spend all their time together, criteria of selection also may be less rigorous.

The population aggregate may be homogeneous so far as economic status is concerned, but not necessarily homogeneous in terms of family, cultural, and ethnic backgrounds. The school is often "a painless substitute for public school for children of wealthy" or would-be wealthy parents and social accelerates.

The political structure is clearly defined in terms of these factors. "Try as we will," says the head mistress of one such school, "we cannot prevent groupings which amount to the 'have's' and 'have-nots.' " She goes on, "And I don't mean just in terms of economic goods. 'What does your father do?' is one of the first questions asked a new girl. 'Where do you live?' meaning what part of town, and 'Do you know _____ _____?' rapidly follow. It's amazing to watch the knowing, calculating looks they portray as they listen to the answers. Cliques form accordingly. Oh, I don't mean they aren't polite to one another. In fact, they are poisonously so, which only establishes the social distance the more. In class work they cooperate beautifully, but it is largely on a secondary contact basis. Sometimes the barriers seem to vanish; then you watch them leave the building or hear them plan gatherings of an intimate sort, and there they are again."

This woman further points out how this operates when offices are to be filled or representatives of the school are chosen. Such a structure makes the network of social relationships even more complex than in the private boarding school, and more discriminating. The "we-feeling" now may depend upon cliques within the larger framework, upon grade level identification, or special projects for outside consumption where differences may be temporarily submerged for the glory of the alma mater. The culture is still a separate one but a more diversified one.

Public schools differ so much in structure and processes that generalizations cannot be made concerning their recognizability as social units. The one-room school, the small town consolidated grade school, the consolidated high school, the suburban schools, and even some small city high schools may have an underlying unity of a sort to mark them off from other social unities.

In the main the following discussions are based upon studies and analyses of social structures and processes within these public schools. The emphasis lies in this direction, advisedly. Those who wish to analyze specialized schools will find a similar approach feasible as a special interest area study.

SOCIAL CLIMATES IN SCHOOLS

Both schools as a whole and classrooms in particular have social climates which not only impinge upon formal learning situations, but also upon those myriads of educational experiences which are by-products forming a substantial part of the school's social world.

In the main these climates are keynoted by those in leadership capacity. If the administrative and supervisory staffs operate under democratic procedures, the tendency is promoted apace in individual classrooms. Likewise laissez-faire or autocratic climates among educational leaders tend to set the temper for classrooms. There are, of course, those stronger souls who prefer to hew their own way, overall policy be what it may.

In the final analysis it is the classroom teacher who implements the social temperature, school policies to the contrary, notwithstanding. For *no philosophy of education, no curriculum, no method is any more effective than the teacher who implements it.*

What then do we know about the social climates in children's classrooms? What are some of the distinguishable effects upon children as to academic and social outcomes? What are the implications for teacher-student interaction?

Waller has insisted that basic to the human relations scheme in any classroom is antagonism. Is this necessarily so? What has been and can be done about social settings?

In the discussion of family atmospheres it was a basic premise that the kind and quality of the social environment was most significant in the "effective learning and becoming" of the child. This further suggested that the adults in the situation (there the parents, here the teachers) set the tonal quality of the social situation.

As in the home, so in the school, there are observable effects upon both students and teachers. Let us examine some selected studies which have been conducted with an eye toward establishing some objective evidence.

First, it is worth knowing how pupils react to personality aspects which operate in interpersonal relations and/or academic pursuits.

One study of interest came as a result of Witty's suggestion to the officials of a radio program (The Quiz Kids) in March 1946 that a prize be awarded to the best response on the theme, "The Teacher Who Has Helped Me Most." These numerous responses were tabulated, organized, and analyzed. From them certain generalizations were drawn. Witty writes:

This emphasis (the mental hygiene approach in the classroom) is the outstanding feature of the letters. These boys and girls appear to be grateful to the school in proportion to the degree that it offers security, individual success, shared experience, and opportunities for personal and social adjustment.[2]

The order of traits which had been mentioned by these students in their responses was:

1. Cooperative, democratic attitude.
2. Kindliness and consideration for the individual.
3. Patience.
4. Wide interests.
5. Personal appearance and pleasing manner.
6. Fairness and impartiality.
7. Sense of humor.
8. Good disposition and consistent behavior.
9. Interest in pupils' problems.
10. Flexibility.

[2] Paul A. Witty, "An Analysis of the Personality Traits of the Effective Teacher," *Journal of Educational Research,* Vol. XL (May 1947), p. 668.

There are social learnings which the school can foster at every developmental level. The progression of such paced learnings contributes to social maturity in outlook and behavior. The very atmosphere in which a child spends successive school years can

Self-reliance and responsibility can begin to develop early.

From the kindergarten up, children learn to help each other.

become a medium which sustains
and develops fine social attitudes.
When parents, pupils, and school
personnel consciously foster and
cherish democratic values, social
learnings have a better chance to
develop and carry over into mature world citizenship.

Self-reliance can be developed in many ways.

Continuity which makes for good, cumulative learning requires consistent guidance in significant social living. The living provides the essential social medium for such learning. The guidance cultivates the social attitudes and dispositions. Recurrent life

situations must actually involve
children in social exploration and
observation, in discussion and cooperative planning, in sharing
and considering others, and enter-
ing wholeheartedly and purpose-
fully into the give and take of
group living.

Playing "roles" is a healthy socialization experience.

Reading and sharing stories are social learning in primary grades.

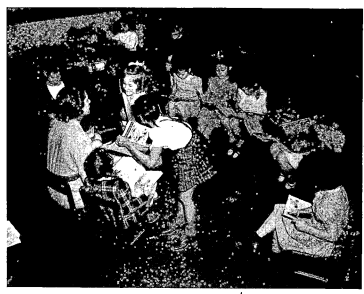

Faith in others and in oneself is fostered by suitable group work.

Group experiments can create mutual respect.

Playing together gives a sense of belonging.

How to work together can be taught in ways suitable for the child's age.

Learning to serve on a committee is important.

Pupils learn skill, self-confidence, and cooperation through music.

Sharing with others broadens the social outlook of all ages.

Children can learn the give
and take of group planning.

Learning concern for safety is a social obligation.

When and how to rest is a necessary learning.

Concentration on doing a good job makes for social competence.

Sharing pleasures of different cultures promotes understanding.

World citizenship is learned by doing.

Continuity of social learning is a day-by-day, year-by-year process of realizing broader horizons, clearer relationships, and deepening insights. Children need to belong to groups in which they can be a part of social processes and have a part in the initiation and projection of social action. Their commitments and responsibilities are the continuities out of which social identification and social competence are developed.

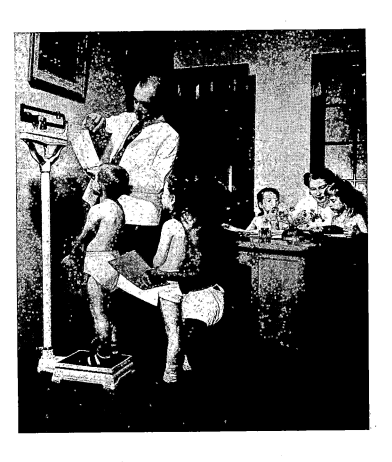

Pupils are proud of their work and school when parents, school doctors, nurses, teachers, and children work continuously together for the optimum development of their common denominator—the child.

Respect for rules makes for social order.

Social learnings are indeed the fundamentals of life adjustment. Nothing less than a continuity of direct experiences in democratic human relations and constructive social aspirations can develop a generation committed to concern for the common good. This is the basic sanction for public education and generous school support.

11. Use of recognition and praise.

12. Unusual proficiency in teaching a particular subject.

In a study made by Hart[3] replies from ten thousand high school seniors were used in which they were asked to describe the best-liked and least-liked teachers they had had. They were also asked to designate the most effective teacher they had ever had. Four out of five declared that the best-liked teacher was also considered the best teacher.

Prescott sums up the analyses and tabulations from Hart's study by saying:

Interestingly enough, teachers are best liked for their helpfulness in facilitating learning. Then come immediately such personality characteristics as cheerfulness, good nature, sense of humor, friendliness, fairness, and sympathetic understanding. In contrast, teachers become the least liked because of the unpleasant effect they produce by being cross, grouchy, or sarcastic, by never smiling, or by losing their tempers. Ineffectiveness as a teacher takes second rank in leading to rejection of a teacher by pupils. Other forms of behavior which produce dislike of a teacher are: being partial, having "pets," "picking on certain pupils," acting superior, aloof, haughty, "snooty," mean, unreasonable, "hard-boiled," intolerant, ill-mannered, being too strict, or failing to recognize pupils outside of class.[4]

It is true that studies such as the two briefly referred to, which give opinions describing desirable personal qualities in teachers, may not be considered as real evidence as to the part that the teacher's personality plays in his effectiveness as a teacher, but there are indications that personality has some influence in education, especially when education is considered to be wider than simply acquiring academic learning as measured by achievement tests.[5]

Harold H. Anderson[6] has conducted and reported revealing and challenging studies of the quality of interpersonal relations in classroom situations. These studies were planned in order to devise suitable measures of the psychological environment of the child in the school and the effects of this environment on the child's be-

[3] From a study by F. W. Hart, *Teachers and Teaching by Ten Thousand High School Seniors* (New York, Macmillan, 1934).

[4] Daniel Prescott, *Emotion and the Educative Process* (Washington, American Council on Education, 1938), pp. 273–274. Used by permission.

[5] From an unpublished paper by Irene Thomas.

[6] Harold H. Anderson, *et al., Studies of Teachers' Classroom Personalities,* Vols. I, II, and III (Stanford, Stanford University Press, 1945–1947).

havior. Public school classrooms were used, and what appeared to be appropriate and reliable methods of observing and recording data were developed.

The investigators first observed a kindergarten group in a play situation where they found these outcomes:

1. Dominative behavior in one child tended to incite dominative behavior in his companion.
2. Socially integrative behavior tended to elicit socially integrative behavior in his companion.
3. Thus dominative and socially integrative behavior were each found to be "circular" in their effects; each tended to produce its like.
4. Dominative behavior, because of its tendency to intensify conflict, was regarded as a "vicious" circle.
5. Socially integrative behavior, because of its tendency to promote spontaneity, security, and understanding, was regarded as socially desirable and came to be known as a "growth circle." [7]

The chief result of this first study was to point out that these kinds of behaviors were occurring and could be described and that further efforts were needed to demonstrate how the behavior of the teacher was related to that of the children. These results furnished tools whereby later studies could be set up.

Essentially Anderson has looked at teacher personality as a contributing factor in creating the classroom atmosphere for learning and has described specifically suggestive kinds of contacts which provide for and limit the kinds of growth possible.

With these situations to work with, Anderson set up a plan to study the interpersonal relations in two second-grade classrooms with specific emphasis upon finding out how the behavior of the particular teacher was related to that of the children. The groups showed very different behavior so it was planned to observe the two groups of children the next year as third graders with different teachers. Again the contacts were recorded as to group or individual contacts on the part of the particular teacher.

At this point a specific description of *dominative behavior* may be helpful. It was considered to be evidenced when the child and the teacher were definitely working *in opposition to* each other.

Conflict, or working against each other, was said to exist when the child by verbal expression or physical action indicated a goal or desire of

[7] Anderson, *op. cit.*, II, p. 23. Used by permission.

his own and the teacher obstructed his pursuit or achievement of that goal or desire by imposing her own wishes or goals.[8]

In other words, she made an attempt to stop his behavior without asking him, without seeking to work out a solution between them. She used her own experience to make a negative decision about the child's indicated wants.

Specific examples of domination with evidence of conflict [9] are such as these:

1. The teacher determines a detail of activity in conflict.
2. The teacher relocates the child.
3. The teacher makes a direct refusal or contradiction; she evades a child's protest or complaint; she postpones without giving a reason or expressing consideration.
4. The teacher registers disapproval, blame, or shame toward the child as a person.
5. The teacher issues warnings, threats, reminders, conditional promises, obstructions, or interruptions.
6. The teachers mete out punishments, such as sending a child from the room or to the principal's office or keeping him after school.

Specific examples of dominative behavior with no evidence of conflict [10] were of the directive type where the teacher was speaking of the routine mechanics of group management such as:

1. The teacher determines the detail of an activity of a routine nature.
2. She repeats warnings, threats, or reminders but shows no evidence of conflict.
3. She calls the members of the class to attention.

A third kind of domination was that found as the teacher and children worked together *with the expressed desire of the child.*[11] The teacher recognizes the child's right to have his opinion, but the child himself does not make the final or the immediate decision. That is left for the teacher. Representative examples of this type of behavior are:

1. The teacher may refuse, deny, or contradict a child's expressed desire with an appropriate explanation.
2. She may postpone and give her reasons.

[8] *Ibid.,* III, p. 22. Used by permission.
[9] Adapted from Anderson, *op. cit.,* III, p. 23.
[10] *Ibid.,* pp. 23–24.
[11] *Ibid.,* pp. 24–25.

3. She may select a child for some kind of an activity on the basis of his expressed interest or request.
4. She may give approval of some required work.
5. She may give her permission for something, a decision reached by her.

This type of action often "sounds" similar to the socially integrative procedure. Its results, however, are quite different.

Aspects of *integrative behavior* were more difficult to define. However, Anderson writes:

Evidence of *working together* consisted of verbal or other expressions which indicated that both teacher and child were pursuing the same goal or were trying to find a common purpose without the imposition of goals, desires, or ideas of the one on the other. This evidence could appear only when the teacher attempted to cooperate with the child in an activity in which he was already engaged, or when the child had already given indication that he voluntarily or spontaneously accepted the teacher's ideas or goals as his own. The "acceptance" of the teacher's goals or problems does not include obedience or conforming under duress.[12]

Anderson singled out two types of integration, that where there was no evidence of working together, and that where there was evidence of working together.

Integration with no evidence of working [13] together he found in the contacts initiated by the teacher but in which she in no way used force or pressure on the child. These contacts were more of an exploratory nature where her aim seemed to be to arouse an expression of an interest on the part of the child who was entirely free to express interest or disinterest. She extended an invitation which the child was free to accept or decline.

Then there was the integrative behavior showing evidence that the teacher and the children were working with each other.[14] Each child was accepted for what he was—a person in the situation because he had given some indication of interest or desire. His status of being accepted as a person in his group was not adversely affected because he made an incorrect or inappropriate solution to a problem. He was not blamed when he made mistakes. There was evidence of joint participation on a common problem. The teacher may have

[12] Anderson, *op. cit.*, III, p. 22. Used by permission.
[13] Adapted from Anderson, *op. cit.*, III, pp. 25–26.
[14] *Ibid.*, pp. 26–27.

initiated the activity but the child pursued the activity without evidence of coercion from the teacher.

Representative examples of this kind of behavior are:

1. The teacher helps the child define, redefine, or advance a problem. This may range from telling a child a word as he reads to help him understand and work out a complex social relationship.
2. The teacher expresses approval, thanks, or acceptance of the spontaneous behavior of the child or of his self-initiated activity.
3. She extends an invitation in response to a child's expressed wish, suggestion, or need.
4. She questions him further concerning an expressed interest or activity.
5. She accepts and admits her responsibility for her own act which is inconvenient, unjust, or unfair.

Several important generalizations can be drawn from the findings of these studies:

1. Domination incites domination.
2. Integrative behavior induces cooperative or integrative behavior.
3. Domination and integrative behavior as defined are psychologically different, and in these investigations they were unrelated to each other.
4. A change in pupil personnel for the two second-grade teachers a second year did not change significantly the pattern of individual teacher behavior with the boys and girls.
5. A change in teacher personnel in the third grade did result in changes in pupil behavior from that found in the same groups the previous year.
6. The main direction of influence seemed to be from teacher to pupil.
7. Teachers tended to meet aggression with aggression. They were inciting resistance and were not systematically breaking up or cutting the "vicious circle" which characterized domination.
8. Teachers were very sporadic in their attempts at introducing socially integrative contacts in efforts to break up the "vicious circles" of dominative behavior.
9. Any difference between the teachers that was significant in the autumn was again significant in the winter when another sampling was made.
10. The range of frequencies of individual contacts showed that individual children in the same room lived in widely different psychological environments.
11. Teachers were doing nothing systematically to reduce conflict by

working with those children who were most in conflict with each other.

12. There seems to be evidence that the teachers were not intellectually aware of the underlying causes of the various kinds of behavior and their own contributions to the making of conditions for such kinds of behavior.

In summary, then, Anderson's study found that children's behavior tends to follow certain circular patterns unless something occurs to break up and change the circle. His investigation indicated that change was due to the kind of leadership offered by the teacher. He also found that the type of leadership offered by the teacher was not at all consistent.

Another kind of study which appraises social climate and its effects upon child behavior is that set up by Lewin and his associates.[15] Experiments covering highly controlled situations were established wherein the group atmospheres were kept constant and consistent. The interpersonal relationships were studied to discover what happened in individual and group behavior under three atmospheres—democratic, autocratic, and laissez-faire club meeting situations were used.

In order to give a clear and brief picture of what the three types of social atmospheres meant in actuality, a description as given in the report of the experiment is presented on page 307.[16]

Possibly at this point it should be added that since the experiment was conducted to find out about aggressive behavior under differing conditions, it would be expected that the autocratic leaders did not forbid aggressive action. Instead their influence was not of the verbal prohibiting kind "but a sort of generalized inhibition or restraining force." They managed it in a sort of positive way.

The authors defined aggressive acts as occurring when one member of a group or one group turned against another member of the group or another group. They suggested that they may be thought of as aggressive acts *within a group* or aggressive acts *against a group.*

[15] Reported by Kurt Lewin, Ronald Lippitt, and Ralph K. White, "Patterns of Aggressive Behavior in Experimentally Created Social Climates," *Journal of Social Psychology* (May 1939), pp. 271–298. See also Florence Greenhoe Robbins, "The Impact of Three Social Climates upon a College Class," *The School Review,* Vol. LX (May 1952).

[16] Lewin, Lippit, and White, *op. cit.,* p. 273. Used by permission.

Authoritarian	*Democratic*	*Laissez-faire*
1. All determination of policy by leader.	All policies a matter of group discussion and assisted by leader.	Complete freedom for group or individual decision, without any leader participation.
2. Techniques and activity steps dictated by the authority one at a time so that future steps were always uncertain to a large degree.	Activity perspective gained during first discussion period. General steps to group goal sketched, and where technical advice was needed, the leader suggested two or three alternative procedures from which choice could be made.	Various materials supplied by leader who made it clear that he would supply information when asked. He took no other part in work discussions.
3. Leader usually dictated the particular work task and work companions of each member.	The members were free to work with whomever they chose, and the division of tasks was left up to the group.	Complete nonparticipation by leader.
4. The dominator was "personal" in his praise and criticism of work of each member, but remained aloof from active group participation except when demonstrating. He was friendly or impersonal rather than openly hostile.	The leader was "objective" or "factminded" in his praise and criticism, and tried to be a regular group member in spirit without doing too much of the work.	Very infrequent comments on member activities unless questioned, and no attempt to participate or interfere with the course of events.

The aggressive acts were recorded so that the number per minute and the kinds of acts were established. Perhaps the strangest and most revealing data were found in the difference between the aggressive tendencies of two autocratic groups. In one there were but two aggressive acts per meeting whereas in the other there were thirty-eight. The apathetic group was described thus:

There was little smiling, joking, freedom of movement, freedom of initiating new projects, etc.; talk was largely confined to the immediate activity in progress, and bodily tension was often manifested. . . . The impression created was not one of discontent by any means, and the activities themselves were apparently enjoyable enough so that the net results for most of the group was more pleasant than unpleasant. Nevertheless, they could not be described as genuinely contented.[17]

The change came, however, when their leader left them alone. Their aggressive actions burst forth ten times as much as formerly. When they changed to the democratic atmosphere, which was their change, the number of their aggressive acts shot tremendously high and then dropped rather suddenly to about the average for other groups in the democratic atmosphere.

Under autocratic leadership the factors determining whether behavior will be aggressive or apathetic rest upon two conditions. The authors explain it thus:

We have apathy when the pressure and restraining forces from without are kept stronger than the forces within the person which lead to emotional expression. . . . Which is stronger depends upon the amount of pressures and the "willingness" of the person to "accept" the pressure.[18]

Several types of aggressive acts within the autocratically controlled group were mentioned. They consisted (1) of composing a letter of resignation which they asked their teacher to give to their leader in the third week of their series of meetings but which they did not give to the leader themselves; (2) of striking; (3) of reciprocal aggression among the members; (4) of rebellious acts; (5) of release behavior when the climate was changed, that is, they used the masks they had made to throw at each other, to kick around, etc.

Hostility was released against another group after a hostile stranger had criticized their work during the absence of their leader. This serious intrusion caused the group to disintegrate. They were restless and tense; there was no respected adult present; they had no absorbing group activity. Therefore, they centered their attention upon a couple of remarks made by members of a laissez-faire group which shared the room with them. A "war" ensued, but it was not labeled as such until quite late in its progress. Later a second "war"

[17] Lewin, Lippit, and White, *op. cit.*, p. 283.
[18] *Ibid.*, p. 297.

started very suddenly, was labeled immediately, and rose to a high verbal pitch within four minutes.

An interesting example of high morale came one day in a democratic group where all were engrossed in painting on glass. The leader was absent. The janitor (a hostile stranger) entered the room and began sweeping, making a great deal of dust. The boys coughed, but they continued to work in spite of the fact that they were almost swept from the room. They stayed on the job until the janitor asked them to get out of their chairs. In sweeping he carelessly broke their glass. They made the expected kinds of remarks, yelling that if their leader were there he would beat the janitor up. Their aggression toward the janitor was verbal, but overtly they needed release so they collectively tore up a wooden sign about their club, giving vent to their feelings by being noisy, using a couple of hammers each, etc.

Out of this experimentation with the three kinds of social climates, the authors found these five factors which play a dominant role in spontaneous aggression:

1. Records show that in the autocratic situations the leader made six times as many directing approaches to the child as were made to him in the democratic situation. This necessity of being a target for so many approaches amounts to social pressure from the leader. It proves annoying and disintegrating and produces a higher state of tension which in turn necessitates some sort of outlet toward some aspect of the environment. The raising of tension is a most important factor in determining spontaneous aggression.

2. The "space of free movement" refers not only to bodily locomotions but to social and mental locomotions. When this space of movement is narrow, it is the same as higher pressure, especially if the group has previously enjoyed a less narrow space of free movement. It is recognized that autocratic leadership grants narrow space of free movement while democracy greatly broadens it. Laissez-faire leadership does not offer an opportunity to its participants to know what comes next or what the structure is and allows various members to interfere in the work activities of other members. Therefore, it limits the space of free movement also.

3. Aggression as the emotional expression of an underlying tension often finds outlets in overt behavior which are unrelated to real purposeful activity and contribute in no way to pushing forward the behavior in which the individual is expected to be engrossed.

4. The need to act which is built up by the higher state of tension may find release in terms of the rigidity of the social position of the per-

son within the group. Autocracy limited the possibilities of changing position in the group much more than democracy. It often seems to make the barriers for leaving the group stronger also. Straining against limiting factors seems to increase tension.

5. Usually the ways of handling tensions deemed appropriate by a culture determine to a great extent how various individuals in that society or culture will handle their tensions.[19]

The experiment also included evaluative statements from the various boys obtained by others outside the club arrangements. They say:

With surprising unaminity the boys agreed in a relative dislike for their autocratic leader regardless of his individual personality. Nineteen of the twenty boys liked their leader in democracy better than their leader in autocracy.[20]

The boys' comments about the leaders were very similar according to the role they played. Seven out of ten cases preferred the laissez-faire leader over the autocratic one. Even disorder seemed preferable to them over a kind of benevolent rigidity.

In considering the concept of the space of free movement on the part of the various children in the autocratic group, it is evident that it is the leader who sets the goal and determines how the goal will be met. This means that each child would have been able to figure out how to reach the goal and also to reach the goal by himself. Indeed, it is appropriate to expect that normal children do have goals of their own, that they do have ideas of how to reach those goals. They have dispositions toward, or readinesses for, some ways of thinking, feeling, and doing which are thwarted when the autocratic leader sets up the appropriate goals and ways of reaching them. These constitute barriers in the child's space of free movement because they are substituted and consist of force in certain directions. Lewin calls such goals induced goals. He writes:

. . . the leader in the democratic group, instead of hindering the children in getting to their own goal, bridges over whatever regions of difficulty might exist. For the democratic group, many paths are open; for the autocratic only one, namely, that determined by the leader.[21]

Careful analysis showed that conversation in the democratic

[19] Lewin, Lippit, and White, *op. cit.,* p. 297.
[20] *Ibid.,* p. 284.
[21] Lewin, *Resolving Social Conflicts* (New York, Harper, 1948), p. 77.

group was characterized by "we" whereas in the autocratic group "I" prevailed.

The patterns of interaction differed in the various groups. They went from the autocratic leader to a child and back to the leader whereas in the democratic group they tended much less frequently to be initiated by the leader and went from child-to-child to child-to-leader, etc. Lewin states that the "style of living" in both atmospheres determined the quality of the child-child relations as well as the child-leader relations. This agrees very closely with the "vicious circle" and the "growth circle" found by Anderson.

Of particular interest were Lewin's statements in regard to the status levels and barriers against change in status in the groups. He found two clearly defined levels of social status in the autocratic group: the leader was the only one having the higher status and maintained the controls completely which set the barriers excluding any other from leadership. All the others were kept on the same low level; they were compelled to compete, to vie with each other, in order to satisfy a normal need to strive for status and prestige. Therefore, each child became a potential threat to every other child, and it was to the advantage of each to suppress the others as thoroughly as possible. In the democratic group no barriers existed against acquiring leadership, and thereby the members were freed to search for status and to explore diversity. This freedom seemed to emerge from the high group feeling which fostered a sense of security, of firm ground from which to grow into individuality. The movie *Autocracy and Democracy* listed in the Appendix shows the study in action.

GROUPS AND GROUPING ARRANGEMENTS AMONG SCHOOL CHILDREN

IMPORTANCE OF GROUP MEMBERSHIP

The people who live together in the microcosm of the school world exhibit all the social structures and processes of the macrocosm of the larger society. It is, therefore, important that we study, within the limits of space, the groups and grouping arrangements of children within the classroom, the ascendancy relationships which occur and their relation to the social climates which teachers establish.

As soon as people aggregate with any regularity for any length of time, action and reaction develop into interaction. In this process lines of communication are established between the persons of the group.

This is as true for classrooms as for any other social group. If the participation is done without reserve, if the nature of the interaction is intimate, usually face-to-face, informal, it is a primary group. And, as has been emphasized many times in earlier pages, the primary groups in which a child operates, as Cooley long ago pointed out, are the significant relations which order his life.

If this is so, all who work or meet with children need to know something not only of peer group arisal and development and impacts outside the home and school but also of the schoolchild's world itself.

It has been indicated that there is discernible a certain process of succession of social groupings as child growth and development proceeds. Each kind of group generally appears at a stage of child development. Many serve their purpose and dissolve naturally as maturation, physical and social, occurs. With the possible exception of such "persisting" groups as the home, each makes its contribution to social development and should lose its importance. If it doesn't, the individual may remain at a retarded developmental stage. Doubtless all of us know adults who never "outgrew" the sorority-girl or frat-man era.

When the child enters school, he is a participant in a uniquely new and important social setting. The group life he experiences there will have a significant bearing upon his personal development, for he can develop for at least six to eight hours of the day only in interaction with his peers and the parent-surrogates, the teachers.

Thus, his sense of happiness and security in the classroom in particular and his child world by implication will be directly related to his group position with his classmates. In fact, within this group life may lie the motivation or lack of it for learning.

In other words, in relation to this group interaction, Jennings says: [22]

In a group he also learns to face, to analyze, and to assess problems in a social context and to develop ways of solving them with others. In interaction with others, furthermore, the broadening of his personal universe takes place; he gets to know his fellows, their values, and ways, and so gradually extends his sensitivity in human relations. His per-

[22] Helen Hull Jennings, *Sociometry in Group Relations* (Washington, American Council on Education, 1948), pp. 4–7. Used by permission.

sonal social maturity is also dependent on interaction with others. Educators have not always realized this. In many schools each child is treated on a strictly individual basis; what he does or does not do is dealt with as his personal responsibility. Tasks are assigned according to this pattern; satisfactions, whether in the form of marks or other recognition, are similarly awarded; and punishments are likewise given as if shortcomings were entirely an individual matter. The child is thus systematically oriented toward standing on his own feet and rising or falling according to personal achievement only. He is not directed toward facing, analyzing, or assessing problems in a social context or developing plans for solving them with others.

This emphasis on independent action has many harmful effects. The more a child succeeds in learning exclusively by and for himself, the greater the loss to him as an individual. Those who are successful learn not only to individualize all achievement and responsibility, but they also learn to cherish exclusiveness in their social relations and to keep others from undermining their position and prestige. In other words, they are learning how to keep group life as sectionized and divided up as possible in order to safeguard their own standing in some part of it. Other less successful children are learning to withdraw and suppress their rebelliousness, to give up trying to exercise their talents, and to acquiesce in a social situation that is largely responsible for their own failures. They may be afraid to enter social doors that are actually open to them and pass up opportunities where their contributions would really be welcome. Both are apt to get distorted views of themselves as individuals and as members of society.

Neither can we overlook the positive role of interpersonal contacts as a psychological necessity. As children mature, their interest in, and affectional relations to, one another broaden parallel to their expanding capacity to get satisfaction from social intercourse. Children need approval from others of their own age possibly more than the approval of their teachers. They need to grow in their ability to appreciate others, to assess themselves through the eyes of others, and to make a place for themselves. They should have opportunities for socialization, for the exchange of ideas, for helping one another, and for exploring one another's personalities. Without such opportunities their perspective will be foreshortened, their skills for contact with others limited, and their initiative in reaching out toward other people inhibited. This development cannot take place naturally when interpersonal contacts are not sanctioned or when natural inclinations and affinities are disregarded in the social arrangements provided.

Teachers often consider it their duty to separate children who show interest in each other because of the assumed interference with their work. Seating plans, working committees, and other arrangements are often set up without regard to students' inclinations toward each other, or even in direct opposition to them. Good conditions for learning are thereby destroyed or at best neutralized, not to speak of other possible consequences such as the expression of thwarted tendencies in giggling or teasing. Many a disciplinary problem arises from the fact that children are taught to live two lives, one officially and the other under cover, in order to satisfy the social needs forbidden by the school.

The same thing applies to the frustration of children's efforts to help each other. Girls and boys may be willing and able to explain things to one another with a patience and understanding beyond the ability of busy teachers to summon. When this inclination is thwarted, it can be exercised by subterfuge only. Thus, the child is taught that he must disregard appeals for help, that he must not openly contribute to the social needs of himself or his classmates—in other words, that he must strictly mind his own business.

Artificial restrictions of this sort will color a child's outlook on everything in school and even life beyond it. Being emotionally fenced in, in this one aspect of his experience, he comes to regard group life and social interaction as something reserved for the unimportant parts of living, possibly as something unpleasant, certainly as something to be avoided in connection with work. Nobody has much opportunity to learn how satisfying give and take can be or to learn the personal release that can be had from joint action.

Academic learning in school cannot be separated from the social atmosphere in which it takes place. Since children are taught in groups, they are bound to affect each other. Their attitudes toward one another and their personal feelings of security and belonging have a lot to do with the way they use their minds. Cleavages, interference with communication, and other tensions usually absorb energy that could be used for positive achievement. Many experiments testify to the fact that when the emotional shocks due to inadequate or discordant group life are removed and advantage is taken of the existing psychological affinities, there usually results a heightening and release of children's intellectual abilities along with a redirection of their thinking processes. These outcomes are related not only to what happens to individual personalities, but also to the play of group or social motivation on performance. Positive interaction in learning allows members of a group to complement one another's capacities and hence contributes to greater total achievement. Individuals can stimulate one another in place of competing with one another. But, above all, group motivation adds an extra stimulus which cannot be set up in individuals by themselves, especially when they may be emotionally conditioned for rivalry instead of collaboration. A basis is thus created for the natural discipline resulting from wanting to please other members in a group, from wanting to perform adequately in the group endeavor.

BASES OF GROUP CHOICES

What do we know about the social processes of students' choices? How do children choose or become chosen? What do their choices mean? How may we study them? These are but a few of the questions usually raised by both prospective teachers and teachers in service.

Until recently intuitive insight provided about the only insight into the social interaction of children within the school as well as elsewhere. At present there is developing, under the title of sociometrics, methodology for investigating the social structure of child groups, their association and communication lives, and the acceptance and rejection patterns which are operating.

A popular device has been the sociometric test and sociogram. Briefly the procedure is to ask children to choose from their companions, first, second, and sometimes third choices, the person or persons whom they prefer for some classroom situation which has real meaning for them. If severe tensions are known to exist, children are also often asked for names of children with whom they would not like to sit or work. The results are then arrayed in what is called a sociogram.

This diagrammatic presentation of data has several advantages. It provides a comprehensive picture of group structure for a given moment of time, and, in turn, it suggests the further needed studies and investigation. In fact, its chief contribution to the teacher who would understand the child society of her classroom is that of a *starting point only*.

Teachers in summer school classes report apalling misuses of so-called sociometrics. Some have made one sociogram and used it to "interpret" child behavior for the rest of the year. Often the sociogram is the only analysis of the children's behavior. The teacher has thus "typed" the child even more perniciously than did the older worship of I.Q. tests. Some have shown no conception of the points made by Jennings in the above excerpt, namely that children play different roles in different situations and occupy different statuses in different situations and contexts unless forced to do otherwise.

"I choose Mary for work period, but for lunch time I like Jo-

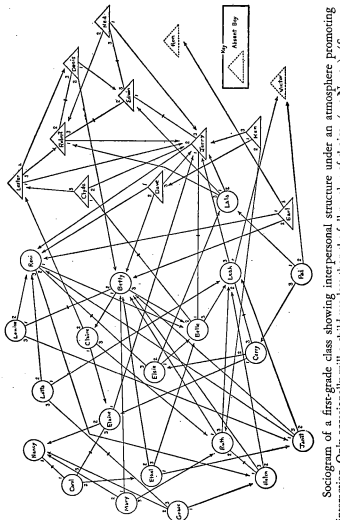

Sociogram of a first-grade class showing interpersonal structure under an atmosphere promoting interaction. Only occasionally will a child use less than the full number of choices (see Nancy). (Source: Helen Hull Jennings, *Sociometry in Group Relations*, Washington, American Council on Education, 1948, p. 77.)

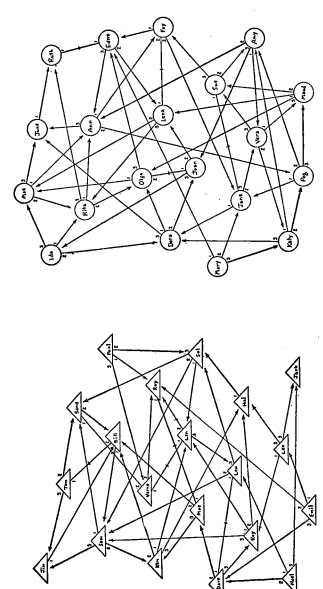

Sociogram of a fifth-grade class showing interpersonal structure under an atmosphere restricting interaction. Note that many of the children in this class have not used their full choice allowance, and one, Jack, has chosen no one. (Source: Helen Hull Jennings, *Sociometry in Group Relations*, Washington, American Council on Education, 1948, p. 80.)

Ann, and when we play games, I like Susie," says a first grader. "And it's funny, Mary wants JoAnn at lunch; so we're all happy."

One further reason for concern may be noted. The method of direct questioning presents a very real danger of promoting social differentiation where little may have existed or of deepening patterns already established.

"Today the teacher said 'Who would you rather sit by?' " says the third grader at dinner. "I said, 'Oh, either Joe, Harry, Sam, or Tubby.' But she insisted on *which* one. I told her I liked 'em all the same, but I had to answer, so I said Tubby. Now that I think of it, I guess I like Tubby best of all and then Joe, and then Sam and Harry."

One teacher with more insight rebelled at giving the tests as suggested by her principal.

I've studied a lot of Prescott's [23] stuff and I decided I'd make sociograms all right, but not by questioning. I read up on how to do anecdotal recordings and got my student teacher to do likewise. Then we took notes on the children's "free choices" for our various activities. We made one sociogram for work periods, one for rest time, one for play period. We made three that year in each area. But as the experts say that was only the beginning. We looked up all the school's cumulative records and then got permission to extend the idea of sending report cards by personal conferences with one or both parents from each family. As a result, I was invited to a number of homes, which helped a lot in working with the children. A number of things surprised me. Children don't always feel about other children the way teachers think they do. I learned a lot too about how to change the group structure, and I acquired a few fears. I've decided that unless a child is a "fringer" or "isolate," or one whose leadership is definitely bad, I won't fool much with him. One girl was the center of all the choices, and this seemed bad to me; so I set up situations which would give others a chance at leadership. Gradually, she was displaced, and the results on her adjustment frightened me. I decided right then I'd help isolates and fringers to become accepted, and, if that process made changes in others positions, it would be O.K. but never again would I tamper with the "accepted" ones.

One need not belabor the points made by this teacher. Her initiative and resourcefulness are inspiring, and her warning notes are not to be taken lightly. Anyone who "tampers" with other peo-

[23] *Helping Teachers Understand Children* (Washington, American Council on Education, 1945).

ple's lives in a professional sense must take responsibility for proper preparation and understanding of the methods he uses. He must be alert to impacts upon groups as well as the ease of securing data.

One must recall that the sociogram gives only a picture of the structure, not the reasons behind it. These reasons must be discovered by using other aids such as the above teacher suggested. Informal and casual interviews with the children, children's themes and diaries, home interviews, further sociograms with data secured less directly again as suggested by the above teacher, plus the school cumulative records will provide a more accurate and usable child and group profile. Analysis and interpretation of data by other competent people is not to be overlooked.

If we may assume, however, that psychological choices have been ascertained in an approved manner, the principle of translation into action is reasonably simple. Each individual should be given the highest degree of satisfaction compatible with maximum happiness for everyone else and maximum stimulation for all. Jennings suggests five rules for carrying out the original agreement.

First, in order to carry out as many expressed wishes as possible, it is generally best to start with the children who have not been chosen at all or only seldom. It is usually better to give an unchosen pupil his own first choice. For example, if David chooses Patty first, Lee second, and Willard third, and no one chooses him; then David should be placed with Patty.

Second, give any pupil in a pair relation the highest reciprocated choice from *his* point of view: his first choice if this is returned, his second if this is returned and his first is not, or his third if this is the only reciprocated choice on his list. For example, if Patty chooses Lynne first, Susan second, and Robert third, but neither Susan nor Robert returns the choice; and if Lynne has chosen Patty second while her first and third choices have not been reciprocated, then both Patty and Lynne will have received optimal treatment if they are put together.

Third, if a child has received choices only from people other than the ones he chose, then give him his first choice. Suppose Paul chooses Edward, Gordon, and Tony in that order, but is chosen by three quite different classmates; the best placement for Paul is with Edward. Fourth, if there have been any rejections, make sure that no such unchosen child is put with those boys and girls who have asked not to be with him. Fifth and last, check the final arrangement to make sure that every child has been placed with at least one of his indicated choices.[24]

[24] Jennings, *op. cit.*, p. 45. Used by permission.

Teachers generally report that though it takes time, realignment of various classroom activities on the bases of psychlogical choices eventuates in more pleasant and more efficient work.

Teachers will need considerable patience and forbearance in the initial stages. These new setups often set children off into gales of laughter and giggling. Once the exploring stage is passed, however, they settle down to work and better work than was done previously.

Among the many teachers who have used sociometric choices and continued their arrangements over a period of time, none have reported more than temporary disturbances, and all have found that their classroom atmosphere and working morale have increased markedly. Teachers should then be patient with children while they learn new skills and accommodate themselves to new methods, especially if these represent radical departures from what they have been used to.[25]

The reasons back of children's choices are of especial interest. Sociometric data suggest that children have much more insight into their needs than is often accorded them. This seems to reach its height when children have operated not only in a democratic school climate, but also in a similar home social climate.

One of the most frequent bases of choice is for the purpose of securing "emotional support to function with greater satisfaction in a given context." [26]

I like Allison because she's always happy. She makes me feel happy too.

He always seems to know if I'm blue and he sympathizes.

Allen is always helping someone. He never seems to mind taking time to explain things.

Janie and I just fit. She has no mother, and I have no father.

I just hate to sit by Bo. He's always getting into trouble himself, and he gets everyone around him in trouble too.

When Sandy is on your committee, nothing gets done. All he wants to do is play cowboy. That's O.K. at recess but no good with our teacher. She likes to see things move.

Such factors as the needs for happiness, sympathy, helpfulness, and similar problems, disruptive persons, able and skilled people, and the like are basic to group choices.

[25] Jennings, *op. cit.,* p. 47.
[26] *Ibid.,* p. 49.

Age levels also influence group membership. At the kindergarten and lower elementary levels, choices are apt to be what are called "chain choices." Mary chooses Sally, who chooses Sara, who chooses Mary. Re-examination of the section on growth rates suggests this may be because of the self-centeredness which is characteristic of these developmental levels. Play is of the parallel kind. As has been said,[27] choices are likely to consist of several chains of one-way relationships with very few mutual choices and no complex networks.

As children progress through the early elementary grades, they become less self-centered, more aware of how their behavior affects others as well as how others affect them. (See Chapter 3.)

In later kindergarten and first grades, girls continue to choose boys and vice versa. Other things being equal, this tends to reverse until about the fifth- and sixth-grade years. From this point on there is a gradual incline in the number of cross sex choices through high school.

This increasing maturity is reflected in the complexity of the choices. As mentioned earlier, around later fourth and fifth and sixth grades "linked chain of mutual association" become more frequent and combine to form clusters. Clique formation is now the commonplace. Here is a means of escape from adult society which is curiously related to that very society.

Not only is sex awareness sharpened, but also companions tend to be chosen on such bases as mentioned in Chapter 4—class status, nationality, religious and racial backgrounds, as well as more specialized criteria, such as which club, sorority or fraternity, and the like.

As children reach preadolescent and adolescent years and levels of development, their choices are often contained within a clique or social circle, or at the most a small number of clique groups. Now, too, there are more reciprocal choices and a clustering of choices about a number of individuals.

The "whys" of choice gradually increase, not only in number, but in subtlety and finesse as social awareness and social facility and capability develop.

[27] *Ibid.,* p. 69.

XIII THE SCHOOL AS A SOCIAL WORLD—SPECIALIZED ASPECTS

ASCENDANCY RELATIONSHIPS—SUGGESTIONS AS TO NEWER CONCEPTS AND A WAY OF STUDYING THEM

THE CONCEPT "LEADERSHIP"

AS WAS mentioned in the discussion on the formation of child groups, lines of association begin appearing almost simultaneously with interaction. These association lines are not merely in terms of choice as to composition of the group members but also in terms of what group position will each person hold.

As someone has said, if two people were placed in absolute isolation, one of the two would shortly assert dominance over the other. It would be done in terms of competition it is true, but also in terms of cooperation, or, more aptly, cooperative-competition. For basic to the very idea of competition as a social process is the idea that it is impersonal, continuous, and in the main carried on according to rules, understood and/or expressed. Such a process has then, as a major part of its concept, cooperation.

Within this frame of reference, people play different roles from time to time largely dependent upon the social situation, its components, needs, facilities, its definition of leader, behavior, etc.

In other words, some people, some children are more dominant in social relationships, some are less so, and some are now dominant and now more submissive. We tend to attach the name "leader" to the more dominant, ascendant person and "follower" or "led" to the more submissive roles played.

What, then, has been, and is, the concept of leadership? What people assume these roles? What are their characteristics? What are their ways of instituting their leadership?

Leadership has been variously defined as "the influencing of opinion," as "the directing of activities of a group," as "acts which make a difference in group effectiveness," and as "actions by people which influence people in a shared direction."

Earlier studies of leadership centered on qualities and characteristics. These have ranged from descriptions of essentials to detailed studies of size, weight, scholastic ability, manner of dress, beauty, etc., as traits of leadership.

Pigors [1] suggests that the essentials of leadership are (*1*) a common cause, (*2*) a leader, (*3*) followers, (*4*) and the current situation.

Terman [2] found leaders as rated by their associates to be either first or last in health, dress, social status, scholastic work, boldness of manner, and speech fluency. As Terman suggests, they stood at one extreme or another in these personal-social characteristics.

Hunter and Jordan [3] in their extensive study of college students found significant differences between leaders and nonleaders in terms of age, weight, and the like. Leaders as compared with nonleaders were significantly younger, were lighter in weight (possibly because of being younger), had parents who were college trained, had parents belonging to the professional classes, had law or journalism as vocational preferences, were superior in tests of intelligence and of vocabulary, and were higher in scholarship.

Lists of leadership qualities are well illustrated by such lists as those by Bernard and Allport.[4]

Bernard's list consists of the following:

1. Striking physical personality.
2. Size.
3. Good looks.
4. Appearance of strength of body.

[1] P. J. W. Pigors, *Leadership or Domination* (Boston, Houghton, 1935), p. 16.
[2] L. M. Terman, "A Preliminary Study in the Psychology and Pedagogy of Leadership," *Pedagogical Seminary and Journal of Genetic Psychology* (1904), pp. 413–451.
[3] E. C. Hunter, and A. N. Jordan, "An Analysis of Qualities Associated with Leadership Among College Students," *Journal of Educational Psychology*, Vol. 30 (1939), pp. 497–509.
[4] L. L. Bernard, *Introduction to Social Psychology* (New York, Holt, 1936), Chap. 34.

5. Appearance of strength of character.
6. Ready speech.
7. Oratorical gift of emotional appeal.
8. Readiness in repartee.
9. Sympathy.
10. Sense of justice.
11. Humanitarianism.
12. Honesty.
13. Good faith.
14. Insight.
15. Courage.
16. Persistence.
17. Good natural ability.
18. Originality.
19. Initiative.
20. Good intellectual training.
21. Soundness of judgment.
22. Mental flexibility.
23. Forethought.
24. Intellectual vision.
25. Moral vision.
26. Positive idealism.
27. Cheerful, even temper.
28. Poise.
29. Self-confidence.
30. Organizing and executive ability.
31. Knowledge of human nature and society.

Allport [5] lists the following:

1. Trait of ascendance.
2. Physical power.
3. High motility.
4. Tonus.
5. Erect, aggressive carriage.
6. Tenacity.
7. Face-to-face mode of address.
8. Reinforcement of energy.
9. Restraint.
10. Inscrutability.
11. Expansiveness in field of action.
12. High intelligence.

[5] F. H. Allport, *Social Psychology* (Boston, Houghton, 1924), pp. 419–424.

13. Understanding.
14. Keenly susceptible to social stimulation.
15. Tact.
16. Zeal.
17. Social participation.
18. Character.
19. Drive.

As Britt [6] once suggested, "it is questionable whether such generalized lists can aid anyone in achieving a position of leadership, for there seems to be a definite specificity in qualifications for leadership. The traits that suit a leader for one purpose do not necessarily suit him for leadership in all activities. To say that a leader is one who has size and good looks may apply in the world of a candidate for political office, but does not necessarily apply to a leader in the world of science. . . . Leadership in any one activity requires a certain amount of skill in that activity as well as evidence of other skills. A person cannot lead in all spheres; he must at times be a follower. In other words, if you wish to analyze the social psychology of leadership so that the materials may be useful to you personally, you should choose some particular situation and then, by observational or experimental methods, make a careful study of leadership in that particular kind of situation." [7]

A PLAN FOR THE ANALYSIS OF LEADERSHIP

In line with this suggestion, we present a paradigm for the analysis of leadership. In the words of Seeman and Morris, this pattern stresses the fact that the group and individual variables commonly examined in leadership studies may be viewed in five ways—as results, concomitants, determiners, or conditioners of the leader's behavior and as criteria for evaluation.

Such an approach to the understanding of status within school groups would be of inestimable value to the teacher and/or counselor with reference to abilities and potentialities. Though the material quoted below is being utilized largely in research of adult groups, its framework is readily adaptable to any age level.

This newer and challenging approach to the study of leadership is being developed in the Ohio State Leadership Studies under

[6] Stewart H. Britt, *Social Psychology of Modern Life* (New York, Farrar and Rinehart, 1941).
[7] *Ibid.*, p. 278.

A Paradigm for the Study of Leadership

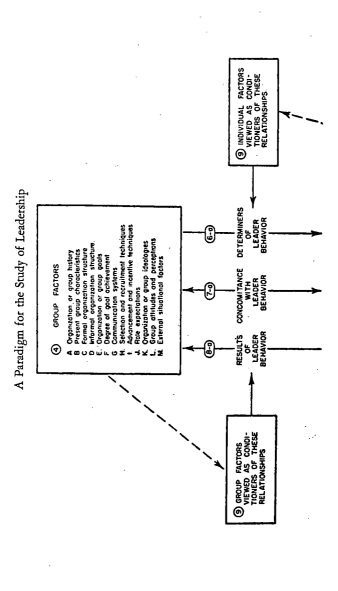

④ GROUP FACTORS

A. Organization or group history
B. Present group characteristics
C. Formal organization structure
D. Informal organization structure
E. Organization or group goals
F. Degree of goal achievement
G. Communication systems
H. Selection and recruitment techniques
I. Advancement and incentive techniques
J. Role expectations
K. Organization or group ideologies
L. Group attitudes and perceptions
M. External situational factors

⑨ INDIVIDUAL FACTORS VIEWED AS CONDITIONERS OF THESE RELATIONSHIPS

⑨ GROUP FACTORS VIEWED AS CONDITIONERS OF THESE RELATIONSHIPS

⑥-⑨ DETERMINERS OF LEADER BEHAVIOR

⑦-⑨ CONCOMITANCE WITH LEADER BEHAVIOR

⑧-⑨ RESULTS OF LEADER BEHAVIOR

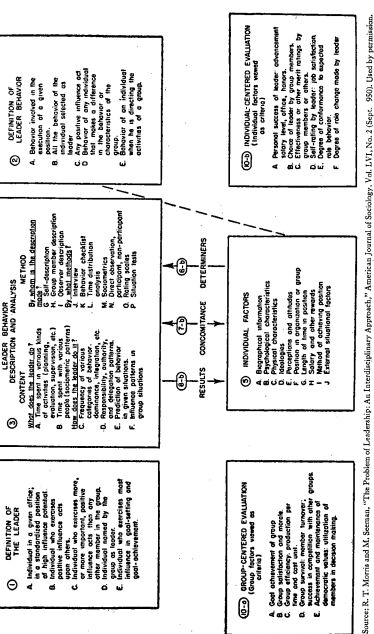

Source: R. T. Morris and M. Seeman, "The Problem of Leadership: An Interdisciplinary Approach," American Journal of Sociology, Vol. LVI, No. 2 (Sept. 950). Used by permission.

the direction of Carroll L. Shartle, *et al.,* Seeman and Morris describe this interdisciplinary approach as follows: [8]

1. Who is the leader? It should not be assumed that the nature of the group under investigation will entirely determine how the leader is to be designated. This is also a function of the theory and definition of leadership involved. It is possible, by one definition, to designate as "leader" the individual in high office who has been chosen for study; while, by another definition, we cannot call him "leader" until he has demonstrably made a difference in the group, i.e., has exercised influence. The problem of designating the leader is of crucial concern in the study of leadership, especially in view of the fact that the office-holder as leader is a common stereotype in our culture.

2. What is defined as leader behavior? The individual designated as leader behaves in accordance with the demands of many roles in addition to that of leader. Clearly some of his behavior is to be considered as leader behavior, and some is not. It seems essential, as methodologies of observation are worked out, to establish theoretically the limits of the phenomena to be observed.

3. How is leader behavior to be described and analyzed? The focus, for the most part, has been on either leader *evaluation* or on the *traits* of leaders, while the leader's behavior has been largely ignored.

The staff of the Ohio State Leadership Studies has made the description of leader behavior one of its chief responsibilities. Instruments designed to observe and analyze the behavior of leaders are being developed. We have found it useful to think in terms of *what* and *how* of leader behavior: on what organizational functions does the leader spend his time [a] and how does he perform these functions? Is he dominant? separated from the group?

Who shall describe the leader's behavior? The description may be made by the leader himself, by his subordinates, by his peers, by his superiors, or by the investigator, either as a participant observer or otherwise. The methods currently being used are listed in the chart: all may be applied to obtain descriptions of leader behavior from the entire range of personnel listed above. One of the instruments currently being analyzed (3K) contains one hundred and fifty items describing

[8] Melvin Seeman and Richard T. Morris, "The Problem of Leadership; An Interdisciplinary Approach," *American Journal of Sociology,* Vol. LVI, No. 2 (September 1950), pp. 152–155. Used by permission.

[a] Ralph M. Stogdill and Carroll L. Shartle have described some of the methods already developed for this type of analysis; cf. their "Methods for Determining Patterns of Leadership Behavior in Relation to Organization Structure and Objectives," *Journal of Applied Psychology,* XXXII (1948), pp. 286–291; and Shartle, "Leadership and Executive Performance," *Personnel,* XXV (1949), pp. 370–380.

leader behavior in terms of nine categories (3C), calling for responses by the leader himself, his subordinates, and others.[b] This instrument can also be used to explore leadership ideologies (What should an ideal leader do?).

4–5. What group and individual factors are significant for leader behavior? The category "group factors" refers to the characteristics of the group in which the individual designated as leader exercised the function of leader. These factors are distinguished from "individual factors" in that the latter refer to the characteristics of the individual designated as leader. The variables listed in these two sections of the chart are suggestive rather than exhaustive. Four major types of variable have been focused upon for present study:

A) *A job analysis and organizational structure approach,* in which the central effort is upon describing *what* leaders actually do (3A and 3B); and on how this is related to organizational structure, e.g., informal work patterns (4D), or echelon level (4C).

B) *A communications and leader effectiveness approach,* in which are examined, first, the relation of leader effectiveness to specific leader differences, e.g., the ability to estimate group opinion (5E) and, second, the relation among multiple criteria for effectiveness, e.g., high group morale (10-aD) and ratings by subordinates (10-bC).

C) *A status factor approach,* in which the emphasis is upon leadership as a status phenomenon with major attention given to exploring the relation of the leader's and followers' behavior to status factors at work in the organization or community, e.g., the relation of leader behavior to commitments about or perceptions of status differences in society (4C and 5E).

D) *A group dimension approach,* which seeks to explore situational differences in leader behavior, e.g., differences in leader operation associated with differences in group size, homogeneity, togetherness, etc. (4B).

6. Why does the leader behave as he does? We are interested here in discovering the group or individual factors which determine differences in leader behavior (6-a, 6-b). As such factors are found, we will be in a better position to test our findings by controlled experimentation in the selection, training, and evaluation of leaders.

7. What phenomena are concomitant with given kinds of leader

[b] A mimeographed staff report on this instrument indicates that the original one hundred and fifty items, classified into nine categories of leader behavior (including domination, organization, initiation, etc.) can be reduced by factor analysis to three major components: goal-attainment behavior, maintenance-of-membership character, and member-interaction facilitation.

behavior? Though the ultimate effort is to isolate the crucial determining variables, all the studies listed in section 4–5 above are primarily, at the present time, studies not of causal but of concomitant relations. To illustrate, Seeman and Morris [c] found, in a study of the relation of general-status attitudes to leadership ideology, that teachers who were committed to maintaining large status differences in a wide variety of social, political, and economic situations were those who wanted most direction, and clear "leader" rather than "member" behavior, from their "ideal superintendent." This suggests a concomitance between the status ideology of superintendents themselves and their behavior as described by subordinates. Seeking out such concomitancies is a vital preparatory step toward the establishment of causal patterns.

8. *What are the results of leader behavior?* The primary concern in describing results of the leader's behavior is with what we have called the "group factors." There are also, however, questions which center on the individual factors as results: Does dominance by the leader (3C) lead to given patterns of advancement for him in an organization (5H)?

9. *What factors serve as conditioners?* Here the individual and group factors are viewed as conditioners of relationships between given leader behavior and other factors. Hemphill [d] found that the reported behavior of "superior" leaders differed significantly in terms of the size of the group in which they functioned. The differences were in the direction of greater tolerance for leader-centered direction in larger groups. These findings suggest that the size of the group is one important factor conditioning the relationship between leader behavior and his evaluation by subordinates. Similarly, the relation suggested in section 8 above between supervision pattern and the communication system in the group may hold only in groups of a given size or in groups having a given type of formal organization.

10. *How are the results of leader behavior evaluated?* Two kinds of criteria can be used: those which evaluate leadership in terms of the results for the group and those which focus simply upon the individual who is the leader.

Criteria for effectiveness may vary systematically with the individual making the evaluation: different people want different things of leadership; or with the situation: what is effective leadership in peace may not be effective leadership in war

[c] These findings are contained in a mimeographed staff report entitled "The Status Correlates of Leader Behavior."

[d] John K. Hemphill, "Group Factors in Leadership. I: Relations Between the Size of the Group and the Behavior of Superior Leaders," *Journal of Social Psychology,* Vol. 32, (December 1950), pp. 11–22.

DEMOCRATIC LEADERSHIP

We are all convinced of the superiority of democratic groups but we frequently are not so aware or convinced of the fact that this superiority is directly related to

. . . appropriate leadership in these groups. And democratic leadership requires attitudes, understandings, and skills which are more, not less, profound and complex than those required by the autocratic leader. These attitudes, understandings, and skills can be learned, but they will not be learned without educational thought and effort.

Too often and too long we have thought and said that leaders are "born, not made" and fully as mythical have assumed that the social situation will automatically provide its own leader. It is high time that proponents of democratic grouping and procedures recognized and accepted the responsibility for training of democratic leadership. The first requisite for this viewpoint is a clear recognition of what is to be developed. What are some leadership functions?

1. It is important that we see "leadership" in terms of functions to be performed in helping groups to grow and operate productively not in terms of qualities inherent in persons. [This means that] one set of leadership functions, then, has to do with services required within the group in helping it to grow to greater maturity.

A. A group must set common goals and purposes. This is done by working through differences among its members. Leadership must help clarify differences, bring in relevant information which will help resolve issues that divide.

B. A group must keep balance between long-range and short-range goals. Leadership must aid here by seeing that one type of goal is not forgotten in planning for another.

C. Groups must be helped to keep plans "realistic," to practice plans before trying them fully, and to test them in practice.

Finally, groups, having planned and acted, must evaluate what they have done. They need help in getting evaluation data, in interpreting it, and in amending cherished plans if evaluation requires it.

2. A second set of leadership functions, therefore, has to do with services required by any group in keeping its processes of planning, acting, and evaluating productive and geared to the changing environment in which it lives and acts.

In the mature group leadership is not resident in any one person but is delegated in terms of different group members, their particular interests and aptitudes. Some functions may even be reserved for the group as a whole.

Principles of Leadership Training

1. Leadership can be learned by children only as they practice the skills of productive group work in a variety of group settings.

This implies extensive experience in student-led groups. But experience in group work is not enough to insure that the skills and understandings are well-recognized or well-learned.

2. Self-evaluation by the group of its own ways of working and group planning to improve the groups' procedures are necessary to insure that leadership functions are adequately understood and practiced by *all* children.

A good starting point for this evaluation is a time when group discussion and action is confused, frustrating, at a stand still.

"The group which discovers out of its own group experience that there is a relation between the language its members use in making a suggestion and the kind of hearing the suggestion receives, that summaries of where we've been and where we seem to be going help keep a group on the beam, that minority or unpopular opinions often contribute much to a groups' thinking, and the right of these opinions to be heard needs to be safeguarded is learning to identify, support and practice the functions of democratic leadership."

One other, often, neglected area of leadership training needs emphasis.

3. New patterns of relationships are frequently resisted by children and adults because they are perceived as threats to self-confidence. Trying out new patterns requires a free and permissive atmosphere in which this ego threat is reduced to a minimum.

This says that "the right to make mistakes" must be a part of group understanding; that consequent criticism is directed in terms of *group maturity* at the *leader* or *member* role not at the person himself.

Role playing [9] may be of great help in such connections, criticisms may be readily accepted under such circumstances because it is the *role* not the *person* which is being evaluated, but the insight and security and skill in new ways of working are just as real and keen.[10]

"FRINGE" RELATIONSHIPS OF THE SCHOOL

Many teacher experience papers bear out Waller's contention that the school social world "contains some hangers-on, some mar-

[9] *See* Appendix, Sociodrama and for examples at earlier years, see also Ruth Cunningham and Madelaine Roberts, "It Takes Experience," *Childhood Education* (January 1948), p. 208 ff.

[10] Kenneth D. Benne, "Leaders Are Made Not Born," *Childhood Education*, Vol. 24 (January 1948), pp. 203–208. Used by permission.

ginal members who from one point of view are members of the school as a social body and from another are complete outsiders, some persons without any fixed legal status in the group but often with a good deal of influence." [11]

The janitor or custodian appears to fill such a role especially in smaller communities. Out of 520 personal experience papers written by returned teachers in educational sociology classes, only 25 did not mention the janitor as a personage to be reckoned with as a "person of power."

This is perhaps all the more significant when it is recalled that 162 papers were written by teachers from communities of 150,000 population to 300,000. The 25 who did not so mention the custodian were from communities of 300,000 or more.

The consensus of opinion seemed to be that if the janitor were on your side, he could do you much good not merely with supervisors and administrators but also with community members. If he did not like you and "the way you kept your room," his opportunity to bear tales was unequaled.

People who work in lunchrooms, corner-store "hang-outs," and the like likewise often influence student thinking and consequent attitude toward teacher activities out of all proportion to their social position.

It has been suggested that this may be due to the fact that these adults represent themselves as harmless and manipulable mother and father substitutes. In so doing they encourage youngsters to establish and carry on a rapport with the older generation at the same time that they are able to "get even" with it by gossip, criticism, and so forth.

School "cops" also fit this fringe roll. Often they are beloved characters for whom alumni ask more often than they do for teachers or administrators.

The influence of alumni is very real, and frequently very potent, as both student participants and observers point out. Their interest is likely to focalize on athletics. At the college and university level they are often carefully courted through alumni associations, class reunions, chain letters, and journals. The object of this attention is not difficult to find. Both contributions to funds, scholarships, and even enrollment are derived from alumni. At the high

[11] W. W. Waller, *Sociology of Teaching* (New York, Wiley, 1932), p. 80. Used by permission.

school level some attempt is made also to maintain the interest of alumni, but, in the main, success is only with the most recent, those who live close about and the very old alumni, who find it a nostalgic release.

One interesting analysis of alumni is presented below:

Indeed, there seems to be an inherent necessity that the better sort of alumni, the more intelligent and the more successful, should always elude the tentacles of the alumni secretary. There are exceptions, of course, but the rule seems to hold. When a man goes back to his alma mater for a reunion, whether that alma mater be a prep school or one of the most advanced professional schools, he does it for a taste of the joys that were his when he was a youngster in school. But if he has attained a satisfactory adjustment of his life on the adult level, he will not be likely to hanker for a revival of adolescent associations. Thus, it is the unadjusted and the failures in life who are in general most enthusiastic about keeping up their school connections; if they have adjusted themselves to adult life, their interests and desires will have moved on irrevocably from their school-day memories. Indeed, it may be argued that a man who after five years still persists in telling stories of his college achievements has failed in life. He may not have failed to secure position, or professional advancement, or wealth, but if his emotions and his intellect have not become involved in situations of life far more interesting than those old situations of school, he has failed in life.

While we are attempting to generalize about alumni, we should state that there seems to be a considerable difference between those alumni who merely hold to the values of school life because that was the most interesting time of their lives and those alumni who break away, are inducted into a rapidly expanding world of adult interests, and afterwards encounter their alma mater in their expanding social world. From this latter group are gathered those excellent individuals who, though weighed down by a thousand and one other interests, persist in serving their alma mater as a means to a wider social service. From this latter class are recruited those lay advisers and administrators without whom it would be very difficult to conduct the work of any school.[12]

Though there may be differences of opinion concerning the inclusion of the school board as a school fringe, the fact remains that it is *in* and *of* the community and *in*, if not *of*, the school social world. Theoretically, it sets and stands for policies and hires a school staff to carry out these policies. Actually in many smaller com-

[12] Waller, *op. cit.*, pp. 84–85.

munities, the school board, composed largely of lay members with little or no specialist training, demands a final voice in matters which require considerable training and which in the opinion of informed people would seem to be matters for staff handling.

It is an easily documented fact that school-board members are chosen with little or no regard for training or experience in educational pursuits. As shown by studies of community conduct codes for teachers, school-board members are apt to translate their role as a highly conservative one. It would be interesting to know what causes a mildly liberal community member to swing sharply conservative once he assumes the role of board member.

SELECTED INTERPERSONAL RELATIONSHIPS WITHIN THE SCHOOL SOCIAL WORLD

STAFF RELATIONSHIPS

The importance of "staff relationship atmospheres" are exceeded in importance, if at all, only by teacher-pupil relationship atmospheres. Obviously, the two are closely related, for few people are able to follow consistently and happily one social atmosphere in one area of interpersonal living and a very different one in other areas.

In earlier days, and in some isolated places still, where single salary scales are not the rule, rivalry and discontent were, and are, often rampant between elementary and high school teachers. This was especially true if both were housed in one building, as in small communities.

Likewise, under the older concept of supervision relationships between classroom teachers and supervisory and administrative people were too often of dubious, if not downright, antagonism and hatred.

These social structures and processes were obviously derivatives from the efficiency complexes which business and industry developed during the era of rapid growth and expansion. It is often said that the army line and staff organization amplified by business and industrial giants has been taken over in toto as the school also became too large, too expanded to be handled by the people as a whole. The pattern of movement from simple, community-wide direction to committees (boards of education) to school superintendents is the usual pattern in the shift from primary to secondary modes of living.[13]

A structural parallel between army and school organization is readily drawn. In the army the line officers are in authority from general to brigadier general to colonels, to majors to captains to lieutenants to sergeants and finally to corporals. The staff officers are specialized experts who can handle technical matters. They are without authority and cannot issue orders though they may have any of the above rankings. Generals issue orders but usually not without consultation with the staff officers.

With some differences, many schools are organized in similar fashion. The executive officer is the superintendent, but he delegates responsibilities to assistant superintendents, principals, vice-principals, and department heads. In the school the staff officers are the psychiatrists, the guidance people, the psychiatric social worker, the librarians, the testing experts, and the like. Their job is an advisory one to the people in the above ranks.

But what is the current scene? What are the attitudes of both teachers and administrators toward "actual and preferred practices?"

A recent doctoral dissertation [14] reveals interesting and challenging factual material on the subject.

After considerable research, Williams devised an inquiry which tested whether school policy formation and implementation was democratic, laissez-faire, or authoritarian, as well as testing the degree or level of development at which the group was working. Authoritarian categories included such characteristics as:

1. The administration decides on policies and announces them to the staff.
2. Individuals who have seniority use their experience and prestige to sway policy formation.
3. The teacher is so much in the background that he contributes little to policy formation.
4. In other than routine matters the administration carries out instructions from the superintendent's office.
5. Irrelevant considerations or fears determine policies used.
6. Factions oppose each other on matters of basic policy.

[13] See Kilpatrick and others, *The Educational Frontier* (New York, Appleton-Century, 1933), p. 221 ff.
[14] Wm. Wendell Williams, done under the direction of Dr. Laura Zirbes and with the approval and aid of the Ohio Education Association, 1950. Used by permission of the author.

7. Precedents and traditions determine policies.
8. The administration uses veto power on matters of policy.

Laissez-faire categories included such characteristics as the following:

1. Mistakes are made without assuming responsibility for actions or conduct.
2. Each teacher handles situations as he sees fit.
3. The administrator handles situations in terms of expediency.
4. Cliques, stool pigeons, suspicions, favors, and "back bitings" influence policy formations.
5. Pressure groups flout or reverse policies by agitating or by influencing public opinion.

Democratic characteristics were as follow:

1. Teachers' expressed preferences are considered as to work that is assigned them.
2. Teachers are given liberties and responsibilities consistent with their individual abilities, interests, and dispositions.
3. The administration secures staff consideration of the problems, issues, and values which need to be considered in policy making.
4. Cooperative concern for the common good is the basis of policies.
5. Teachers are given opportunity to question or suggest policies.
6. The administrator works with his teachers. Suggestions take the place of commands.
7. Teachers are permitted and expected to share in the forming of school policies.
8. Committees are established to formulate policies which will be presented to the entire staff.
9. Staff meetings are planned ahead of time on a cooperative basis.
10. Members of the faculty help formulate the issues to be discussed in staff meetings.
11. Matters are discussed pro and con, put to a vote, and the majority decision becomes policy.

In county secondary schools administrators felt by slightly higher scores (95) than teachers (89) that democracy prevailed in their systems activities. In the county elementary schools there was so small a difference in administrators (97) and teachers opinions (98) as to be negligible. Secondary school administrators and teachers were farther apart in their opinions.

In exempted villages the elementary teachers gave the school a score of only 92 whereas administrators gave a 99 score. Secondary teachers and administrators presented scores of 92 and 99, respectively, also showing greatest consistency in opinion.

In city systems elementary teachers and administrators were again close together as were secondary people with a score of 91 for teachers and 90 for administrators.[15]

Further breakdowns of the over-all findings allow for several conclusions from the Williams study.

1. Policy formation (and by implication) policy implementation is increasingly coming to be regarded as the joint responsibility of teachers and administrators.

2. The enthusiasm of teachers for participation in policy formation rises or falls according to the degree to which they are permitted to take part in the process.

3. There is an inverse relationship between staff participation and administrative administration. As staff participation increases, administrative participation decreases.

4. Both teachers and administrators feel that free discussion of needed policies is of paramount importance.

5. Most administrators and teachers feel that majority vote is very democratic and very satisfactory.

6. Very few schools strive for consensus in arriving at desired policies.

7. Committees form a major role for study of problems and in the presentation of recommended solutions for them.

8. Actual practice falls far below beliefs and desires of both teachers and administrators.

9. Teachers and administrators in about equal numbers believe in cooperative procedures, although administrators are slightly more enthusiastic than are teachers.

10. Administrators as a whole are slightly more anxious to move toward democratic procedures than are teachers.

11. There is a very close relationship between the goals sought by the administrators and those sought by teachers.

12. Both desire an increase in teacher participation.

13. There is little difference between attitudes of the two groups on policy formation.

14. Often administrators do not realize their use of dictatorial methods, or teachers do not realize their actions as participants in administration.

[15] Scores represent amount accorded out of a possible 120 points.

15. After policies are set up, it is often felt that teachers should help administer them more than they do.

16. The democratic staff process provides almost unanimously experiences that are effective, satisfying, while undemocratic procedures provide experiences which are unsatisfactory and ineffective.

17. Staff agenda need to be prepared and presented to teachers well in advance of staff meeting.

18. When changes in policy are desired, democratic procedures are more frequently used than undemocratic or doubtful procedures.

19. In-service training is provided through democratic staff participation.

20. There should be a continual evaluation of policies which have been formed.

21. There is need for a basic set of values to guide formation of school policies.

22. No one person has enough ability and information to supervise and administrate a school at its highest efficiency.

23. Staff members are more effective when they feel that they are an accepted part of the school organization and not just pawns of a supreme administration.

24. Only 29 percent of the schools that were studied have definite written policies.

25. Where there is not cooperative procedure in administration of school policies, the teachers alone administer the policies twice as often as do the administrators.

26. There is practically no variation in the degree of democracy thought to be present in the exempted village, the county, and the city schools.

27. Exempted schools are more democratic than small community schools in their staff policy-making procedures, while city schools are least democratic.

28. Administrators feel schools to be more democratic than do teachers.

29. There is a definite preference for democratic organization rather than authoritarian or laissez-faire.

30. Often the administrator or a board member stifles the desire of a staff to participate in policy by having earlier reversed or disregarded staff decisions.

31. Veto power on the part of the administration is used sparingly.

32. It is believed that in large staffs committees should first study and analyze the problems, then present tentative findings to the entire staff for further study.

33. The most democratic policies now in use are those which concern school trips, guidance, assembly programs, and textbook selections. The least are those which concern corporal punishment, school accidents, religious instruction, and school budgets.

TEACHER SOCIAL ROLES

Heretofore we have spoken of teacher living in terms of interpersonal contacts with children as related to effects of teacher personality and social climate upon children.

It is now necessary to consider the backgrounds of classroom teachers. Who are they? Where are they on the social-cultural status scheme? What is expected of them as persons in the school's community life?

Though the social position of the teacher varies somewhat in terms of regions of the United States, size of communities, and the personal-social characteristics of the individual, teachers are derived largely from middle-class backgrounds. Some studies suggest their orientation to be largely lower-middle and upper-lower with main emphasis upon lower-middle and middle-middle. This is said to be especially true of the Middle West and the Far West.

In studies of social backgrounds of teachers, parent occupations are largely farmers and businessmen, usually small business owners.

In one study of women students in teachers' colleges Methodist and Baptist religious denominations accounted for more than half of these would-be teachers. These denominations more than any other in this country are middle class.

Elsbree and others have considered these backgrounds as dangerously limiting factors. "Coming as they do mostly from lower-middle class, they bear all the marks of the relatively unfavored social and economic group. To fill in these cultural gaps in the experiences of teachers is a task of considerable magnitude." [16]

[16] Willard S. Elsbree, *The American Teacher* (New York, American Book, 1939), p. 555.

With such backgrounds in evidence, it is safe to say that teaching has been "chosen" by many people because it served as a possible social elevator for those who elected to be teachers. Though there may have been historically disagreement as to its rating as a profession, it has until very recently been the profession requiring least formal training.

With such backgrounds teachers tend to present, perpetuate, and enforce middle-class mores, attitudes, and skills. This very often results in penalization of lower-class children. One who is on his or her way up, unless he thoroughly understands such sociological factors and backgrounds, will see only as "bad" and "nasty," the child who uses the language and techniques of his lower-class level within the schoolroom and on the playground.

The expectations and anticipations established for middle-class youngsters may well be not only impossible but undesirable and frustrating to him, as described in Chapters 4 and 5.

Since few upper-class children appear in public schools, they escape this impact in the main. It is true that their teachers in private schools are also largely middle class, but there teacher role and function is restricted to teachings which have upper-class value.

It has been said that like other professions

teaching is regulated by at least two basic kinds of controls—by laws imposed from the outside and by codes of ethics developed within the teaching group. More than in other professions, there is a third, and perhaps even more rigorous type of control in teaching. This consists of the attitudes, values, expectancies, and norms of the public—the type of control which defines the kind of person a teacher should be and thus determines to some extent the characteristics of those who enter the profession. These factors likewise play a part in deciding who shall continue in the profession and are therefore instrumental in forming the "teacher" as an occupational type. Although the teacher type has never been expirically delineated, some of its elements have been analyzed by a few students.[17]

This study has attempted to answer this question by securing replies to the inquiry: "Should the following types of persons be employed to teach in the public schools of your community?"

In Table 1 employability quotients have been arrayed from highest positive to lowest negative response, using school board member totals

[17] Florence Greenhoe, *Community Contacts and Participation of 9,122 Teachers Selected as a National Sample* (Washington, American Council on Public Affairs, 1941), p. 28.

as a base. Inspection reveals a number of generalized findings. For instance, female applicants who are married are definitely disapproved of by school-board members (− 32.1), only mildly reacted against by lay persons (−12.0), definitely approved by students training to be teachers (12.4). More likely than not, the student vote in the last instance is probably based upon anticipated competition with married women for teaching positions.

TABLE 1

EMPLOYABILITY QUOTIENTS OF POTENTIAL APPLICANTS FOR TEACHING POSITIONS IN THE PUBLIC SCHOOLS OF THE NATION

	As Rated by			
Potential applicant for teaching position	*356 Sch-board members*	*2,095 Lay persons*	*9,122 Pub. Sch. teachers*	*3,054 Educ. Stud'ts.*
1. A known Protestant	76.5	84.9	93.5	93.5
2. Native-born, foreign name	56.3	73.2	88.5	89.9
3. Non-local resident	48.3	46.0	78.4	89.1
4. City-reared person	45.8	66.6	85.4	90.8
5. Out-of-state applicant	15.4	27.5	69.4	64.9
6. A known Catholic	−21.3	9.5	53.1	68.0
7. A known pacifist	−22.8	5.3	29.7	40.4
8. A married woman	−32.1	−12.0	36.5	12.4
9. A known Jew	−41.3	2.3	44.8	41.5
10. A known militarist	−62.0	−50.1	−42.1	−25.0
11. A light Negro	−82.1	−54.2	−54.2	−33.6
12. A dark Negro	−85.7	−66.0	−63.4	−49.4
13. A known radical	−88.0	−72.5	−63.6	−48.2
14. Person in bad health	−93.3	−87.9	−54.7	−89.6
15. A known Communist	−94.1	−83.2	−77.5	−57.9

Light Negroes and dark Negroes are significantly differentiated in only one instance—the response of the community group—a finding contrary to common-sense expectations and probably due to the tendency to think of Negro teacher applicants as seeking positions, not in "the schools of your community," as stated in the instructions, but in Negro schools.

Source: Florence Greenhoe, *Community Contacts and Participation of Teachers* (Washington, American Council on Public Affairs, 1941), p. 32.

A nonlocal resident is favored more by school-board members than by community lay representatives, a rating position not duplicated on any other item in the entire list.

In the words of one Southern student, "The only place Negroes would be employed to teach would be in colored schools, and I naturally assumed this was the meaning of the question."

Attention may be called to one final comparison of scores. Apparently school-board members would employ a person in bad health in preference to a known Communist, though the difference in score is so small as to lack significance.

In many instances the reactions of school-board members are so different from the young people among whom they may be expected to find teachers for their schools as to be a matter of grave concern. Evidence also indicates that the longer students are in college the more liberal they tend to become, a fact which we have singled out for sociological interpretation.

Various writers have called attention to the several types of mores and to their coercive power. One set of moral codes is the "organizational mores," the approved ways and sanctions on which our social system rests, i.e., competitive labor, representative democracy, compulsory education, race prejudice, and nationalism. A second set comprises the humanitarian mores, the urges for social betterment, public welfare, and charitable activities. A third set of mores is the scientific, defined as "the assumption of order in nature, a faith in man's power to predict and control natural processes, and a courage to make known the findings and implications of research."

The mores have obvious effects upon each of the four rating types discussed in this study. Lay persons, especially those of the so-called middle class, are the carriers and transmitters of the mores par excellence. School-board members are enforcers of the mores in respect to school and community relations, and if our findings are generally valid, these same board members are overly conservative in their attitudes. That is, they cling more closely to traditional beliefs and practice than do community lay representatives. Presumably, this arises from two major sets of circumstances. School-board members are usually fairly well advanced in years, and advanced age has a position correlation with a desire to preserve the status quo. Secondly, school-board members are in general a property-owning group, and wealth makes for conservatism.

Students are born into the organizational mores of their communities. As indicated earlier, the vast majority of students who are training to become teachers are from the villages and small towns of the nation. They absorb their origional mores as a matter of course, and they come to college as representatives of the moral system which has influenced their formative years. At college, and especially in education and arts courses, they come in contact with liberalism and its emphasis on democracy, humanitarianism, and social idealism. They develop the relatively liberal views which account for the scores and rank order position in the present survey. What happens when these students seek employment as teachers, or when, having secured a first position, they are again caught up in small-town community life, is told, in part, by the study on conduct codes for teachers.[18]

[18] Florence Greenhoe, *op. cit.,* pp. 37–39.

With perhaps a few unimportant exceptions, conduct codes for teachers have been objects of scientific study only during the present decade. Prior to 1930, the literature shows no quantitative investigations and the case studies to be found are mostly in the form of autobiographical records such as *The Hoosier Schoolmaster.* The first fairly systematic study is the work by Howard K. Beale.[19] A careful study of Beale's volume reveals that community controls apply in nine major respects:

1. They frequently indicate where teachers must not live, for example with certain families, in an apartment, or outside the local community.
2. They prescribe appropriate dress for teachers, including facial make-up, hair coiffure, and style of dress.
3. They define many of the teacher's leisure-time pursuits, such as dancing, card playing, smoking, and drinking.
4. They regulate associations between teachers and members of the opposite sex who may be students, town persons, or teachers.
5. They bring pressure to bear on teachers to participate in such approved community activities as teaching a Sunday school class and contributing to worthy causes; and they seek to enjoin teachers from participating in disapproved activities and movements, such as the Teachers Union, an affiliate of the American Federation of Labor.
6. They prescribe extracurricular activities in which the community takes a strong interest, such as competitive athletic contests, school celebrations, musicals, etc.
7. They seek to regulate the time teachers spend in the school community by reacting against week-end trips or limiting the number of such trips.
8. They forbid running for political office by teachers, and they indicate disapproval of participation in politics, especially in issues affecting the school.
9. They clearly indicate that teachers are expected to attend institutes or summer schools; at times they enforce this view through promotions or adjustments in salary schedule.

The same community attitudes, frequently found in materials published by other investigators, are also evident in the cases cited in the present study. Apparently codes vary by localities, are stronger

[19] Howard K. Beale, *Are American Teachers Free?* (New York, Scribners, 1936).

in small communities than in large cities, are more rigid for women than for men, and are everywhere undergoing liberalization as a consequence of urbanization.

Reaction of four rating groups to teacher behavior are presented in Table 2. These data find basic interpretation in terms of a sociology of social control.

In sociological theory social control is usually distinguished from physical control. By the latter is meant the manipulation of another person by sheer physical force, such as carrying a child off the street and out of the pathway of automobiles. Social control, on the contrary, accomplishes the same end by and through the "cooperation" of the person involved; that is, the person responds to some such stimulation as a command, threat, or explanation and takes himself off the street. Used in this sense, social control is of two fundamental types: formal and informal. By formal control we mean the kind of stimuli and pressures which are exerted by laws and official rules having the sanction of the punishing power vested in the state or in any of its governing bodies. Informal control connotes the nonlegal forms of manipulation—praise, blame, rewards, suggestions, etc. While teachers are subjected to both formal and informal control, the present study has been limited to the latter type.

From time to time one is impressed with the manner in which college students training to become teachers think of themselves as "free souls." They live in an atmosphere of semi-anonymity and limited personal responsibility. They come and go and govern their conduct by the liberal and tolerant standards of the "college crowd." Conditioned to this way of life, they are unprepared for the situation which will confront them as teachers. For one thing, they become "public personages" in the small community. Moreover, they become heirs to the community controls worked out long ago and passed along as part of the town's heritage. By one means or another, they are made familiar with community expectations and this control process continues as long as they are teachers. Our purposes have been to examine, in more detail than has been done, the various areas in which community controls operate and to canvass the adjustment patterns which the teachers themselves report. The most obvious implication of a practical nature is the teacher's conception of self as developed in reference to conduct taboos. If teachers feel that their freedom as citizens is unduly limited, they grow restless and unhappy and cannot, therefore, do their best work.[20]

[20] Florence Greenhoe, *op. cit.,* pp. 60–61.

TABLE 2

NET APPROVAL AND DISAPPROVAL REACTIONS OF REPRESENTATIVE GROUPS TO TEACHER BEHAVIOR

Teacher Behavior	As Rated By					
	356 School-board Members		9,122 Teachers		1,363 Students	
	Male [1]	Female	Male	Female	Male	Female
1. Owning an automobile	61.3	60.0	64.4	59.6	81.0	79.3
2. Dating a town person	31.7	28.9	49.7	46.5	65.8	64.2
3. Dating another teacher	19.6	19.5	35.2	40.5	67.3	66.7
4. Leaving area over week-ends [2]	0.8	0.9	9.9	5.5	5.8	−6.7
5. Pay for coaching, speaking, etc.	−2.8	−3.1	30.4	29.0	23.3	21.8
6. Single teachers living in apartment	−6.2	−11.2	24.6	24.5	36.4	29.7
7. Buying clothes, etc., outside area	−8.5	19.4	−4.3	−4.0	−1.6	−1.5
8. Smoking in private	−9.8	−46.2	11.5	11.2	35.0	1.4
9. Not attending church	−9.9	−69.0	−54.8	−54.5	−61.6	−62.2
10. Playing cards for money	−18.2	−56.6	−69.2	−70.0	−72.3	−77.6
11. Joining Teachers Union	−22.5	−23.1	9.1	8.5	22.2	22.4
12. Dancing at public dances	−23.9	−26.4	5.7	4.2	25.7	19.0
13. Playing pool or billiards	−25.0	−38.2	−8.0	−17.8	−3.6	−47.2
14. Living outside community	−27.2	−29.7	−11.7	−10.8	−37.4	−39.1
15. Teaching controversial issues [3]	−34.9	−36.7	−1.2	−1.4	34.2	32.9
16. Smoking in public	−48.1	−80.7	−25.2	−61.0	−16.1	−66.7
17. Playing cards for fun	−48.1	16.9	54.3	54.5	66.8	76.1
18. Making a political speech	−55.7	−55.9	−34.9	−40.5	−53.7	−60.3
19. Running for political office	−56.1	−56.4	−33.4	−34.2	−58.4	−57.7
20. Drinking alcoholic liquors	−80.1	−81.3	−71.8	−73.2	−76.5	−76.7
21. Dating a student	−86.0	−65.7	−84.4	−86.4	−68.8	−76.7
22. Use of rouge, etc., by a woman		0.4		45.5		65.3
23. Woman teaching after marriage [4]		−43.2		4.7		−25.5

[1] Male (teacher) female (teacher). [2] Item reads in questionnaire "leaving community often over week-ends." [3] Item reads "teaching controversial social issues in the classroom." [4] Item reads "A woman who continues to teach after marriage."

Source: F. Greenhoe, *Community Contacts and Participation of Teachers* (Washington, American Council on Public Affairs, 1941), p. 51.

SUMMARY

T H E   S C H O O L is like an organism.[21] Every aspect is interdependent with every other. Anything which affects one aspect has repercussions on all other aspects. It is in truth the microcosm of the macrocosm. Within its patterns of living operate all the social structures and processes of the microcosm which are reproduced or reflected in terms of the young.

Ostensibly schools are set up and conducted for the youth of the land. In reality, this conception is far from attainment in many schools. As one visits, listens, and observes, one too frequently comes away with the impression that schools are often run so that teachers may have jobs.

Those who would work in the complex interrelated, interdependent social world of the school need to give attention to a study of its basic structures and processes. This needs to be done not merely in terms of what is but also in terms of what research shows are possibilities for constant appraisal, reappraisal and replanning in the light of the larger social world, its tempo of change, needs, and general backgrounds.

Of equal importance is the study and understanding of the interpersonal relationships within school life, such as teacher-pupil, teacher-teacher, teacher-community, and "fringe."

The specialized culture of the young is very real and very satisfying for those who live within it. And this specialized culture is perhaps the agency most effective in binding personalities together to form a school.[22]

The following chapter will attempt an analysis of that culture which rises as a product of the school's social world.

TEACHING AND STUDY AIDS

1. Consider the problem of social climate within the classroom. Which kind of climate will you choose to use? How will you go about implementing it? If you have chosen a specific field or grade level, organize a project for the actual *setting up of some experiences* for children which would be in line with your aims?
2. If you are interested in the democratic atmosphere, relate what you

[21] Waller, *op. cit.*
[22] *Ibid.*, p. 13.

think would be worth-while experiences for teacher-education programs to provide for prospective teachers. Have you had any such experiences?

3. How does the concept of democratic leadership differ from other concepts of leadership with which you are familiar?

4. Apply the paradigm to a school situation in which you are or have functioned. Do you find it useful? Why or why not?

5. Students often make the remark that lists of leadership characteristics are of little interest to them since they only include what democratic school people want for all well-adjusted children. They then say that they are interested in training not for leadership or fellowship per se but for "participation." What is your reaction to this viewpoint? How would such a viewpoint alter motivation for children?

6. Individually or in groups investigate teacher to teacher relationships and/or teacher to supervisor and administrator relationships.

7. The "preadolescent" years have been least studied of any of the stages of child development. People who will teach or otherwise deal with this age level will be interested in reading Blair and Burton, *Growth and Development of the Preadolescent* (New York, Appleton-Century-Crofts, 1951).

   A. Analyze the volume and any additional materials in terms of behavior peculiar to this level.

   B. behavior needing understanding and insight

   C. methods for dealing with preadolescent adjustment problems

8. Read, compare, and evaluate the work of Cunningham as told in, Ruth Cunningham, *Understanding Group Behavior of Boys and Girls* (New York, Teachers College Columbia Publications, Columbia University, 1951).

SELECTED READING REFERENCES

Anderson, Harold, et al, *Studies of Teachers' Classroom Personalities,* Psychology monographs, Stanford (Stanford University Press, 1946).

Ash, F., *Effect of Teacher Adjustment upon Personality Adjustment,* University of Iowa Study, Sims Progressive Research, 1944, No. 76. Study Series No. 408.

Baxter, Bernice and Cassidy, Rosalind., *Group Experience, the Democratic Way* (New York, Harper, 1943). I. Group Leadership; II. Face-to-Face Group: Its Emergence and Guidance; III. Individuals in Groups; IV. Preparation for Tomorrow's Leadership.

Cook, Lloyd Allen, and Cook, Elaine Forsyth, *A Sociological Approach to Education* (New York, McGraw-Hill, 1950).

Counsellbaum, Stella, "Building Democracy Through Extra Curricular Clubs," *Education,* Vol. 68 (November 1947), pp. 62–68.

Cuber, J. F., "Changing Courtship and Marriage Customs," *Annals of the American Academy of Political and Social Science,* Vol. 229 (1943), pp. 30–38.

Cummings, Howard H. (ed.), "Improving Human Relations," *National Council for the Social Studies* (Washington, National Education Association, November 1949).

Davis, R. G., "Group Therapy and Social Acceptance in a First-Second Grade," Bibliography F. Ed. Sch., Vol. 49 (December 1948), pp. 219–223.

DuVall, Everett. *Personality and Social Group Work, an Individual Approach* (New York, Association Press, 1943). I. The Individual and the Group; VIII. Leadership as Relationship.

Greenhoe, Florence, *Community Contacts and Participation of Teachers,* (Washington, American Council on Public Affairs, 1941).

Harnly, Paul W., and others, *Improving Intergroup Relations in School and Community Life* (Lincoln, Neb., The North Central Association of Secondary Schools and Colleges, 1946).

Havighurst, Robert J., Developmental Tasks in Education (Chicago, University of Chicago Press, 1951).

Hopkins, Thomas, "Techniques in Human Relations," *Teachers College Record,* Vol. XLVII (November 1945), pp. 89–97.

Kirkendall, Lester A., *Factors Related to the Changes in School Adjustment of High School Pupils,* Contributions to Education, No. 705 (New York, Bureau of Publications, Teachers College, Columbia University, 1937).

Kirkpatrick, C., and Coplow, T., "Courtship in a Group of Minnesota Students" *American Journal of Sociology,* Vol. 51 (1945), pp. 114–125.

Lee, Doris, and Lee, J. Murray, *The Child and His Curriculum* (New York, Appleton-Century-Crofts, 1950).

Lewin, Kurt, "Experiments on Autocratic and Democratic Atmospheres," *Social Frontier,* Vol. 4 (July 1938), pp. 316–319.

Mangus, A. R., "Four Marks of a Mature Teacher," *Portfolio of Teaching Techniques,* Staff of Educator's Washington Dispatch.

McCandless, Boyd R., "Changing Relationships between Dominance and Social Acceptability during Group Democratization" *American Journal Orthopsychiatry,* Vol. 12, (1942), pp. 529–535.

Mitchell, Lucy Sprague, *Our Children and Our Schools* (New York, Simon and Schuster, 1951).

Northway, Mary L., Frankel, Esther, and Potashin, Reva, "Personality and Sociometric Status," *Sociometry Monograph* (New York, Beacon House, 1947).

Olson, W. C., "Human Relations in the Classroom," *National Education Association Journal,* Vol. 36 (December 1947), pp. 640–641.

Reed, Mary F., *Follow-up Studies of the Effects of Dominative and Integrative Contacts in Children's Behavior* (Stanford, Stanford University Press, 1946).

Shapiro, Leo, and Goldenberg, Benjamin, "Promising Practices in Intergroup Education," *NEA Journal,* Vol. XXXVII (February 1948), pp. 96–97.

Slavson, S. R., *Character Education in a Democracy* (New York, Association Press, 1939). I. Conflict between Character and Culture; II. Social Roots of "Human Nature," III. Education for a Dynamic Society; IV. Education for Social Action.

————, *Introduction to Group Therapy* (New York, Commonwealth Fund, 1943). I. Principles; V. Problem of Grouping; VI. Function of the Adult.

Symonds, Percival, "Personality of Teachers," *Journal of Educational Research* (May 1948), pp. 652–661.

Watson, Goodwin, *Action for Unity* (New York, Harper, 1947).

Wickman, E. K. *Children's Behavior and Teacher's Attitudes.* New York, Commonwealth Fund, 1937).

Zirbes, Laura, "The Emotional Climate of Schools," *The Educational Method* (January 1935).

XIV THE SCHOOL'S CULTURE

THE SCHOOL'S SEPARATE CULTURE

Teachers have always known that it was not necessary for the students of strange customs to cross the seas to find material. Folklore and myth, tradition, taboo, magic rites, ceremonials of all sorts, collective representations, participation mystique, all abound in the front yard of every school, and occasionally they creep upstairs and are incorporated into the more formal portions of school life.

There are, in the school, complex rituals of personal relationships, a set of folkways, mores, and irrational sanctions, a moral code based upon them. There are games, which are sublimated wars, teams, and an elaborate set of ceremonies concerning them. There are traditions, and traditionalists waging their world-old battle against innovators. There are laws, and there is the problem of enforcing them. There is *Sittlichkeit*. There are specialized societies with a rigid structure and a limited membership. There are no reproductive groups, but there are customs regulating the relations of the sexes. All these things make up a world that is different from the world of adults.[1]

IN AN EARLIER SECTION it has been suggested that the school is a locus for cultural diffusion, that the school transmits the culture from one generation to another as well as skills, attitudes, and prejudices; yet these social products are seldom passed on intact. For the child does not experience these things as do the adults who are attempting to transmit the norms and customs of behavior.

In terms of his physical, physiological, mental-emotional, and social-cultural maturity quotient, he sees them differently than

[1] W. W. Waller, *Sociology of Teaching* (New York, Wiley, 1932), p. 103. Used by permission.

adults. Very early in life he experiences the world in terms of very small, simple wholes which are extended, as has been said, by a series of "Aha moments." The results of these insightful moments build his selfhood.

This seems to say that the norms and patterns of childhood arise in part at least from "imperfectly experienced adult situations."

The culture pattern followed out by children may be a survival, for when culture changes, it often happens that what was formerly a serious activity for adults is continued in the play of children. Indian fighting, sword play, Hallowe'en festivities, fairy tales, and the use of the bow and arrow have lost their worth in the adult world, but they have retained a certain value in the mental world of childhood. Sometimes economic activities survive and are continued in play because they have great intrinsic interest and have disappeared from the adult world only because they were unable to hold their own in competition with more efficient and prosaic means of getting a living. This has been true of hunting and fishing. There is in the development process a gradual evolution in the complexity of social situations and of the adjustment which the person makes to them; the fact that these social situations sometimes reproduce the actual situations of an earlier state of society has led some commonsense observers to believe in the theory of recapitulation.[2]

This separate culture of the young is easiest seen and studied in peer groupings and within the school. The unsupervised playground probably approaches "pure child culture" most closely. The cultural forms within the school pattern are the next best objects of study.

This suggests that such differences in perception and conceptualization may well lead to conflict between the adults who are attempting to induct the child into society and the child who sees otherwise.

As pointed out by Kingsley Davis, this is true at all age levels,[3] but often painfully so at adolescence. It is often suggested that awareness of this potential conflict has caused those who were able to project themselves back into the child's world[4] with intensity and understanding to attempt "to make the transition easier by presenting to children a finely graded and continuously evolving culture, organized into ever more complex configurations."

[2] Waller, *op. cit.*, p. 105.
[3] Kingsley Davis, "The Sociology of Parent-Youth Conflict," *American Sociological Review* (August 1940), pp. 523–535.
[4] Waller, *op. cit.*, p. 107.

Recent curricula and teaching methods are evidence that educators understand this important principle and are attempting to bridge these gaps by meaningful activity programs within the academic field.

But this recognition is not so new at that. The history of the growth and development of "extracurricular activities" is the story of teacher recognition of the factor. The difference is largely in the point of focus.

Educators of other times and of other schools of thought today are trying consciously, or unconsciously, to keep academic things intact and meet the needs through a whole galaxy of "school activities." In the main these are "teacher-initiated" and "teacher-managed," at least in the beginning. Should the young attempt to take them over and mold them to suit themselves to free them from stifling, adult domination, the ensuing conflict negates much of the intended ameliorating influence. Youth is charged with insubordination, impudence, lack of appreciation, and "wanting to run everything."

Waller spoke tellingly when he wrote, "So completely is the individual immersed in his own age and social level that he often has difficulty in realizing that any other kind of culture exists." [5]

One can only conclude that adults who experience violent and continued conflict with children and youth are so bound by their adult views that they forget the thoughts and feelings of their younger years.

The resiliency of childhood allows it to set up a buffer subculture of its own. As emphasized earlier, this has two main centers of orientation: child peer groups, especially those unsupervised (at least ostensibly) by adults and the school. In the former children are free to set up their activities largely in terms of their own desires and devices. The culture of the school, however, "is a curious melange of the work of young artisans making culture for themselves and old artisans making culture for the young; it is also mingled with such bits of the greater culture as children have been able to appropriate." [6]

This culture may be studied from many vantage points. For our purposes, we have selected traditions, ceremonies, and activities.

[5] Waller, *op. cit.,* p. 106.
[6] *Ibid.,* p. 107.

TRADITIONS, CEREMONIES, AND ACTIVITIES

The traditions of the school appear to derive from several sources. As evidenced in conduct codes for teachers, there is a body of tradition which comes from the school's community, a purely outside tradition, but a powerful one. These traditions are concerned with the community's expectations of the role to be filled by the school in the socialization of its children. Suffice it to say that the very existence and insistence upon schools themselves is a western tradition.

The "outside" tradition defines also at least for nonschool adult community members, the status positions of teachers and students.

Teachers shall be older than students or at least able to appear older and in command of the situation at all times.

The old shall teach the young, and not that the young shall ever teach the old, which would be at least equally justifiable in a world that changes so rapidly that an education twenty years old is out of date.[7]

Teachers and students are expected to maintain a discernible social distance and the penalty for failure to do so is for the teacher, at least, a loss of status and prestige in both the student world and the adult world. (For example, see reactions to teachers dating students, etc., in Chapter 8.)

Teachers are also expected to treat all students with equal attention, respect, and opportunities. Favoritism is the cardinal sin.

What is sometimes termed intermingled tradition is that derived partly from outside and partly from inside the school.

In so far as this tradition of teachers is derived from outside a particular school, it is drawn by teachers from the general culture and from association with members of the teaching profession everywhere. In so far as it is a purely local product, it is produced by the teachers in the institution and is passed on from one teacher to another. We may mention some cardinal points of the teacher tradition as it is usually encountered, making due allowance for local variations. There is a teacher morality, and this morality regulates minutely the teacher's relations with his students and with other teachers; it affects his relations with other teachers, especially where the standing of those teachers with students might be affected. There is a character ideal of the teacher; nearly every group which lives long in one stereotyped relation with other

[7] Waller, *op. cit.*, p. 108.

groups produces its character ideal, and this ideal for teachers is clearly observable. Teachers have likewise a certain traditional attitude toward each other. The most obvious manifestation of the traditional attitude is the ceremoniousness of teachers toward each other and toward the administration of the school. It seems clear that this is the ceremoniousness of a fighting group which does not care to endanger its prestige with underlings by allowing any informality to arise within itself. Another interesting observation that has often been made about particular groups of teachers is that they discriminate markedly between veterans and new men. This distinction is in the folkways. Occasionally there is a more or less definite ceremony of initiation, more rarely, actual hazing.[8]

Traditions within the school have been originated by both teachers and students. In some instances teachers originate traditions because they were a part of their own background or because they seem to give cultural respectability to the institution. Or they act as means of gaining popularity with students and/or as means of controlling students' behavior.

Traditions set up and carried out by students vary in structure and process between schools, but have certain basic characteristics which can be mentioned.

Student-teacher relationships come within this area. In the earlier grades children "like" the teacher, and there is customarily no disgrace in behaving toward her as a veritable mother surrogate. If the teacher is a man, he is openly declared a father surrogate. By some more erotically precocious girls and boys he may unashamedly be spoken of as a later love object.

In later elementary and high school, however, one likes the teacher but not too well, at least openly, unless, of course, it is a permissive atmosphere with democratic implementation.

Student to student loyalty is a strong tradition. Many youngsters suffer undeserved punishment rather than "squeal" on their budies. While giving information concerning others may be taboo, just as strong feeling exists if in a democratic framework wrongdoers "admit" mistakes and one does not. For example,

Never again can we trust Joey. We all admitted we played with the dry ice when we weren't supposed to, but Joey. He lied on his cub scout honor, and, Mother, he raised his hand to God. No more Joey for us boys.

[8] *Ibid.*, pp. 108–109.

Green hats for freshmen, school letters for upper classmen, jeans, sweaters, T-shirts, low-heeled shoes and bobbysox, sweaters and skirts with pearl necklaces, plus many, many more clothes choices are part of the tradition of dress. And woe betide the child who dresses other than in the designated tradition of dress.

Language, or as someone has said *slanguage,* is also traditional not only within the school but also within maturation levels. Once a pleasing object or experience was "hot stuff," "tricky," "sweet," and more recently "neat," "nifty," "mellow." As Whyte suggests for *Street Corner Society,* so too the school child is surrounded by a language which to the uninitiated is often unintelligible.

Some high schools and many colleges and universities carry rigidly enforced traditions of where different grade levels may walk, sit, to whom they may speak, and certain services which one class level must perform for another. These traditions involve a sanction of mores proportions. For the school pupil, they are *right, necessary,* and *true.*

Every school population has ceremonies for implementing traditions. Sometimes they consist of simple informal things, such as slaps on the shoulder, verbal signs of passing from novitiate to member, or just payment of dues.

Again the ceremonies may be formal, replete with symbolism, such as initiation ceremonies, mock trials, hell weeks, and the like. Shudder the novice may, but refuse to perform, however outlandishly, he will not, as some tragedies from fraternity initiations will illustrate.

Whether the activity is athletics, clubs, or secret societies, the traditions take on stability and immortality as they are carried out through the rituals and ceremonies of the school's activities. Because of the limiting factor of space two examples of school culture as shown in structure and processes will illustrate the point.

FRATERNITIES AS A SCHOOL CULTURAL PHENOMENON

A student probably joins a sorority or fraternity, not because he feels identity with that group, not so much because he thinks he is like that group, but because he wants to be like it. Such a group holds prestige value for him. He has heard fraternity mentioned in such ways that it holds "glamour" for him. There is the matter of secrecy, the desire to participate in activities that are not for the mob. The fraternity holds prestige values because it has been so closely identified with college life. Fraternities have drawn within their membership individuals who, themselves, have high status and prestige value. They hold such status and value because they have excelled in areas which are of concern to youth, such as athletics. Alumni become famous writers, actors, governors, businessmen. The prestige which these individuals carry is shed upon the group to which they belong—to the whole state, or university, but, in particular, to the intimate in-group, the fraternity. The individual's own ego expands in the reflected glory of the campus hero. To belong to such and such a fraternity makes X a marked man; to him is attached the prestige of the group.[9]

The term "fraternity" itself carries prestige value, largely because of its association with the values of school life. Added prestige is given by the use of Greek letters. The Greeks were a classic people, great in art, literature, athletics, war, politics, philosophy, etc.

The fraternity has what may be called polarity. It is a fixed thing on the high school or college campus. It has a name, a history, a ritual. To the lonely boy or girl coming to the campus, it beckons because of its offer of security, the provision of an intimate we-circle of closely interacting personalities. In it the individual may sink himself, and feel that he is anchored, that he belongs.

Fraternities more or less control many of the activities of the university which are most meaningful to the student. This control may extend to such things as athletics, the school publications, extracurricular activities, social functions. Organized power and strength have their own prestige values.

A fraternity is also a unity of interacting personalities. This is to say that it is more than a solid entity, totally given to singleness of purpose. We have said that individuals seek membership in a fraternity not because they *are* like that group but because they *want to be* like it. Within limits the fraternity draws its members from a variety of social sources, those members having different backgrounds. The fraternity has its own culture—its characteristic traditions, values, attitudes. It has a history. There may well be a fraternity type of personality. The incoming new member does not represent this type of personality. Without knowing exactly what it is doing, the fraternity immediately sets about shaping each individual into the fraternity-type personality. A process of socializa-

[9] From an unpublished paper by Herbert Lohrman.

tion goes on which is analogous to the same process in the family. By individual counseling, through "round table" discussion, by bull session, by precept and example the neophyte is shaped into the fraternity personality. He is rewarded by approval or other techniques; he is punished by ridicule, by "lecture," and even by the paddle. He learns what sort of girls he may date—those whom he may date for college affairs and dates—and those whom he may sexually exploit. He learns the proper attitude toward the professor, the apple polisher, the independent, other fraternities. He learns what clothes and jewelry are taboo.

Ordinarily, it is not difficult to mold the personality into proper form. The individual seeks the approval of his group and its constituent members. He reacts easily to suggestion, imitates consciously and automatically mannerisms, dress effects, etc. He stands always ready to defend the group against outsiders, against certain allegations directed at his fraternity or fraternities in general. He comes to hold all the symbolisms of fraternity in high value—the pin, the "boy gives girl pin" complex, the hand clasp, the ritual, the whistle, the sentiment that we must stick together and pull together. The inner workings of campus politics come to be entrancing to him, and he defends them for all he is worth.

But in still another sense the fraternity is a group of interacting personalities. If there are group purposes, group values, group techniques, there are also individual purposes and values. There are statuses within the fraternity. Some of them will be official statuses usually achieved in some manner. There are certainly ascribed statuses that are assigned to the freshman pledge. Status may derive from the holding of office, or from some other factor: wealth, athletic ability, scholastic ability, wit, and the like. The members hold attitudes toward each other as well as toward the group as an entity. Fraternities sometimes pluck a "lemon"—a member who outwardly conforms to fraternity standards, but whose personality pattern does not fit in with those of a number of the group. There may also be groups or cliques within the larger group.

Between the members there will be behavior derived from varying attitudes toward one another. There will be rivalry, competition, sometimes open conflict.

There are then those attitudes of institutionalism which govern the behavior of the member in all outside relationships. These attitudes and their attendant behavior patterns, make him a fraternity man—both in the eyes of outsiders and of the in-members. There will also be types or patterns of behavior within the group which are governed by the institutional attitudes, such as those with respect to the conduct of fraternity business and fraternity order, the performance of certain social functions, the support of a brother because he is a brother, the glowing response to the achievements of a fraternity brother (the pride felt in the fact that Governor Blah is an alumnus member).

On the other hand are those attitudes which motivate individualistic behavior. These are manifested in the interplay between personalities, in the seeking of status within the group, the playing of roles of various kinds.

Much the same structure and similar processes are to be observed in the school club with several exceptions. Few clubs have the lure of secrecy, with all its symbols, rituals, and the like. Some may have longevity, but fewer will have the cultural prestige hangover of the Greek letter society.

Likewise the control exerted over the individual member is not likely to be so potent as in the sorority-fraternity exclusiveness construct. It may well be in fact as well as in theory that the social-cultural interpretation of the term Club as over against the more controversial terms sorority and/or fraternity, sets the stage for its "halo" among nonmembers as well as members.

ATHLETICS AS A SCHOOL CULTURAL PHENOMENON

As has often been pointed out by analysts of school activities, "their catch-on," their appeal is directly related to the spontaneity of their base. In other words, do the activities have behavior patterns which have such intrinsic interest for students that they will gladly brook faculty connections?

The sorority-fraternity appeal as discussed previously is one of intrinsic interest sans, in large measure, faculty intervention. Many have hazarded the guess that the escape from adult domination is one of the secret society's greatest appeals to adolescents, and at the same time one of its greatest potential dangers.

We should now like to pay attention to one area of school activities which seems most successful in providing the spontaneous base just mentioned to the extent that adult connections are accepted by students. An important factor in this is the "set form," as Waller called it, which individuals can observe on the basic assumption that the "group welfare and prestige" are at stake. And from this observance can and must come "merit and distinction" in the eyes of both the whole school and outside adults as well.

For the athlete who plays the game, the forms to be observed such as training rules, long, arduous practices, even the often tedious trips not to mention the grueling minutes of the game are well recompensed by the shouts of his name as he scores, by the we-group spirit and enthusiasm of his classmates, by the respect and admiration of the townspeople, and finally by the letters, sweaters, banquets, and press releases which show him to be the maker and carrier of glory for his old alma mater.

But what of the substitute, the "fall guy" for the first stringer? At least he has identification with the glamor, the honor, and in defeat, the sorrow, and commisseration of the defeated but unbowed contenders. The spectator also can and must feel a similar identification if there is to be "support" for the team.

Here too, form and merit enter into the planning. Cheering sections are carefully organized, drilled, even uniformed sometimes. Booster clubs assume considerable prestige as not merely those who provide "things," follow the team, and generally display loyalty, but also as keepers of the school's good sportsmanship reputation.

Whichever game is considered is surrounded by form, and this form is handed on from one school generation of players and spectators to another with very few variations. Uniforms, plays, yells, rituals such as rallies, after-the-game dances become traditional and are part and parcel of the form and merit concepts.

A student paper illustrates this individal and groupal identification which occurs and under what circumstances.

I always loved athletic competition, and on the sand-lot I could manage rather well. But I could never make the team in high school. I trained twice as conscientiously as most of the first team (who always boasted they never trained at all), I worked at practice until I was weak from exhaustion, and I was sure I "internalized perfection of response" for several special roles, but somehow the coaches always thought that I was willing and "a great help to morale," but I wasn't quite in form, they said. So I played the bench throughout high school. But I was never bitter. We played football at night under the lights, and nothing could be more thrilling. The colors, the yells, the feeling of something bigger and more important than you personally, did something to all of us. When Waller says a game is a sublimated fight, I think he's right. The cheerleaders work people into a frenzy with their Fight, Fight, Fight yells, the crowd echoes in a roar, the coach tells you to go in and "fight 'em to a standstill," and when we were losing, we sang, "We'll go down fighting."

While this is fine for the spirit of the team and the school, it can also be a detriment. Rivalries between small towns as between big universities can become so intense that to lose that game may mean a coach's job. As a result he often keeps star players playing when to do so endangers their future health.

This game as a fight business is further shown by the ways of controlling the situation. There are elaborate sets of rules for every game and penalties for infractions plus a referee and in most situations now, more than one referee. It's hardly safe to be *The* referee on a tight basketball game floor or on a football field.

Yes, I think athletics is the most developed, detailed, formalized, and most loved and participated in school cultural pattern. Bands, school papers, language clubs, and class plays are fine and surely worthwhile, and I was on the staff or had parts in all of them while I was in school, but I would have given up every one of them if I could have carried that ball over the goal line just once each football season!

SCHOOL CULTURE IN TERMS OF PROCESSES OF SOCIAL INTERACTIONS

AS ONE STUDIES the over-all social-cultural process of social interaction, he finds that it breaks down into several subprocesses.

All of these subprocesses operate within the social and cultural world of the school. Some writers are interested mainly in analyzing from the viewpoint of conflict as the basic process. Social educational analysis is more concerned with what Park and Burgess earlier designated as cultural process or the interpretation of persons and groups, with the goal of sharing experience and history.

In the words of Park and Burgess, "Assimilation is the process of interpenetration and fusion in which persons and groups acquire the memories, sentiments, and attitudes of other persons and groups, and by sharing their experience and history, are incorporated with them in a common cultural life In so far as assimilation denotes, this sharing of tradition, this intimate participation in common

The school comprises a child's social and cultural worlds. It is his place of work, the site of his romance, his scene of social siftings and sortings, and his place of social experimentation in all the social processes he will use later as an adult.

experiences, assimilation, is central in the historical and cultural processes." [10]

Accommodation, on the other hand, is a living arrangement which has been worked out through compromise, systems of dominance and submission, and the like. "Accommodation has been described as a process of adjustment, that is, an organization of social relations and attitudes to prevent or to reduce conflict, to control competition, and to maintain a basis of security in the social order for persons and groups of divergent interest and types to carry on together their varied life activities. Accommodation in the sense of the composition of conflict is invariably the goal of the political process." [11]

It will help us to grasp the meaning of the school as a social-cultural institution if we try to place it with regard to these processes. To be strictly accurate, we must think of these processes as going on within the school as well as without it, of the school as a microcosm that mirrors the macrocasm.

When the political process is still in the stage of overt conflict, various conflict groups attempt to use the schools for passing on their truth to the unbiased younger generation. Sectarian schools are for the most part established for this purpose, but it is perhaps only of the worst of these that Ross's aphorism that they are means of conducting children into society through a tunnel holds true. Economic groups are able to influence profoundly the policies of established schools, and on occasion to establish chairs and schools for the promulgation of their doctrines. In a leading eastern college is a chair that was endowed for teaching the fallacies of socialism. One of the greatest of the business schools was established, at least in part, as a means of crushing out various heresies concerning the protective tariff.

The list of those who have sought to use the tax-supported schools as channels for their doctrines is almost as long as the list of those who have axes to grind. Prohibitionists, professional reformers, political parties, public utilities, sectarians, moralists, advocates of the open shop, labor unions, socialists, antivivisectionists, jingoes, chauvinists, and patrioteers—all have sought to control the curriculum, the composition of the teaching staff, and the method of instruction.

Opposing groups work out various compromises by virtue of which the schools can be made acceptable to all parties. Thus the school is shot

[10] R. E. Park and E. W. Burgess, *Introduction to Science of Sociology* (Chicago, University of Chicago Press, 1924), pp. 735–736.
[11] *Ibid.,* pp. 735–736.

through with accommodations, some of which have grown so old that their original purpose has been forgotten.

In that assimilation of group to group which Park and Burgess think of as characterizing the cultural process, the schools play a most important part. That is particularly true of the schools of a nation which, like ours, is seeking to amalgamate into one whole the representatives of many diverse cultures. The main burden of Americanization falls upon the public schools, and there is every likelihood that it will continue to do so. The schools Americanize by immersing the young in the culture and tradition of the country, by inducing them to participate as much as possible in the activities of the American arena. The things that the children of the foreign born learn at school, and on the streets before and after school, are often in conflict with the tradition which their parents are trying to transmit to them. Children usually learn to speak English better than their parents, and they more rapidly acquire a superficial familiarity with American life, so that frequently they feel superior to the parents and are most unwilling to take advice from them. Since the home plays a large part in the formation of law-abiding attitudes, and since the view of American life which these children get is at best incomplete and distorted, Americanization through the schools usually entails a certain amount of disorganization for the second generation of immigrants. Adult education of immigrants has also been organized on a wide scale. Though less immediately effective, it is yet a very powerful means of leading the immigrant to the participation in American culture from which Americanization results.

The common experiences of a group of people living together under any circumstances which give a semblance of unity operate to give the group that sense of a common past which is the mark of assimilation. Time is of the essence of the cultural process. There is, however, in the cultural process a many-sided interchange of attitudes and definitions of situations, of techniques and knowledge concerning the elements of culture. It is this process of transmission and interchange which we shall have particularly in mind when we speak of the cultural process from this point on. The school serves as a medium in which this interchange takes place.

The ordinary school does not serve as a center of inventions, although there are many institutions of higher learning which, through the support of experimentation and research, are taking over this function. The ordinary school does not share in this, but serves rather as a very important subcenter in the process of cultural diffusion.

Particularly on the mental side of culture it is the task of the schools to mediate new things to the local community. Sociologists have found that many of the unadjustments in modern society are traceable to what is known as cultural lag, to the fact that nonmaterial, or adaptive culture, does not change so rapidly as material culture. Thus our systems of law, religion, and morals are authentic antiques, but our automobiles and radios and talking pictures are modern. Much of the maladjustment of society is due to this failure of the machinery of social control to change with a rapidity equaling that of mechanical culture.

The existence of cultural lag is ascribable to a number of factors. There is a low rate of invention in nonmaterial culture. And it is also true that new ideas spread slowly and meet with much opposition because many of them are against the mores. The schools could do much to accelerate the diffusion of nonmaterial culture, but they have not usually cared to assume this function.

We come now to the second phase of the cultural process, which consists of the transmission of attitudes, techniques, and knowledge to the younger persons of the community. This process is incidental to the succession of generations and is necessitated by the fact that all men are born 'equally ignorant. Much of the work of forming the young is done by other institutions, and certainly the family is more significant in child life than the school, but the importance of the school in the cultural process seems to be increasing; its formal position has always been central in the process, and there are indications that the actual significance of the school in child life is not destined to diminish.

The amount of schooling which children undergo foreshadows, and some would say determines, their future earning capacity and the level of society on which they will find their life. A crude selection, then, goes on in the schools, a social selection of those destined to fulfill certain predetermined social functions.

Partly it is the schools themselves which select. The native intelligence of children sets certain absolute limits to their achievements. No amount of schooling can make the moron perform satisfactorily above his fated level. The schools, by their curriculum which must be mastered before the student can pass on, sift and resift their human materials, selecting on the basis of intelligence chiefly, but allowing considerable weight to other qualities such as a pleasing manner, emotional stability, and diligence.

The schools must sort all the human material that comes to them, but they do not subject all children to the same kind of sorting process. Other things being equal, the schools tend to bring children at least up to an intellectual level which will enable them to function in the same economic and social stratum as their parents. But the children of the poor tend to drop out early, and very frequently for reasons quite other than incapacity to learn; they drop out because their labor is needed at home, because they are ashamed to attend school in shabby clothes, because there is no tradition in their group of going beyond the literacy stage in education. Equally important with economic factors are the social assets of a family, its standing in the community, its level of cultural participation, its traditions and ambitions—these factors likewise limit social mobility.

The functions of the school as an agency of the cultural process and as a channel of vertical mobility are sometimes blended; indeed, these two functions in their individual reference are often indistinguishable. Education brings one into touch with the main stream of culture. The aspiring student embraces this wider cultural participation in the hope that it will make of him something somehow different. Yet this being different is indissolubly connected with having a different place in society. A university confronts a gifted freshman as a vast array of cultural riches; he may appropriate these and realize himself in learning to use them. The cultural process, which must start anew with every generation, automatically assigns men to their proper posts. The manner and extent to which they assimilate the cultural heritage determine the niche they will fit into in the social structure.

One of the important things that the school does is to separate individuals into classes corresponding roughly to certain occupational and social strata. When the matter is pragmatically considered, that conclusion seems inescapable. One is tempted to inquire whether this view of education corresponds with that social philosophy which is known as democratic theory and which is regarded as the fundamental orientation point for discussion of social policy in our society.[12]

We turn now to a consideration of child-school-community relationships and how they may, and in many instances have been, beamed toward the assimilative end result of social interaction.

TEACHING AND STUDY AIDS

1. Make a study of "the school culture" of which you are a part. Select a set of traditions, ceremonies and/or activities and analyze their impact upon you as a social individual, upon a specific group of which you are a member.
2. Make a study of such school political structures as the student senate or other student governing bodies. How do they reflect the larger culture? How are they unique as cultural products of the young?
3. Study the problem of high school and college secret societies. Have you read the book or seen the movie "Take Care of My Little Girl"? What are its implications for school culture?
4. Have you ever been a student where teachers tried initiating activi-

[12] Waller, *op. cit.*, pp. 16–22.

ties and traditions as a means of control? Discuss and analyze the situation and its outcomes?

5. The area of Pressure Groups and their impact on school culture merits extended study. A panel discussion would doubtless be interesting and instructive.

6. Analyze school songs, jokes and rallies, and initiations as cultural forms.

7. How are school athletics an attempt at a culture of the young?

8. Read the entire article by Willard Waller, "The Rating and Dating Complex," *American Sociological Review,* Vol. 2 (1937), pp. 727–734. Relate his findings to your high school and your college. Where do you agree? Where disagree? Some people do not agree with Waller's generalizations, can you think of ways to gather data from your own college world on this topic?

SELECTED READING REFERENCES

Allport, Gordon, "The Psychology of Participation," *Psychological Review,* Vol. 52 (1945), pp. 117–132.

Brown, Francis J., *Educational Sociology* (New York, Prentice-Hall, 1947), Chaps. 11, 12, 13, 14.

——, *Sociology of Childhood* (New York, Prentice-Hall, 1939).

Cook, Lloyd Allen and Elaine Forsythe, *A Sociological Approach to Education* (New York, McGraw-Hill, 1950).

Cupps, R. D., "Dating at the University of Washington," *Marriage and Family Living,* Vol. 9 (May 1947), pp. 30–31.

Griffin, Alan, *Freedom American Style* (New York, Holt, 1940).

Mead, Margaret, *The School in American Culture* (Cambridge, Harvard University Press, 1950).

Roucek, Joseph D. *Sociological Foundations of Education* (New York, Crowell, 1942).

Smucker, Orden, "The Campus Clique as an Agency of Socialization," *Journal of Educational Sociology,* Vol. 21 (November 1947), pp. 163–168.

Strang, Ruth, *Group Activities in College and Secondary School* (New York, Harper, 1946).

Waller, Willard, *The Sociology of Teaching* (New York, Wiley, 1932).

II

Integration of the Child, School, and Community—or—The Community Approach to Education

XV

THE COMMUNITY
APPROACH TO EDUCATION

WE HAVE ASSUMED in this treatise that the rearing of children is *the* most important job of this or any other generation. But this does not mean merely bringing them to physical maturity unharmed. For a child to be well adjusted it is necessary to help him at every maturity level to live easily and comfortably with other normal persons to attain behavior patterns and attitudes that do not differ too greatly from the standards of right and wrong, and to be personally happy and socially useful. Such a person lives up to a high level of his potentialities, and continues his process of social growth and development in the direction of social, emotional, intellectual and moral maturity.[1]

In other words, mental health and maturity are as important, many would argue more so, than mere physical health. Obviously the two are so interrelated as to be inseparable.

Today the need for such child rearing is accentuated a thousandfold by the level of development of the society and culture in which children must live and grow. The statistical evidences of the need are not of the nature to inspire complacency.

Beyond the evidences of personality conflict and maladjustment evidenced in such areas as divorce, mental disease increases, and the like, lie equally disturbing data concerning the mental hygiene aspects of children themselves.

One reputable research into the mental health quotients of

[1] A. R. Mangus and J. R. Seeley, *Mental Health Needs in a Rural and Semi-Rural Area of Ohio, 1950* (Columbus, Division of Mental Hygiene of the Ohio State Department of Public Welfare, 1950).

children and adults in a county will illustrate. It must be borne in mind that the study is of a rural and semirural area where folklore has it that we may expect adjustment and happiness in greater degree than an urban milieu is expected to afford.

The following paragraphs summarize some of the major findings with respect to the prevalence of mental hygiene problems: [2]

A. What did the draft reveal?

Based on the record of one of the two local draft boards which, between them, covered the county, it was estimated that at least 10 percent of the men of military age (18–37) had personality disorders serious enough to disqualify them for effective military service. This included those rejected with some personality disorder as the leading cause for disqualification. This group alone made up 6.3 percent of all the men examined and 23.6 percent of all those rejected.

It should be remembered that the Army psychiatrist at the induction station based his judgment very largely on the man's civilian record of adjustment. Most of these men, therefore, were more or less seriously maladjusted in civilian life.

It may be assumed that many of those who were rejected for obvious and disqualifying physical defects at the local board were also notably lacking in mental health, though they had no psychiatric examination. Many others were rejected for a variety of physical difficulties which in all probability were bodily manifestations of personality disorders. Finally, a considerable number of men whose emotional difficulties were not detected by psychiatric examiners, or not considered serious enough to bar them from service, had to be discharged later because of "nervous breakdown."

In addition to rejections for personality disorders, 1 man in each 100 of those examined had to be rejected because of mental and educational deficiency. One in each 200 was epileptic, and was disqualified for that reason.

B. What did the study of school children show?

A rough screening, with tests and ratings, of all third- and sixth-grade children provided a basis for an evaluation of their mental health. It was found that:

(1) At least 18 percent of all third graders in all schools

[2] Mangus and Seeley, *op. cit.*, pp. 11–13. Used by permission.

in the county were poorly adjusted and in need of some kind of mental health aids. An even higher proportion of the sixth-grade children showed evidences of poor mental health. In that grade it was estimated that about 21 percent were poorly adjusted children.

On the basis of these percentages it was estimated that more than 1,200 poorly adjusted children are to be found in the first eight grades of the Miami County Public Schools.

What General Conclusions were reached as a result of the study?

About *one in every five* elementary school children in Miami County presents evidences of poor mental health of some degree of seriousness. Large numbers of these children are evidently maladjusted to a very serious degree and are in grave need of specialized guidance services to meet their mental health needs. Many are less seriously maladjusted and may somehow "get by" without specialized help, although they, too, could profit if it were available.

Mental health problems were much more prevalent among boys then among girls.

Such problems were especially acute among children who were retarded in their school progress and whose advanced age made them misfits in their class.

C. What was shown by the study of juvenile delinquency?

From 1940 through 1945, a six-year period, 1,168 delinquency cases were brought before the County Juvenile Court for official or unofficial action. Juvenile delinquency cases brought to court reached a peak in 1943 when 260 cases were subjected to court action. That was nearly 4 percent of all children of juvenile court age. These figures do not reveal the total prevalence of delinquency, since the larger number of offenses involving children are dealt with by schools, by parents, by law enforcement officers, and by other authorities.

Juvenile delinquency is considered a mental hygiene problem since many children are offenders because of personality distortions or undergo distortion as a consequence of the treatment their behavior provokes. Misconduct in children is often a way of reacting to inner conflicts and frustrations. These, in turn, may reflect external pressures and deprivations which leave basic emotional and social needs unmet. Delinquent behavior is often a substitute gratification for real but unmet needs of the child.

This study confirms the conclusion of many other studies which show that personality disorders occur as often among farm people as they do among nonfarm residents, and perhaps more often. Estimates of maladjustment among elementary school children in Miami County showed two interesting things in this regard:

A. At both the third- and sixth-grade levels the incidence of maladjustment, as estimated on the basis of tests and ratings, was less among farm children than among those from nonfarm homes.

B. But the advantage enjoyed by the farm children was much less among sixth graders than among those in the third grade.

The draft board records showed that the rejection rate generally was higher for farm men than for nonfarm men. It was also found that the incidence of personality disorders was greater among farm workers than among other registrants. This study points to the conclusion that, from the point of view of mental health, farm residence is probably an advantage for younger children, but that the advantage is lost with increasing age. Among men of military age, those in other occupations have the advantage over those concerned with farming. This may be due in part at least to migration of disproportionately large numbers of better adjusted youths away from farms and from farm occupations.

If it is true that basically unhappy, frustrated, children tend to become adults with similar risks, and if it is also true as it seems to be, that happy well-adjusted children, free from severe tension and strain, tend to become happy well-adjusted, efficient adults, the importance of both home, school, and community cooperation in child rearing becomes readily apparent. With this viewpoint few would disagree though some few people and groups will still maintain that "raising kids is their own business," and "they don't need any help from crack-brained educators and outsiders." Equally eloquent was the teacher-student who replied:

And believe me their children show the results. Such youngsters are often the social isolates and rejects in the school world.

Heretofore, we have suggested a point of view toward childhood and have pointed out how it may be implemented in child life associations, such as family, peer groups, and classroom situations. This kind of discussion has been parallel with that of pointing out the "what is" aspects of relationships. We need now to consider the interaction of all these influences—the integration of school and community always with reference to the growing, developing organism, the child.

TRADITIONAL—PROGRESSIVE-COMMUNITY APPROACHES

AS WE HAVE SAID at some length in Chapter 11, schools have always played both a receptive and a directive role in social change. Sometimes it has been done rather blindly, sometimes with clarity of insight and purpose. It is doubtless true, however, that whatever the case in high places, the classroom teacher has too often merely gone along.

Today and for the future it must be otherwise. Each teacher who comes into contact with youth needs to be aware of his philosophy of education and living, needs to be familiar with its implications not only from the standpoint of curriculum building and methods of instruction, but also from the standpoint of impact upon child growth and development.

It is the bias here that the community approach is a natural and logical outgrowth of other approaches which may have suited their eras of evolvement. This is to say that in the light of the social trends mentioned above, it appears to offer the most satisfying and fruitful means of inducting the child into adulthood in a changing world. This says also that there may be other modes, perhaps already originating, which will replace this approach as changes continue to occur.

May we then consider the three approaches mentioned in terms of their (*1*) conceptions of the child and his role in school and community, (*2*) conceptions of the teacher and his role in the classroom, and (*3*) conceptions of the school and its role within the school community.

By implication, many of these concepts have been explained earlier. The purpose in coming to them again is to sharpen and review and to point a way and course of action.

The traditional school conceives of the child as a miniature adult. This means in effect that he may be expected to be and do much as adults with the exception of feats of skill. Bolted down desks, protracted periods of sitting quietly at these desks, selection of subject matter and activities all are evidence of this concept of childhood. In short, as you see the child so will you arrange his school plant setting, his learning outcome expectations and ways of proceeding to accomplish them.

"The child is a vacuum," quoth one education professor in his pompous fashion. "Yours is a great responsibility. You must so fill that vacuum with worthwhile facts and ideas that he will have them ready to hand when the occasion arises."

Or listen to one who phrased it a bit differently. "The child is a slate on which the teacher writes. Guard well that you write only the great from our heritage." A lá the Great Books, one is tempted to suspect.

Or again. "The child is a sponge. He increases in stature as he absorbs."

Such statements point readily to a further concept of the child. He is considered the carrier, the transmitter of the culture per se, and its potential enacter. The teachers' function then is so to cull the heritage and so meticulously to arrange and indoctrinate it as to cause the status quo to be perpetuated.

Such a school is a place of learning to be sure but not necessarily of education. Bode's remark is classic when he wrote: "At the turn of the century there were those who began to see the child otherwise and as important to do something about it." [3]

As is often the case, when the break with tradition set a new social movement in motion, the swing for a while was toward the opposite extreme. So-called progressive educators regarded the child in no way similar to a miniature adult but considered him a being in his own right. In the effort to shake off the excess baggage which had been characteristic of traditional education, there was a tend-

---

[3] Boyd Bode, a public lecture. For examples see *Thirty Schools Tell Their Story,* Progressive Education Publications (New York, Harper, 1943); also The Ohio State University, University High School Class of 1938, *Were We Guinea Pigs?* (New York, Holt, 1938).

ency to swing to the opposite pole and assume the meeting of pupil interests, likes and immediate needs as the basic factors in his education. The role of the teacher was now that of friend and guide, rather than that of disciplinarian as in the cultural transmission oriented school.

As might be expected, some teachers became merely glorified fellow student-travelers in laissez-faire situations which were mistakenly set up in the name of democratic education.

There were from the first in the movement, however, those who did not confuse the woods and the trees, who recognized that child-centered did not mean child-licensed; who were aware of the sociological fact that the "musts" of the culture were ever present as well as student likes, interests, and needs. These people were also well aware that the job of education was not an either/or stampede but a challenge and opportunity to consider the needs and interests of *both* adult society and young society and to provide induction for the young into adult society not blindly as mere culture carriers, but as dynamic, thinking societal members. These educators were interested in so educating that the young would be able, critically, to appraise personal and societal needs and interests, to enact them where they stood the tests of time, change, and the current social scene, and to be unafraid to revise them when lags became apparent.

Unlike the alarmists' predictions, such education (sometimes referred to as progressive education with a small "p") has not turned out incompetents in the three R's or revolutionists who wish merely to tear apart or continually to emasculate the culture with no constructive attitudes of mind. Nor has it built cynics, agnostics, and atheists as predicted.

Instead, the studies point to people who have performed creditably in college and on the job, who have been rated as superior in such personal-social traits as initiative, social responsibility, and concern for the rights and privileges of others and who are able and willing to take a stand and whatever consequences may result.

Among those more far sighted there gradually developed the cognizance that the child-centered approach needed broadening. There arose an emphasis upon what was called the "community school." Here the attempt was to consider the "whole child," not merely as an individual but also in relation to community social order and processes of social interaction.

In a number of instances this relating process became so concerned with the local community as to become bogged down in its problems and concerns with little or no integration with the larger whole.

Sometimes the concept of education became lost along the way, and schools tended to become largely service institutions. This is not to imply that the interactional position of the school and community should not allow for service projects. It does say that when the activity has reached the place where it is no longer a learning experience for children, it should be replaced by something which does possess learning potentialities for the child group.

An example of the above will serve to illustrate. A visitor watched the boys in the shop program "fixing" Model T Ford trucks, of which there were quite a number in this relatively isolated community.

"How long have you been repairing Ford trucks?" the visitor asked.

"All year," replied the principal proudly.

"How long will you continue to repair them?"

"As long as they need it," was the reply.

Even a cursory observer could see that the students involved had passed both the period of maximum learning and interest. Several were obviously bored and resentful of "working for nothing."

The *Community Approach* to education has a chance to miss many of these pitfalls of the more restricted so-called community school. In a community approach the school is conceived of as *one* agency which must interact, plan, and carry out plans in connection with *all other* agencies within the community. Where need exists, schools and school people will be quick to pick up the ball and start the thinking and acting. Once that function has been discharged, however, they will be ready and willing to release the authority and the activity itself, if need be, to others who may carry it on as well or better. In fact, community social education implies the educating of children, youth, and adults to the level where they do just that—assume the continuance of an activity, leaving the school and school people free to foster real education for others and in other needed areas of which there is never a dearth in a continually changing social world.

This is not a new or novel theory. Many so-called "community schools" have followed this policy, and for a long time. If the literature is read carefully, however, it is possible to point out many instances where the *school* was the containment of the idea and insisted upon maintaining such a position rather than assuming the role of a community participant.

CRITERIA OF A COMMUNITY SCHOOL APPROACH

IN ORDER TO TEST whether or not a school has a community approach, it is necessary to build a set of criteria. A particular school might reach the goal in all or most of these. Another school might reach but one or two, but it would still realize some of the potentialities of a community approach to education. From the literature and observation in a number of community-oriented schools, the following criteria have been evolved:

1. A community school is a cooperative enterprise, involving shared undertaking. There is opportunity for democracy to function through participation in planning, decision making, executing, and evaluating. Opportunity is given to all to help set goals and make choices, and guidance is given to all to help assure the carrying through with the choices made. Further, a community school cooperates with other agencies in promoting services for all the age groups in the area.
2. A community school is available and friendly, easy to get to, and into. Not only does it serve as the center of a natural area geographically, but must serve as the center of a group of people sharing a common interest.
3. A community school has people in it, all ages, all times. The facilities of a school plant are in use other than the school hours. The auditorium, gymnasium, school grounds serve many people of all ages and at all times.
4. A community school lays stress on human interrelations and makes a human needs approach to learning. It is still responsible for transmitting any of the cultural heritage that youth needs but evaluates the success of the learning in terms of changes in the individual and in the environment. "It is a dynamic social agency pointed specifically toward the enrichment of life for the

men, women, and children living in the geographical area in-fluenced by the school in question." [4]

5. A community school uses the resources of the community as the content of education. The school still takes the responsibility for the traditional subject matter but through the use of community resources, both human and material, translates and interprets that subject matter that it may be vital to the individual as he lives in his community. From first hand experiences an insight into the social and economic assets and limitations of the community is gained, from which more desirable social attitudes develop in terms of sensitivity to needs and knowledge of ways to take action.

6. A community school relates local life and values to the world community. The participation in near by experiences are inter-preted to show their interrelation with the larger area. The beginning will be with the need at hand, it must go beyond the immediate community.

7. A community school finds a way to do things, other than talk. Beyond the vision of desirable changes and attitudes that should be gained must be purposeful planning to achieve them. The degree of success will depend on the proportion of people who share in the idea, its implementation, and its continuance.

In the following accounts compiled from the literature and from direct observation, the attention is directed to the initial ac-tivities of schools in the community approach direction. Some of the programs have been in existence for a number of years and are well known throughout the country. Others are quite recent and several have not been described in writing before.[5]

Round Valley [6]

Round Valley is a village of 1,000 population with about one fourth of them being Indians. The school principal and faculty felt that the citizens were poorly informed regarding the school system and what it was trying to do for the children. It was proposed that a community

[4] Adapted from Willard E. Goslin, "The Characteristics of a Community School," *Forthcoming Developments in American Education,* W. C. Reavis, ed., (Chicago, University of Chicago Press, 1946), pp. 90–93.

[5] Committee members working on this interest were Mildred Swearingen, Katherine Boylan, and Janet White.

[6] R. L. Sharp, "School Public Relations Via a Community Council," *American School Board Journal* (August 1947).

council which would study school procedures and policies might be a successful way of interpreting what was then current and of obtaining community suggestion for next steps in the work of the school.

The principal called a meeting for the purpose of forming a council, requesting each of the 16 civic organizations to send a representative. A chairman and secretary were elected, after which the principal became an ordinary participant.

The council during the first year began with a study of school matters, such as report cards and the need for establishing a kindergarten. Recreation for school youth and adults soon became the focus of attention. Still within the first year, night classes were organized. Between the night classes and the adult phase of the recreation program, there were more adults using the school plant at night than there were children using it in the day.

The plans for the immediate future included work on medical service. The town had no doctor or dentist, and periodic dental service was already being arranged through the school. The council also was beginning to study some problems of race relationships.

Round Valley meets at least six of the criteria listed of a community school. It should be noted that the first steps were made when a small group of people took action upon an immediate problem. The people were not aware, at that time, that they were launching a community school. Rather, one problem after another was taken up; more and more people were involved; success with small plans led to longer range planning. Now, anyone can look back and see that a community school approach has developed gradually. As important, the school and school people have played the role of participants on equal bases with other organizations within the community.

Panama City[7]

Parker Grove School, located just outside of Panana City, enrolls approximately 300 pupils in grades 1 to 8. The school is situated near the center of a fairly distinct community. The homes are small and rather scattered, with space for gardens and pastures. Filling station-grocery stores serve the immediate needs of the people, but the main shopping center is in Panama City, about 8 miles distant. There are no libraries or forms of organized recreation.

In the spring of 1945 the faculty of the school discussed the advantages that would accrue to the pupils if the school library were kept open during the summer, one afternoon each week. The suggestion was then discussed with the P.T.A. The plan finally worked out for that summer included three parts: (A) the use of the library, (B) the

[7] Reported from direct observation.

establishment of a crafts room, (C) a pre-school roundup of first-grade pupils. Teachers and P.T.A. mothers both contributed time and effort.

The work met with so much success and such an enthusiastic response from the pupils that the second summer all three phases of the work were expanded. Members of the community other than parents were drawn in to help with the crafts work. More and more adults began to take advantage of the library and crafts opportunities.

An interesting fact in regard to the second summer was that all of the teachers were going to be away at summer school. After the middle of June the parents carried on the work by themselves.

The Sloan Project in Applied Economics [8]

The Sloan Project in Applied Economics has as its ultimate goal the improvement of living through the school program. In its experimental aspects, the Project is attempting to find out through long-range observation and experiment how specifically children are influenced in their daily living by what they study in school regarding three basic areas—food, shelter, and clothing. The many schools cooperating with the Sloan Project almost invariably develop into community schools, since the ultimate aims of the community school and the Project are almost identical.

In most schools the work starts with something that can be done within the classroom or building itself—the beautification of the building or grounds, improvement of ventilation, care of the clothing the pupils are wearing, providing of a hot dish to supplement packed lunches of the school which has no lunch program. Schoolwide projects are often undertaken involving committee work. No matter what the point of departure is, work soon extends into the community and enlists more and more community organizations and lay people, often, at first, in search for information and help. The help of County Agents and Home Demonstration Agents is frequently used almost from the start.

In many instances the work of the schools in food, clothing, or housing has led to the formation of a school community health council which involves all the agencies having a contribution to make to the health of people, regardless of age level. In a number of cases the Health Councils have broadened their scope to include recreation and their other matters.

Geneva [9]

Geneva is a three-teacher school in an agricultural region. Most of the children are transported to the neat brick school house. Adult mem-

---

[8] *School-Community Cooperation for Better Living* (Gainsville, University of Florida Press, 1947).

[9] Reported from direct observation.

bers of most of the families work on the celery farms in the area.

The principal and his wife, who is the primary teacher, lived in the area and taught in the school for a number of years. They came to know the families well, to see the needs of children, and to realize that the school could do more toward improving the quality of living for these children than it had in the past. Because the need for a more varied diet was apparent, the principal and middle-grade teacher planned a school vegetable garden with the pupils. While the garden work was going on, a lunch program was inaugurated. The school did not wait for lunchroom equipment but began with what cups and spoons could be brought from home. A cow was secured later, and the pupils learned how to care for the animal and the milk.

In subsequent years the children also undertook garden and household projects at home and reported progress at school. The teachers made several visits a year to the homes to help with the projects and visit with parents. Parents, meanwhile, were coming to the school to assist with sewing and with canning for the lunchroom.

Later years saw a widening of a variety of undertakings. The children's lives were barren of any music experiences, and so a small school orchestra was gradually developed.

Parker District School [10]

In 1923 fourteen small elementary schools forming a semicircle around Greenville, South Carolina, were consolidated into one district. A major reason for the reorganization of the districts was the hope that a high school could be established that would appeal to the youth of the area. Previous to 1918 there had been no high school at all. In 1924 the high school enrolled 55 pupils and was housed in three rooms.

In an effort to find out what a really appealing program would be like, the entire faculty engaged in intensive curriculum study with the purpose of revision. Specialists in curriculum revision were brought in then to lead the faculty study groups at intervals during the year. A summer camp was held for further faculty study. Some teachers traveled to other states to visit schools that had already embarked on curriculum revision. Effort after effort was made to increase teacher vision. One observer reported that it was hoped to fit the school to the needs of the child by fitting the teacher to the needs of the child.

Centers of interest and units of work were the first year modifications resulting from the study of child needs. This study of needs led the faculty to the point of view that "American schools exist only to help improve the quality of the people's living and to help each person achieve the happiest and most useful life of which he is capable." The

[10] *Parker District School Serves Its People* (Greenville, S. C., 1942).

school is to work in and with the community for this improvement of the quality of living.

The subsequent activities are reflected in the growth of the school and its facilities. It now [1942] accommodates 1,400 pupils and is composed of 12 building units, which show its variety of service to the community: a three-story classroom building; an annex for the library; a cafeteria; conference rooms; a vocational building including arts and crafts shop; a gymnasium; an athletic field arranged for variety of sports, day and night; a maternity shelter where mothers can receive prenatal, delivery, and postnatal care; a museum; gardens; a warehouse with a wood working department; an annex for a music room and recreational hall; and a year around camp. Adults have access to these facilities and share in planning next steps.

The San Diego, California, Community School Camp [11]

About seven years ago the idea for a public, year-round camp in San Diego County came from a group of nature-loving citizens. In it they saw possibilities for healthful development. Parent-teacher groups, county and city superintendents of schools, a member of the County Board of Supervisors, plus some individuals, sponsored the idea. From this group a five-member board was formed which negotiated for the land and buildings.

The program started the first year with boys and girls from the sixth grades. Land has since been secured for a second camp which will be part of the high school curriculum. In this second camp, the high school youth will devote half of the time to a work experience, the other half to study and recreation.

The community has become very much aware of the program and its benefits, and consequently proud of its part in the enterprise.

The two aims of the project have been: (1) to make democracy real and understandable to boys and girls through experiences in out-of-doors living, and (2) to give every child of appropriate ages a camp experience.

In the summer the camp has been available to other groups such as 4 H Clubs, Boys' Clubs, and church groups.

Curriculum Planning on a Community Basis [12]

A curriculum-planning workshop was the means by which the

[11] Edwin Pumala, "The San Diego, California, Community School Camp," *The Bulletin of the National Association of Secondary School Principals* (May 1947), pp. 100–105.
[12] Johnie Christian, "Curriculum Planning on a Community Basis," *Educational Administration and Supervision,* Vol. IV (January 1947), pp. 43–48; "Community Participates in Curriculum Building," *Texas Outlook,* Vol. XXXXI, (February 1947), pp. 12–13.

small village of Joshua, Texas, moved toward community thinking. Curriculum planning was the concern of a group of homemaking teachers in service. The year before Joshua had discontinued its program of homemaking but had retained the teacher. This teacher was a member of the workshop. She presented the situation as a real problem which gave an opportunity for the workshop members to share in thinking about ways of solving it.

The teacher had the support of the superintendent, and with him appointed an advisory council of people who were interested in better family living. This group had representatives from the high school student body, teachers, administration, school board, and parents. The members of the workshop met for discussion, did much reading, and had meetings at Joshua once a week. At the first meeting the superintendent described the school and the economic and social factors affecting it.

At the second meeting all interested adults and high school students were invited. The discussion was broken into three groups, the adults, the high school boys, and the high school girls. One community need that was brought out by all the discussion groups, and especially from the boys, was the great need of suitable recreation within the village.

By the next meeting in Joshua, the workshop members found that the community members had already started work on this recreational problem. The first venture was a field for soft ball. Before the ball field was ready, the community had broadened its efforts to include recreational activities for all age groups.

Through this approach to the curriculum study, the community awakened to its own possibilities. Interests that had only been the concern of the school became the responsibility of the community.

The Community Cooperates [13]

In Groton, Connecticut, a small town of 5,000, the community agencies joined with the school to improve the recreational facilities for youth.

A civic organization offered to sponsor a town Hallowe'en party. The superintendent recognized the possibilities for aiding youth and wrote to every agency in the community.

At the first meeting, which had a better response than had been expected, a Youth Council was formed. The superintendent was elected as acting chairman. The school board voted to let the Youth Council use the school auditorium and gymnasium, which made possible a recreational program of dancing, basketball, badminton, table tennis, wrestling, all under proper supervision.

[13] Victor E. Leonard, "The School Cooperates," *The School Executive*, Vol. 66 (December 1946), p. 40.

Other community-wide parties followed. An adult dramatic club was formed which included the mayor, school teachers, and civic leaders. Several all-community events took place during the first year, such as a hobby show and an "International Fair" with contributions from descendants of many nationalities.

A monthly calendar that listed all of the community's activities followed later.

Juvenile delinquency has decreased to a great extent. The youth, the parents, and the school have all undergone a change of attitude.

Mexico's School Made Society [14]

The Mexican government's attempt to better the living conditions of its inhabitants started with the revision of Article 3 of the Mexican Constitution. This revision gives us the background for Mexican progress which is slow but sure.

Article 3.[15] The education imparted by the State shall be a socialistic one and, in addition excluding all religious doctrine, shall combat fanaticism and prejudices by organizing its instruction and activities in a way that shall permit the creation in youth of an exact and rational concept of the Universe and of social life.

Only the State—Federation, States, Municipalities—shall impart primary, secondary, and normal education. Authorization may be conceded to individuals who desire to impart education in any of the aforementioned three levels in conformity, in every case, with the following norms:

I. The teachings and activities of private plants must adjust themselves without exception to that indicated in the initial paragraph of this Article and shall be in charge of persons who, in the opinion of the State, shall have sufficient professional preparation and a morality and ideology that is suitable to and in keeping with this precept. In view of this, religious corporations, the ministers of cults, the organizations which preferably or exclusively carry on educational activities, and the associations or societies bound directly or indirectly to the propaganda of a religious creed shall in no way intervene in primary, secondary, or normal schools, nor shall they be permitted to assist these financially.

II. The formation of plans, programmes, and methods of teaching shall in every case rest in the State.

[14] George C. Booth, *Mexico's School Made Society* (Stanford, Stanford University Press, 1941).

[15] George I. Sanchez, translator, *Mexico: A Revolution by Education*, The Viking Press, 1939, pp. 102–3. Used by permission.

III. Private plants shall not be permitted to function without first, and in each case, having obtained the express authorization of the public power.

IV. The State may at any time revoke the authorization granted (to private individuals or organizations). There shall be no judgment or recourse whatsoever against such revocation.

The same norms shall govern the education of whatever type or grade that is imparted to workers or peasants.

Primary education shall be obligatory, and the State shall impart it gratuitously.

The State may, at its discretion and at any time, withdraw recognition of official validity to the studies made in private plants.

The Congress of the Union, in the interest of unifying and co-ordinating education throughout the Republic, shall promulgate the necessary laws destined to distribute the social educative function between the Federation and the States and Municipalities, to fix the financial apportionments corresponding to that public service, and to indicate the sanctions (penalties) applicable to those functionaries who do not comply with, or force compliance to, the respective dispositions, as well as to all those who violate them.

The Highlander Folk School [16]

The Highlander Folk School is located in the community of Summerfield on the Cumberland Mountain. Six hundred fifteen farms make up this community.

The Highlander Folk School was guided by the belief that our economy, which is rapidly becoming collectivized, can be made the basis for a genuine democracy and that the final attainment and protection of the fullest rights of the masses can come only through their own economic and political organizations. With this goal constantly in mind, they set to work. A large house, in which the founder of the elementary school had lived and worked, served as a community center and residence for two teachers. Social evenings when young men and old gathered to sing familiar songs and to talk and play games were the first organized activities of the school. Only one student from outside the community had come to attend the residence term for workers, later he was joined by others. Scheduled classes did not occur until several weeks after the arrival of the students.

The wife of a neighboring farmer, in remarking about her unruly

[16] Myles Horton, "The Highlander Folk School," *The Community School*, Samuel Everett, ed. (New York, Appleton-Century, 1938).

child, started a discussion about psychology with one of the students and a teacher. As a result of this, a class in psychology for adults was announced. Gradually more and more classes were started.

Out of the first years' experience grew a threefold program consisting, first, of community work, second, of a residence program of short courses and week-end conference, and third, of extension work. Members of the community participate as students or co-workers in all phases of the program.

Arthurdale [17]

Arthurdale, West Virginia, is one of the better known community schools. It differs from others in that it was started with the vision that the school would be the center for use and learning of the community. Even in the preparation of the first rooms that were to house the school, the fathers, mothers, teachers, and children worked together. At the very outset, before the building was ready to be occupied, the school belonged to the community.

Arthurdale is located in a worn out mine area. The miners for whom the project was built had been out of work from three to seven years. In dealing with people who had had so very many difficulties there were many problems to be met. The health of the members of this group was the first to get attention. The school felt this need, and, because there were no other agencies responsible for this, took it up. This health program included the babies and the older people as well as the children of school age.

The first year of the project included attention to this health situation, provision for recreation facilities for people of all ages, establishment of a night school, a farm cooperative, and a summer program.

Shaker Heights [18]

The first venture toward community thinking in Shaker Heights, Ohio, was the establishing of a summer recreation program. For ten weeks of the summer vacation the schools and playgrounds are open for the children under trained leaders assisted by high school students. Games, sports, swimming, dramatics, story telling, and ceramics are offered.

The school plants are used for many adult classes of badminton, table tennis, rifle shooting, ceramics, swimming, study groups. One school has a daily session of Hebrew sponsored by a near-by synagogue. Many church groups use the auditoriums for recreational meetings.

[17] Elsie Clapp, *Community Schools in Action* (New York, Viking, 1939).
[18] Reported from direct observation, 1949.

Recently the school joined with the public library in sponsoring a study of books dealing with current world problems.

Several years ago the parents were invited to work with the staff on committees in setting up a new curriculum. These committees had as a basis the answers to questionnaires sent to all children in grades six, nine, and twelve, and to their parents. Discussions on the needs of children and the needs of society were followed by conferences on experiences to meet these needs, evaluation of the results of these experiences, and a final one on a program of studies that could be set up.

Shaker Heights has a Community Council which includes representatives from most of the organized groups of the area. The school has two members, one from the administration and one from the Teachers' Association. This group with other organizations joined in a celebration that commemorated the one-hundred twenty-fifth anniversary of the founding of the original Shaker Colony from which the village took its name.

While there is a rather common social and economic status, there is great need for a more inclusive program that will bring the entire community into a closer relationship.

Collins Grove [19]

Collins Grove, a rural community of around thirty-two families located about ten miles outside of Greensboro, North Carolina, was selected for a community-school program after a survey of various communities was made by Miss F. Parker, a sociology instructor at Bennett College in Greensboro. It was the most retarded community in the area and needed the most help. Its inhabitants had no electricity, no water close to their homes and very little sanitation.

A door-to-door questionnaire campaign was conducted by the Bennet College group as the first step in its program. It was found that each family had from two to three children at home; one family with fourteen children lived in two rooms. The family cash incomes were primarily derived from crops plus wages earned by some residents with jobs in Greensboro.

The first problem to be attacked was health. After some progress was made in that direction, demonstrations for cooking and making home furnishings were given. Recreational programs and educational forums were also set up. Work in this community was conducted in the religious as well as the social and economic spheres.

The people in Collins Grove readily accepted guidance. They dug wells, installed out-houses, remodeled some of their homes, and painted other buildings. They are progressing toward a better life by working with the students and faculty from Bennett College.

[19] Reported from direct observation.

Mt. Tabor [20]

Mt. Tabor, about seven miles southeast of Greensboro, was picked by Bennett College as the second community in which school-community relationships would be developed. Its inhabitants, about fifty in number, would be classified as progressive. At first their attitude was one of indifference to the college project. They felt that for their entertainment and extra activities they would go into Greensboro.

To obtain a true picture of the community, we made a door-to-door canvass and met the people, saw their homes, and received needed information. We did find that most people in the community wanted food demonstrations, sewing information, political information, and other social events. In order to establish such a program, a place large enough had to be found. Since there was no school, the only building in the community for a meeting of any size was the church. (The children attended a school which took care of a number of communities.)

Here, in the church, the program was started, and by the end of the year every person in the community was playing an active roll.

The School Lunchroom [21]

The change in the lunchroom in the nine elementary schools of Orange, Texas, came about through the cooperative planning by the faculty and representative community groups. The lunchrooms have become laboratories for learning and living.

In revising the curriculum, the philosophy agreed upon called for the application of reputable practices in child development to all phases of school life. This made it necessary to include the lunchrooms in the instructional program. Out of this has come understanding, practices, and personal satisfactions.

The practices included the development of a broader concept of nutrition and education, a better concept of health instruction, a reorganizing of the plan of instruction so that the lunchroom would tie in with all areas of learning, and work experiences extending the home-school relations to include the lunchroom.

The only criterion which was set up was that the school lunchroom, as an area of living, should contribute to the child's *total* growth and development. It should be a functional part of school and community living.

The study of foods and food combination led to a study of vegetables and fruits in season, which developed an understanding of some of the problems of production, transportation, and prices of food. '

[20] Reported from direct observation.
[21] Essie Young, "The School Lunchroom," *Educational Leadership,* Vol. IV (February 1947), pp. 314–320.

To prove that balanced meals were better than lunches bought at hamburger joints led to an experiment with white rats. The rapid decline of rats fed on hamburgers and soft drinks influenced many to eat in the school lunchroom.

The relationship between the home and school has kept pace with this program. Each Friday the menus for the next week are sent home. This enables mothers to supplement the school meals, and also gives suggestions to mothers whose children do not eat at school.

An attitude of friendliness and good will is apparent as teachers, pupils, parents, and administrators work on new problems.

A Community College in Action [22]

The Rochester Community College of Rochester, Minnesota, is a department of the junior college. Up until 1944, what adult education there was, was handled through the senior high school. A few classes were sponsored, mostly in the commercial field.

When the work was turned over to the junior college, the faculty study of the situation was turned over to a faculty committee. After studying the area, this committee came to the conclusion that the community was ready for a much extended program.

Through the Community College teachers may pursue professional studies while in service. At the close of the war the need arose for helping the veterans make the most of their G.I. rights. One thing that has grown out of this is job training for veterans. Training in the college has been given which relates to this apprentice work.

An economic and social survey of Rochester was made; the expense of which was carried by the Board of Education and the Chamber of Commerce. The results are being used for integrating and improving the economy of that city, and to acquaint people with the city. Several special projects are under way, such as a community canning center, research projects, lecture series, and study and discussion groups of such questions as the emotional development of the elementary-grade child and home planning.

Piney Woods School [23]

Piney Woods Country Life School, near Jackson, Mississippi, was founded in 1909 by Laurence Clifton Jones on a pine stump with three illiterate pupils and $1.65 cash. The school now has a $250,000 plant, 1,700 acres of well-tended land, and an enrollment of 440 pupils ranging in age from 6 to 40, drawn from 15 states and one foreign country.

[22] Emil Heintz, *The School Executive,* Vol. 66 (March 1947), p. 47.
[23] From Nelson Antrim Crawford, "The Little Professor of Piney Woods," *The Rotarian* (October 1945).

It has sent out to rural communities thousands of trained farmers, mechanics, and housekeepers and hundreds of practical competent teachers. In addition, it has carried the gospel of good farming, healthful home-making, sensible religion, and has stimulated social life for Negroes for miles around.

Piney woods has never departed from its original ideal of education for poor children. If a boy or girl can pay, the charge is $20 a month including board and room; most of the students pay what they can and earn the rest of their way by working.

Through the extension department of the school, reaching 15,000 Negroes annually, and the influence of its graduates, three fourths of the colored farmers in two adjacent counties own land, as against less than 5 percent when Piney Woods was started. Twenty home economics graduates are now housekeepers for well-to-do families at $75 to $175 a month. Others teach in 26 states.

The Wool Market School [24]

In Harrison County, Mississippi, about eight miles from the Gulf of Mexico and in a typical southern Mississippi rural community, may be found the Wool Market Consolidated School. Three medium sized one-teacher schools were done away with to form this one.

The people of the community felt that a more extensive program could be carried out with interests all brought together and not divided threefold.

This consolidated school was located near the trading store and other businesses. Extensive programs of community betterment were inaugurated. People in the community began to take active interest in community gatherings and entertainments. After some time noted progressive changes were seen in this community.

The Benjamin Franklin High School [25]

This is a school for boys in the city of New York. Established in 1935, it has functioned from the beginning with a determination to become an integral part of its community and to provide ways and means by which the school and community might work together for the good of the children and of the community at large.

As a first move, the school undertook to secure adequate information about the East Harlem neighborhood in which it is located. All available data on the East Harlem community were studied thoroughly. Statistical information of all kinds was assembled, and a series of maps

[24] *Lincoln Library of Essential Information* (Buffalo, N. Y., Frontier Press, 1935).

[25] Leonard Covello, "The Benjamin Franklin High School," *The Community School* by Samuel Everett (New York, Appleton-Century, 1938).

showing racial distribution in the community was prepared. Likewise, social maps were drawn showing the location of every school, church, social and civic agency. These provided a background of information for those who were undertaking the task of transforming all necessary details into a program humanly helpful in which the emphasis is placed not on records, statistics and routine plans but upon human values both in the school and in the community.

A Community Advisory Council was created to bring about effectual cooperation between the various social agencies and the school. Through this council the extramural, or neighborhood activities of the school, are carried forward. In addition, there are various faculty committees, not ordinarily a part of the routine school program. Through these committees the regular school program is linked to the larger community program, thereby greatly extending the school's sphere of activity and influence.

Savannah [26]

The Armstrong Junior College in Savannah, Georgia, organized in 1935, has maintained the attitude that its responsibility to the city and community does not end with the classroom instruction of the young people. The college has developed many ways of augmenting its program with activities of benefit to the townspeople. The initiative was apparently taken by the college, but the activities are carried on through community-college cooperation.

The Forum is one of the most popular features of the program. The director is a member of the faculty, and he is assisted with arrangments and selection of subjects and speakers by an advisory committee composed of citizens of the community and students.

The Playhouse is another successful activity. It is directed by a Senior Board whose members are chosen from both the community and college on the basis of work done in the theater.

Facilities of the college are available to Savannah organizations at a minimum charge to cover utilities and janitor service.

Other activities include veterans' guidance, evening classes, Red Cross service, home economics services, chemical research, and service of faculty members in community organizations.

QUALIFICATIONS OF COMMUNITY TEACHERS

THE MEMBERS of the staff—their attitudes, beliefs, training, experience, and skills—will have such a bearing on the possible

[26] J. P. Olson, "Going Beyond the Classroom," *Junior College Journal* (March 1946), pp. 303–305.

development of a community school that they deserve some attention at this point. An individual deeply committed to the idea that the teaching of subject matter and skill represents the basic function of the school, and attainment in such areas a satisfactory end of education, will find himself unhappy in a situation where a community school is being developed. As is the case with the school, no particular pattern can be sketched for successful teachers in a community school. Three or four qualities of successful teachers and leaders in community schools though do seem to stand out in importance. The individual must be at home in the culture in which he finds himself. Such maturity means that the individual understands the environmental forces at work around him. He must have adequate knowledge of the historical development of our nation and its institutions, and of the particular community of which he is a part. Such a worker must have a high level of belief in education and see in it a force for both individual and community improvement. He must have a philosophy of education compatible with the best we know in the fields of freedom and democracy.

Then there are certain things which community teachers in rural as well as urban areas should have.

1. Teachers should develop effective and well-balanced personalities for the enrichment of their own living and for aiding others better to develop well-balanced personalities for themselves.

2. Teachers should become persons rich in firsthand experience and in broader understanding of the many aspects of our culture in order better to advance the experience and understanding of others.

3. Teachers should obtain an expert understanding of the process of human living, growing, learning at all ages, and should become competent in acting upon this understanding in teaching situations.

4. Teachers should obtain an understanding of and practice in the democratic process in all areas of living and should become competent in guiding young people to utilize such democratic process in their own living.

5. Teachers should become expert in utilizing their enriched experiences in guiding the process of living, growing, and learning in young people.

6. Teachers should develop an adequate working philosophy of life and education.

7. Teachers should be stimulated to desire continuous professional growth.

8. Teachers should become scholars willing constantly to use the resources and methods of critical inquiry in the fields of human knowledge relevant to their responsibilities as individuals and as professional workers in teaching and guiding students to use similar resources and methods in facing their own problems of living.[27]

OBSERVATIONS AND TENTATIVE CONCLUSIONS CONCERNING THE ROLE OF THE SCHOOL IN THE COMMUNITY APPROACH

1. In every case some one sees a need of the people about which action can be taken.

2. Usually the school takes the initial step. This was true of sixteen of the twenty cases studied. In only four did the original incentive come from outside.

3. There is a wide variety of procedure, but always with the common goal, to fulfill a need.

4. There are records of more small than large communities, of the ones we have observed all but three are of towns and small villages.

5. In the small community the school is often the only formal agency; therefore, it is natural for it to assume some of the responsibility that would be designated to other agencies in a larger community or to a community council.

6. Health and recreation are needs which always clearly require cooperative planning. The activities involve other people or agencies increasingly.

7. The use of the school plant is a common way of beginning.

8. No one kind of physical setting is indispensible to a beginning. The limitations of the situation will, of course, influence the activities undertaken. In planning future building, space should be provided for educational activities that are to serve all ages.

9. The principal or superintendent is a key figure in the initial steps. Although he may soon relinquish active leadership, any

[27] E. S. Evenden and R. Freeman Butts, eds., *Columbia University Cooperative Program for the Pre-Service Education of Teachers* (New York, Bureau of Publications, Teachers College, Columbia University, 1942), pp. 29-32.

indifference on his part will hinder and may even destroy the vision or enthusiasm of co-workers.

10. Community schools are indigenous; there are no patterns that can be transferred. In the twenty communities reviewed, four showed health as the initial step; four, recreation; three, curriculum planning; and nine could not be grouped at all. Even this classification does not give any indication of the various activities and outcomes. The one common outcome was the improvement of the quality of living.

11. Some undertakings involve only a few people; others involve thousands. Some phases of work are completed in a few days; others go on for years. Some projects arise out of a classroom incident; others require months of pre-planning. Whatever the differences according to size of community or project, however, the ways of furthering work and purpose usually show six major processes: [28] organization, research, interpretation, publicity, cooperation, pressure.

These processes vary tremendously in application but they can usually be seen in community action, and it makes for clarity of thinking and future action to recognize them.

A. *Organization* is a way of giving strength and permanency to ideas and impulses. In the simplest instances, as far as number of people, the organization may not have actual form. In a one-teacher school the teacher and an interested parent, home demonstration agent, nurse, or the students themselves may be the planners. In a large urban setting organization may involve community councils, other organizations, and the enlisting of influential persons in the community.

B. *Research* is the technique of finding facts and rests on the assumption that one must know reality before he can have any well-grounded hope of controlling it. Even the smallest undertakings require careful analysis of the situation first lest absurd blunders be made in estimating the relative importance of needs.

C. *Interpretation* is the process of relating evidence to group policy and procedure. Facts do not always reveal their own meanings and care has to be exercised in planning action suggested by the facts. Thus, to use a very simple illustration, the

[28] Lloyd A. Cook, *Community Action and the School* (Columbus, The Ohio State University, 1941), p. 9.

need of children in an isolated school for milk might lead to hasty plans for securing and delivering milk, without proper provision for caring for it (some kind of refrigeration), or without any provision for coordinated educational activities that would extend the values beyond the actual drinking of the milk.

D. *Publicity* is sometimes described as "a way of reaching the public with the facts." Here the small community has an advantage. Through direct conversation the facts are transmitted. A high proportion of the people know about the plans first hand and are helping develop them. While a city has more avenues of appeal, the spreading of information takes on many aspects of a campaign. At best, it is a case of a few persons trying to tell many people about plans already developed.

THE ROLE OF THE COMMUNITY SCHOOL APPROACH

JUST AS THE TRENDS in education have led to the need for a broader concept of the function of the school today, so does an analysis of the social forces at work in the community lead to a similar conclusion. Everett has said, "The potential evils of a technological civilization can be transformed into human assets only by the cooperative creation of community life patterns within which socially significant growth of personality is guaranteed to all persons." [29]

The community school offers one channel or agency for such "cooperative creation." Through it common concerns can be preserved and developed and experiences that cut across class lines can be shared. Greater community integration can be attained.

Many experiences which children and adults encounter are divisive in nature, setting group against group or individual against individual. Through the community school, however, both children and adults can experience the satisfaction that comes from organizing the efforts of many people toward the solution of a common problem. The influence of the community school is cohesive, pulling people together, rather than divisive, and can be, therefore, highly significant in present day society.

[29] Samuel Everett, *The Community School* (New York, Appleton-Century, 1938), p. 53.

Furthermore, there is a growing conviction among many thoughtful people that the democratic way of life is something not merely to be defended and protected but also to be extended by intelligent planning and persistent effort. Important as have been the contributions of the past to democratic living, its full potentialities have yet to be achieved. The extension of the democratic way of life demands a high level of individual initiative and responsibility and a high level of understanding among groups and skill in working together. The community school can aid in this extension since its activities help provide practice in cooperative undertakings, and lead to the development of the very qualities needed for improved democratic living.

TEACHING AND STUDY AIDS

1. It is sometimes said that it is fairly easy to carry on the community approach in smaller towns and rural areas. Canvass the literature for evidence for and against this assumption.
2. Think of the high school to which you went. How could it have employed the community approach?
3. If possible show the movie, *Playtown—U. S. A.* Study the roles of the teacher and the school in light of this chapter discussion. Notice the step-by-step social planning. How were these processes similar or dissimilar to those suggested by Cook?
4. See Olsen's book, *School and Community,* for further discussion and clarification of the concepts *traditional, progressive, community school.*

SELECTED READING REFERENCES

Angell, Robert C., *The Integration of American Society* (New York, McGraw-Hill, 1941).

Baruch, Dorothy, *Parents and Children Go to School* (Chicago, Scott, 1939).

Chambers, M. M., *The Community and Its Young People* (Washington, American Council on Education, 1940).

Cheskie, Sophie V., "A Flexible Pattern for Adult Education." *The Nations Schools,* Vol. 43, No. 4 (April 1950).

Christian, Johnie, "Curriculum Planning on a Community Basis," *Educational Administration and Supervision,* Vol. IV (January 1947), pp. 43–48; "Community Participates in Curriculum Building," *Texas Outlook,* Vol. XXXXI (February 1947), pp. 12–13.

Clapp, Elsie, *Community Schools in Action* (New York, Viking, 1939).

Cook, Lloyd A., *Community Action and the School* (Columbus, The Ohio State University, 1941).

———, *Community Backgrounds of Education* (New York, McGraw-Hill, 1938).

———, and Elaine Forsythe Cook, *A Sociological Approach to Education* (New York, McGraw-Hill, 1950).

Coons, P. W., "School-Community Relations: A Report on a Poll of 67 Educators," *Social Education,* Vol. 14 (May 1950), pp. 223–225.

Crawford, Nelson Antrim, "The Little Professor of Piney Woods," *The Rotarian* (October 1945).

Department of National Elementary School Principals, "Building Community Understanding of the School," a cooperative set of materials in *Elementary School Principal's Bulletin,* 24th Yearbook, Vol. 25 (Washington, National Education Association, 1945–1946).

Englehart, Fred, *Planning the Community School* (New York, American Book, 1940).

Everett, Samuel, *The Community School* (New York, Appleton-Century, 1938).

———, *School and Community Meet* (New York, Hinds, Hayden and Eldredge, 1948).

Goslin, Willard E., "The Characteristics of a Community School," *Forthcoming Developments in American Education,* William C. Reavis, ed., (Chicago, University of Chicago Press, 1946).

Heintz, Emil, "A Community College in Action," *The School Executive,* Vol. 66, No. 7 (March 1947).

Jeffers, Ruth Arnold, "An Orientation Conference for Parents, It Pays," *West Virginia Educational Bulletin,* Vol. XV, No. 5 (January 1948).

Leonard, Paul, "The School Cooperates," *The School Executive* (December 1946), p. 40.

Mangus, A. R. and R. H. Woodward, *An Analysis of the Mental Health of Elementary School Children* (Columbus, Division of Mental Hygiene of the Ohio State Department of Public Welfare, 1948).

———, *An Analysis of the Mental Health of High School Students* (Columbus, Division of Mental Hygiene of the Ohio State Department of Public Welfare, July 1949).

Moehlman, A. B., "Why a Community School?" *The Nations Schools* (March, 1944).

New Jersey State Teachers College at Trenton, *Student Leadership in Community Clubs,* Studies in Education, No. 5 (Trenton, 1940).

Olsen, E. G., *School and Community* (New York, Prentice-Hall, 1946).

Project in Applied Economics, *School-Community Cooperation for Better Living* (Gainsville, University of Florida, 1947).

Pumala, Edwin, "The San Diego, California, Community School Camp,"

The Bulletin of the National Association of Secondary School Principals (May 1947), pp. 100–105.

Reavis, W. C., ed., *Forthcoming Developments in American Education* (Chicago, University of Chicago Press, 1946).

Rice, Theodore, "Leadership through Group Dynamics," *Nations Schools,* Vol. 43, No. 5 (May 1949), pp. 31–32.

Sharp, R. L., "School Public Relations Via A Community Council," *American School Board Journal* (August 1947).

Stolen, A. T., "Duluth Schools Provide Experiences in Community Life," *Nations Schools,* Vol. 45, No. 4 (April 1950), pp. 44–46.

Stone, Sybil A., et al., *Children in the Community* (Washington, Government Printing Office, 1946).

Whitcomb, Mildred E., "Play—the word that makes Milwaukee famous today," *Nations Schools,* Vol. 43, No. 6 (June 1949), pp. 24–27.

Wofford, K. V., *Teaching in Small Schools* (New York, Macmillan, 1947).

Young, Essie, "The School Lunchroom," *Educational Leadership,* Vol. IV (February 1947), pp. 314–320.

XVI INTERPRETING THE SCHOOL TO HOME AND COMMUNITY

> Since to live well men must live in society, the content of the
> good life is the life of society . . . and education is the
> process of leading the young most effectively to learn and live
> the good life.
>
> WILLIAM H. KILPATRICK
> *Modern Education: Its*
> *Proper Task*

THE RESPONSIBILITIES of the school as a social institution take on new meaning when the task of education is interpreted in its social setting. Formerly when the major aim of education was knowledge, schools could operate largely in isolation from their social content. As education has become increasingly a social life process, however, the schools must become even more articulate with the social situation from which they emerge.[1] This chapter is concerned with the school responsibility to provide adequate social interpretation of its function in society.

RELATIONSHIP OF SCHOOL INTERPRETATION TO EDUCATIONAL TRENDS

THE MEANING OF SCHOOL INTERPRETATION

Social institutions like the school grow out of cultural needs and have the obligation to change as such needs become more clearly defined or are replaced by new ones. Social interpretation

[1] From an unpublished paper by Victor Lawhead.

is largely an instrument for keeping an institution close to this responsibility. Arthur Moehlman suggests that school interpretation may be considered:

> . . . as that activity whereby the institution is made aware of community conditions and needs and the factual informational service whereby the people are kept continuously informed of the purpose, value, conditions, and needs of their educational program.[2]

This definition suggests at once the reciprocal nature of such interpretation. Since this concept is relatively recent in origin and is more comprehensive than the earlier functions of "publicity" and "public relations," it seems pertinent to sketch briefly the relationship of this expanding concept to its earlier antecedents.

PUBLICITY, PUBLIC RELATIONS, AND SCHOOL INTERPRETATION

At the time when the school's primary relationship to the community centered upon the necessity for continued support, desirable publicity was considered the major focus of attention of these institutions. The school recognized its problem as one of building timely good will in order to gain budget approvals, tax levies, and bond issues. The on-going process of school-community cooperation on educational problems was seldom included in the relationship.

In the decade of the 1920's when practices of industrial management influenced greatly the operation of schools, the concept of publicity enlarged to become known as "public relations." This was the era when school curricula reflected the job analysis procedures of development and when industrial line-staff organization of personnel became firmly planted in the public school. Like industrial concerns the schools recognized the value of continued public approval of enterprises with which the people shared only slight participation. Public relations implied informative services, but it did not imply directly any institutional ethics respecting community and institutional responsibilities. As Moehlman points out, "the commercial exploitation of public relations by professional

[2] Arthur Moehlman, *Social Interpretation* (New York, Appleton-Century, 1938), p. 104.

counselors employed by individuals and corporations to direct their propaganda programs has made this term synonymous with propaganda." [3] The situation in which public relations programs were launched could hardly be described as the genuine, democratic participation we conceive of today.

The social disorders which accompanied the economic depression brought into sharp focus the actual disparity between the school and the people. When schools failed to meet the needs of youth in a contractual economy, citizens took renewed interest in the school program and in many cases assumed their rightful role in demanding that the school assume its social responsibilities. Here were the major beginnings of the "community school" and the life-centered curriculum. This changing relationship between the school and the community placed upon the schools the additional interpretive function of understanding the community and being understood by the community.

PURPOSES OF A SCHOOL INTERPRETATION PROGRAM

The reciprocal nature of school interpretation has been emphasized in the foregoing section. Actually, the expanded concept implies a series of purposes which would logically follow should a school consider seriously a program of school interpretation. Stated briefly these may include:

1. To enlist community interest in, and support of, the school program.
2. To understand the community so that the role and function of the school can be determined by the specific community backgrounds of the pupils.
3. To foster democratic values through intelligent participation by youth and adults in community enterprises.
4. To inform the public of changes and new developments in the educational field.
5. To understand the community in order that the school may readapt its program in the light of the changing services of other community agencies.

Further clarification of these purposes will be made in a subsequent section.

[3] *Ibid.,* p. 105.

THE MEDIA THROUGH WHICH THE SCHOOLS ARE INTERPRETED

INTERPRETATION THROUGH THE PUPILS

Pupils constitute the most important personnel group that can interpret the schools to the community. In a section of James Bossard's *The Sociology of Child Development* called "School Life in Retrospect," Eleanor S. Boll makes a convincing analysis of the significance of school situations in the lives of boys and girls. In studying twenty-one autobiographies for insight into the crucial aspects of school life, she recognized five types of situations which seemed to dominate the interpretations:

1. Beginning school or changing to a new school were experienced as crisis situations.
2. The apparent differences in backgrounds emerged so that pupils often became identified as children of certain parents.
3. The adjustments placed upon immigrant children in an American School.
4. The awakening of the protectively reared and sensitive child to certain crudities of life.
5. The classroom as a little world of romance.[4]

As suggested by these situations, the child is really a postgraduate in community relations when he enters the school. When he leaves its doors, both daily and at graduation, he interprets to the public in terms of what the school has done to him.

It seems important in this respect to realize the limiting factors associated with having the schools interpreted largely by children and youth. Even among adults the general impressions of school life are those gained earlier at immature ages and usually in terms of what has been called "traditional education." For this reason the schools, in order to assure adequate interpretation, must make serious efforts to bring patrons closer to the school program.

ROLE OF SPECIAL SCHOOL EVENTS

Some of the most convenient times to provide adult interpretation are occasions of special school events such as athletic contests,

[4] James H. Bossard, *The Sociology of Child Development* (New York, Harper, 1948), pp. 461–465. Used by permission.

concerts, and dramatic productions. In some school situations such occasions offer the only opportunity to bring the adult citizenry into the school building. Without attempting to stage an artificial front, the school should make special effort to provide desirable school interpretation at such times. Some *pupil-planned* and *-directed* methods for interpreting the school to the home are these taken from actual experiences in one public school.

A. "Let's-Get-Acquainted" evening: *1.* Preplanning period of several days; *2.* reception of guests at 5:00 o'clock; *3.* recreation period shared by host's and guests; *4.* dinner planned by children and prepared and served by mothers; *5.* sharing of original written expression (poems, stories, and reports) and of music in the classroom; *6.* dramatization, original and completely produced by the group, for parents.

B. Open house—"The School in Action." The role played by the child in a genuine "Open House" situation, should be the leading role. The parents and friends who visit should feel free to ask questions, but never to disturb group work without reason. Teachers should be in the background, guiding and helping but never lecturing or otherwise "showing off." The children from one classroom may be scattered over the school engaged in various activities—creative art, group discussion, or pursuit of a more traditional subject, such as arithmetic. The key to a successful "Open House" is to keep it a natural and honest interpretation of the school in action.

C. Hobby fairs have provided occasions for some of the most fruitful interpretations.

D. Art exhibits especially when you can observe "growths" of various sorts interest not only parents but others.

E. Dramatizations in assemblies or on special holiday occasions never fail to pack the auditoriums.

F. School concerts of all varieties are of prime interest to all community members.

G. Athletic contests need little comment in our recreation- and sports-conscious world.

H. Mothers' teas and informal parties by rooms or grades for parents promote social intercourse of a highly desirable sort.

I. Where parents sponsor trips, hikes, and picnics the results have been gratifying indeed.

The logical question in response to such suggestions is, "What are the values if any, to children, of this kind of procedure?" From a social educational standpoint, the following values could be stated.

1. The realization of the need of interpretation on the part of the child.
2. Experience in setting up of meaningful aims and planning a course of action.
3. Development of both oral and written and visual expression.
4. Experience of working cooperatively.
5. The sensing and experiencing of real-life public response.
6. The realization that he, the child, and his school are of vital importance to community members.
7. The creation of a growing awareness and respect for community problems, thus making him an active, "caring" citizen both as a child and as a later adult of another school's community.

YOUTH ORGANIZATIONS

In many schools youth organizations as the Y.M.C.A., Y.W.C.A., and Scouts conduct activities in the extracurricular program of the school. These enterprises develop close relationships between the schools and adult youth leaders in the social agencies of the community. Because participation in such activity is not compulsory, there develop splendid opportunities for democratic leadership, group planning and action. In many schools the "extracurricular" program is the only aspect of school life in which the pupils are given a measure of responsibility in planning and carrying out programs of action. These experiences, because they are more meaningful to the boy and girl than those in the traditional academic classroom, are the experiences which are subject to the greatest amount of discussion and evaluation in the family situation! The average parent usually knows a great deal more about this aspect of the school program than about the instructional emphasis!

Schools alert to the importance of the social orientation of the child are introducing a problem-focused curriculum which makes group endeavor a positive aspect rather than an extracurricular aspect of the school program. Such a curriculum makes possible choice situations similar to those existent in the nonacademic experiences of the pupil. The therapeutic advantages of such a curriculum are vividly outlined by Helen Jennings in the following passage.

> Teachers often consider it their duty to separate children who show interest in each other because of the assumed interference with their work. . . . Seating plans, working committees, and other arrangements are often set up without regard to the students' inclinations toward each other. . . . Many a disciplinary problem arises from the fact that children are taught to live two lives, one officially and the other under cover, in order to satisfy the social needs forbidden by the school.[5]

The interpretative values are obvious in a situation where the school engages actively through its curriculum to provide desirable social orientation.

EDUCATIONAL PUBLICITY

While educational publicity is no longer considered synonymous with school interpretation, it still remains a significant aspect of it. The public school as a democratic social institution belonging to the people has to operate on the central tendency of public opinion. This implies that public opinion must be informed of changes and new developments in the education field. This is especially important where those members of the school's community are citizens but not parents of the current school population. Many of these people vote *no* on issues through misunderstanding of the true workings of the school. If they cannot or will not come to the school, the school must go to them.

The public press and the news broadcast offer the widest circulation for this kind of educational publicity. Since the school is dependent upon the press for desirable publicity, it should take steps to insure this outcome. Publicity releases offer an excellent means of telling the public what is taking place in the schools, what may be expected, and what changes have occurred. In order to get newspapers to give adequate attention to such releases, Benjamin Fine, educational news editor of *The New York Times* makes the following suggestions:

[5] Helen Jennings, *Sociometry in Group Relations* (Washington, American Council on Education, 1948), pp. 5–6. Used by permission.

1. Copy should be on white paper 8½ x 11 inches.
2. Release should be clearly typewritten.
3. Release dates must appear at top of first page.
4. Name of school should appear in the upper left hand corner of the first page.
5. Release must be double or triple spaced, on one side of paper only.
6. Copy should start halfway down first page.
7. Pages must be numbered.
8. The word "more" should appear on the bottom of a page to indicate that copy is unfinished.
9. Finish of story is indicated by "end mark."
10. Each paragraph is ended on one page.
11. Copy should be written in good English.[6]

Wherever and whenever possible, pupil participation should be encouraged since in these mass media the child is also the top-notch salesman of universal advertising appeal in the school's community. Accordingly, many schools have used pupil participation on established programs with a gradual increase in originality and scope until pupils have often worked up to their own programs.

With television in its inceptive stages and "free performers" in demand, the school has its greatest opportunity for contacting the public. Many phases of school life are readily adaptable to television. Activities such as music, oral interpretation, art, dramatization, and dancing can be made popular.

Store displays are another medium used with success in some schools. Groups of children demonstrating some school activity are "set up" in large community stores. To show the study of pottery in a sixth grade, a group of children was installed in a large department store. The children actually turned a potter's wheel and made pottery. When questioned as to what that had to do with school, they could answer quickly and thoroughly, explaining just how this study was correlated with the so-called traditional subjects in which the questioners were so interested.

REPORTS TO PARENTS

Periodic reports of pupil progress made to his parents provide a direct contact through which the school is interpreted to lay citi-

[6] Adapted from a list in Benjamin Fine's *Educational Publicity* (New York, Harper, 1943), pp. 29–39.

zens. Few schools, however, capitalize sufficiently upon this opportunity to interpret school purposes.

Reasons for Sending Reports

The school must send reports to provide the information necessary for a sound working relationship between the school and the home in the guidance of the child. Reports personalize the education and guidance of the children, and in this way they are an aid to better home-school and community relations. This allows the parents and the community to "see" what goes on in the school so that all can understand the reasons and needs for the practices which are carried on in the school in terms of the school's objectives.

Content of a Good Report

In order to attain the objectives that we have set up for our reports to parents, we must establish some criteria for judging and evaluating our reports in terms of these objectives. Since school people are seeking to promote greater understanding by parents of the school's purposes and to establish more cordial relations between the home and the school, they need to use a type of report which the parents understand. This can be accomplished either by educating them and the community to the "school-made" reporting system or having them help establish a reporting system together with the school. The school should furnish information of specific ways in which parents may assist in achieving the educational aims and objectives. Providing space on the report for parent's reciprocal comments can be a way of handling this. The report should include the objectives of the school and adequate description of the quality, quantity, and variety of children's activities. The report would, of course, have to be flexible in this respect to allow for explanations appropriate to the maturity level of the group. Furnishing all of this information in reports to parents would help them get a comprehensive picture of their child's development.

The child is, of course, the subject of the report, and his feelings and reactions to the report are extremely important. Not only do we want to gain the understanding and support of the parents and the community, but also we want to add to the child's interest in school activities and his enthusiasm for further learning. The report should not only "inform on" but also should "contribute to" the balanced physical, social, emotional, and mental development.

The report should be put on a constructive basis with positive rather than negative statements. We must seek to encourage wholesome self-analysis by children of their own strengths and weaknesses in relation to their general progress. If the child shares in the reporting, he will better understand what and how he is doing. This practice will build his respect for the teacher's integrity and a trust in her understanding of him as an individual as well as a part of the group. We should try to reduce undesirable "competition between" and "comparison of" children, and compare children against their own progress and potential abilities. If children's difficulties and strengths are diagnosed in specific terms and given definite suggestions for their elimination, reports will be of more value because they can be used as a device for guidance by both the parents and the teacher.

The teacher herself must be considered when one discusses reports and reporting. She wants something which will require a minimum of time in developing. Some schools supply free school time for teachers to work on such matters, and this helps considerably. If such an arrangement is lacking, she needs something brief yet complete and all inclusive, accurate, and closely related to the accumulative record. This kind of report can be used as a type of record in the child's personal file and will aid in readjustment in case of a transfer.

Reports Currently in Use

Written reports may be in the form of notes, letters, or printed forms. Progress periodicals are probably the most important type of written report to be considered. These may be a letter, check list, formal grade card, child-written self-analysis progress evaluation, or a combination of these.

The letter report is gaining more and more popularity. It is flexible and allows for individual differences. Essential factors can be emphasized, and parents can be made aware of the interrelation of physical, social, emotional, and mental development. The letter, however, does have some disadvantages in that it is very subjective and reflects the teacher's personality to a great extent. It takes a longer time to prepare an adequate letter than to fill in a printed form on the child's progress. Poorly written letters create an unfavorable attitude, and not all teachers are able to write good letters. "The success of letter reports depends on the skill of the reporter in portraying the child's needs in such a way as to secure the parent's sympathetic cooperation and help." [7] It probably would be better for a teacher to use the type which best achieves the objectives of the school and is in line with her own abilities.

A general outline or basis for a "good" letter would include: beginning with encouraging news, closing with an attitude of optimism, soliciting cooperation in solving problems if any exist, evaluating growth in all areas of development, comparing growth with previous efforts of the same child, speaking of achievements in terms of his own ability, suggesting solutions, giving advice in matters pertaining to health, and, in general, treating the letter as a professional diagnosis. [8]

In case this sounds ideal not real, two sample letters are presented below as astute examples of the above criteria.

Mr. and Mrs. John Doe
50 Parkwood Ave.
Columbia, Ohio

Dear Mr. and Mrs. Doe:

Marian has been a most pleasant, helpful and cooperative member of the first grade group. Marian is friendly toward others and well liked by the children. She takes an active part in all of the group work and play. She is very mature socially and is thoughtful of others and concerned about the group as a whole. Marian is very independent in her thinking and acting and very responsible for her own conduct. She is a creative child and has contributed very much to the group enterprises with her creative ideas and consistent planning.

Marian has a good amount of energy, is active in work and play, eats well, relaxes well at rest time, and seems to be quite free from signs of tension. She has excellent muscular coordination and is skillful in games and physical activity.

Marian's work habits and attitudes are excellent. She gives very good attention to all kinds of group work and instruction. She takes part in an interested manner and shows a great desire to learn and achieve. She is always ready to try more advanced and challenging things. Her work is carefully done, plans are thoughtfully made, and

[7] Willard S. Elsbree, *Pupil Progress in the Elementary School,* p. 78. New York, Teachers College, Columbia University, 1943.
[8] Ruth Strang, *Reporting to Parents* (New York, Bureau of Publications, Teachers College, Columbia University, 1947).

she consistently completes that which she undertakes. She is sensible in requesting help when it is needed but not dependent upon adults.

Marian has a good store of general information which she uses well in meeting group and individual problems. She expresses her ideas easily and clearly and considers the contributions of others. Marian has done some independent writing as well as writing in manuscript from copy. She writes rapidly and with good letter form. She is able to spell a good many words needed in her writing.

Marian is interested in science and a good thinker in working out science problems. She enjoys music, sings well, and is active in rhythms and dancing. She also participates freely in dramatization and enjoys it very much.

Marian has a very good understanding of numbers and works problems dealing with number and measurement very readily. She has made excellent progress in learning to read. She reads very independently for a first grade child and with good comprehension and speed. She is able to use phonetic help in finding out unfamiliar words.

It has been a pleasure to work with Marian this year. She appears to have enjoyed her first grade work and is well ready to do second grade work in her next school experience.

> Very truly yours,
> SUSAN HANE
> *First Grade Teacher*

Dear Mr. and Mrs. Blank:

SOCIAL STUDIES

Since the last report to you, the eleventh grade has made a study of several problems of current interest. They examined the organizational set-up of the U.N. and discussed some of the problems that needed to be settled. Because the class felt that the United States must accept leadership in helping rebuild the world, we studied those countries which fought the war just ended. We noted their geographical location, their economy and their trade with the United States. We discussed the trend toward specialization and the significance of rapid communication and came to the conclusion that this is one world. We agreed that we must learn to live in it.

We took some time to examine the three political philosophies that appear to have made considerable headway since the turn of the century. We have examined the bases of fascism, communism, and socialism, and have gone into some detail as to how they were organized and what they intended to accomplish. We examined their economic concepts and then took each one and compared it with our way of life.

Because labor and management were running into difficulties, the class decided to study labor-management relations. We traced the relation between the two from the end of World War I and then went into a discussion of terms. We clarified such terms as overproduction, underconsumption, money wages, real wages, inflation, mediation, etc. We noted some of the acts passed by Congress relative to the problems of labor and management and then discussed the way in which the two attempt to come to some satisfactory agreement. We examined the basis of the dispute between the G.M. and the U.A.W. because they were still attempting to negotiate a settlement when we were discussing this problem.

Blank has done mediocre work throughout the year. He may have done much better had he not have been absent so much. He does not find studying too easy and make-up work becomes doubly hard. His written work has been fairly consistent and usually has indicated a good grasp of what he was supposed to do. His tests have not shown the same thoroughness, however.

He has never entered into discussion when we have been considering a problem. He does not appear to be interested in expressing himself. I wish he would make a conscious effort to develop the ability to state his point. It would serve him well, and he needs it.

Blank has completed his assignments in social studies in a manner that makes it possible for me to say that they are satisfactory. I hope he will be able to cut down his absences next year and do better and more consistent work.

ENGLISH

Whenever I think of Blank, I am reminded of the continuous descriptions Blank wrote of his fishing experiences. There was often a touch of humor in them. He never seemed to want to relate what he and others might be doing in a group of boys and girls. I believe Blank finds it difficult to express himself. He also is very quiet in class. At the time of writing this letter, three weeks before the close of school, he has done very little work for the quarter. This is not a very encouraging report, I know. Perhaps his own physical growth, by next year, will help Blank be more sure of himself.

MATHEMATICS

Blank has done poor work in mathematics. He depends on other students to do his thinking for him. He lacks direction when he has a job to do, and he does not exert will power to keep himself steadfastly at a task until he completes it. He has not contributed to group development of new concepts. The assignments he has met have been done with the aid of other persons.

RELATED ARTS

Blank's work in this area has shown some improvement as far as his finding a real challenge in his work is concerned. Though he definitely has been hampered by material shortages, he has pursued his work diligently and made worth-while substitutions in material and alterations in his plans as situations changed. In this work, he has been both pleasant and affable to work with and has made quite some progress in the quality of his relationships during the school year. In general, we are quite pleased with his development this year.

PHYSICAL EDUCATION

Blank evidently has been more interested in tennis than he has been in any other sport because Mr. B—— reports that he has worked hard and that his game has improved a great deal. Evidently there was less of the lack of concentration which has characterized him before.

Sincerely,
THE STAFF

The descriptive check list has several advantages in that it avoids comparison between children and it reduces the number of marking symbols, thus making it easily completed by the teacher. However, many important items are likely to be omitted, and special gifts or needs cannot be emphasized.

The formal grade card has long been used to show school achievement with reference to grade standards. It can be shown in percentages, letter or number symbols, or "satisfactory" and "unsatisfactory." The card may include a space for comments, an invitation to parents to talk with the teacher, and an absent-tardy report. The traditional "grade card" has had some bad effects on children. Rather than being a device for guidance, it has been reason for punishment. It is often said to have contributed to truancy, to have made children unhappy and maladjusted, and to have failed to convey *helpful* information. Yet, it is still used in many systems, and teachers can only supplement it with other reports in order to meet their objectives.

Child-written progress evaluation reports are very good as a supplementary report. They help the child clarify things in his own mind. He can then evaluate and replan in the light of his findings.

There are many other types of supplementary reports which can be, and are, used. Many of them are necessary only in particular cases. In systems where letters are written, fewer supplementary reports are needed. These supplementary reports include the health report (nutrition, eyes, teeth, general doctor's examination), psychologist's report, speech report, behavior and social development report, personality report, school and room press printed material (handbooks, annuals, magazines, programs, and newspapers), the objectives and plans for class group activities, and the whole school philosophy.

Oral reports may be in the form of *casual or unplanned contacts,* or individual planned conferences. Many times the teacher does not realize what an opportunity she is passing up when she does not make the most of what we call "casual contacts" with parents. This type of meeting may take place in any number of ways, such as phone calls about the child, meetings when the parent comes with or for the child, or even a chance meeting in one of the stores in the neighborhood. At times like this, the teacher who is "on her toes" can do much to build rapport.

Though casual meetings are quite essential for good parent-teacher relationships, conferences should not be completely on an incidental or emergency basis. Planned individual conferences should be regularly scheduled with all the parents. These conferences may be used to supplement written reports and are often much more valuable than any form of written report. At these conferences the progress of the individual child can be evaluated in terms of the child's own needs and abilities and free from the competitive or comparative element.

The following principles are essential to the success of any conference:

A. There must be a reason for the conference.
B. The teacher must be relaxed and able to put parent at ease.
C. The point of the conference must be arrived at quickly.
D. The teacher should listen and not dominate the conversation.
E. Family quarrels should be omitted.

F. When the purposes have been attained, the interview should be culminated courteously so that the parent will have a feeling of having been helpful and will want to confer again.[9]

Much can be accomplished from the *group meeting* which has been carefully planned by the teacher to meet the needs of the parents and to be of real educational value to them. When the teacher meets parents as a group, she can talk about problems which she might not be able to discuss with an individual. Parent meetings should be informal, and the teacher should appear at ease, but they must be quite carefully planned on the teacher's part. Definite objectives should be set as to what should be accomplished. The teacher will not always be the leader nor does she need to talk at every meeting. The supervisors, the principal, the school doctor or nurse, or the school psychologist are logical leaders for some of the meetings. Several of the meetings should be discussion meetings with the teacher as the moderator. As Gesell has said, "Such arrangements would tend to humanize school practice and counteract the tendencies toward regimentation which are so inconsistent with a democratic culture." [10]

The *home visit* is included under planned conferences because it should definitely be planned in line with the time which is convenient for the parent. The conventional home visit must be treated with much discretion. Some homes are not proud of their economic status and surroundings, and some parents are ashamed of themselves. The teacher should not force herself upon these particular parents. But, if the teacher feels that the way is clear for a successful home visit, there is little which can do more toward the desired rapport.

Trends in Reporting to Parents

The trend seems to be away from the formal routine card toward diagnostic letters, personal notes, and conferences, with a greater emphasis upon reporting social and emotional development. Reporting is done less frequently and more comprehensively. In style there is a change from negative statements to a positive and constructive type of statement. Rather than reporting in terms of

[9] Dechent W. Wills and W. H. Stegeman, *Living in the Kindergarten* (Chicago, Fallett, 1950), p. 331.
[10] Arnold Gesell and Frances Ilg, *The Child from Five to Ten* (New York, Harper, 1946), p. 37.

group norms, we are thinking now in terms of individual progress and comparing the child against his own previous progress. In this way the report tends to be child-centered rather than subject-matter-centered because the teacher is supplementing descriptive anecdotal material to show character and personality development as well as growth in academic subject matter. Rather than just passing judgments, teachers are trying to analyze difficulties and to make concrete suggestions for improvement in their reports. Pupils are now helping evaluate their own progress, and parents are asked to do reciprocal reporting. Finally, teachers are tending to diagnose achievement in terms of the school's objectives.

Transition to a Better Reporting System

We must make our reporting a continuous process. If the teacher will keep diary records, work samples, reports of conferences, test results, observations, case studies, home visit reports, interviews, and a cumulative record, she will have an up-to-date record of all phases of the child's development and background at her finger tips. The child too can keep work samples, and the administration should keep a permanent cumulative pupil personnel record folder to which the teacher can refer. With this information the teacher should be able to make an honest, inclusive, and understandable report. If the present program of reporting is unsatisfactory, a new program can be developed cooperatively with the parents, the child, and the school. In this way it can be kept in harmony with the curriculum practices and the changing needs of the pupil and the community as a whole.

As Strang has suggested, if parents and teachers get together to discuss and understand the problem, get essential information, put committees to work, prepare a tentative form, introduce the tentative form, try it out, and then evaluate and revise in terms of behavior changes in pupils and the improved relationships between the home, school and the child, a very effective program can be worked out.

Such an experiment occurred in the Woolridge Schools in Dallas, Texas. The school called the parents together and had a September discussion meeting. Reporting was one topic for discussion. They went through the problem finding and solving process described by Strang, and after the year of experimentation, they evaluated together and revised accordingly. The parents approved of the reporting system devised, and they were ready to respond and cooperate with the school philosophy and objectives they had set for themselves to meet their own needs. What better way to interpret the school?

PARENT EDUCATION

The optimal development of the child can only be achieved to the degree that school staff and parents interact cooperatively to provide like environments for child development. If this unity is to be realized, parents will need not only to become more familiar with the philosophy, policies, and practices of the school but also to become more familiar with their children. These needs can be met through an intensive program of parent education. This educational program can be carried out in many ways.

Discussion Groups

Most people who work in the field of parent education agree that small group discussions are a "must" in parent education. Here parents find others who face similar problems with children and often one may give and gain hints which are of great practical value. Care must be taken, however, by discussion leaders that these sessions do not turn into merely routine queries about materials and the like.

Some schools have set up a *grade group organization* in which the parents of the children in a given grade meet as a discussion group to work on problems concerning the age group in that room. Each grade group elects a representative to act on a parent council which draws these organizations together so that important issues might be known to all groups. Schools which have tried this procedure report enthusiastically on its success.

In many cities *child study groups* have organized for the purpose of discussing problems pertinent to the parent-child relationship. Through these discussions parents can become familiar with the modern theories and practices concerning child care and child development.

The city of St. Louis has organized a *Council for Parent Education* which uses friendly discussion, led by a trained psychiatrist, "to stop juvenile delinquency before it begins." As soon as a youngster's unusual behavior attracts his teacher's attention, his mother is invited to join one of several small informal groups where the behavior problems are analyzed, and strategy is set up for attacking the problems.

Many parents would welcome such trained help in handling their children. There are some educators who may object to using behavior problems as a means of contact with the parent; yet, there are some parents who will respond more readily in cases where their child is greatly concerned.

The *clinical analysis* type of discussion is another approach that is valuable. Parents meet to analyze and discuss some area of the curriculum, such as art or arithmetic. The teachers in those areas explain the methods used in the school and actual samples of work done by the children are exhibited with the names hidden, so that parents can study the work objectively. Through this study parents can see how capabilities vary for different children and for different age levels. This helps the parent to understand the abilities of his own child in relation to others.

A concomitant good derived from any group discussion approach is the emotional uplift experienced by the parents who participate. The "feeling of belonging" is a most worth-while experience for many. This is true especially for mothers who have allowed their social connections to lapse during the years of childbearing and child rearing. First, they have too often given up "all" for the child only to find themselves overprotecting and overmanaging the child to both his and their detriment.

Parent-Teacher Associations

An active P.T.A. (Parent-Teacher Association) can be utilized to promote parent-teacher understanding. The parent and teacher should learn to know and understand each other first as people, then as the parent or teacher of "Sally." The local P.T.A. can demonstrate to parents and interested citizens in the community what is really being done in the schools. Programs dealing with the life of the school can be presented by the students, assisted by the teachers who know the underlying philosophy and can suggest ways of interpreting that philosophy to the general public.

Classroom Observation

One of the best ways to familiarize the parent with the teaching methods used in the school is to permit them to observe in the classroom. These observations will also be valuable to the parent as a means of analyzing his or her child in relationship with other children and with the teacher. If the parent can *see* how "Johnny" is getting along there will be no need to ask the age-old question, "How is Johnny getting along in school?"

Playground Observation

By observing the play activities of the children, the parent can see whether his or her child has good play habits. It is possible to see whether the child is overly aggressive or whether the child is overly shy and does not take part. This observation may show the parent the need for guiding the child in building good play attitudes.

Parent Handbooks

Many schools publish a *parent handbook* as a means of informing parents about school practices. These books usually contain a statement of the school philosophy and aims. General information concerning the school policies can be included, e.g., entrance requirements, method of registration, school hours, vacation dates, safety practices, health rules, report cards, lunchroom facilities, etc.

Parent Reading Lists

Oftentimes parents do not have access to books which will aid them in understanding their children. The school can help by setting up a reading shelf for parents or by making a list of good reading materials with sources indicated. Parents may wish to share their own books by putting them on the reading shelf for others to use.

Some of the following books might be included in such a reading program:

Baruch, Dorothy W., *Parents and Children Go to School* (Chicago, Scott, 1939).

The Faculty of the University School, *How Children Develop* (Columbus, The Ohio State University, 1949).

Fisher, Dorothy, and Sidonie Gruenberg, *Our Children, A Handbook for Parents* (New York, Viking, 1932).

Hockett, John A. and E. W. Jacobsen, *Modern Practices in the Elementary School* (Boston, Ginn, 1943).

Meek, Lois H., *Your Child's Development and Guidance Told in Pictures* (Philadelphia, Lippincott, 1940).

Patri, Angelo, *How to Help Your Children Grow Up,* (Chicago, Rand-McNally, 1948).

Reynolds, Martha May, *Children from Seeds to Saplings* (New York, McGraw-Hill, 1939).

Ribble, Margaretha A., *The Rights of Infants* (New York, Columbia University Press, 1943).

Sait, Una B., *New Horizons for the Family* (New York, Macmillan, 1938).

Strain, Frances Bruce, *The Normal Sex Interests of Children: from Infancy to Childhood* (New York, Appleton-Century-Crofts, 1948).

Since the problem of money must be considered here, many schools would lack necessary funds for buying books for parent use. There are, however, inexpensive or free pamphlets which can be easily distributed to parents. Pamphlets are known by all who teach to be effective teaching aids. They are usually written simply, vividly, and briefly. Often these days they are beautifully illustrated. Thus the busy layman may read and learn with pleasure.

Many organizations publish excellent materials for adult education. The following list contains just a few suggestions as to where one can obtain pertinent materials:

American Education Fellowship, 289 Fourth Ave., New York 10, New York. *Know Your Children,* 1945—$0.25.

American Medical Association, 535 N. Dearborn St., Chicago 10, Ill.

The Child in the Family, 1945—$0.10; *Protecting the Health of the Child,* 1939—$0.10; *Sex Education for the Preschool Child,* 1945—$0.15; *The Story of Life,* 1945—$0.25.

American Study Association of America, 221 W. 57 St., New York 19, New York. *What Makes a Good Home,* 1944—$0.15.

Extension Service, Iowa State College of Agriculture and Mechanic Arts, Ames, Iowa. *Constructive Discipline,* 1940—free; *Home and School: Partners in Education,* 1940—free.

Extension Service, School of Home Economics, Ohio State University, Columbus 10, Ohio. *Guiding Behavior of Children,* 1943—free; *Helping Children to Learn,* 1944—free.

Parents' Magazine Inc., 52 Vanderbilt Ave., New York 17, New York. *Ten Commandments for Parents*—free; *Grow With Your Child,* 1945–1946—free.

United States Department of Labor, Children's Bureau, Washington 25, D. C. *Your Child from One to Six,* 1945—$0.15.

MEDIA OF RECIPROCAL INTERPRETATION— SCHOOL-COMMUNITY

COMMUNITY COUNCILS

The reciprocal nature of social interpretation in which an institution is made aware of community conditions and needs is well illustrated through the community council. Where one exists, such a *coordinating council* offers direct channels for social interpretation between the schools and other social agencies. The need for this type of council is clearly stated by Nisonger:

> This movement toward the organization of councils has grown out of our efforts to keep up with the rapidly changing society. New organizations have been springing up to meet new social needs at a rapidly accelerated rate. These organizations have their own specific programs and each works largely independent of the other. As a result there is much over-lapping and often conflict.
>
> Even with this multiplicity of programs many community needs remain unmet. There is need in every community for some organization such as a council to study the needs of the community as a whole and assist in coordinating the program of existing agencies.[11]

Educational needs like other social needs are met by many agencies other than the school. A coordinating council can facilitate social interpretation by informing the school of changing community conditions in order that the school may readapt its program in the light of the changing services of other community agencies. An example in point relates the need in many schools of re-examining the vocational education program in view of increased vocational training by industrial concerns.

Added impetus has been given to the movement toward community councils to study educational needs. Aroused by the continuing nationwide crisis in public schools, a group of prominent men and women have formed a National Citizens Commission for the Public Schools. The commission, which has received initial financial support from the Carnegie Corporation and the General

[11] Herschel W. Nisonger, *The Role of the School in Community Education* (Columbus, Bureau of Special and Adult Education, The Ohio State University, 1940), p. 27. Used by permission.

Education Board, "will act as a clearing house to enable one group of laymen working for better schools to benefit from the experiences of others" [12]

EDUCATIONAL AND FISCAL REPORTS OF SUPERINTENDENTS

Many school systems give serious attention to the annual reports made public by the superintendent of schools. Where printing facilities are available in the high school the slight cost of such a report is well worth the expenditure in view of the interpretive potential of such literature. By using charts and diagrams to illustrate fiscal data, pupil attendance, and other statistical information, the content of such reports can be vitalized for lay education. Some administrators may, as is the case in Cincinnati, choose to publish two reports one financial and the other descriptive of the school program. The latter type of report offers a splendid opportunity to inform the public of the schools' purposes, needs, and accomplishments.

THE TEACHER AS A COMMUNITY PARTICIPANT

Lloyd A. Cook has pointed out effectively the difficulties in the fact that "conduct codes for teachers find their basic interpretation in the sociology of the stranger." [13] A few schools have sought to remedy this situation by encouraging teacher membership in civic clubs. To do this the building administrators attempt to assign flexible teaching schedules, particularly in the early afternoon to allow teacher participation in luncheon meetings of such organizations. All such civic clubs engage in childhood and youth programs which often bear directly on a school program. In a study of youth needs and services in a small city, one student encountered an instance in which a civic group interested in youth employment was completely unaware of a related project being conducted by the business education department of the school. Had there been closer relationship between school personnel and members of this service organization, this lack of coordination could not have existed.

[12] Benjamin Fine, "Education in Review," *The New York Times* (May 15, 1949), Section IV, p. 7.
[13] Lloyd A. Cook, *Community Backgrounds of Education* (New York, McGraw-Hill, 1938), p. 308.

LAY ADVISORY COMMISSIONS

For many years educators have recognized that the legally organized school board does not represent the numerous interests included in the community. As a lay group it provides only a limited interpretative function. In order to utilize a liason group to bring the school closer to the citizens of the community, school officials have appointed lay advisory commissions to serve in an extra-legal capacity. These commissions according to Moehlman receive institutional interpretation from the school and "their reactions and points of view . . . may be considered as community interpretation for the organizational group." [14] The appointment of an advisory commission does not relieve the superintendent and the board of school trustees of their legal responsibilities; therefore, the decisions of such a group are subject to final review. However, they do relieve school officials of much of the task of sounding out community opinion regarding proposed changes in the school program, unmet educational needs, and points for cooperative action between the schools and other social agencies.

SUMMARY

IF THE COMMUNITY APPROACH to education is to be maintained, the interpreting of the school to the community and the community to the school is of extraordinary importance. The classroom teacher can help the issue along by the course of study, by taking the school into the community, and vice versa. In view of our urbanized culture, however, with its drift from primary to secondary modes of living, these interpretations cannot be left to just the classroom and chance.

Teachers and administrators are increasingly aware of this. One of the most heartening concrete evidences comes especially in summer school classes. Each term the class chooses this area for intensive study and reporting by one of its groups.

As one school superintendent phrased it, "I've looked into the behind-the-scene facts in several of these places where there has been so much school trouble, and I've decided it's brewed by a minority who dragged others along out of fear and misinformation. It's our job to get the facts out first for the good of everyone."

[14] Arthur B. Moehlman, *op. cit.,* p. 350.

TEACHING AND STUDY AIDS

1. Operating on the assumption that the community can and should be included in school processes, some administrators have invited laymen to participate in not only appraisal of the school but in planning of program. Read some accounts such as *Laymen Help Plan the Curriculum* (Washington, Association for Supervision and Curriculum Development, National Education Association, 1946). How would these procedures work in your community? Give a critical analysis.

2. Outline a plan for your community which would utilize the resources you know it has, for reciprocal interpretation between community and school.

3. Check the Selected Readings concerning special interest area reports such as School Publications as Interpreters of the School. See Moehlman, Rice, Waller, and Fedder as first helps.

SELECTED READING REFERENCES

Adams, Fay, *Educating America's Children* (New York, Ronald, 1946).

Bain, Winifred, *Parents Look at Modern Education* (New York, Appleton-Century, 1936).

Baldwin, Sara E., and Osborne, Ernest G., *Home-School Relations, Philosophy, and Practice* (New York, Progressive Education Association, 1935).

Baruch, Dorothy, *Parents and Children Go to School* (New York, Scott, 1939).

Blackburn, Laura, *School Publications* (New York, Macmillan, 1928).

Burr, J. B., Harding, L. W., Jacobs, L. B., *Student Teaching in the Elementary School* (New York, Appleton-Century-Crofts, 1950).

Butterworth, Julian E., *The P.T.A. and Its Work* (New York, Macmillan, 1929).

Clapp, Elsie Ripley, *Community Schools in Action* (New York, Viking, 1939).

Cook, Lloyd Allen, *Community Backgrounds of Education* (New York, McGraw-Hill, 1938).

———, and Cook, Elaine F., *A Sociological Approach to Education* (New York, McGraw-Hill, 1950).

De Lima, Agnes, *The Little Red School House* (New York, Macmillan, 1942).

Department of Elementary School Principals, *Building Community Understanding of the School,* Bulletin 23, Part 3 (Washington, National Education Association, 1945).

Dillon, Ina K., "Community Cooperation for Improving the Child's World," *Childhood Education,* Vol. 21 (September 1944).

Driscoll, Gertrude, *How to Study the Behavior of Children* (New York, Bureau of Publications, Teachers College, Columbia University, 1941).

Educational Policies Commission, *EDUCATION for ALL American Children* (Washington, National Education Association, 1948).

Elsbree, Willard, *Pupil Progress in the Elementary School* (New York, Bureau of Publications, Teachers College, Columbia University, 1943).

Evans, R. O., *Practices, Trends and Issues in Reporting to Parents* (New York, Bureau of Publications, Teachers College, Columbia University, 1938).

Fedder, Ruth, *Guiding Homeroom and Club Activities* (New York, McGraw-Hill, 1949).

Fisk, R. S., *Public Understanding of What Good Schools Can Do* (New York, Bureau of Publications, Teachers College, Columbia University, 1945).

Foster, Josephine C., and Headley, Neith E., *Education in the Kindergarten* (New York, American Book, 1948).

Frank, Lawrence K., "New Ways to Reach Parents," *Child Study*, Vol. XXIV (Summer–Fall 1947).

Freund, Annis Leeds, "When Parents Help at School," *Childhood Education*, Vol. 19 (December 1942).

Gabbard, Hazel F., "Parent Participation in the School Program," *School Life*, Vol. 30 (December 1947).

Gantz, Ralph M., "Report Cards that Tell the Story," *The Nations Schools*, Vol. XXVIII (August 1941), pp. 51–53.

Gruenberg, Sidonie M., *The Use of Radio in Parent Education* (Chicago, University of Chicago Press, 1939).

Hanna, Paul R., *Youth Serves the Community* (New York, Appleton-Century-Crofts, 1950).

Hausser, E. W., "Marks that Aid in Guidance," *The Nations Schools* Vol. XXXVI (December 1945), p. 25.

Hildreth, Gertrude, *Child Growth Through Education* (New York, Ronald, 1948).

Hill, E. B., "Guiding Principles for P.T.A.," *National Parent-Teacher*, Vol. 33 (June 1939) pp. 34–36.

Hopkins, L. Thomas, *Interaction: The Democratic Process* (Boston, Heath, 1941).

————, and others, *Integration: Its Meaning and Application* (New York, Appleton-Century, 1937).

Irons, H. S., *The Development of Characteristics in Superintendent's Annual Reports to the Board and to the Public*, Doctor's Thesis, University of Pittsburgh, B, Vol. 39, No. 2 (1943).

Jenkins, Gladys, Shacter, Helen, Bauer, William, *These are Your Children* (Chicago, Scott, 1949).

Lee, J. Murray, and Doris M. Lee, *The Child and His Curriculum* (New York, Appleton-Century-Crofts, 1950).

Leonard, Edith M., Miles, Lillian E., Vanderkar, Catherine S., *The Child at Home and School* (New York, American Book, 1944).

Lewin, Kurt, "The Dynamics of Group Action," *Educational Leadership,* Vol. 1 (January 1944).

Lissim and Silbert, "When Parents Learn With Children," *Childhood Education* (January 1950).

Mason, Martha Sprague, *Parents and Teachers* (New York, Ginn, 1928).

McKown, Harry C., *Extracurricular Activities* (New York, Macmillan, 1948).

Mendenhall, Charles B., and Arisman, Kenneth. *Secondary Education* (New York, Sloane, 1951).

Moehlman, Arthur B., *Social Interpretation* (New York, Appleton-Century, 1938).

Nisonger, Herschel W., *Special and Adult Education* (Columbus, The Ohio State University Press, 1940).

Norton, Edith, "Parent Education in the Nursery School," *Childhood Education International* (1949).

Olsen, Edward G., *School and Community* (New York, Prentice-Hall, 1945).

————, *School and Community Programs* (New York, Prentice-Hall, 1949).

Primary Bulletin, The Curriculum Bulletin 95 (Cincinnati, Cincinnati Public Schools, 1947).

Reeder, W. G., *An Introduction to Public School Relations* (New York, Macmillan, 1937).

Rice, A. H., ed., *Today's Techniques,* First yearbook (Detroit, School Public Relations Association, 1943).

Sherer, Lorraine, *Their First Years at School* (Los Angeles, Los Angeles County Board of Education, 1939).

Stern, Edith M., "Can Talk Cure Delinquency?" *Woman's Home Companion* (June 1950).

Stiles, Lindley J., "Up to Date Reporting" *School Executive,* Vol. LXVI (January 1946), pp. 50–52.

Stout, Dorman G., *Teacher and Community* (Yonkers-on-Hudson, World Book, 1941).

Strang, Ruth, *Educational Guidance: Its Theory and Practice* (New York, Bureau of Publications, Teachers College, Columbia University, 1947).

Strang, Ruth, *Reporting to Parents* (New York, Bureau of Publications, Teachers College, Columbia University, 1947).

————, *The Role of the Teacher in Personnel Work* (New York, Bureau of Publications, Teachers College, Columbia University, 1945).

————, "What Did You Get on Your Report Card?" *National Parent-Teacher* (March 1950).

Traxler, Arthur E., *Techniques of Guidance* (New York, Harper, 1945).

Tyler, Ralph, "The Character of a Modern Educational Program," *The Elementary School Journal*, Vol. XLVIII (November 1947).

The University of Texas Publication, *Grouping, Marking and Reporting to Parents,* Woolridge School (Austin, University of Texas Press, February 1950).

Van Nice, C. R., *Teacher Teamwork with a Problem Public* (Topeka, Kan., School Activities Publishing, 1940).

Waller, J. F., *Public Relations for Public Schools* (Trenton, N. J., MacCrellish and Quigley, 1933).

Walser, Frank, *The Art of Conference* (New York, Harper, 1947).

Warner, W. L., and Havighurst, R. J., *Who Shall Be Educated?* (New York, Harper, 1947).

EPILOGUE

HERE IS A CHILD, another, and still another; all centuries old in biological inheritance; all breathtakingly new in social inheritance; all unique, none like any other; all the community's stake in immortality.

How shall we regard this child, and this child? Shall we see him as miniature adult, transmitter of the status quo per se, a candidate for societal membership? Or shall we view him as an out-reaching, dynamic organism, who is in no way like an adult; one who grows, develops at his own rate in terms of his own potential; who on the continuum of experience needs go from dependence through independence to interdependence; who *is* a citizen with all the rights, privileges, and responsibilities such societal membership implies but always in terms of his maturity, not ours?

How shall we treat this child, and this and this? Shall we assume he has no interests, no needs, save those we prescribe for him? Or shall we study what his individual differential is; see him as a person in his own right, listen when he speaks that we may hear his needs, his hopes, his fears, his worries, his plans? Shall we then help him to see himself ever in relation to his peers, his elders and their needs, hopes, fears, worries, and plans?

For thus he forms his patterns of thinking, his ideas, attitudes, and prejudices. And as the patterns form, so, too, do the roles emerge which he will play. For only when he experiences "generalized others" will he be able to see himself, deal with himself, and appraise and reconstruct that self.

Shall we cause him to sit long periods, to listen and repeat, to store up knowledge for another vague day, to do as he is bidden and make no comment, to prepare for living? Shall we reward him extrinsically when his struggles carry him past our goals and punish him if he rebels, is indifferent, or is unable to reach the prizes we offer? Or shall we let him grow, sometimes stumble, regain his footing, and, by guidance, help him toward greater maturity in family, peer, and other adult relations.

This child is our life now and for the future. Shall we see him in his fate-appointed place whether it be squalid or enriched? Shall we leave him there to battle as best he may the social forces of a swiftly changing, disjointed social world?

Or shall we hold him inviolate, worthy of the best democracy can offer; as challenging our creative resources one and all; as worthy of community attention, planning, action, that he may attain his optimal development and in time provide the same for others without regard for creed or color?

Here is our common denominator—the child. In terms of him only is social telesis worthwhile. Eliminate or crush him and we die. Misdirect him and we betray not only him but ourselves, society as a whole. Cherish him, tread lightly lest we stunt his vast creative powers, take thought that these powers be guided into ways of intelligence, and reciprocal relations, that he learn inviolability of others through his own experience, and the immortality of democracy is assured.

APPENDIXES

A | SOCIAL EDUCATION

STUDENT BULLETIN[1]

I. COURSE PLANNING, ORGANIZATION, AND APPRAISAL

THIS BULLETIN is an attempt to bring together for your inspection some basic facts concerning courses in educational sociology. It is not meant to be a hard and fast outline. When student needs and interests so direct, we shall set up additional or substitute units or practices. Likewise, it does not mean that your course has not been carefully thought through and planned. It does mean that though there is a central core which has been organized by the instructor, there are areas in which student help and planning are both useful and desirable.

The basic assumption is that students are not only able but also willing to plan under guidance and to carry through those plans. One of our first tasks then is to set up our objectives. In order that we may know where we are, where we are going, and whither along we have come, we need to think together concerning basic aims for our course. In the main these goals tend to arrange themselves in terms of general class objectives and possible personal outcomes.

Will you, therefore, carefully inspect such materials as will be given you at the first meeting and come to class prepared to share in the decisions such as course aims, course procedures, appraisal procedures, and the like.

[1] The bulletin presented is a reproduction of the one given to students in educational sociology at The Ohio State University.

In any social studies class there are at least three major areas which should be affected. These include *information, values,* and *ability to interpret critically* social data of a live-a-day world. Perhaps these will be a good starting point for our discussion.

Simply because a pattern of instruction is interested in the individual in relation to groups does not mean it has no interest in so-called "academic" achievements. Vast increments of knowledge are to be desired. We ask only in a social education approach that they have direct bearing and relation upon the attitudes, biases, prejudices, and value system of the person encountering them. And that the above experiences be related to methods of handling data which are continually bombarding one through all the various media of communication, from comics through radio to television.

These three general objectives are suggested as valid for any social science course. Students have often pointed out that they are not merely goals to hold in mind as we plan and replan but serve as criteria for appraising both individual and groupal course outcomes.

Beyond them is the consideration of specific aims in terms of the specific course area and the final more personal outcomes of the individual. The specific area aims are the teacher's and students' concern.

A few possible personal outcomes are listed below merely as a basis for further thinking.

1. Appreciation of the democratic process in solving problems; greater skill in directing this process.
2. Considerable development of "work skills" such as ability to organize materials, to generalize, to make applications, and to interpret critically.
3. Increased social sensitivity and responsibility through group work and committee work as contrasted with work of an entirely individual nature.
4. New viewpoints regarding the social aspects of child personality, its organization, disorganization, and guidance.
5. Richer experience in visualizing the school as a child and adult service and welfare institution.
6. Increased skill in solving problems via scientific methods.
7. Insight into self—one's personal growth, strengths, and weaknesses in reference especially to factors of competency in teachers.

II. COURSE PROCEDURE

There are a number of procedures open to us. We may elect a lecture course, a class discussion technic, project procedures, or a combination procedure. Classes in Educational Sociology have tried various methods. The favorite pattern has been a combination of lecture, discussion, and projects. When conducted on this basis, class is conceived of not as a passive learning situation but as a clearing house for student problems, a testing place for new views, ideas, skills, and experiences. Lectures are then used for special purposes only, such as orientation at the beginning of the course, for presenting special materials, or for synthesis at the close of the course.

Considerable experimentation has convinced us that in committee work our principle of greatest number is five. This number is sizable enough to allow the project group to plan nearly any type of clever presentation from a dramatization to a debate, a round table discussion, or a panel performance. In the busy college world it is not unwieldy in terms of planning committee meetings. Getting five people or less together in one place at one time is a possibility. These groups must be "working groups." If the number is larger, in a term or semester span of time too much time has to be spent in the adjustment of interpersonal relationships. While this adjustment period is a valuable learning period, we wish to make the phase as short as possible to allow heavy concentration on the area of new data and skills.

If such a scheme is approved by students (and the writer freely admits hoping you will give it a "try"), project groups are composed of from two to five members. Individual projects are allowed if circumstances warrant. These groups investigate, work out, write up, and present experiments and/or activities within our field. Projects may be selected from the list given or devised by the group with the instructor's approval.

The groups are organized in class complete with chairman and secretary. At the first conference with the instructor "starting lists" of references are given plus basic help in outlining or planning of the project.

As many conferences are granted as are needed, but once the outline or plan is OK'ed, students are expected to be "on their own."

Modes of write-up and presentation may be chosen by the group. In the past clever presentations have included debates, panel discussions, one-act plays, "Information Please" programs, juries of experts, as well as the class report, etc.

Field trips are not required but are urged, especially in connection with project work. A complete Community Inventory of Social Agencies in Columbus is at your disposal in the instructor's office. (This was a "continuing" project once upon a time.)

Reading reports as such are not assigned. Oral reports on subjects of interest will occur as we go from unit to unit. Others are oriented about project work.

The class file contains copies of study forms, such as questionnaires, schedules, rating scales, etc. Also available are sample copies of tests, and project write-ups.

III. PROJECTS AND PROBLEMS

This section lists a number of topics which are suitable for term projects or problems. The list is suggestive only, and usually the best studies are made by students who revise or adapt a project to suit themselves.

The write-up of the project may be done individually or as a group. Completed projects, typed on $8\frac{1}{2}$ by 11 paper, should be handed in at least one week before the end of the term. They are the property of the department and are filed in class case file. The file also contains samples of study forms. Both sets of materials are available for student inspection on the assumption that social waste is inexcusable. That is to say that well-done student papers are valuable resources of both information, techniques of study, illustrative material, and bibliographies.

Some Topic Suggestions

A. **The Area of Educational Sociology**

1. An historical view of educational sociology.
2. Contributions of educational sociology to educational philosophy and practices.
3. Devices for appraising learning outcomes.
4. Relationships of educational sociology to other social sciences.

B. **Studies Concerning Child Orientation**

1. A critical study of theories of personality arisal and development.
2. Relation of language and thought in personality development.

3. The dynamics of learning.
4. Value systems of childhood.
5. Value conflicts of adolescence, origins, nature of, programs for resolving conflicts.
6. Homes as cultural worlds for children: sibling relationships, special situations as broken home, adoptive home.
7. Sex education.
8. Mental hygiene goals for children.
9. Camping as a socializing agency.
10. Study of acculturation in preliterate societies.
11. How can we improve the quality of family life?
12. Adjustment problems of the exceptional child.
13. Adjustment problems of the handicapped child.
14. The bi-lingual child.
15. The child between two cultures—marginal man.
16. Religious experiences of children.
17. Imaginary companions.
18. Painting and personality.
19. The effect of the quality of family life upon mental health.
20. Special concerns of the preschool child; the child from six to twelve; the adolescent.
21. Children's guests.
22. The role of family table talk.
23. The "fringes" of the family circle.
24. Mechanisms of personality adjustment.
25. Bibliotherapy and the child.
26. Play therapy, dramatic play.
27. Comics, movies, radio, and television in relation to acculturation of children.

C. The School as a Social World

28. Rating and dating complexes.
29. The case for and against sororities and fraternities.
30. The school as a cultural matrix.
31. Impact of teacher personality upon students.
32. Social climates in the classroom.
33. Social distance in the school.
34. The "marginal" child.
35. The social isolate—social reject—social assimilate.
36. Class and caste in the school social world.
37. Ceremonies, mores, and rituals as social phenomena.
38. Good and bad teachers.
39. The school's community.

D. Community Study

40. Interpreting the school to the community.
41. Parent-teacher relations.
42. The social status of the teacher.
43. The teacher as a sociological stranger.
44. Pressure groups and the school.
45. School trips.
46. Using community resources.
47. Leadership techniques.
48. Sociography of the community.
49. Conduct codes for teachers.
50. The community coordinating council.
51. Community institutions and welfare institutions such as courts, community chest, newspaper organizations, department stores, settlement houses, etc.
52. Three educational theories: traditional, progressivism, essentialism
53. Means and methods of group process education.
54. A plan of group study.
55. The changing community.
56. Attitude changes, values, social skills as goals of education.
57. Media of mass impression and social control.
58. A study of my home community.

IV. APPRAISAL

Since we must assign grades, we must consider modes of evaluating learning outcomes.

How shall we weight the parts of the course is usually one of the first student questions. Each class discusses and votes its own fate. Past patterns have included the following weighting arrangements. You may have other suggestions:

Class discussion	1	1	1	1
Projects	1	2	1	2
Tests	1	1	2	2

How *many tests* shall we have? Here the class may choose from a number of possibilities:

1. Midterm and final
2. Two midterms and final
3. Weekly quizzes

    4. Three midterms and a final
    5. Three midterms mutually exclusive, etc.

What *kind* of tests shall we have? The class shares in planning each test pattern. It is the custom to vote on each test as it comes up. Thus, if a pattern has not proved satisfactory, it may be shifted somewhat.

How many questions shall we write in the time allotted? Included below are some samples of test questions. Will you study them carefully and come to class prepared to evaluate them critically prior to choosing a first test pattern? It is felt that under these circumstances people will not be penalized by meeting "new kind of question," at the time of the test.

Test Questions

Some people are sure they "do better" on objective questions, others are just as sure they perform better on subjective questions. Though research belies both extremes, it is deemed a worthy part of the learning situation to work with test formation, its results, and consequent replanning.

Since many or often most of the people who study Educational Sociology will one day be teachers, it is a "must" that they be familiar with the mechanics of forming test questions.

Experience is also desirable with tests which try to get at outcomes other than sheer factual material. Given below then are "samples" of kinds of test questions.

A. Discussion Questions

These types of questions need little by way of illustration. They take three forms—essay, problem, and short answer essay.

    Essay Example. Write clearly, completely, but concisely.
    1. What is your theory of personality development?
    Problem Example. A birth notice as follows:
        Born to: Mr. and Mrs. A. Average—a son, 110 Blenheim Road, Columbus, Ohio
                  or
        Born to Mr. and Mrs. Above Average—a girl, 2113 W. Beechwold, Columbus, Ohio
    Choose one set of the factors we have discussed as child orientation

agencies. Trace developmentally the imaginary children at least to teen age.

Short Answer Essay. Explain the following concepts in not more than 75 words.

       1. The socialized being
       2. Social role
       3. Class

What are the strengths and weaknesses of each kind of question?

B. Check Type Questions

Check questions demand specific, discriminating replies. Examples included here are the multiple choice, the matching, the completion, the true-false, the logical incoordinate.

Multiple Choice Example: Place a check mark on the blank or blanks which make the statement true.

1. A culture trait is: ——*a.* pattern of the group; ——*b.* single combination of habits and ideas meeting a situation; ——*c.* such as our political system; ——*d.* use of matches.
2. The ethos of a culture: ——*a.* the addition of its cultural traits; ——*b.* is its distinguishing patterns; ——*c.* furnishes the yardstick for judging other cultures; ——*d.* is an absolute thing.

Matching Examples: Select the concept on the right which best describes the concept on the left. Concepts may be used more than once.

SOCIAL PHENOMENA	SOCIOLOGICAL CONCEPTS
——totality of human traits and attributes	*1.* play pursuits
——organization of traits into functional patterns	*2.* cultural forms
——body of heritages to which individual is heir	*3.* ecology
——revaluation of old friends and relationships	*4.* primary group
——Stanley assimilated gang culture; his brother rejected it	*5.* assimilation
——compulsory activity with utilitarian end	*6.* personality integration
——age, sex, race, social status, etc.	*7.* differential response
	8. work
	9. marginal man
	10. effective environment
	11. variables
	12. majority group
	13. original nature

——boy's gang   *14.* world expansion
——to believe oneself victim of   *15.* rationalization
fate   *16.* adolescence
——one's unique set of potentiali- *17.* personality
ties

Completion Example: Complete the blanks in the following
statements.

    1. The book *Elmtown* is written by _____ and
is about _____.

    2. A community survey treats data _____.

True-false: Encircle correct letters. T means true, F means
false, D means doubtful. If you check *doubtful,* explain what makes
it so.

    T   F   D   *1.* Science has proved that the universe is orderly.

    T   F   D   *2.* Sociology is both a descriptive and a generalizing
science.

    T   F   D   *3.* Science can deal only with what man can observe
with his senses.

    T   F   D   *4.* Human beings have always and everywhere char-
acteristically lived in groups.

    T   F   D   *5.* Man learns through reflection; animals learn through
imitation.

Logical Incoordinate Example: Cross out any concepts which
in the logic of the classification do not apply.

    1. Horizontal, democratic, authoritarian, vertical socialistic, com-
munity-wide.

    2. Organization, disorganization, research, interpretation, publicity,
cooperation pressure, conflict.

    3. Actual participants, community survey, community spirit, com-
munity activities, potential participants.

    4. Middle States, Far Western States, Northeastern States, the
Southern States, Southwestern States.

    5. Social base map, social survey, life history, score card, statistics.

Discuss the strengths and weaknesses of each type of question.

C. Questions Testing Values and Ability to Draw Conclusions from Sets of Data

    1. Application of Principles. Example.

Problem: "Yuki"

A large high school in California has a large number of foreign-born boys and girls among its students. One of these was Yuki, a well-dressed, gentle, and friendly Japanese girl. She spoke good English and made a wonderful record in scholarship during her high school career. At the end her academic record was better than any of the other students in her class. Since the best student usually becomes the valedictorian of the graduating class, the principal decided to make her the valedictorian. Immediately a storm of protest broke loose. Newspapers took it up; citizens called on the principal and threatened him; classmates announced they would not appear on the platform with a Japanese girl as their leader.

The principal's reply to these protests was that Yuki should lead the class or else there would be no valedictorian.

What is your feeling about the decision of the principal?

Conclusions: (Check one or more conclusions with which you agree).

—— A. He was right in doing what he did.
—— B. He was probably right, but it was an impractical and foolish thing to do.
—— C. The principal should have let the faculty and the students participate in making the decision.
—— D. He should not have decided to have a girl of an alien race for the school valedictorian.

Reasons: Indicate the reasons which you would accept in support of the conclusion or conclusions you have checked above by writing the appropriate letters in the margin. Write in any additional reasons which seem important to you.

—— 1. School is no place to fight out the issue of racial equality.
—— 2. The high school students must learn not to let race prejudice affect their behavior.
—— 3. Race prejudice is inborn and it is no use to try to do anything about it.
—— 4. The Japanese should be made to feel grateful that they can go to an American school. There is no point in making them feel superior.
—— 5. It is an established tradition that the best student in the class should be the valedictorian.
—— 6. We should not let a Japanese girl get the honors which rightfully belong to the Americans.
—— 7. In a democracy there should be no racial discrimination.
—— 8. The community and the students probably had some very good reasons for feeling as they did towards Yuki.

—— 9. Japanese are too cocky anyway.

——10. Had the principal yielded to the community pressure, he would have supported unreasonable race prejudice.

——11. The parents who pay the taxes have the right to determine what the school should or should not do.

——12. It would have been unfair to deprive Yuki of her due reward.

——13. The community and the students were unreasonable in their protests.

——14. In cases such as these, it is most expedient to try to reform the community before raising the issue.

——15. Schools are especially responsible for cultivating a democratic spirit.

——16. The principle of social equality of all races is all right in theory, but it is impossible to act on it in all practical situations.

2. Interpretation of Data. Example.

Among the most important of all skills and abilities which a student needs to develop are those involved in reflective thinking. Our approach to these abilities has been made via "interpretation of data" tests. Here is one exercise which is relevant to the purposes and content of our course. Read instructions carefully before answering.

To warrant any inference of truth or falsity, mark *D;* if data suggest statement is probably false, mark it *PF;* if data show statement is false, mark it *F;* if data show statement true, mark it *T.*

COMMUNITY CLEARING HOUSE, J. P. MCEVOY; *The Kiwanis,*
December, 1939.

Twenty years ago when August Vollmer, professor of criminology at the University of California, became chief of police at Berkeley, he asked himself the question: "Instead of a dozen welfare organizations working on youth problems, why not a community agency to coordinate effort and prevent useless duplication?" Today there are 420 community coordinating councils functioning from coast to coast, in big cities, small towns and villages.

Who starts these councils? The local newspaper editor, a minister or a priest, the president of a women's club, the head of the American Legion. In one tough Los Angeles district it was a plumber. But in every case it is an individual who has proved his leadership in his organization or in civic affairs.

How does the council function? Its first job is to decide on the most pressing problem. It may be the elimination of a slum district, as in Cleveland; or it may be a shake-up of the local government; it may be a community swimming pool, as in Mojave, in the desert. The range of activities can be glimpsed from the program of the smallest in Alturas, a town of 250 in California. Its recent good deeds include providing a municipal ice-skating pond, a summer camp for Scouts, a nursery school, organizing a discussion group and a dramatic club, securing a children's corner at the library, and sponsoring a women's dance class.

What Councils can do when they really go to town is shown by results in Los Angeles county. In 1931 some 6,000 children passed through the juvenile court; in 1937, a few over 3,700. The decrease closely corresponds to the number of children who went through the adjustment committees of the coordinating Councils. If you accept Juvenile Judge Fox's estimate that it costs taxpayers $200 to put a child through juvenile court, a saving of $460,000 can be chalked up to the Council's credit in this county alone.

——1. The growth of the councils is evidence that citizens are taking responsibility back into their own hands.
——2. Community coordinating councils are an outgrowth of the last quarter century.
——3. A community council does not effect a cure; it provides mechanics for community integration if groups concerned elect to cooperate.
——4. The councils are local in origin and follow no set pattern in aims or organization.
——5. If no one else initiates a council, the superintendent of schools should take the initiative if there is need of one in the community.
——6. Delinquency prevention is the sole aim of such an organization.
——7. One barrier to council success is the failure of leadership to win locality support.
——8. The community council is a good approach if democracy means concern for individual welfare, faith in decision of the people, and a respect for cooperative effort.

What are the strengths and weaknesses of these types of questions?

Preparing a Test Pattern for this Course

Questions to Consider. We come now to several points on which our class should reach a decision. What kind of question, or combination of more than one kind of question, do we need to test the learning outcomes expected in this course? What shall be the time length (ten minute quiz, full period test, etc.) of our exams? How many exams shall we have this quarter? At what intervals?

After a test has been scored, shall all scores be arrayed on the blackboard? How shall these numbers be translated, finally, into letters as required by the university? Shall the papers be returned to students and that period spent in a critical review of the examination? What other evidences of student achievement should be considered in determining a final grade for the course? What weight should be assigned to test grades?

After much experience, it seems well to advise that if an objective or combination objective and essay test is chosen, four or five questions are enough for a 50-minute period. Students often choose to write four out of five questions. Sometimes the teacher has exercised a doubtful prerogative and required one essay question. Students are then free to select any other three.

Preparing for the Test

Suggestions Worth Thinking Over. Since this *Bulletin* will be given to you prior to any major test in the course, it may be helpful to outline some rules found useful in preparing for examination. It has been suggested that a student should:

1. Frame questions which he would ask if he were the teacher. He must be certain he can answer them.
2. Discuss the work with fellow students and argue the issues involved.
3. Set up review periods well ahead of the exam, yet not fail to review summary notes just before the test.
4. Ask that a class period be devoted to review and then use this time as an apportunity to clarify doubtful points.

D. Project and Course Appraisal Forms

As mentioned earlier, students are both willing and able to share in such evaluation and appraisal. Under proper social climates in the classroom they provide instructive and constructive comments and criticism.

The first form is one used for rating committee project presentations in class. Both the teacher and the audience rates the group and the group rates itself. It is a most educative experience for the

. committee to "take stock" and appraise its own work. The results are
compiled and reported back to the committee at the earliest possible date.

     If we are to maintain a situational approach we must be anx-
ious and willing to appraise both *course structure and course proc-*
esses. Over a period of ten years, student committees and instructors
have framed, tried, abandoned, and reframed many such forms.
Though the ones presented below are not considered final in any
sense, they are proving useful as guides for constant planning and
replanning.

APPRAISAL OF PROJECT--GROUP REPORTS
                          Individual Rating Blank No. 1

  1. Rate each speaker or discussant separately
     and immediately after he has completed his
     participation.
  2. Add the points given to each participant and
     report his score.
  3. If a participant merits an A grade, his final
     score should be 50 to 40; B, 39 to 30; C, 29
     to 20; D, 19 to 10; E, 9 to 0.
  4. Please be discriminating in your reactions,
     giving credit where credit is due, and vice
     versa. Your ratings are confidential; only
     class averages will be reported.
  5. Complete your appraisal and turn in this
     sheet before you leave class.

Criteria for Report Rating	Total Possible Points	Points Awarded to Each Speaker				
		1st	2nd	3rd	4th	5th
1. Did the speaker delimit and define the problem clearly?	5					
2. Did the speaker explain his methods of study?	5					
3. Did the speaker go beyond his data?	11					
4. Was the report well organized?	9					
5. Was the time wisely divided						

```
    between partici-
    pants?                      6
6.  Was the report in-
    teresting as well
    as instructive?             7
7.  Were teaching aids
    used to advantage?          7
    Average score for          ──
        group                  50
```
Topic of general report.........................
Name of first speaker............................
Name of second speaker...........................
Name of third speaker............................
Name of fourth speaker...........................
Name of fifth speaker............................
Your name as rater...............................
Date of this rating..............................
Grade of rater (Filled in by instructor)........

APPRAISAL FORM FOR PROJECT—GROUP REPORTING AS A
GROUP   Blank No. 2

Often people choose to present their work by
some method which makes blank number 1 unwieldy
since it is set up for more individual reporting. They may then inform the class that they
have worked as a group, want to be graded as a
group and choose form 2 for their rating blank.

Instructions: Please hold in mind the following
criteria for appraising the group as a whole.

If a participant merits an A grade, his final
score should be 50 to 40; B, 39 to 30; C, 29 to
20; D, 19 to 10; E, 9 to 0. Please be discriminating in your reactions, giving credit where
credit is due, and vice versa. Your ratings are
confidential; only class averages will be reported.

Complete your evaluation and turn in this sheet
before you leave class.

Criteria for Rating Report	Total Possible Points	Points Awarded
1. Was the subject properly de-limited and aims clearly de-fined?	6	

2. Were methods of study care-
   fully delineated?   6   ___
3. Were generalizations properly
   documented or did they go be-
   yond study data?   12   ___
4. Was the presentation unified,
   well-organized, and coopera-
   tion evident?   10   ___
5. Was the presentation inter-
   esting as well as instructive?   8   ___
6. Were teaching aids utilized
   to advantage?   8   ___

                  Group Score   50

Date of rating.................................
Name of rater..................................
Grade of rater (Filled in by instructor).......

Educational Sociology

Section_____   Sex M – F
                         Last Test Grade____

I

General Rating of Course

Directions: Check the one answer in each series
(reading across page) which most nearly represents your point of view.

As compared with OTHER courses I am taking this
quarter, this course is:

1. More interesting____   Less interesting   ____
                           about the same____
2. More instructive____   Less instructive   ____
                           about the same____
3. More difficult   ____   Less difficult   ____
                           about the same____
4. More practical   ____   Less practical   ____
                           about the same____
5. Better taught   ____   More poorly taught____
                           about the same____

II

Teacher Personality and Organization of Course

Place a check mark (√) before all words or
phrases which are true as a rule of your in-

structor. There is provided under each division
a space for any additional comment of your own.

Teacher Personality

_____ 6. Good sense of humor.
_____ 7. Sarcastic, boastful, overcritical.
_____ 8. Understands student needs and problems.
_____ 9. Lacks poise; ill at ease.
_____10. Interested in student views.
_____11. Personal appearance not pleasing.
_____12. Treats students as mature persons.
_____13. Has peculiar mannerisms, annoying ges-
          tures.
_____14. Has genuine enthusiasm for the subject.
_____15. _____.

Class Discussion

_____16. Provides ample opportunity for discus-
          sion.
_____17. Lets discussion run off on side issues.
_____18. Effective in integrating discussion.
_____19. Thinks his opinions are always right and
          final.
_____20. Clarifies issues; all sides brought into
          open.
_____21. Too much time used by a few students.
_____22. Encourages all to participate in discus-
          sions.
_____23. Illustrations not practical, poorly
          chosen.
_____24. Concerned with important topics.
_____25. _____.

Assignments, Teaching Materials, Course Planning

_____26. Students share in planning the course.
_____27. Assignments too long and too difficult.
_____28. Encourages wide range of voluntary read-
          ing.
_____29. Too many written papers assigned.
_____30. Tests fairly graded.
_____31. Too many tests are given.
_____32. Too much required reading.

_____33. Feel free to discuss grades with teacher.

_____34. _____.

Out-of-Class Conferences and Contacts

_____35. Teacher is friendly and helpful in out-
          of-class contacts.
_____36. Seldom available for conferences.
_____37. Keeps office hours as announced.
_____38. Confidential information told to others.

_____39. _____.

III

This course would be improved by:

_____40. Closer adherence to the textbook.
_____41. Fewer lecture sessions.
_____42. More lecture sessions.
_____43. More motion pictures.
_____44. More outside speakers.
_____45. More field trips.

_____46. _____.

_____47. _____.

IV

Y N 48. Would you approve of a book fee to pur-
        chase new books for class use?
Y N 49. Did you read any of the bibliography
        books?
Y N 50. About how many?
51. In your opinion, what could be done to im-
    prove the discussion sections; the committee
    work and presentations:

52. What are some topics which you think should
    have been discussed, but which were not dis-
    cussed, or discussed insufficiently?
53. Did you confer with your instructors about
    your work or personal problems? If not, why
    not?

54. Did you develop any new friendships in _____
    _____this class?   Boy or girl?____
    _____through project work? Boy or girl?____
55. Did you learn to dislike anyone in this
    class?____ Do you know why?____
56. Remarks: General comments on course not
    covered in the above._____

TEACHING AND STUDY AIDS

1. After reading the above suggestions for course organization, procedure and appraisal, form a committee to investigate what other people are thinking and doing about this issue. The following references will give you a start:

Better Than Rating, Pamphlet by Association for Supervision and Curriculum Development, N. E. A., 1201 Sixteenth Street, N. W., Washington, 6, D. C.

Cook, Lloyd A., and Koeninger, Rupert, "'Measuring Learning Outcomes in Introductory Sociology Courses," *Journal of Educational Sociology,* Vol. 14 (December 1939), pp. 208–225.

Greenhoe, Florence, "Contributions of Community Sociology to Teacher-Training," *Journal of Educational Sociology,* Vol. 13, No. 8 (April 1940).

Hamilton, Samuel L., *What It Takes to Make Good in College* (New York, Public Affairs Committee, 1941).

Hartshorne, Hugh, *From School to College: A Study of the Transition Experience* (New Haven, Yale University Press, 1939).

Jayne, Clarence D., "A Study of the Relationships between Teaching Procedures and Educational Outcomes," *Journal of Experimental Education,* Vol. 14 (December 1945), pp. 103–134.

2. Conditions will vary practices. How much of the above organizational pattern could apply to your situation?

B

SOME GENERAL TEACH-ING-STUDY AIDS AND RESOURCES

I. MAGAZINES. SOME MAGAZINES WHOSE CONTENT WILL AFFORD RESOURCES ON STUDY OF CHILDREN, SCHOOL, COMMUNITY INCLUDE:

Adult Education Journal
American Journal of Sociology
American Sociological Review
The Child
Child Development
Child Study
Childhood Education
Education Digest
Educational Administration and Supervision
Elementary School Journal
Experimental Education
Hygeia

International Journal of Religious Education
Journal of Educational Sociology
Marriage and Family Living
National Parent-Teacher
Parents Magazine
School Life
School Review
Social Education
Social Forces
Sociology and Social Research

II. INDEXES OF ARTICLES AND RESEARCH

Child Development Abstracts
Education Index
Journal of Educational Research
Periodical Index
Readers Guide
Review of Educational Research
Psychological Abstracts

Research Relating to Children, an Inventory of Studies in Progress. Children's Bureau, Federal Security Agency, Washington, D. C.

III. AGENCIES AND ASSOCIATIONS WHO PUB-LISH PAMPHLETS, ETC.

The Association for Family Living, 28 East Jackson Street, Chicago 4, Ill.

Association for Supervision and Curriculum Development, N.E.A., 1201 Sixteenth Street, N. W., Washington, D. C., 6.

The Child Study Association of America, Washington, D. C.

Community Service Society, 105 East 22nd Street, New York 1, N. Y.

National Council on Family Relations, 5757 South Drexel Avenue, Chicago 37, Ill.

New York Committee on Mental Hygiene of the State Charities Aid Association, 105 E. 22nd Street, New York 10, N. Y.

Public Affairs Committee, 22 East 38th Street, New York 16, New York.

IV. RESEARCH CENTERS AND CLINICS

Brush Foundation, Western Reserve University, Cleveland, Ohio

Child Welfare Research Station, University of Iowa, Iowa City, Iowa

Experimental School, University of Michigan, Ann Arbor, Mich.

Fels Institute, Antioch College, Yellow Springs, Ohio

Gesell Institute of Child Development, New Haven, Conn.

Institute for Juvenile Research, Chicago, Ill.

Institute of Child Welfare, University of California, Berkeley, Calif.

Institute of Child Welfare, University of Minnesota, Minneapolis, Minn.

Judge Baker Clinic, Boston, Mass.

Merrill-Palmer School, Detroit, Mich.

Philadelphia Child Guidance Center, Philadelphia, Penn.

V. SIXTEEN-MILLIMETER MOVIES

Schools with funds for teaching aids may wish to purchase the films listed below. If this is not feasible, they may be rented or borrowed from state departments of education film libraries or as in Ohio from the Mental Hygiene Information Service of the Department of Welfare, 1210 State Office Building, Columbus, 15, Ohio.

1. Role Playing in Human Relations Training

Training film which demonstrates the spontaneous enactment of human relations situations as an educational method as well as how to develop the skills needed in the use of role playing.

RUNNING TIME: 25 minutes, sound, black and white.

2. Preface to a Life

Produced for The National Institute of Mental Health of the U. S. Public Health Service. The film opens upon Michael Thompson, a newborn baby—a human being with certain unique potentialities. The development of his personality will be greatly influenced by the experiences he has with parents, friends, and teachers, for they will largely determine the kind of adult Michael will be. The camera follows a series of episodes in his early life, using typical situations that occur during childhood as illustrations of how parental attitudes mold a sound or unhealthy mental outlook in the child. In one set of episodes we watch the mother, who tries to do everything for Michael instead of letting him face new situations or deal with his problems in his own way. In another set of episodes we follow the father whose aspirations for his child make him push Michael ahead at too fast a pace. Finally, in an alternative to both attitudes, we see Michael allowed to develop as an individual, accepted for what he is and appreciated for himself alone. It is this last Michael who is best equipped for success in his marriage and his career and is able, in spite of the usual problems, to live a creative and satisfying life.

RUNNING TIME: 29 minutes, sound, black and white.

3. Know Your Baby

Produced by the National Film Board of Canada. This film illustrates do's and don'ts in the care of the new baby. It stresses the importance of proper food, clothing, bedding, bathing and "burping." This sympathetic subject stresses the fact that the new baby's constant claims upon his mother's time and attention may be resented by the other children in the family unless care is taken by the parents to prevent them from feeling "neglected." Various ways of developing the interest and participation of brothers and sisters in the care of the new infant are recommended.

RUNNING TIME: 10 minutes, sound, kodachrome.

4. *Emergence of Personality*

Produced by Encyclopedia Britannica Films, Inc. This film is a combined forum version of three films listed as: *Baby Meets His Parents, Helping the Child to Face the Don'ts,* and *Helping the Child to Accept the Do's.* It explains how the developing personality of the child is influenced by the manner in which his parents provide for his basic needs and prepare him for social living.

This film is recommended for adult study and discussion groups such as mothers' clubs, women's clubs, parent-teacher associations, child study classes, etc.

RUNNING TIME: 30 minutes, sound, black and white.

5. *Your Children and You*

Produced by the British Ministry of Information. This film concerns the care of young children from the first months to the age of four or five. It realistically portrays the struggles of average imperfect parents and average imperfect children. Although the film is mainly a counsel of perfection, the suggestions are practical and parents could adopt them all without growing wings.

RUNNING TIME: 30 minutes, sound, black and white.

6. *Problem Child*

Produced by the American Academy of Pediatrics and made possible by a grant from the Pet Milk Company. This film concerns the behavior of the preschool child. At the age of two, Sandra is active, alert, bursting with curiosity. She is, as her mother said, "into everything." When her great aunt called her a "problem child," her parents took her to a doctor for advice and consultation. The doctor watched Sandra's behavior and then reviewed her first two years. He discusses the keys to mental health and something of the psychology of growth, pointing out that each child has his own individual growth pattern. Sandra's "problems" are simply a part of her growth pattern and part of the normal learning process. The film emphasizes the five fundamental growth needs of the child: A feeling of security, unqualified acceptance by his parents, a chance to develop a feeling of usefulness, standards of behavior appropriate to his age and mental development, and a chance to grow according to his own pattern.

RUNNING TIME: 27 minutes, sound, black and white.

7. *A Start in Life*

Produced by the British Ministry of Information. This film broadly outlines what is being done in Britain to ensure that every child receives adequate care from birth, the benefit of a full education, and a healthy and happy preparation for adult life.

RUNNING TIME: 22 minutes, sound, black and white.

8. *Human Beginnings*

An Eddie Albert production made under the supervision of Dr. Lester F. Beck, University of Oregon. This film concerns the attitudes of six-year-olds with the advent of a new baby brother or sister. Some children are delighted; others are confused and hostile. The film shows how these children, in a normal classroom situation, develop a warm wholesome attitude toward the idea of a new baby in the family.

Recommended uses: Elementary school classes, college courses, adult education groups.

RUNNING TIME: 22 minutes, sound, kodachrome.

9. *Why Won't Tommy Eat?*

Produced by the National Film Board of Canada. This film concerns the problem of children who won't eat and what can be done about it. Tommy should be hungry, but we see him just picking at his food. Going back to early babyhood, the film traces in detail how eating habits are formed. We see how individual likes and dislikes must be taken into consideration and that the worst habit of all is the permanent battle over food. After this analysis we find Tommy still sitting by his well-filled plate. In despair his mother takes him to the doctor, who explains that she is really the problem. She realizes that she has been tense, impatient, with Tommy from the start. Now it will take painstaking care to build a new atmosphere of cooperation and friendliness, to learn understanding of Tommy's personal requirements at meal times, and all the time.

RUNNING TIME: 19 minutes, sound, kodachrome.

10. *Problem Children*

Produced by The Ohio State Division of Mental Hygiene in cooperation with The Ohio State University and the University School. This film tells the story of two "problem children" of junior high age: Roy, an aggressive show-off, who is in trouble because of the things he does; and Jimmy, shy and introverted, who gets into trouble because of the things he does not do. The film stresses the point that these are not "problem children," but children with problems that have grown out of their individual home, school, and play relationships. The effect of these relations on the mental health and the personality development of the two boys is discussed. The film shows how parents and school together can work toward solution of such problems and can help children to grow to useful, well-adjusted adulthood.

RUNNING TIME: 20 minutes, sound, black and white.

11. Human Growth

Produced by E. C. Brown Trust in collaboration with the University of Oregon. This film (A) demonstrates for parents how sex education can be handled smoothly, intelligently, and in a socially acceptable manner in schools; (B) provides the classroom teacher with a suitable instructional aid for presenting the biological facts of sex as a part of human growth and development; (C) establishes, through identification, an exemplary teacher-pupil relationship conducive to easy classroom discussion.

This film is planned primarily for classroom use in grades six to nine, and is accompanied by twenty slides for teaching and discussion purposes. However, it has broad application, in adult and college courses, particularly those in family-life education, child study, mental and social hygiene, and teacher training.

RUNNING TIME: 19 minutes, sound, kodachrome.

12. Learning to Understand Children, Parts I and II

Produced by the McGraw-Hill Book Company, Inc. These two films record the case history of a maladjusted girl of fifteen. Ada Adams, mentally above the average of her ninth-grade class, is shown as a shy, backward student, handicapped by a poor home environment, and totally incapable of making the adjustment to her fellow students and to her work in school. The films trace the diagnosis of Ada's problems by a sympathetic English teacher and the remedial techniques she works out to reorient the girl to her proper place among her schoolmates. While Miss Brown's efforts are in no way intended as a blueprint to be followed explicitly, her careful analysis of Ada's personality, her cultivation of a successful pupil-teacher relationship, her conferences with Ada's mother and her other teachers, and the outlining of a plan which will give Ada's latent abilities an opportunity to develop—all are offered as acceptable and successful techniques for approaching similar cases of maladjustment.

RUNNING TIME: Part I, 21 minutes; Part II, 23 minutes, sound, black and white.

13. *Shy Guy*

Produced by Coronel Instructional Films in collaboration with Dr. Alice M. Sowers, Director of the Family Life Institute of the University of Oklahoma. This is a motivational film designed to treat the problem of shyness as it affects the adolescent. A teen-age boy whose family has moved to a strange community finds himself at a loss in a new high school. He is started on the road to friendly association with the aid of some timely advice from his father, who helps him to see that he must practice some of the principles he observes among students who are well-adjusted. The film is valuable for general use with junior and senior high school pupils and for teacher-training and parent-teacher groups.

RUNNING TIME: 15 minutes, sound, black and white.

14. *The Feeling of Rejection*

Produced by the National Film Board of Canada for the Canadian Department of National Health and Welfare. This film is the case history of a young woman who learned in childhood not to risk disapproval by taking independent action, showing the harmful effects of her inability to engage in normal competition, and analyzing the causes of her trouble. While outwardly seeming a quiet, not unusual girl, Margaret at 23 is afraid to stand up for herself in ordinary situations at home and at work. Flashbacks to her early years show how childhood conditioning contributed to her failure to develop into a self-reliant adult. Through private discussions with a psychiatrist and later through "group psychotherapy," she gains an understanding of the origin of her difficulties and becomes able to take part with confidence and satisfaction in the world of her fellow men.

RUNNING TIME: 23 minutes, sound, black and white.

15. *The Feeling of Hostility*

Produced by the National Film Board of Canada for the Canadian Department of National Health and Welfare. This film dramatizes factors producing resentment and hostility in personal relationships. The death of one parent results in over dependence on the remaining parent. The latter's remarriage discourages the child, Clare, in giving love and seeking affectional relationships.

This film is primarily intended to be used by psychiatrists for showings to groups of patients. Recommended also for college use in psychology, sociology, social service, nursing, teacher training, and similar courses. It is suitable for parent audiences, particularly if accompanied by a competent speaker. It is recommended for general interest audiences, if accompanied by professional explanation.

RUNNING TIME: 32 minutes, sound, black and white.

16. Over-Dependency

Produced by the National Film Board of Canada for the Canadian Department of National Health and Welfare. This film is the case history of Jimmy, an attractive young man whose life is crippled by behavior patterns carried over from a too dependent childhood. When we first see Jimmy, he is sick, though we later learn, his illness has no physical cause. He finds it difficult to face and deal with the ordinary problems of life and takes frequent refuge in the comforting of his mother, sister, and wife. But, through the patient retracing of childhood experiences in talks with a doctor, Jimmy comes to understand the emotional causes of his illness and fear, and he takes hold of life with new confidence.

Recommended for use by students of psychology, psychiatry, sociology, social service, nursing, and teacher-training and by parents, child study groups, teachers and medical organizations.

RUNNING TIME: 32 minutes, sound, black and white.

17. Broader Concept of Method, Part I

This picture presents a frank picture of the conventional teacher-dominated, lesson-hearing type of recitation and shows typical effects of this method upon student attitudes, responses, and learning. The film then shows alternative techniques to achieve broader educational objectives. In the class shown in this film an atmosphere of freedom of discussion leads to a suggestion for a class project that is readily accepted by the students.

RUNNING TIME: 13 minutes, sound, black and white.

18. Broader Concept of Method, Part II

This film continues the development of the project that was initiated by the class in Part I.

RUNNING TIME: 19 minutes, sound, black and white.

19. Teacher as Observer and Guide

Presents actual classroom practice, directs attention to the importance of the teacher as an observer and guide of pupil growth.

RUNNING TIME: 20 minutes, sound, black and white.

20. The City

This film ably shows the transition from primary to secondary modes of living, the problems and possible means of solution. Impacts of modern living upon personality are also emphasized. American Documentary Films.

RUNNING TIME: 30 minutes, sound, black and white.

21. *Autocracy and Democracy*

This film shows the experimental study of differing social climates of group. Film illustrates differences in group organized democratically, autocratically, and on a laissez-faire basis. Then the social climate of each group is changed, and the changes which took place within each group are noted and compared.

RUNNING TIME: 40 minutes, sound, black and white.

22. *Pre-School Adventures*

Activities in preschool laboratories of Iowa Child Welfare Research Station, showing major objectives in child developments.

RUNNING TIME: 42 minutes, silent, color.

23. *Problem Children*

This film concerns school adjustment problems and home background of two boys, one an over-aggressive bully and the other a shy and timid child.

RUNNING TIME: 20 minutes, sound, black and white.

24. *Wilson Dam School*

This film describes the progressive technique of this school.

RUNNING TIME: 22 minutes, sound, black and white.

25. *Brotherhood of Man*

That differences between the human races are superficial, accidental, and environmental are portrayed in this film. It explains that the differing skins of the races of mankind mean nothing. It shows how, through the driftings of the first peoples of the earth, there developed the three separate races of mankind. Further points out there are four distinct types of blood but all are found in all races and therefore, its difference has no racial relevance.

RUNNING TIME: 9 minutes, sound, black and white.

26. *House I Live In*

This academy award picture starring Frank Sinatra develops the theme of understanding religious and racial problems.

RUNNING TIME: 11 minutes, sound, black and white.

27. It's Your America

Against the background of war, Jeff comes to know the meaning of a free country, all from the Lincoln-head penny. From the words and symbols he realizes why we fought the war.

RUNNING TIME: 35 minutes, sound, black and white.

28. Frustration Play Techniques

A study of normal personality development in young children, and a demonstration of effect of intrusions, blocking and hostility games in the diagnosis of normal personality.

RUNNING TIME: 35 minutes, sound, black and white.

29. Near Home

The teaching techniques of a British social studies teacher. The community approach to education.

RUNNING TIME: 25 minutes, sound, black and white.

30. Playtown, U. S. A.

What a community did with the cooperation of the schools in providing recreational facilities for the children to reduce juvenile delinquency is the central theme. The film is especially useful for showing steps in social planning. Athletic Institute, Chicago.

RUNNING TIME: 45 minutes, sound, color.

31. Play Is Our Business

Produced by Play Schools of America in New York City. It shows what can be accomplished in underprivileged neighborhoods by Play Schools.

RUNNING TIME: 34 minutes, sound, black and white.

32. $1000 for Recreation

This film is invaluable for impressing people with the need for the community approach in planning for community welfare. It goes well with *Playtown, U. S. A.* Athletic Institute, Chicago.

RUNNING TIME: 23 minutes, sound, color.

33. Leadership for Leisure

This film shows how important trained leadership is to a community enterprise and what its omission will do. Athletic Institute, Chicago.

RUNNING TIME: 25 minutes, sound, color.

VI. RECORDINGS

Usually borrowers must provide their own record playing equipment. All recordings require 16-inch play-back at 33⅓ r.p.m. Recordings may be used for group meetings, teaching purposes, etc., *but not for broadcast. Unauthorized use of these recordings for broadcast can result in prosecution by their producers.*

1. Hi, Neighbor!

Produced by The National Mental Health Foundation. A series of ten 15-minute recordings, featuring Eddie Albert as narrator, calling attention to the mental health aspects of family life. By showing how specific personality problems can be solved through effective use of nonpsychiatric community resources, the series gives a practical approach to the continuing problem of safeguarding and promoting mental health. The plays do not minimize the role of the professional worker; rather, they attempt to provide listeners with ideas for solving the "little" problems of their daily lives so that the little problems do not snowball into big ones requiring professional help.

2. The Tenth Man

Produced by The National Mental Health Foundation. A series of thirteen 15-minute dramatic recordings designed to foster a better understanding of America's Tenth Man—the one person out of every ten who will need help for emotional problems.

3. Which World for Susan

A single, short dramatic recording of 13 minutes, 10 seconds from the above series, *The Tenth Man.* The central figure in this sketch is Susan, a 15-year-old high school girl who has been cut off from many normal social contacts. As a result she has taken to day dreaming, living in a world of fantasy instead of reality.

This recording is accompanied by a good discussion guide and is particularly suitable for parent groups, PTA's, and others interested in the problems of adolescence.

4. For These We Speak

Produced by The National Mental Health Foundation. A series of eight 15-minute recordings, dramatizing the problems of the mentally ill.

5. The Inquiring Parent

Produced by The National Committee for Mental Hygiene. A series of fourteen, 15-minute, interview type programs in which Dr.

Luther E. Woodward, well-known psychologist, discusses with parents ways of handling normal problems of children. Includes such topics as comic books, sex education, teen-age problems, allowances, etc.

6. *Mind in the Shadow*

The Columbia Broadcasting System's famed documentary program on mental illness, originally broadcast over the CBS network on February 2, 1949. A full hour-long program. It highlights the need for eliminating prejudice and fear and for attacking the problems of inadequate care for the mentally sick.

7. *The Impact of Culture on Personality Development in the United States.*

Produced by the Museum of Natural History. Running time: 12 minutes.

VII. OTHER SUGGESTED RESOURCES

For Club and Group Work:

1. *Guideposts to Mental Health*

A set of leaflets explaining the principles of good mental hygiene in daily living, prepared by the New York State Department of Mental Hygiene, $7.84 per 100 sets. The set of seven leaflets follows the gradual development of the personality from birth to old age, showing each period of life blending into the next in a continuous process of change and preparation for the future. Write to: State Department of Mental Hygiene, State Office Building, Albany 1, New York.

2. *Do We Forget Our Mentally Ill?*

A guide to action published in the December 1948 issue of *Platform* by the Club and Educational Bureaus of *Newsweek,* 25 cents a copy. Write to: *Newsweek,* Club and Educational Bureaus, 152 West 42nd Street, New York 18, New York.

3. *Where Do You Take Your Troubles?*

A program package for women's clubs prepared by the *Woman's Home Companion.* Write to: The Woman's Home Companion, 640 Fifth Avenue, New York 19, New York.

4. *Temperate Zone*

Three plays for parents about the emotional climate of the home, published by the National Committee for Mental Hygiene, producing packets $4.50 each. Planned for parent meetings, they should be followed by group discussion, for which a discussion guide is provided. Write to: National Committee for Mental Hygiene, 1790 Broadway, New York 19, New York.

5. *The Universal Heckler*

A mental hygiene play dealing with anxiety and its influence on human behavior. One of a series of scripts for community plays prepared by the American Theatre Wing, each script 25 cents. Write to: The American Theatre Wing, 730 Fifth Avenue, New York 19, New York.

6. *The Ins and Outs*

A 20-minute play for and about teen agers published by the National Committee for Mental Hygiene, producing packets $2.00 each. Dealing with the relationships of the "Ins" (those who belong to a group) with an "Out" who tries to belong but is excluded, it is planned for use in junior and senior high school classes and is accompanied by a discussion guide. Write to: National Committee for Mental Hygiene, 1790 Broadway, New York 19, New York.

7. *Parents' Ways with Children*

Four series of dramatizations and outlines for discussion groups published by the Elizabeth McCormick Memorial Fund, covering these topics: the preschool child, the school child, the adolescent, and child welfare. Complete set of all four series, $4.25. Each series may be purchased separately. Write to: Elizabeth McCormick Memorial Fund, 848 North Dearborn Street, Chicago 10, Illinois.

8. *Catalogue of Mental Health Pamphlets and Reprints*

A comprehensive listing of materials prepared and distributed by more than 60 federal, state, and voluntary agencies, compiled by the Publications and Reports Branch of the National Institute of Mental Health. Write to: Public Health Service, Federal Security Agency, Washington 25, D. C.

9. *Audiovisual Aids for Mental Hygiene and Related Areas*

Prepared by Elias Katz, Ph.D., and distributed by the New York State Department of Mental Hygiene. A list of charts and posters, exhibits and displays, film strips, and motion pictures, giving their sources. Write to: Division of Publications, New York State Department of Mental Hygiene, State Office Building, Albany, New York.

ONE SCHOOL'S STATEMENT OF ITS SOCIAL EDUCA-TION PROGRAM

C

THE CHARACTERISTICS OF A DEMOCRATIC SOCIETY AND THE DEMOCRATIC PERSONALITY

THE PHILOSOPHY AND PURPOSES OF THE UNIVERSITY SCHOOL [1]

A WAY of elaborating the meaning of democracy is to analyze the characteristics of an ideal democratic society and an ideal democratic personality. The staff has endeavored to make these analyses and have set up the characteristics in parallel columns. Attention has been called to the relationship of the individual personality and the society. The understanding of this interrelatedness is necessary to conceive of democracy as a way of life. The characteristics represent goals toward which we are striving rather than ends which we have already achieved.

I. MAINTAINING PERSONAL HEALTH AND PROMOTING HEALTHFUL LIVING

CHARACTERISTICS OF A DEMOCRATIC SOCIETY	CHARACTERISTICS OF A DEMOCRATIC PERSONALITY
A democratic society is concerned with the health of all of its members. There is increased sensitivity to the need for developing optimum physical health and freedom from anxiety and fear through the development of appropriate understandings, atti-	In order to maintain personal health and promote healthful living in the democratic society of which he is a member, the individual, using the method of intelligence in dealing with his problems and the problems of the group, seeks to:

[1] Prepared by the Faculty of the University School (Columbus, College of Education Press, The Ohio State University, 1948). Used by permission.

tudes, and habits. A democratic society seeks to promote healthful living conditions for all of its members by the use of the method of intelligence in dealing with problems of personal and community health and by cooperative planning for:

1. Sanitary, comfortable, well-designed homes.
2. Control and elimination of contagious and infectious diseases.
3. Adequate recreational facilities.
4. Programs of physical fitness in the school and community.

5. Adequate medical care.

6. Opportunity for out-of-doors life.
7. Safe and sanitary conditions for work.

1. Follow consistently and intelligently a program of good health practices.
2. Understand his basic needs of food, clothing, and shelter, and to meet them satisfactorily.
3. Establish a rhythm of work, rest, and relaxation.
4. Control emotions such as fear, worry, hate, jealousy, and joy.
5. Protect himself against infection.

6. Develop vigor, muscle tone, and reserves of energy.
7. Understand a wide range of variability that can exist within the concepts of normality and accept his own personal variations.
8. Understand his sex role and maintain good sexual adjustments.
9. Develop a zeal for promoting healthful living in the immediate and wider community.

II. ACHIEVING AND MAINTAINING A SENSE OF SECURITY

CHARACTERISTICS OF A DEMOCRATIC SOCIETY

A democratic society is concerned with the conditions of living which promote a sense of security for all its members. This implies:
1. Conditions of work which promote a feeling of social responsibility for the quality of work done.

CHARACTERISTICS OF A DEMOCRATIC PERSONALITY

In order to attain optimum development and growth in his sense of security in family, school, and wider community relationships, the individual:
1. Seeks to maintain affectionate relations with his parents and feels himself a part of the family group.

2. Cooperative planning and working together for the improvement of social and economic life.

3. Opportunities to secure sufficient economic goods to insure reasonable stability and a feeling of economic well-being now and in the future.

4. A feeling that the work which one does actually counts in enriching and improving social living.

5. Freedom in choosing work that holds a promise for social good and is best suited to one's abilities and interests.

6. Conditions of family and group life that help the individual achieve a sense of belonging.

7. Freedom of assembly and communication.

2. Seeks to establish sound relationships and to achieve status in an expanding social environment as relationships with his family develop and change.

3. Gradually achieves confidence through venturing into new social situations which contribute to his growth, and is able to make new friends.

4. Seeks acceptance by his age-mates, gradually develops a sense of belonging to the group, and forms friendships with members of both sexes.

5. Achieves self-confidence and poise in social and recreational situations.

6. Seeks increasing economic independence through participation in the economic life of family and community groups.

7. Has faith in his ability to grow and to enrich life for himself and others.

8. Believes that social and economic conditions can be bettered by man through the use of intelligence and cooperative endeavor.

9. Entertains new ideas and opinions, proposes courses of action, and assumes responsibility for his own beliefs and acts.

III. DEVELOPING AND MAINTAINING A SENSE OF ACHIEVEMENT

CHARACTERISTICS OF A
DEMOCRATIC SOCIETY

A democratic society recognizes that all of its members

CHARACTERISTICS OF A
DEMOCRATIC PERSONALITY

In order to develop a sense of satisfaction which comes through should possess a sense of satisfaction in accomplishment. It therefore seeks to provide:

1. Opportunities for successful participation in group activities directed toward common ends.

2. Adequate facilities for universal education.

3. A recognition of the social contributions of the individual to the life of the immediate and wider community.

4. Adequate facilities for games, sports, arts, crafts, and the like, and the opportunity to carry on creative activities.

5. A democratic way of life that is constantly being improved by the cooperative planning and participation of all.

6. Opportunity for each individual continuously to improve his status in economic and social life and increase his effectiveness as a contributing member of society on the level of his abilities, interests, and maturity.

7. An economic system that is organized so that each individual may become continuously more effective as a consumer of goods and services.

8. Opportunities for the participation of all in the political life of the community, state, and nation.

meeting social situations and life problems successfully, the individual seeks to:

1. Recognize his own needs and set valid goals for his efforts.

2. Make wise choices in terms of his own needs and the common good.

3. Plan, initiate, and carry activities to completion.

4. Evaluate the extent of his success in solving problems and achieving goals.

5. Participate constructively in socially significant activities in school, at home, and in community groups, and feel that his participation is worthwhile.

6. Live and work harmoniously with others, expressing in his group relations those attitudes which characterize a democratic personality.

7. Express his ideas and the ideas of his group effectively, using the various media of communication.

8. Engage successfully in a number of games, sports, hobbies, and creative activities.

9. Think clearly and effectively in solving both personal and group problems.

A. Do careful exploratory thinking in analyzing situations and identifying and defining problems.
B. Formulate hypotheses or suggested courses of action.
C. Assemble, select, and organize facts relevant to those hypotheses.
D. Judge hypotheses in terms of a sufficient range of data, and in light of consequences.
E. Integrate results of his investigation into an effective plan or solution.
F. Modify plans in terms of newly discovered facts or changing conditions.
G. Test decisions through action.
10. Discriminate between that which is socially desirable and will enrich life by extending the common good, and that which will impoverish life.

IV. DEVELOPING AND MAINTAINING EVER WIDENING AND DEEPENING INTERESTS AND APPRECIATIONS

CHARACTERISTICS OF A DEMOCRATIC SOCIETY

A democratic society is concerned that the living of all of its citizens be continuously enriched by the extension of the range of interests and appreciations. To meet this concern it aspires that all of its members seek:

1. Wholesome family life which promotes growth in interests and appreciations.

CHARACTERISTICS OF A DEMOCRATIC PERSONALITY

The democratic individual:

1. Develops a wide range of interests and appreciations and seeks continuously to extend and enrich them.

2. Understands and values the cultural heritage as a means of improving contemporary living.

2. Contacts with institutions and organizations which afford opportunities for the cultivation of interests and appreciations, including schools, churches, museums, libraries, musical organizations, recreational agencies, and the like.

3. Opportunities to extend the understandings and appreciations of the contributions of science, art, literature, and technology, to contemporary living.

4. Opportunities to understand and utilize the contributions that past cultures have made to the enrichment of living.

5. The fruits of creative effort and technological development for the purpose of enhancing personal and social living.

6. Opportunities for finding new interests and appreciations through vocations.

7. Experiences with freedom of choice which are meaningful to the individual.

8. Opportunities for wide contacts with cultures other than one's own.

3. Values creative activities as a means of enriching group life, and as a contribution to a happy, balanced personal life.

4. Cooperates with others in ventures which will provide opportunities for expanding and deepening interests and appreciations.

5. Utilizes his vocation as a means of discovering new interests and enhancing appreciation.

V. ACHIEVING A SOCIAL OUTLOOK ON LIFE

CHARACTERISTICS OF A DEMOCRATIC SOCIETY

A democratic society is one whose members consciously strive to understand more clearly and refine its basic ideals, and to apply them to the enrichment of living. To this end:

CHARACTERISTICS OF A DEMOCRATIC PERSONALITY

In a democratic society each member should develop a consistent and unified outlook on life and grow in sensitivity to the values and ideals of our democratic society, to the end that they affect behavior and constitute personal character. Such individuals:

1. Its members have mutual concern for optimal development, e.g., health, security, achievement, interests.

2. Its members seek to extend the use of the method of intelligence to the solution of problems of living in all areas, including the personal, social, aesthetic, civic, and economic.

3. Its members provide for the extension of common concerns through cooperative planning and working together for the improvement of living.

1. Respects the personality of others and accepts differences in interests, capacities, beliefs, standards, and customs.

2. Believes that every person should have the opportunity to develop to the extent of his capacities, regardless of race, color, class, family, occupations, wealth, sex, or place of residence.

3. Believes in the freedom of all individuals to think and act independently and creatively, so long as their actions extend the common good.

4. Believes in freedom of social interaction—to come and go, to converse, to assemble, to speak in public, and to listen without fear.

5. Endeavors to extend those freedoms to every member of society.

6. Has faith in the common man's capacity for intelligent judgment and action, and believes that each individual can make some contribution to group life.

THE GENERAL AND CONTINUING POINTS OF EMPHASIS

Implementing its statement on philosophy and purposes, and keeping in mind its view of the characteristics of the democratic society and democratic personality, the University School staff believes that certain types of curricular experiences should be emphasized at all levels in the school program. These experiences may be regarded as "threads of continuity" that give unity to experience, and hence are the concern of all teachers in every phase of the life of the school. Some of these "threads" are directly related to the major values of democratic living, while others are less directly related to such values even though they are of great significance in the development of all youth in all cultures. For the purpose of analysis, those continuous experiences are divided into two groups as follows:

A. **Continuous Curriculum Experiences Directly Related to Democratic Values:**

1. *Developing social sensitivity.* Experiences which develop an awareness of and responsiveness to, human values should be the constant concern of the school. Democracy is based upon the mutual respect for personality. This implies that each person will respect differences in social or racial groups and strive to elicit the unique contributions of others to the common good.

2. *Developing cooperativeness.* The school program should provide continuous opportunities for young people to work together toward common ends. This includes cooperative planning of programs in every area of school life, and the carrying out and evaluation of such programs.

3. *Developing the ability and zeal to utilize the method of intelligence in solving all problems of human concern.* The method of intelligence in a narrow sense includes the following factors: (A) recognizing problems, (B) formulating hypotheses, (C) discovering and organizing data, (D) arriving at tentative conclusions and acting upon them. In a wider sense it also means striving to employ reflective thinking in as many areas of living as possible, to develop a consistent pattern of behavior, and to regard truth as tentative and experimental, rather than absolute.

4. *Developing creativeness.* So far as possible, the school should provide experiences which demand novel adjustments to situations rather than those which emphasize routine and repetition. Good citizenship calls for individuals who have the ability to synthesize elements of experience, that are seemingly unrelated, into unified wholes. Such experiences are not confined solely to the arts but should characterize every area of school life.

5. *Developing skills in democratic living.* Students should learn to choose leaders in terms of the qualities needed for the particular job at hand. All students should have opportunities for leadership at their level and all should be able to cooperate with leaders. All should have a growing understanding of how to enlist effective participation for common ends by enabling all to take part in defining goals and in selecting their own part in working toward goals. Leaders should become increasingly skillful at distributing responsibilities in terms of the abilities, interests, and preferences of individuals so that all may participate effectively. Before the end of the high school years

these experiences in democratic participation should have reached out beyond the school into the community at many points.

6. *Interpreting democracy.* It is not enough that young people should live democratically. They should know what they are about, in the sense that they should become increasingly aware of the value of such living, not only within the school but in life outside of the school. This does not imply dreary "talks" by the teacher on the meaning of democracy, but rather that the democratic life of the school shall be so dynamically related to life outside that the students will be led to understand its meaning, and seek to extend it to all situations in which they are involved.

7. *Developing self-direction.* All experiences should be such as to aid in the process of "growing up," by which is meant the gradual development of mature relationship with others, that is, the cultivation of a growing sense of responsibility for one's own development in the light of a consistent set of values.

B. **Continuous Curriculum Experiences Implied by Democratic Values:**

1. *Developing communication skills and appreciations.* A democratic philosophy implies that all avenues of communication be free and open. In its narrower sense this may refer to the verbal skills of reading, writing, and speaking. In its broader reference it applies to all media that communicate human experience, including verbal languages, music, art, and the language of quantity.

2. *Developing skills in measurement and the use of quantitative symbols.* Recognizing that the language of number provides one of the major instruments for the organization of experience, opportunities must be provided for the development of mathematical skills and ability to apply them.

3. *Developing skills in utilizing goods and services.* In its widest sense this includes skill in using not only consumer goods, but also of such things as radio and movie programs and other forms of recreation and entertainment.

4. *Promoting social adjustments.* This may include establishing satisfactory relationships among members of the immediate school group and improving personal relationships such as boy-girl and family, and helping the individual find his place in the wider community.

5. *Promoting health and safety.* In a school devoted to the philosophy of optimum development of the individual, attention must be given enabling him to understand his biological nature and needs, and the opportunities and means his culture provides for satisfying these needs and maintaining life at the maximum level of physical efficiency.

6. *Developing vocational adjustments and standards.* The individual must have opportunity to investigate and explore the vocational opportunities open to one of his skills and capacities. This may range from becoming acquainted with various occupations at the lower levels of the school, to actual participation at the upper levels.
7. *Developing adequate recreational outlets.* It should be the function of the school not only to develop vocational interests, but also to develop recreational interests and hobbies, together with a knowledge of games that permit adequate physical activities leading to a healthy and well rounded personality at all stages of development.
8. *Developing standards of personal appearance and grooming.* While the major emphasis here must be made by one area, all teachers should be concerned with maintaining and developing standards in their class groups.

SUMMARY

In order to implement these general and continuing points of emphasis, it is necessary to provide a school program which will afford the finest opportunity for personal development and social living. To this end a school staff interested in both child development and social progress, and expert in the various fields of knowledge, is constantly on the alert to refine and improve the program of the school.

The basic idea which underlies the program is that the school should be the finest possible illustration of democratic living. This means that the program must be so organized and administered that youth will have an opportunity to learn to live democratically by the actual process of living together. Thus the school becomes not merely a preparation for life in a democratic society, but a social institution dedicated to the democratic way of life. This way of living together is difficult to explain in brief. Essentially, however, it means first that the school, through all that it does, strives to develop the capacities of each student. To this end it studies his physical, emotional, and intellectual needs, his interests and talents, and helps him grow normally along these lines. Second, the school recognizes that people develop only as they live and work with other people. Hence, cooperative planning, working, and evaluation are stressed to the fullest possible extent. Third, the school seeks to help each child grow in the ability to use reflective thinking in solving his problems, rather than to accept conclusions blindly. To this end, students are placed in situations which involve the making of choices: they are helped in making wise choices and in assuming responsibility for them. The program of democratic living within the school is the basis on which each student is encouraged and helped to develop and continuously to reconstruct and refine a philosophy of life. This process is carried on not only through the experience of living together, but also through considering, with the help of teachers, the full implications of the life of the school for the improvement of democratic living outside the school.

Conceived in this frame of reference, all relationships in the school should be the finest conceivable examples of democratic forces at work. The school should endeavor to preserve and continually reinterpret and recreate the democratic way of life, which has made public education possible. The University school has as its basic purpose the creating of a living and learning situation which will provide for the maximum development of the individual and the group in a democratic setting.

For the reader interested in accounts of the school's program in action, the following publications may be of value:

PRINTED MATERIALS

Class of 1938, University High School, The Ohio State University, *Were We Guinea Pigs?* (New York, Holt, 1938).

The Faculty of The University School, *How Children Develop: A Revision of Child Development Study.* Adventures in Education, University School Series No. 3 (Columbus, The Ohio State University, 1946).

Gilchrist, Robert S., Kahn, Lothar, and Haas, Robert. *Building Friendly Relations,* Adventures in Education, University School Series, No. 4 (Columbus, The Ohio State University, 1947).

Progressive Education Association, *Thirty Schools Tell Their Story, Adventures in American Education,* Vol. V. "University School of Ohio State University, Columbus, Ohio," (New York, Harper, 1943), pp. 738–758.

MIMEOGRAPHED MATERIALS

The Faculty of The Ohio State University School, *Curricular Experiences, Lower School,* rev. ed. (Columbus, The Ohio State University, 1948), Mimeographed.

The Faculty of The Ohio State University School, *Curricular Experiences, Upper School,* rev. ed. (Columbus, The Ohio State University, 1948), Mimeographed.

SELECTED EMPHASES CUR-
RENTLY USED FOR INTE-
GRATION OF CHILD,
SCHOOL, AND COMMUNITY

IT HAS BEEN a basic assumption throughout this discussion that the way to happy adulthood is to take up the slack in childhood adjustment. On the basis of this theory both cities, counties, and states have established child guidance centers. And in certain schools of education there is greater and greater emphasis upon the understanding of personality development, the recognition of unhealthy mental hygiene signs and the will to do something about them when recognized.

The signs that the child needs help are not always evident. In one sense children are luckier when they try to solve their problems by obvious misconduct. Parents and teachers then know at least that problems are too acute to be ignored. Whether these people know what to do is then the crucial point, but at least as Redl says, "they are not ignored." More pitiful are those whose troubles show in behavior patterns adults are not forced to notice. It is for these children that teachers should be especially alert. For as Redl says:

> Teachers occupy a strategic point in the life histories of disturbed children. They are often the first adults able to be objective who come in contact with children. Teachers may be the only trained people who ever observe an individual's conduct. Therefore, their skill in detecting deep-rooted difficulties and in taking the steps which will bring competent help may be decisive in the life of many a child.[1]

[1] Fritz Redl and W. W. Wattenberg, *The Mental Hygiene of Teaching* (New York, Harcourt, Brace, 1951), p. 339. Used by permission.

How shall teachers find indications of child needs is the next logical consideration. Redl lists five criteria as bases for teacher decision.

1. *Persistence of difficulty.* All children engage in misconduct at various times. The seriously disturbed child by contrast is likely to have difficulties which last for long periods.
2. *Behavior which does not yield to usual measures.* Teachers are ordinarily quite skillful in dealing with problem behavior of normal children. When a teacher who has had fairly consistent success in handling a particular type of behavior is at wits' end over one child, there is a strong suspicion the youngster needs help.
3. *Compulsive Conduct.* Seriously disturbed children simply cannot help but do certain things, even though there is no good rational reason—(they are)—the victims of psychological forces beyond the scope of regular classroom handling.
4. *Weak realization of reality.* Loss of contact with reality (excessive daydreaming), rage, suspicion, are all signs that a young person's actions are being determined largely by imaginary conception, which is the clearest sign of mental disease.
5. *Existence of objective difficulties.* These include such problems as arise when a child's size, physical, or learning ability, is all out of range of that of his classmates. Homes which are unstable emotionally as described in Chapter 5 also impose "heavy psychological burdens on children." [2]

PROCEDURES IN DEALING WITH THOSE WHO HAVE PROBLEMS

THE ROUTINE METHOD of dealing with these children, youth, and adults has been to administer a battery of tests in an attempt to gain a "profile" of the individual. Fortunately the day seems about over when *a* test, such as a so-called intelligence test is administered as the main or sole means of diagnosis and treatment.

Astute testers make every effort to see that the child involved is not panic stricken by tests. A relaxed, permissive atmosphere must prevail if the results are to be real measures, not panic-stricken emotional deeds.

Medical examination seems a good startingpoint, since extreme apathy may be traced to endocrine malfunctions as well as to feel-

[2] *Ibid.,* pp. 340–342.

ings of rejection and the like. Intelligence tests are a next logical kind of check-up on the child. Such tests as the Ohio State *Intelligence Test* which are not concerned with time limits and their frustrations appear to yield best results. Once a child is suspected as a seriously disturbed child, group test scores should not be relied upon.

The child's social adjustment quotients can be obtained by other tests which may be given in the classroom. Friendship, work committee, and play choices may be charted as shown in Chapter 12 in sociograms.

The Guess Who Test, The Wishing Well Test and the *Mooney Problem Check List* [3] are among the better tests of this sort. Since we have emphasized the need for knowledge of social status background, the *Sims* Score Card for scoring economic status may prove useful. The Fels Institute Test [4] on Parent-Child Relations, always reveals a wealth of information concerning interpersonal interactions among family members. Some students have used the *California Test of Personality* advantageously. Perhaps the most useful social acceptance test at the present time is the *Washburne Social Acceptance Inventory*. Projection tests such as *Rorschach* and *Thematic Apperception* tests also point out basic personality patterns of behavior.

It is important to remember, however, that one must have considerable knowledge both on how to give tests and how to interpret tests if he is to use them effectively and without actual harm to the student. For this reason such testing is usually done by the school psychologist or child guidance clinic.

What may teachers do about these problems once delineated is the next question?

The usual process in view of limited time per pupil and the need for specialized knowledge and technique is to "refer" the child to outside help such as the *visiting teacher,* the *school social worker, family agencies, child guidance centers,* the *school psychologist* or possibly *special schools.*

There are other procedures open also to the alert classroom teacher. Since these considerations are not so commonly known or indulged in by teachers and parents, we are selecting a few such areas to describe at some length.

[3] Samples of these tests may be obtained from the Bureau of Educational Research, The Ohio State University, Columbus.

[4] Fels Institute, Antioch College, Yellow Springs, Ohio.

The reader may well say that there is much overlapping, and he will be right. The main purpose in so presenting these avenues is that the people who are their proponents have done their experiential and experimental work from that point of view and in such a manner have written about it. All have subscribed to the basic tenets of the democratic creed and have accordingly keyed their climates in terms of the worth, dignity, and optimal development of children. No one is expendable in a democracy.

These approaches are in no way exhaustive, but selected on the basis of current movements and interests of teachers. While many of the activities suggest the need of a clinical setting, their *principles* without exception may be employed by all who deal with children and youth.

Likewise, there is no attempt to be exhaustive in reviewing methods of child study and therapy, rather it has been the aim to present newer and often less known attempts at understanding and adjustment.

THE PLAY THERAPY APPROACH TO CHILD STUDY

THE INTEREST in the play therapy approach to child and youth adjustment is a development of the last fifteen to twenty years. Though technically speaking it is an area for trained clinical workers, its principles have implications for the alert teacher and parent.

The approach appears to have developed from the realization that psychoanalytic methods were not successful with children because of their dependence upon the ability of the patient to express himself verbally. As Anna Freud has said,

> Everything is lacking in the situation of the child, which seems indispensable to that of the adult: insight into the illness, the voluntary decision, and the will to cure.[5]

Another danger in the analytic approach is that the therapist usually has some preconceived notion as to causes and may fit the child's problem into one of these handy classifications. Landisberg states: "Most earlier therapeutic work with children revolved

[5] T. Landisberg, *An Investigation Into the Nature of Non-Directive Play Therapy*, M. A. thesis. The Ohio State University, 1945, p. 2.

around the remodeling of parents and environment, completely excluding the dynamic growth potentialities of children." [6]

Play therapy may be directive or nondirective and applied to an individual or a group. Its nondirective form is most usable in the classroom or home.

It is based upon the fact that play is the child's "natural medium of self-expression" and its main objective is to aid the child in adjusting satisfactorily by gaining insight into his own behavior. Thus, it assumes that the child has within himself not only the ability to solve his own problems satisfactorily, but that he also has the growth impulse which makes mature behavior more satisfying to him than immature and unacceptable behavior.

Under such an approach the child is accepted as he is, without evaluation or pressure to change. Concern is with the immediate situation and the growth which is possible through the treatment of that situation.

Carl Rogers, who has been eminent as a definer and implementer of the approach lists four basic assumptions thusly:

1. The individual possesses a drive toward growth, health and adjustment.
2. Nondirective therapy stresses the emotional aspects of adjustment rather than the intellectual ones.
3. The method is principally concerned with the immediate situation rather than the emotional situations of childhood.
4. The treatment relationship itself is a growth experience.

Under the guidance of Rogers, Axline implemented these assumptions in her work with the Counselling Center of the University of Chicago.[8]

Axline's eight basic principles for implementing Rogers' basic assumptions are as follows:

1. The therapist must develop a warm, friendly relationship with the child in which good rapport is established as soon as possible.
2. The therapist accepts the child exactly as he is.

[6] *Ibid.*

[7] Carl Rogers, *Counseling and Psychotherapy* (Boston, Houghton Mifflin, 1942), pp. 1–25.

[8] Virginia M. Axline, *Play Therapy* (Boston, Houghton Mifflin, 1947), p. 75–76. Materials from Axline used by permission.

3. The therapist establishes a feeling of permissiveness in the relationship so that the child feels free to express his feelings completely.
4. The therapist is alert to recognize the feelings the child is expressing and to reflect these feelings back to him in such a manner that he gains insight into his behavior.
5. The therapist maintains a deep respect for the child's ability to solve his own problems if given the opportunity to do so. The responsibility to make choices and to institute change is the child's.
6. The therapist does not attempt to direct the child's actions or conversation in any manner. The child leads the way: the therapist follows.
7. The therapist does not attempt to hurry the therapy along. It is a gradual process and is recognized as such by the therapist.
8. The therapist establishes only those limitations that are necessary to another and therapy to the world of reality and to make the child aware of his responsibility in the relationship.

While it is desirable, it is not absolutely necessary to have a room set aside and furnished for the playroom. This is an indication of the vast possibilities of utilizing play therapy techniques with very small budget and space appropriations. Successful work has been reported from mere corners of a classroom or an unused nursery or kindergarten room.

Play materials which have been used with varying degrees of success include: nursing bottles; a doll family; a doll house with furniture; toy soldiers and army equipment; toy animals; play house materials, including table, chairs, cot, doll bed, stove, tin dishes, pans, spoons, doll clothes, clothesline, clothespins, and clothes basket; a didee doll; a large rag doll; puppets; a puppet screen; crayons; clay; finger paints; sand; water; toy guns; peg-pounding sets; wooden mallet; paper dolls; little cars; airplanes; a table; an easel; an enamel top table for finger painting and clay work; toy telephone; shelves; basin; small broom; mop; rags; drawing paper; finger painting paper; old newspapers; inexpensive cutting paper; pictures of people, houses, animals, and other objects; and empty berry baskets to smash. Checker games have been used with some success, but they are not the best type of material for expressive play. Likewise, mechanical toys are not suggested because the mechanics often get in the way of creative play.

Most needs exhibited by children can be met through the toys selected. The child may adapt the clay and drawing materials to any use he desires. The dolls provide opportunity for him to express affection, sex curiosity, and many other attitudes. Although almost any medium can be used for the expression of aggressive play, sand is a particularly excellent one. It can be "snow," "water," "burying ground," or "bombs."

For purposes of illustration, excerpts from three of Axline's case histories are presented below. The first two show the procedure in the individual therapy situation. The third is an example of group therapy which is somewhat different.

The Clay Man

Case of Joann—Age Six—Excerpt from Fourth Contact

Joann comes into the playroom, sits down at the clay table, plays with the clay. She is usually very quiet and does very little talking. Every time she comes in she plays with the clay and makes the same thing—a figure of a man carrying a cane. Each time, after he is finished, awful things happen to him. He is pounded full of holes, beaten with a stick, run over by the toy truck, buried under a pile of blocks. The fourth time the clay figures emerges, the therapist says, "Here comes that man again."

Joann: Yes. (Her voice intense, determined.)

Therapist: The man with the cane.

Joann: Yes. (She begins to punch him full of holes.)

Therapist: You're putting holes in the clay man.

Joann: Stab. Stab. Stab.

Therapist: You're stabbing him.

Joann: (in small voice): Ouch, you hurt me. (Voice changes.) I don't care. I want to hurt you.

Therapist: The clay man is crying because he is hurt.

Joann: (interrupting): I want to hurt him.

Therapist: You want to hurt him?

Joann: (emphatically): I don't like him.

Therapist: You don't like him?

Joann: I don't like him. I hate him. Look. This hole went clear through him. It went in his front and out his back.

Therapist: He gets holes punched clear through him. You fix him.

Joann: Yes. I'll tear his head off.

Therapist: You'll even tear his head off.

Joann: I know. I know. I'll put him clear down in the bottom of the jar and then I'll put the clay in on top of him and he'll

smother. (She tears him into little pieces and gouges her thumb through the clay and carefully puts the pieces down in the bottom of the jar and then covers it with all the rest of the clay.)
·*Therapist:* You tore him into little pieces and buried him in the bottom of the jar.
(Joann nods and smiles at the therapist. Then she goes over to the baby doll, pretends to feed it, holds it tenderly in her arms, puts it to bed, sets the table, and plays house very quietly.)

This was the pattern of Joann's behavior while in the playroom. She always made the clay man, tore him up, got rid of him, and then played with the baby doll. This continued through the the seventh interview and then she stopped making the clay man. She sometimes played with the clay, but made cats or toy dishes or candles. She was very fond of the doll and continued with this play.

COMMENTS

Joann was referred for play therapy because she seemed nervous, tense, withdrawn. What the real significance of this clay man was remained a mystery for a long time. Joann's father had been dead for three years, and she lived with her mother and a 10-year-old sister. There were no men in the family circle. However, her play seemed to indicate that she did have it in for some man. At the time of her play, identity of the man seemed unimportant. Joann never named him. The therapist did not pry into his identity, as it seemed important to Joann that she hide him behind anonymity. Finally Joann stopped making him. She showed considerable improvement in her attitude and behavior.

Later, after the therapy contacts had been terminated, the therapist met the mother, who told her that she was contemplating getting married again. "The only drawback," said the mother, "is the fact that he is a cripple and carries a cane. Joann acts as if she is afraid of him."

That seemed to be the explanation of the man with the cane. This man's intrusion into Joann's home must have been the reason for the terrible treatment he always got at Joann's hands.[9]

Sheila Straightens Her Rival's Hair

Case of Sheila—Age Seven—Excerpt from Fifth Contact

Sheila comes into the playroom, immediately picks up the nursing bottle and either holds it in her hand when she isn't sucking it or sets it on the table within easy reach. She comes over and

[9] Axline, *op. cit.,* pp. 180–182.

sits down at the table across from the therapist. She pulls the crayons and drawing paper toward her and begins to draw.

Sheila: Look, this is a clock. See, here are the numbers and here
are the hands and here are the insides of the clock.

Therapist: You drew all of it.

Sheila: Now you just watch this. (She bends over the paper and
draws a head with lots of long, red, curly hair.) Write down
here for me, "Mrs. B. (the house-mother) said, 'I don't want to
wash this awful hair.'" (Sheila laughs as the therapist writes
that down.)

Therapist: The house-mother doesn't like her hair. She doesn't
like to have to wash it.

Sheila: (picking up the black crayon and streaking through the
red hair): Look how dirty it is? Mrs. B. said, "I don't want to
wash this awful, dirty, old red hair!" This kind of bushy hair
ought to be red. Her eyes blue, huh? Shirley has red hair and
blue eyes. She's pretty too. And she's happy. But, I'm going to
make her cry. I'm going to draw three of her and they are all
going to be crying.

Therapist: Shirley has pretty red hair and blue eyes and she is
happy, but you are going to make her cry three times.

Sheila: Yeah. You just watch me. (Draws two more heads.) Look
at these tears. Aren't they big? Splash. Splash. Splash. Splash.

Therapist: You really are making her cry. You've fixed it so she
isn't happy now.

Sheila: I'll say not. And now I'm going to take the curl out of her
hair. See? (She draws very straight hair over the curls.)

Therapist: You wish she had straight hair?

Sheila: I sure do. It's straight now, though. See. And now you
look! (She takes her red crayon and draws long red lines down
the face.) Ha! I scratch her face. Now when her mother comes
she won't know her.

Therapist: You don't like having Shirley's mother come to see her.
You've scratched her face and taken the curl out of her hair so
her mother won't know her.

Sheila: (bitterly): Her mommy came last night to see her and
brought her a bag of candy, and Shirley wouldn't give me any.

Therapist: Shirley wouldn't give you any of her candy and you
didn't like that and you fixed her.

Sheila: (smiling): Look here. (She draws a brown ball in Shirley's
hair.) Chewing gum in her hair! (Sheila is quite happy about
it.)

Therapist: You've put some chewing gum in her hair. You're
spoiling those red curls.

Sheila: They aren't pretty now, are they?

Therapist: They aren't pretty now.

Sheila: (laughing happily): Now write, "Cry, baby, cry, wipe your teary eye, point to the east, point to the west, point to the one that you like best." and then you write up here like Shirley says it—write, "I like Sheila the best!" (Therapist does as she is asked.)

Therapist: You really want Shirley to like you?

Sheila: (sighing): Yeah! (She picks up the bottle and sucks on it contentedly.)

COMMENTS

Sheila was referred for play therapy because she was aggres- sive, jealous, quarrelsome, sullen, and antagonistic to every sug- gestion. She had been placed in the private children's home when she was four years old. Her parents had been divorced. The mother had remarried and had moved to another town and seldom came to see Sheila. The father was in the navy and too far away to come and see her. She never heard directly from him, although the ma- tron at the home said that he did send money to the home for them to buy "whatever extras the children were allowed."

This is a rather simple example of how children will use the play period to express the feelings that are close to them. Shriley was a very pretty little girl with beautiful long, red curls. Her mother came to visit her every night, and she managed to main- tain a good mother-daughter relationship even though she had been forced to place Shirley in the children's home temporarily after her father had died. Everyone loved Shirley. She was a quiet, sweet, well-behaved little girl, inclined to be smug and self- centered. On the other hand, Sheila was a very unattractive child, with stringy mouse-colored hair, and hazel eyes. She was above average in intelligence, but was failing in school because of her troublesome behavior.

Her favorite toy while in the playroom was the nursing bot- tle. Every time she came into the room she snatched up the bottle and sucked on it intermittently during the whole therapy hour.

In the rather pathetic incident related above, the child draws her antagonism for her rival in the home. Her jealousy was so close to the surface that she acted out her feeling with the crayons —three times for added emphasis. It may seem that jealousy over pretty curls is a trivial thing, but to Sheila it was very important. It seemed to do her good to get this feeling out of her system, because she was able at the end of the hour to express a positive feeling about Shirley. She said she wished that Shirley liked her.[10]

This example also illustrates the channeling of behavior into socially acceptable outlets.

Richard, Jack, and Philip Gain Courage from One Another

This example of group therapy shows how the children in a group sometimes gain courage to do things that ordinarily they might be a bit reluctant to do.

Richard, Jack, and Philip were eight and nine years old. They went to the same school, were in the same grade, and were very good friends. The therapist saw all three of them individually for several weeks before they were placed in the group at their request. Their problems were similar—bed wetting, negativism, failure in school. Richard arrived first. While waiting for the others, he got out the checkers and asked the therapist to play a game with him. She did. During the play, Richard talked about school and the games they play at recess. He seemed very calm and relaxed. Then Jack came in. He sat down at the table.

Jack: Where's the nursing bottle? (He reaches over and gets one.)
Richard: Get me one. (Jack hands him one.)
Jack: Hurry up with that old game. (The game is finished as quickly as possible.)
Jack: (sitting down across from the therapist and pushing Richard off the chair): Let me play!
Therapist: You want to play a game of checkers like Richard did?
Richard: (sucking on nursing bottle): Me 'ittle baby.
Jack: (grinning): Yeah. Me, too. Play me a game of fast checkers.
Therapist: You want me to play with you?
Jack: Yes. Come on. (Arranges the checkers.)
Richard: He wants you to play with him because you just played with me.
Jack: Sure. You wanted to play with her, didn't you?
Richard: And because I did it, you want to do the same thing.
Jack: I like to do the same thing you do. I'm jealous. (He laughs.)
Richard: You're jealous all right. (Laughs.) So am I.

(The therapist plays the game with Jack and shortens it to a minimum. Richard and Jack talk back and forth about one another's attitudes. The therapist missed getting this in her notes because of the game, but it certainly was accurate evaluation of

[10] Axline, *op. cit.,* pp. 178–180.

one another's motives. Finally, halfway through the game Richard gets down on the floor and begins to crawl.)

Richard: Me baby. Tum pway!

(Jack got up, left the game unfinished, and got down and crawled around after Richard. Richard lay down on his back and drank from the bottle. Philip came in and got a nursing bottle too. The three boys spent the rest of the hour crawling around on the floor, talking baby talk, and finally squirting water on one another. They laughed and had a hilarious time. When the hour was up Richard said goodbye to the therapist and left. Philip and Jack poured the remainder of the water in their bottles on the floor and ran out. Jack came back in with the mop that stood in the hall and, with much giggling, mopped up the water and then he left.)

COMMENTS

This excerpt shows the suggestive element that is sometimes present in a group situation. One boy wants to do something because another has done it. Of these three boys only Jack had previously had the courage to pour the water on the floor. It may have been that the similarity of their problems caused the similarity of their actions in the playroom.

As has been pointed out, checker games are not the best kind of material for expressive play, but this contact shows the possibilities of even this type of material when the permissiveness and freedom of the relationship are established. One of the disadvantages of this sort of game, when used in group therapy, is the possibility of the therapist being drawn into the play with one individual and consequently centering the therapy around one child in the group.[11]

The people who are closely associated with our schools today know that the primary need for the successful education of the children is sound mental health for all. A teacher who is frustrated and worried, cannot do a satisfactory job. A child whose emotional life is in conflict and turmoil is not a satisfactory pupil.

Thus far play therapy has been used chiefly in clinics to which children are brought. These children are considered socially maladjusted or have learning blocks. But more and more teachers and parents are becoming interested in learning about and experimenting with the basic principles of play therapy.

[11] Axline, *op. cit.,* pp. 208–210.

Winifred Tom, who investigated its implications for kindergarten education, sums up her study in these words: [12]

1. By providing for play, teachers are helping children to live well with themselves and with others . . . play is a process by which children grow and mature. Play develops muscles and coordination as children engage in running, skipping, climbing, galloping. Play builds creative imagination as children (at whatever age) manipulate play materials and rearrange possibilities to suit their individual desires. Play helps children become acquainted with their physical and social environments as they reproduce and dramatize their daily experiences. Play rounds out personality as it gives children the opportunity to be what they want to be in a world of adults and restrictions. . . . As Hymes says: [a] Good play can lessen the feelings of fear and anger and inadequacy. It can provide power—not so that children will learn it and use it, ruthlessly, but so that children can have it and not be drawn into seeking it unreasonably, unconsciously, deviously, all the rest of their days. It can provide control, so that children do not have to bring a load of fear to all they do. It can provide a safe world for the feelings, so that children do not have to carry confusion inside of them, ever ready to pop out unreasonably and inappropriately. It can provide a world where, for a time, cleanliness and order and politeness and respect do not have the standing that they do in real life,—not so that the child can learn to escape the force of these desirable patterns, but so that he can learn to accept them comfortably, easily, gladly. Here is a major learning. Through good play, children can learn to live with others and learn to live in this world as this world operates.

2. Play therapy has possibilities for solving minor problems as well as deep-seated maladjustments . . . play goes on whether under guidance or not. A teacher cannot assume the role of a clinical therapist, in a classroom situation, . . . (she can, however, if aware of play therapy principles) use children's play as a lead to where guidance is needed. . . . The use of play therapy then could extend to the prevention of serious maladjustment through timely detection and referral of the child, . . . and when the problem seems more immediate or less deep-seated, the opportunity to play is itself a remedy.

[12] Winifred K. Y. Tom, *Play Therapy: Its Implications for Kindergarten Education,* M. A. thesis, The Ohio State University, 1949, under guidance of Dr. Leland B. Jacobs, Professor in Elementary Education. Used by permission.
[a] J. L. Hymes, Jr. "Why Play Is Important," *Parents Magazine,* Vol. 24. (November 1947), pp. 124–125.

Though the study was done in relation to kindergarten education, the implications are much the same for all ages. If special emphasis seems to be beamed, at elementary years, this is done advisedly. Personality difficulties do not spring full blown, as from the forehead of Jove, at early or later adolescence. They grow slowly but steadily from infancy and childhood bases. Prevention in these years is our greatest hope. For here we may hope to take up the slack. There is no period of greater teacher importance than these years in the development of the self. Elementary teachers are second only to parents in impact upon this development. Theirs is a great and thrilling responsibility.

A DANCE APPROACH TO CHILD ADJUSTMENT

DANCE THERAPY

ONE OF THE NEWER and equally fascinating developments in study and therapy with children is the area of body movement and rhythm. Though the dance in one form or another is as ancient as social living itself, its history is an intriguing tale of an often "discriminated against" area.

After its severance from religious ritual it has most frequently been associated with licentiousness in entertainment. Schillinger [14] points out that in Egypt the influence of the Near East and the Orient was early seen in the entertainment dancers hired by the nobles for their pleasure. The history of the dance in the Roman era is one intimately connected with all forms of entertainment, especially those of the culturally debauched period of the Empire. It is this ancient connection which present-day artists and teachers of dance are still fighting to break. The layman's general attitude toward the dance is that it is either of the ballroom or of the music hall—or at best the spectacle of the ballet. In the last thirty years, since the time of Isadora Duncan, great strides have been made in the recognition of the dance as art form, though the work is just begun.

Likewise the study and use of body movement, rhythm, and the dance as a means to self-insight into needs and possibilities is an even more recent development. It appears to be most used and with most success in kindergarten and elementary grades. Where

[14] Edna Schillinger: "American Opinions on Dancing," *Health and Education,* Vol. 17, No. 6 (June 1946), p. 337.

FUNCTIONS OF THE TEACHER	PRINCIPLES WHICH GUIDE PRACTICE
A. To develop a warm friendly relationship with children	1. Good rapport must be established. 2. Children need affection and attention.
B. To accept children emotionally, rejecting none as hopeless or unworthy.	1. Each individual is worthy of respect. 2. Each child should be guided to alienate emotional problems.
C. To create a permissive atmosphere for expression.	1. Children have many problems resulting from want of love and care, from unreleased emotions and tensions, from wanting to achieve independence, from conflicts within the family.
D. To recognize and reflect feelings expressed by children.	1. The child is capable of gaining insight into his own behavior. 2. The child is capable of understanding his own emotional problems.
E. To respect children's ability to solve problems.	1. The child is capable of solving his own problems if given opportunity to do so.
F. To let children grow at their own rate, in their own pattern.	1. Each individual is unique, has potentialities to be developed. 2. Each individual develops within his own growth pattern.
G. To let children work at their own speed.	1. Frustrations, inhibitions are often caused by impatient adults, time pressures, unnatural demands, external rewards, etc.
H. To establish limitations	1. Permissiveness does not include willful injury of self or property. 2. Permissiveness implies distinctions between liberty and license.

Play Therapy [13]

DIRECT EXPERIENCES	VICARIOUS EXPERIENCES
1. Meet people, be interested in them.	1. Read Adams, *Educating America's Children*.
2. Develop attitude of friendliness.	
3. Observe good teachers at work with children.	
1. Respect people in spite of their faults.	1. Read, Johnson, *People in Quandries*.
2. Accept people as they are, try to understand behavior.	English & Pearson, *Emotional Problems of Living*.
3. Work with children in small groups or individually.	American Council of Education, *Helping Teachers Understand Children*.
1. See psychiatrist or psychologist. Express feelings. Get help in analyzing own behavior and attitudes.	1. Read, Axline, *Play Therapy*. Alschuler, *Painting and Personality*. Allen, *Psycho-therapy and Children*.
2. Help equip a play environment.	
3. Study children's art work.	
4. Watch and listen to children engaged in dramatic play.	
1. Practice reflecting feelings to adults and children.	1. See movie, *Snake Pit*.
2. Observe play therapy sessions.	
1. Observe children working in a permissive and non-permissive environment.	1. Read, Asco, *Toward Better Teaching*. Rosenblats, *Literature as Exploration*.
2. Help children think reflectively on stories heard, movies seen, and in solving problems.	
1. Make sociograms.	1. Read: Olson, *Child Development*.
2. Keep anecdotal records.	
1. Work out time schedule for a classroom. Allow children time to work and clean up.	1. Lectures, conferences, discussions on curriculum building, time scheduling, etc.
1. Take charge of work period.	1. Use films, filmstrips, slides, pictures, charts, etc.
2. Observe techniques used by teachers in giving help to children who seek it.	

[13] Winifred K. Y. Tom. *op. cit.,* p. 123.

the atmosphere is relaxed, permissive, and democratic, the very young and slightly older children respond freely to the suggestion of the music teacher or physical education teacher that they "act out" or just "do" what the music says. Though research studies are at present not completed in the area, there are those who are using this approach to help children and adolescents to release tensions, to do away with self-consciousness, and to attain poise.

In urging a dance approach to education, Barbara Mack[15] suggests that the concept implies a number of things not only in teaching the dance as an art but as an aid to personal adjustment. This concept would,

1. Rid the dance of that strange aura of mysticism which has so long kept it from functioning in the day-to-day living of students.
2. It would no longer need to be an exalted form of art reserved for those whose life work it is.
3. It would assume its rightful place as a means of communicative expression inherent in each of us.
4. Evaluation of teacher competency and student progress would be based, not on performance relative to theatrical or concert standards, but on the contribution of the activity to the total education of the student.

Even more important, the focus of dance activity would be on the student, which is where the focus for any kind of education should be. The criterion for the conduct of dance activities would be the needs of the student. The teacher would ask herself daily: "What is it I want for Mary and Susan and Patrick, and what do they want for themselves?" And then: "How can I help them to attain these goals through movement?"

Are these goals to be technical or performance skills? They may be if Mary and Susan and Patrick have examined their own interests and desires and found those to be paramount. It is more likely, however, that Mary and Susan and Patrick would want and need other attitudes, understandings, and skills more urgently in order to be the competent, integrated, happy young women and men they want and need to be. Regardless of their professional or vocational goals, they need to understand themselves and their as-

[15] Barbara Mack, "A Dance Approach to Education," *Health, Physical Education, and Recreation,* Vol. 20, No. 10 (December 1949), p. 640.

sociates more completely. They need to learn to work effectively
and creatively both alone and with others. They need to look at
themselves and their accomplishments critically and objectively,
with the complete assurance that they and their contributions are
not only accepted, but welcomed and esteemed. They need to learn
of the depth of feeling—the true impetus for dance—within each
of them, and of the satisfaction of communicating that inner wealth
to others through total body movement.

Actual methods for a "dance approach to education" are as
varied as the individual situations themselves. Each girl or boy has
a personality uniquely his own, the result of all that she or he, and
she or he alone, has experienced. Each girl or boy will respond differently and to different kinds of situations in terms of the peculiar
conditionings which are his or hers. Some students will accept and
use the stimulation of music; others will find their motivation in a
painting. Some will find movement a substitute for words in the
telling of a story; while others will discover that movement can
transcend the spoken language in the expression of an emotional
experience. The implication here is that the dance opportunities for
any group of girls or boys need to be varied so that each girl or boy
may find at least one stimulus for release in movement in terms of
which he or she can then translate other problems. Some students
will always think and understand in terms of rhythm, others in
terms of dramatic idea, etc.

Similarly, the activity itself needs to be varied. Most students
feel the need for a basic understanding of how the body works along
with opportunities to make that body express their own ideas and
feelings.

The real crux of the method problem lies in the extent to
which the student can be led to an understanding of his or her
own needs and of the possibilities for meeting those needs through
dance activity. Many a conscientious student has labored through
technique sessions and has busily created fine dance studies in answer to teacher-posed problems, without ever seeing the activity
in terms of his or her own physical-social-emotional development.
Because of limitations of time and numbers, the teacher has felt
that she must "get the group moving" as quickly as possible. It may
be that haste needs to be made more slowly here, for only as the
class discusses and sets its own objectives can the teacher have any
assurance that her students are more than dutifully carrying out

assigned tasks. Time spent in enlisting class interest and commitment to self-assigned goals may pay rich dividends in actual growth. Any learning activity needs to be purposeful to the participants if it is to achieve its aims.*

As individuals move toward their objectives, they need time to assess their own progress, to set new goals, and to plan ways to reach those goals. Those who are interested will find much stimulating material concerning this medium in such materials as: Gertrude G. Bunzel and Joseph H. Bunzel, "Psychokenetics and Dance Therapy," *Health and Physical Education,* March 1948, Vol. 10, No. 3. The Bunzels elaborate on field methods and courses of study by developmental levels.

Though body movement as a means of personal adjustment, as illustrated by the above, is in its initial stages of development, it offers a challenge as a means of catharsis, release of tension through interpreting needs in a new medium, and educative outcomes such as better coordination at all levels. As coordination increases, skills such as reading, writing, and the like profit often in marked and seemingly sudden fashion. Continued research and experimentation in the area are highly desirable.

SCHOOL CAMPING

SINCE THE BEGINNING of the school camping movement the philosophy of its administrators has been "bringing the children back to the land" [16] through a learning by doing program. A well-balanced educational program in the classroom includes group planning, sharing, discussion and evaluation. These are essentials of camp living also. A program of nature study and science can get off to a better start if the boys and girls, under guidance, are able to see the out-of-doors as a resource in studying and solving problems.[17]

Today the opinion that children need a wider range of experience within the school program is commonly held by educators. When instructional procedures are confined to the classroom, many fundamental learnings and contacts essential to a well-rounded de-

* Adapted from Mack, *op. cit.* By permission.
[16] *Proceedings (A.A.H.P.E.R.) Year Book* (Washington, American Association of Health, Physical Education and Recreation, 1949), p. 254.
[17] Helen K. Makintosh, *Camping and Outdoor Experiences* (Washington, Government Printing Office, 1947).

velopment of the child are not available to him. This was effectively pointed out by John Dewey recently when he said, "The average American child seldom comes in direct contact with nature. In school he learns a few dates from books, to press a button, to step on an accelerator; but he is in danger of losing contact with primitive realities—with the world, with the space about us, with fields, with rivers, with the problems of getting shelter and of obtaining food that have always conditioned life and that still do." [18]

New York City was one of the first to experiment with this new type of education. In 1934 the city public schools in cooperation with other public agencies decided to try a new plan. They started with the summer play school that was scheduled for two days a week until the middle of August. From that time on until school opened in September, the camp was open every day. A number of private schools in various parts of the country maintain summer camps which provide for some of the children and staff members a continuity of experience. In some of these schools, like the Manumit School of Pawling, New York, and the Oogantz School of Pennsylvania, the school work of the winter is closely related to summer activities. In others, there is no apparent continuity, but the opportunity for teachers to know youngsters in various kinds of situations makes a real contribution to a better understanding of the whole child, and thus better educational procedures.

An extensive discussion of one state's program in action, including such important details as objectives, organization and evaluations, is to be found in Appendix C.

ROLE PLAYING AS AN ADJUSTMENT TECHNIQUE

THE PLAYING of roles (sociodramà) as a newer means of group discussion of a problem is increasing in popularity. Owing to its flexibility in structure and function, it can be used at any age level and with most areas of discussion.

To begin a sociodrama, the group needs a problem of common interest. Unless the situation is completely unstructured, the teacher-leader will know the general area of concern, for example, a campus problem, school discipline, school-community relations,

[18] Lloyd B. Sharp and Ernest G. Osborne, *Schools and Camping,* Reprinted from *Progressive Education* (April 1940).

faculty attitudes, and so on. As problems are named by group members, they are listed on a blackboard, after which the leader makes a selection of the most suitable for study. All of this must be done with dispatch, else time will permit little demonstration. Other things at all equal, it is best to work on a process involving various persons in a series of interrelated acts.

To illustrate what has been said, consider a concrete case. Among the problems listed by a graduate class in education, one concerned a Negro teacher in a Detroit school. This problem was contributed by the principal of the school who seemed to have no inhibitions in discussing it. The Negro teacher was a Wayne University senior, a math major and an honors' student. She was described as a very well-appearing person, cooperative and professional in her outlook. She was the first and only colored teacher in this all-white school, hired in an emergency situation on a half-year contract and without tenure. These facts were contributed by the principal in response to the leader's request for "more information" about the teacher. The principal was guided in the narration and kept from telling how the problem developed or how it all came out.

With this background sketched, the principal was asked if he had interviewed the teacher applicant before accepting her on the staff. His affirmative reply created a situation for the first sociodrama. What would this interview be like? Assuming that all credentials were in order, recommendations good, etc. what would the applicant be asked? What would she ask about? How would the interview be conducted? And then, to get things going, who will be the principal in this case? The teacher applicant? As each participant was selected, his orientation was tested by a few questions on the school situation, his role, and the like.

After this scene had been run, the class was asked for comments. What was good about it? What could be done better? When hands went up on the second question, a student was invited to show the class what he had in mind, to play a character part, and the interview was run again. By this time, the atmosphere had changed from one of doubt and embarrassment to that of serious problem solving, with students taking turns at showing the class how the situation should be handled. Few discussants saw any unusual problem in the case, treating it as a rather routine job-seeking interview. Finally, a Negro student in the principal's role depicted a new level of sensitivity when he began a line of questions on how the teacher would react to prejudice, on whether she could do good work if conditions were adverse.

At about this point, the real principal was asked to tell what had happened next in the case. He was stopped as soon as he had said that "pupils began to talk about the teacher." "What did they say? Did some disagree?" We ran this scene several different times, sounding out class ideas as to feeling tones in the school. Next, the principal said, "A boy told his mother about the teacher and she came storming into my office, demanding the teacher's discharge." This scene differed from others in that it called for expressive action of an emotional sort, hence was most revealing of student role-playing ability. It raised, of course, a very crucial question for all teachers, namely: how does one handle an angry parent, a parent with whom it is impossible to reason?

Other scenes followed, ending with a community meeting called by the president of the school board, the final action in the real-life case. The class was asked to cast this meeting, to say who had a stake in the matter and should be represented. To keep thought clear, the teacher-leader drew a blank diagram on the board, similar to Figure 32. As the class named individuals (teacher, principal, mother, etc.) the interests (P.T.A. Property Owners' Association, C.I.O., N.A.A.C.P., Urban League) they were written in, an exercise that always proves to be a good test of what students know about the community where they live.

In addition to its wide applicability, the sociodrama is unique in the skill training it provides. Consider a single composite category, one much neglected in conventional teacher education, face-to-face communication skills. We do not mean the academic patter of the classroom but rather the ways in which people, via voice, words, and gestures, relate themselves to people, seek to give them the guidance they may need.

Given a recording of student participation in several sociodramas, what can be said about voice characteristics? The speed of sound, rhythm, pitch, intensity, quality, and changes? Next, what is the literal meaning of words, the precision of language as a tool of thought? Third, the projective significance of words? Does word usage tend to further thought, offering wide choice ranges, or does it stop thinking, closing doors before they are fully opened? In the fourth place, what is the structure of the language— pedantic, immature, florid, illiterate, compulsive, confused? Fifth, what of its emotional content—slips of the tongue, guarded values, irrelevant wanderings, sudden shifts in ideas, repetitions, idiosyncratic usages? Obviously, such analysis has a place in teacher-leader training. It can provide a firm foundation for much group and individual guidance work.[19]

[19] Lloyd Allen Cook and Elaine Forsyth Cook, *A Sociological Approach to Education* (New York, McGraw-Hill, 1950). Used by permission.

Additional information on sociodrama may be secured from the reading list at the end of the chapter as well as a movie entitled *Role-Playing.* The movie is put out under the auspices of the National Education Association in cooperation with the University of Michigan and the Institute of Group Dynamics at Bethel, Maine. It demonstrates objectives, techniques and actual scenes from the Bethel training center.

BIBLIOTHERAPY

ANOTHER AREA of interest and expansion is that of bibliotherapy. This is a big name for the practice of having children use reading as a means of preventing and solving personal problems of adjustment. To some extent this has always been done, but recent work in the field gives promise of a scientific approach to the use of books.

At present bibliotheraphy is developing along two main lines. The first is its use in hospitals as an aid in return to mental and physical health. The second, and our concern, is its use in education to prevent and alleviate mental hygiene problems. In this connection its purpose is much the same as that of counseling or psychotherapy, namely, to assist the individual to change attitudes and behavior into socially acceptable channels.

Where education aims at the whole child, simply reading books for the sake of reading books is of little moment. Such a usage does not contribute assistance in a mental hygiene light. Reading materials can, however, be used both for the normal child who may be experiencing mild behavior difficulties as well as in special classes in psychological adjustment.

For example, Mrs. Edna D. Baxter has worked with such classes in the elementary schools of Englewood, Colorado. The classes met once or twice a week with discussion and activity centered around certain social adjustments which the children needed to make, such as getting along with playmates, parents, and teachers. In these classes work books were used by the children under teacher guidance.

Interesting experiments are reported by Dr. Moore of the Catholic University of America. He used stories in which a particular child's problem was featured incidentally.

Where adolescents and adults are concerned, books seem most

useful in presenting value concepts and structuring of them into a philosophy of life.

Writings which reveal this relatively new approach include: a series of articles by Alice Bryan to be found in the *Journal,* Vol. LXIV and LXV and entitled: "Can There Be a Science of Bibliotherapy?" October 1939; "Personal Adjustment through Reading," August 1939; "Psychology of the Reader," January 1939; and "The Reader as a Person," February 1940.

For a systematic treatment of this more insightful approach to all literature, read and enjoy Louise Rosenblatt's, *Literature as Exploration* with special emphasis on part three, "Sensitivity as a Basis for Insightful Adjustment."

ART EXPERIENCES AS A MEANS OF PERSONALITY INTEGRATION

MANY PEOPLE are increasingly interested in art activity as one important aspect of full mental, emotional, and social growth and adjustment. Many, too, are coming to think and say that in line with this viewpoint art education must shift its emphasis from the merely artistic product to the arts as a process of human action and social development. Where this has been done in classrooms, in homes, and in therapy situations, exciting results have been obtained.

In the relaxed atmosphere of such an art room or corner the child may find the freedom he needs, in his choice of paint, materials, and subjects. Here teachers allow freedom in the child's work, since they are chiefly concerned with his creative growth; here the art work of many is displayed rather than the work of one or two outstanding children. Such a situation provides a great and exciting field of expression, exploration, release, and enjoyment.

One teacher reports that over a two-year period she worked with a child who stuttered so badly he could scarcely speak in his regular classroom. In the permissive atmosphere of art work, this child not only spoke often but with no hesitation. Hospitals also have found creative art activity to have curative values.

Something which can be of such mental health value in a curative fashion is worthy of extended analysis and use as a preventive and educative measure. To teachers using art as such means, art becomes an organized body of experiences dealing with the meeting of human needs through the use of materials and participation in situations full of information, appreciation, and feeling. These experiences contribute greatly to integrative living. Art, then, is seen to be an active agent in curriculum integration, thus contributing much to the realization of the broad objectives of general education. It becomes a powerful educational instrument in such fundamental tasks as the promotion of democratic living (the planning, sharing, contributing, and evaluating processes) in the learning group. It accomplishes much toward the integration of the pupil's personality as it frees him from tensions, affords him a sense of achievement, and gives him a feeling of personal worth. It can vitalize the curriculum by achieving integration, motivation, enrichment, and balance in teaching. It is functional art and art to be used by all that will reach these heights.

Creative learning and expression can open the way to functional learning which is so necessary for the total development of the person, and it is in this respect that art can make valued contributions. "When arts are pushed into a minor place, it is the emotional side of human life which suffers." [20] Art functions in the pupil's lives through their informational experiences and activities that accomplish individual and social objectives such as:

1. The development of a social organization in which children work together democratically toward common values and goals, and respect the work and rights of others.
2. The attainment of increased art knowledge through creative activities.
3. The increased understanding of ideas developed as a result of school experiences.
4. The increased ability to use tools and materials.
5. The development of hand skills necessary to art experiences.
6. The development of muscular control in using art skills and mediums.
7. The understanding of the safety aspect in the handling of tools.
8. The ability to critically evaluate one's own work and that of others.
9. The growing appreciation of good workmanship.
10. The ability to develop qualities of leadership.
11. The increasing understanding of sources of aid in solving problems which arise.

[20] James L. Mursell, "The Arts in American Education," *Teachers College Record,* Vol. 46 (February 1945), pp. 285–292.

12. The increased responsibility for the care and economical use of art materials.

It thus becomes a part of the school's planning to set up experiences which will provide opportunities for the child to reconstruct his previous experiences for further learning situations. The concept of developing readiness enters in here, as some children obviously do not have a sufficient base of previous experiences upon which to operate. This lack must be remedied by the teacher's providing many meaningful experiences which will help the child to mature. In Mursell's philosophy of an art program we find the idea of "the elaboration of a common policy which would liberate, inform, cultivate, and guide the emotional side of living." [21] He would bring out this philosophy in the development of a three point program:

1. Promote individual artistic creative activities on the part of the pupils on the most ambitious scale possible. Unless the arts are possessed as personal possessions they instantly lose their power, and the individual creative endeavor is an avenue to the personal possession of the arts for which there is no adequate substitute.
2. Promote activities in the way of artistic participation. The experience of actually projecting works of art in one's own proper person and through one's endeavors, is another essential means of getting hold of the arts as personal and intimate possessions. . . .
3. Promote appreciative experiences on the most comprehensive scale possible, another essential avenue to possession.[22]

This program to foster creative expression is seen to have three major purposes or goals:

1. The development of self-expression, aided by:
   A. Successful and shared experiences.
   B. Self-adjustment to experiences.
   C. Personality growth.
   D. Values attained from one's finished products.
   E. Satisfaction in the ability to use the art techniques as needed.

[21] James L. Mursell, "The Arts in American Education," *Teachers College Record,* Vol. 46 (February 1945), p. 288.
[22] *Ibid.,* pp. 288–289.

2. The ever-growing appreciation and enjoyment of the arts.
   A. The child's own experiences which deal with art information and skills enable him to appreciate the art of others, even to that of the masters.
   B. Real enjoyment is vital to integrative experiences.
   C. It would provide means for using leisure time advantageously.
   D. Appreciation is world-wide, helping to integrate all peoples in a common understanding.
3. Understanding and interpreting phases of living.
   A. It helps the child to see others' viewpoints and problems, as well as his own.
   B. It is an excellent aid in understanding international aspects of living.
   C. Mutual recognition of values are gained.
   D. It gives feeling tones to living.

Hockett and Jacobson see as an outgrowth of this creative activity these personal values; self-reliance, persistence, enthusiasm, intellectual honesty, intellectual adventurousness, constructive use of leisure, appreciation, and means of expression.[23]

Victor D'Amico's popular answers to the twenty questions parents most often ask about are worthy of careful consideration. Children's art work is suggestive of the way in which art may become an integrating principle for the child, the adult and society.[24]

SELECTED READING REFERENCES

Adlerblum, E. D., "Know Your Child Through His Play," *Parents Magazine,* Vol. 22 (November 1947), pp. 24–25.

Agricultural Extension Service, *Guiding Behavior of Children,* Bulletin No. 184 (Columbus, The Ohio State University, 1948).

Allen, Frederick, H., *Psychotherapy with Children* (New York, Norton, 1942), Part III, Therapeutic Processes and Factors that Interfere with Therapy.

Alschuler, Rose H., and Heinig, Christine, *Play, the Child's Response to Life* (Boston, Houghton, 1936), pp. 1–20.

[23] John Alpheus Hockett and Einor William Jacobson, *Modern Practices in the Elementary School* (New York, Ginn, 1943).

[24] Victor D'Amico, Director, Educational Program For Schools, Museum of Modern Art, New York, "Start Your Child's Creative Art Experiences," *Family Circle Magazine* (August 1950), p. 24.

Axline, Virginia M., *Play Therapy* (Boston, Houghton, 1947).

Berenburg, S. R., "Watching Your Child's Play Needs," *American Home,* Vol. 41 (December 1948), pp. 76–78.

Bixler, Ray, *Non-Directive Play Therapy,* M. A. thesis, The Ohio State University, 1942.

Carroll, J. S., "Camping Education and the Extended Year," *School Management,* Vol. 18 (April 1949), p. 12.

Clark, L. S., and Donaldson, G. W., "Camping Is a Natural," *School Executive,* Vol. 67 (June 1948), pp. 43–44.

Combs, Arthur W., "Basic Aspects of Non-Directive Therapy," *The American Journal of Orthopsychiatry,* Vol. XVI, No. 4 (October 1946).

Crook, E., "Camps That Are Different," *Parents Magazine,* Vol. 23 (May 1948), pp. 30–31.

Davis, J. E., *Play and Mental Health* (New York, Harness, 1948).

Donaldson, G. W., and Clark, L. S., "Two Weeks of School in the Woods," *National Elementary Principal,* Vol. 28 (February 1949), pp. 11–15.

Gilbert, H. B., and Wrightstone, J. W., "Education's New Look: Camping," *School Executive,* Vol. 67 (June 1948), pp. 31–34.

Henry, Jules and Zunia, *Doll Play of Pilaga Indian Children,* Research Monograph No. 4 (American Orthopsychiatric Association, 1944).

Hosking, E., "Children's Work and Play Experiences in a School Camp," *Childhood Education,* Vol. 25 (December 1948), pp. 166–169.

Hubbard, R. A., "Three Teachers Start a School Camp," *National Elementary Principal,* Vol. 28 (February 1949), pp. 36–38.

Hymes, J. L., Jr., "Why Play Is Important," *Parents Magazine,* Vol. 24 (November 1949), pp. 42–43.

Jackson, L., and Todd, K., *Child Treatment and Therapy of Play* (London, Methuen, 1946).

Jennings, Helen H., *Leadership and Isolation* (New York, Longmans, Green, 1950).

———, "Sociometry and Social Theory," *American Sociological Review,* Vol. VI, No. 1–6 (1941), pp. 512–522.

Kawin, E., *The Wise Choice of Toys* (Chicago, University of Chicago Press, 1934).

Law, S. G., *Therapy through Interview* (New York, McGraw-Hill, 1948).

Lee, J. Murray and Lee, Dorris M., "Guiding Creative Experiences in Dramatic Play," *The Child and His Curriculum* (New York, Appleton-Century, 1940), pp. 577–584.

Makintosh, Helen K., *Camping and Outdoor Experiences* (Washington, Government Printing Office, 1946).

"Mental Hygiene Functions and Possibilities of Play and Physical Education," *Elementary School Journal,* Vol. 50 (December 1949), pp. 196–200.

Miller, Helen E., "Play Therapy for the Problem Child," *Public Health Nursing,* Vol. 39 (June 1947), pp. 294–296.

Mitchell, Harriet, B. A., R. N., *Play and Play Materials for the Pre-School Child* (Ottawa, The Canadian Council on Child and Family Welfare, 1934).

Moreno, J. L., *Psychodrama* (New York, Beacon House, 1946).

———, *Sociodrama,* Psychodrama Monograph No. 1 (New York, Beacon House, 1944).

Muench, George A., "Implications of Play Therapy for Educational Practice," *Educational Administration and Supervision* (April 1949).

Peavy, G. D., "Handicapped Child as a Playground Problem," *American Childhood,* Vol. 24 (October 1938).

Proceedings (A.A.H.P.E.R.) Year Book (Washington, D. C., American Association of Health, Physical Education, and Recreation, 1949), p. 254.

Robertson, M. M., "A-Camping They Will Go," *National Parent-Teacher,* Vol. 42 (July 1948), pp. 25–27.

Rogerson, C. H., *Play Therapy in Childhood* (London, Oxford University Press, 1949).

Seaman, P., "Camping in Southern California," *Recreation,* Vol. 4 (February 1948).

Shoobs, Nahum E., *Psychodrama in the Schools,* Psychodrama Monograph No. 10 (New York, Beacon House, 1944).

Slavson, S. R., *An Introduction to Group Therapy* (New York, The Commonwealth Fund, 1943).

Smith, J. W., "Education Goes Camping," *School Executive,* Vol. 68 (September 1948), pp. 45–46.

———, "Overview of School Camping in Michigan," National Elementary Principal, Vol. 28 (February 1949), pp. 34–35.

Solby, Bruno, "The Psychodramatic Approach to Marriage Problems," *American Sociological Review,* Vol. VI, No. 1–6, (1941), pp. 523–530.

Studebaker, J. W., "Camping in Education and Education in Camping: School Camps," *Social Life,* Vol. 30 (July 1948), pp. 2–3.

"The Place of Camping in Education" (Committee Report), *Journal of the American Association for Health, Physical Education, and Recreation,* Vol. 21, No. 1 (January 1950), pp. 46–47.

Tom, Winifred, *Play Therapy,* M. A. thesis, The Ohio State University, 1949.

E | A STATE CAMPING PRO-GRAM IN ACTION

IN MICHIGAN the growing awareness that the out-of-doors should be used more extensively in the growing-up process of youth has led many to feel that there is a need for special action in camping and outdoor education.

This realization has prompted the Departments of Public Instruction and Conservation to enter into a joint educational enterprise.[1] With financial aid from the W. K. Kellogg Foundation, it was proposed to approach the camping conservation and outdoor education problem by enlarging the experimental Division of Health, Physical Education, Recreation, School Camping, and Outdoor Education of the Department of Public Instruction to embrace the joint experimental project and to associate it more directly with the combined effort of the department in harmonization and coordination of those areas concerned with the health and better living of people. This fitted well into the state pattern because the schools of the state were already cooperating with the department in carrying forward the division mentioned, and were sharing in its financing by making some funds available to the State Board of Education. This had been done through an appropriation by the Michigan High School Athletic Association representing all the secondary schools of the state and approved by the Michigan Secondary School Principals.[2]

Camping as part of the educational program of the community

[1] Eugene B. Elliott and Julian W. Smith, "The Michigan Program in Action," *The Bulletin of the National Association of Secondary-School Principals.* Vol. 31, No. 147 (May 1947). Materials cited from this article by permission.
[2] *Ibid.,* p. 61.

school was recognized by the Michigan Legislature in 1945 when it enacted Act 170, enabling school districts to purchase, maintain, and equip camps to carry out an educational and recreational program. The act took into account the fact that schools might wish to join in a camping program to serve a larger area than was usually covered by the individual schools and made provisions for such a joint endeavor. Local schools in the state may thus recognize camping as an essential part of the curriculum in expending school funds for this program.[3]

Michigan interested in camping and outdoor education has centered much attention on the problems of pre-service and in-service training of teachers. Camping administrator and counselor courses have been offered for some time in several Michigan colleges and universities, but actual on-the-job training is more recent.[4]

There is no prescribed pattern of camping or any other form of outdoor education that is being urged or recommended for all schools. Rather the approach has been to suggest that each school use the out-of-doors to meet its local needs, building upon programs already in operation. The local planning programs can best be described by outlining some of the patterns and schools.

1. Camp Property Owned by a School or Groups of Schools

A board of education in Michigan, under Act 170, P. A. 1945, may purchase property and build a camp in the same manner as it would a regular school plant. This was done in Cadillac, Michigan. The program is being extended to include more youth and to identify it more closely with school programs.[5]

2. Camp Property Owned by a Governmental Unit

In this type of a situation, the facilities can be made available to the whole county. Nearly 500 youth of Iron County last year (1946) had the privilege of educational camping because the public saw the need and because some leaders saw the possibilities for using resources already available without any appreciable outlay of cash.[6]

[3] Elliott and Smith, *op. cit.*, p. 65.
[4] *Ibid.*, p. 66.
[5] *Ibid.*, p. 68.
[6] *Ibid.*, p. 69.

3. Camps Owned by Private or Community Agencies Which Are Made Available for School Camps

At the present time many of the schools of southwestern Michigan have had experience by using the W. K. Kellogg Foundation camps at Pine Lake, Clear Lake, and St. Mary's Lake. St. Mary's Lake Camp is leased to a camp board in Calhoun County, and an extensive year-round camping program has been carried on for the schools. The Mott Foundation has provided a camp for Flint for a number of years. Another variation in this category of camping is a camp which was purchased and developed by the Parent-Teachers Association and other community clubs connected with Tappan Junior High School, Ann Arbor. The deed to the camp is held by the board of education but interested community groups are still participating in further development and expansion of its use.[7]

4. A Camp under the Direction of a College

There are a number of situations where a college or university owns or operates a camp, combining teacher training in a camp situation. A situation of this kind is found at Clear Lake Camp where the W. K. Kellogg Foundation has leased the camp to Western Michigan College of Education. In these camps plans are now under way for extending the use of the camp to include more youth and identify it more closely with the educational program of the school and the teacher training program of the institution involved.[8]

5. The Use of State Lands for Camping

The greatest possible opportunity for extending camping to large numbers of youth will be the use of state-owned facilities which, in Michigan, are under the direction of the Conservation Department. These will include recreation areas, game areas, group camps, and other state lands. Consideration is being given now to the development of policies so that such lands may be available to schools. It is possible, in some cases, that schools may be able to erect temporary buildings; in other instances, camps already maintained and operated by the Conservation Department can be made available for the use of schools. The schools of Huron County, Michigan, the 4-H Clubs, and other agencies are developing a camping program for the county.[9]

[7] *Ibid.*, pp. 69–70.
[8] *Ibid.*, p. 70.
[9] *Ibid.*, p. 71.

6. Day Camping

Day camping is possible and will then reach nearly every school program, as well as recreation departments, social agencies, and other organizations. It is a simple way of utilizing the out-of-doors to supplement classroom instruction, in addition to providing for the development of outdoor skills and to making possible many direct learning experiences. There have been a number of day camp programs in operation, but special effort is now being made to extend them for greater use by schools and other agencies.[10]

7. School Forests

There are many tracts of land in Michigan under the direction of schools, known as school forests. Such lands are made available to schools for reforestation. They constitute a valuable resource for out-door education, serving ι   ιboratory of the school. Muskegon, Michigan, has a school farm which includes a forest. The school conservation club has made frequent use of it, and ways are being worked out to include a broader educational program.[11]

8. The School Site as an Outdoor Laboratory

Some boards of education, in acquiring new school sites, are selecting those that include woodlots or land suitable for the development of a natural setting. Such a combination of facilities will provide for outdoor education and camping as a part of the community school program. Waterford Township, near Pontiac, has a thirty-acre tract where a new school will be built. Twenty acres of the land are wooded, with a stream flowing through the area. The school staff and a community group are planning for the use of this site to include many forms of outdoor education, camping, and recreation.[12]

SCHOOL CAMP PROGRAM

THE FOLLOWING OUTLINE is presented both as a summary and as a means of helping the reader visualize the aims, objectives, organization, program, and evaluations of a school camp program as a part of the educational plan.

[10] Elliott and Smith, *op. cit.,* p. 71.
[11] *Ibid.,* p. 72.
[12] *Ibid.,* p. 72.

I. **AIMS**

The general aim is to provide and utilize opportunities for wholesome, rich, and happy experiences in the out-of-doors that would contribute to the total education of the child.

   A. Four specific aims

      1. To help each child to grow and live happily as a member of the group and community.

      2. To create a desire for worth-while experiences.

      3. To practice healthful living and safety precautions.

      4. To develop an appreciation and enjoyment of the beauty of creative expression.

II. **OBJECTIVES**

The New York City Schools set up those objectives for camping, and they are consonant with the objectives of education.[13]

   A. To improve physical health.

   B. To improve mental health.

   C. To improve social relationships.

   D. To guide and develop desirable interests and aptitudes.

   E. To gain integrating knowledges and skills.

III. **ORGANIZATION**

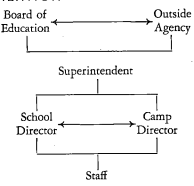

IV. **FINANCING**

The responsibility for financing the school camp programs is assumed by the Board of Education. However, there are some boards who have accepted the financial aid of different educacational foundations to further their programs.

[13] *Extending Education Through Camping,* Report of the School Camp Experiment (New York, Life Camps, Inc., 1948), p. 110.

V. TEACHER EDUCATION FOR CAMPING

Teacher education for camping in many ways is just good teacher education. Strong emphasis should be placed on the doing and participating. The good camp counselor is first a good teacher, and second, one who is an interested and informed individual of the learning potential in the outdoors and the camping environment.

A. Criteria for a good teacher education program.[14]
    1. The place of Camping in Education. Potential values of camping as an integral part of the education program should be explored. The understanding and appreciation of those values.
    2. Experiences in Camping Situations. These again could well be a part of the preparation of all teachers because of the unequal opportunity to observe children in "round-the-clock" living. This time spent in camp in watching, working, playing and living with children could count toward the psychology requirements of most colleges and universities.
    3. Outdoor Courses. The thought here is that "outdoor" science, "outdoor" arts and crafts, "outdoor" music and dramatics, etc., should either be established as special courses or incorporated into existing courses. These would stimulate a good trend in the program of the regular classroom.
    4. Camp Internship. The time involved here would be longer than indicated in "B." It would be comparable to practice teaching and should probably last for a period of 8 to 12 weeks.

VI. PROGRAM

Various schools hold their camps at different times of the year. Today the camping experiences are being planned and carried out during the academic year. In this way the students plan their camp, execute their plans, and evaluate their experiences as a part of their curriculum study. In most cases the campers are children from the fifth, sixth, seventh, and eighth grades. Sometimes two different grades go to camp together, and sometimes each grade goes alone.

[14] "The Place of Camping in Education," (Committee Report), *Journal of the American Association for Health, Physical Education and Recreation,* Vol. 21, No. 1 (January, 1950), pp. 46–47.

A. **Precamp program**

The precamp program takes place in the school and is integrated with the curriculum.
  1. Precamp planning
       Discussions by parents, teachers, and pupils of camp program, responsibilities, and objectives.
         A. Methods used for introducing the camping experience.
               (1) Discussions
               (2) Movies
               (3) Slides
               (4) Home visits
  2. School and camp program integration.
       The following information was taken from the Report of the School Camp Experiment.[15]

CAMP EXPERIENCES AND ACTIVITIES	AREAS OF CURRICULUM
Setting goals for group living, respecting other's rights, care of communal property, rotating duties	Pupil participation and practical arts
Living in groups of varied ethnic and religious backgrounds, cooperating in group endeavors	Pupil participation and language arts
Studying the history of the locale	Social studies
Reconstructing pioneer days by—outdoor living, sleeping, building shelters, fires, camp sites	Social studies and practical arts
Caring for one's person	Health and practical arts
Caring for communal property	Practical arts and health
Participating in varied physical activities	Practical arts, health and physical education
Observing safety measures	Safety
Exploring the camp area	Science
Finding worth-while interests	Science, health, and fine arts
Trying out new tools and equipment	Practical arts
Collecting specimens; exhibiting finds	Science
Analyzing camping problems	Science and arithmetic
Anticipating camping needs	Arithmetic

[15] "Extending Education Through Camping," *op. cit.,* pp. 47–53.

Substantiating finds	Language arts
Summarizing findings	Language arts
Learning how to use tools and equipment	Practical arts
Learning how to make and when to use different types of fires	Science
Learning how to cook outdoors	Practical arts
Learning how to prepare menus	Health, practical arts, and arithmetic
Getting acquainted with new skills	Science, arithmetic, and health .
Observing beauty in nature	Science and fine arts
Listening to the sounds of nature	Science, music, and language arts
Singing	Music
Expressing ideas through the hands and mind	Fine arts and language arts
Living together as a family	Pupil participation and language arts
Living as a group in a community	Pupil participation, and language arts
Participating in social activities	Pupil participation and language arts
Observing social amenities	Pupil participation and language arts
Realizing the need for desirable work habits	Pupil participation and practical arts
Understanding interrelationships and contributions made by all who serve in the world of work	Social studies

   3. Postcamp evaluation
      A. Did the program provide opportunity for:
            (1) the children to plan, execute, and evaluate the experiences?
            (2) the child to gain closer contacts and better understandings of the outdoors?
            (3) integration of activities?
            (4) discovery, adventure, and direct experience?

    (5) cooperation rather than competition?
    (6) a new way of learning interesting things?
    (7) development of new interest in the surround-
         ing environment?
    (8) the development of the whole child?
    (9) democratic and healthful living?
   (10) practicing manners and good social conduct?

If a camping program is to serve its purposes, it must be an integrated part of the school program. The children and teacher must plan
for the experience together at the school before camping time. The
teacher should be with the children at the camp. She may be one of
the staff or may go as a camper herself, but she should be with the
children. She could not do a good follow-up program if she did not
know what happened to the children at camp.

Some schools plan their camping experience on the last week of
the school year. We do not feel this is wise because the opportunity
for a follow-up program is gone. While no statistical study has been
made the following conclusions have been drawn by teachers and
counselors in the school camps.[16]

    1. The camping situation is one in which educators can learn
       much of value concerning pupils.
    2. There are evidences of growth in such desirable habits as com-
       pleting one's job; caring for one's person; caring for shelters.
    3. There are instances of growth in such knowledges and skills as
       identifying birds and their calls, recognizing animals, insects
       and stars, cooking, serving, fire-building, table manners, swim-
       ming, etc.
    4. There are evidences of growth in desirable attitudes.
    5. There are evidences of desirable intergroup relationships.
    6. There are evidences of growth of abiding interests so that pupils
       will be able to direct their leisure time activities purposefully.

These kinds of outcomes are closely related to the personal adjustment outcomes in which we are so interested. Freed from tensions
of various sorts, children and youth have a chance to develop insight
into both themselves and situations which affect them.

Another newer and also challenging type of camping is that of
family camping. Under the sponsorship of settlement houses, specific
churches, and American Friends Service Committee and occasional
schools, there have been significant attempts in the area of family
camping.

[16] "Extending Education Through Camping," *op. cit.,* pp. 79–82.

INDEXES

INDEX OF NAMES

INDEX OF SUBJECTS